QVI ▲ MISCVIT
VTILE ▲ DVLCI

Festschrift Essays for
Paul Lachlan MacKendrick

Paul Lachlan MacKendrick

QVI ▴ MISCVIT VTILE ▴ DVLCI

Festschrift Essays for
Paul Lachlan MacKendrick

Edited by

GARETH SCHMELING
University of Florida

&

JON D. MIKALSON
University of Virginia

BOLCHAZY-CARDUCCI PUBLISHERS, INC.
Wauconda, Illinois
1998

GENERAL EDITOR
Laurie K. Haight

CONTRIBUTING EDITOR
Gaby Huebner

TYPOGRAPHY
Diane E. Smith
Scholarly Typesetting

COVER DESIGN
Charlene M. Hernandez

COVER ILLUSTRATION
Athens: The Acropolis
Photograph by Raymond V. Schoder, S.J.
© 1987 Bolchazy-Carducci Publishers, Inc.

© Copyright 1998
BOLCHAZY-CARDUCCI PUBLISHERS, INC.
1000 Brown Street, Unit 101
Wauconda, IL 60084

ISBN 0-86516-406-1

Printed in the United States of America
by United Graphics
1998

Library of Congress Cataloging-in-Publication Data

Qui miscuit utile dulci : festschrift essays for Paul Lachlan
    MacKendrick / edited by Gareth Schmeling and Jon D. Mikalson.
        p.   cm.
    Includes bibliographical references.
    ISBN 0-86516-406-1 (alk. paper)
    1. Civilization, Classical. 2. Classical antiquities.
3. Classical philology. 4. MacKendrick, Paul Lachlan, 1914-   -
-Bibliography. I. Schmeling, Gareth L. II. Mikalson, Jon D.,
1943-   . III. MacKendrick, Paul Lachlan, 1914-   .
DE71.Q5 1997
938--dc21   97-326620
                                                             CIP

TABLE OF CONTENTS

PREFACE

The essays by students and colleagues of Paul MacKendrick are gathered here to recognize the career of a distinguished classicist. The *Tabula Gratulatoria* contains a list of well-wishers; the editors apologize for all omissions.

Paul MacKendrick was born on 11 February 1914, the son of Ralph and Sarah (Harvey) MacKendrick, in Taunton, MA, where he attended Hopewell Grammar (1926) and Taunton High School (1930). In 1934 he graduated with an A.B. degree from Harvard University, was elected to ΦBK, and gave the Latin commencement address. In what would prove to be a regular itinerary, he crossed the Atlantic for Europe, and in the years 1934–1936 was a student at Balliol—he returned often to Balliol and to Churchill College, Cambridge. Back at Harvard he received an A.M. degree in 1937, and in 1938 a Ph.D. under Sterling Dow with a dissertation entitled *de gente Attica Eumolpidarum*.

From 1938–1941 Paul was Instructor in Latin at Phillips Academy, Andover, and then like many men his age entered the military. After growing up in the Great Depression he served his country throughout the Second Great War: he has remained ever since a stout un-reconstructed Roosevelt Democrat. The U.S. Navy taught him Portuguese (which would prove useful later for *The Iberian Stones Speak*), spying, shipping him across the Atlantic to Sicily and the Azores, and acted the part of ablative of attendant circumstance for him with his wife-to-be, Dotty. Paul returned to Harvard as Instructor for one year, and then in 1946 was appointed assistant professor at the University of Wisconsin-Madison, an intense relationship which would last almost forty years. He was promoted to associate professor in 1948, full professor in 1952, and named Lily Ross Taylor Professor in 1975, a position he held until retirement in 1984.

Though born and educated on the East coast, Paul is a Wisconsin man: he bleeds Badger (Cardinal) red. He believes in the "Wisconsin idea" of education, and, in addition to teaching Classics courses, regularly lectured in the freshmen-sophomore program called Integrated Liberal Studies (ILS). More than professional, he was serious about his teaching. Classics mattered; it was of immediate importance for living. He was Director of the Summer Session of the American Academy in Rome (1956–1959), ΦBK Visiting Scholar, Visiting Professor and External Examiner at the University of Ibadan, Nigeria, Visiting Professor at the University of Florida.

He has been awarded Fulbright and Guggenheim Fellowships, served as Secretary-Treasurer of the American Philological Association (1956–1959), and been elected President of the Classical Association of the Middle West and South (1969–1970).

We suppose that a collection of essays for Paul MacKendrick should have been entitled *Saxa Loquuntur*—in imitation of his best known works. But Paul was interested in many areas — the diversity of these collected essays reflects some of those interests: long before it was fashionable to do so, Paul employed anthropological methodology to combine the various skill areas in Classics (epigraphy, archaeology, literature, philosophy, history) to help to put together all the *tesserae* in the Classics mosaic. As students we joked that *Romans on the Rhine* might have been entitled *The Rhinestones Speak* and that *The Romans in France* might have been *de Gaulle Stones Speak*. But we were envious as hell and knew a *ludi magister* when we met one. Papers graded in great detail in red ink in that minute hand of his and signed PLM demanded our attention.

Gareth Schmeling

TABVLA · GRATVLATORIA

Isobel J. and Eric C. Baade
Charles Babcock
Balliol College
Hazel Barnes
Herbert W. and
  Janice M. Benario
Emmett L. Bennett, Jr.
J.D. Bishop
Alan Boegehold
Glen Bowersock
Fred Brenk
Edwin L. Brown
Jeffrey Buller
William M. Calder, III
Mortimer Chambers
Marshall Clagett
Robert Cromey
John Crook
Judith de Luce
H. A. Drake
Andrew Dyck
Victor Estevez
Barbara Fowler
James Franklin
Ernst Fredricksmeyer
Katherine Geffcken

Edward George
Peter Green
Kathryn Gutzwiller
David Hahm
Charles Henderson, Jr.
Joy King
M. Owen Lee
Fannie J. Lemoine
Lydia and John Lenaghan
Dean Linder
Ramsay MacMullen
Patricia Marquardt
Ralph Mathisen
Alexander McKay
Jon D. Mikalson
Chester and
  Mary Ann Natunewicz
Thomas Nevin
Helen North
Martin Ostwald
Paul Plass
Norman Pratt
Michael Putnam
Antony Raubitschek
Joyce Reynolds
Lawrence Richardson, jr

Robert J. Rowland, Jr.
Harry Rutledge
Gareth and
  Karen Schmeling
Kathryn Sinkovich
Kathryn Stallard

Susan Stevens
Arthur F. Stocker
Dana F. Sutton
Homer A. Thompson
Peter Wiseman

PUBLISHED WORKS OF
PAUL LACHLAN MACKENDRICK

(prepared by Craig Dethloff and Catherine O'Hanlon)

1938

"The Folklore of Athenian Democracy," resumé in *TAPA* 69 (1938) XLIII.

De Gente Attica Eumolpidarum, Dissertation, Harvard University, resumé in *HSCP* 49 (1938) 271–273.

1939

"The ἐργαστῖναι and the Attic γένη," resumé in *TAPA* 70 (1939) XXXIX.

1942

(with R. Westgate), "Juvenal and Swift," *CJ* 37 (1942) 468–482.

1948

"Cicero's Ideal Orator: Truth and Propaganda," *CJ* 43 (1948) 339–347.

1950

"The Great Gatsby and Trimalchio," *CJ* 45 (1950) 307–314.

1951

"A Renaissance Odyssey: the Life of Cyriac of Ancona," *C&M* 13 (1951) 131–145.

1952

"Roman Colonization," *Phoenix* 6 (1952) 139–146.

(ed. by Paul MacKendrick and Herbert Howe), *Classics in Translation*. Vol. I, Greek Literature, Vol. II, Latin Literature (Madison: University of Wisconsin Press, 1952). [Often reprinted in paperback]

1954

"Herodotus: the Making of a World Historian," *CW* 47 (1954) 145–152.

"Demetrius of Phalerum, Cato, and the *Adelphoe*," *RFIC* 32 (1954) 18–35.

"T.S. Eliot and the Alexandrians," *CJ* 49 (1954) 7–13.

"Asphodel, White Wine, and Enriched Thunderbolts," *G&R*, 2nd series 1 (1945) 1–11.

"Cicero, Livy and Roman Colonisation," *Athenaeum* 32 (1954) 201–249.

1956

"Roman Town Planning," *Archaeology* 9 (1956) 126–133.

"Kipling and the Nature of the Classical," *CJ* 52 (1956) 67–76.

1958

The Roman Mind at Work (Princeton: Van Nostrand, 1958).

1959

"The Pleasures of Pedagogy," *CJ* 54 (1959) 194–200.

1960

The Mute Stones Speak: the Story of Archaeology in Italy (New York: St. Martin's Press, 1960).

1962

The Greek Stones Speak: the Story of Archaeology in Greek Lands (New York: St. Martin's Press, 1962).

1963

"Herodotus, 1954–1963," *CW* 56 (1963) 269–275.

1965

"Some Books on the Etruscans," *CW* 58 (1965) 45–46.

1966

"Meander on the Mississippi: the Classics in America," *Phrontisterion* 4 (1966) 41–46.

The Mute Stones Speak: the Story of Archaeology in Italy (New York: New American Library, Mentor Book, April 1966). [paperback reprint of 1960 edition]

The Greek Stones Speak: the Story of Archaeology in Greek Lands (New York: New American Library, Mentor Book, April 1966). [paperback reprint of 1962 edition]

1967

Roms steinernes Erbe: Römische Archäologie in Italien (Wiesbaden: Brockhaus, 1967). [German edition of 1960 English edition]

1968

"Love Among the Ruins. A Study of Propertius," *Nigeria and the Classics* 10 (1967–68) 1–12.

Western Civilization (New York: American Heritage Publishing Co., 1968)

1969

"Herodotus 1963–1969," *CW* 63 (1969) 37–44.

The Iberian Stones Speak: Archaeology in Spain and Portugal (New York: Funk and Wagnalls, 1969).

The Athenian Aristocracy, 399–31 B.C. (Cambridge: Harvard University Press for Oberlin College, 1969).

1970

Romans on the Rhine: Archaeology in Germany (New York: Funk and Wagnalls, 1970).

1972

Deutschlands römische Erbe (Wiesbaden: Brockhaus, 1972). [German edition of 1970 English edition]

Roman France (New York: St. Martin's, 1972).

1975

The Dacian Stones Speak (Chapel Hall: University of North Carolina Press, 1975).

1976

The Mute Stones Speak: the Story of Archaeology in Italy (New York: Norton, 1976). [hardcover and paperback reprints of 1960 edition]

1980

The North African Stones Speak (Chapel Hill: University of North Carolina Press, 1980).

1981

The Greek Stones Speak: the Story of Archaeology in Greek Lands, 2nd edition (New York: Norton, 1981). [first edition 1962]

1983

The Mute Stones Speak: the Story of Archaeology in Italy, 2nd edition (New York: Norton, 1983). [first edition 1960]

1984

"An Aristocratic Reformer: Kleisthenes and After," in ed. K.J. Rigsby, *Studies Presented to Sterling Dow on his Eightieth Birthday*, *GRBS* Supplement X (Durham: Duke University Press, 1984) 193–202.

1987

"The Romans in Burgundy," in eds. C.Crumley and W. Marquardt, *Regional Dynamics: Burgundian Landscapes in Historical Perspective* (San Diego: Academic Press, 1987) 431–445.

1989

The Philosophical Books of Cicero (London: Duckworth, 1989).

1995

The Speeches of Cicero: Context, Law, Rhetoric (London: Duckworth, 1995).

The Red Stones Speak: Porphyry Discs in the Pavements of Roman Churches

Isobel J. and Eric C. Baade

The type of pavement called "cosmatesque" is named for the Cosmati family (or guild), which seems to have held a kind of monopoly in this sort of work in the twelfth and thirteenth centuries. At any rate all that is signed is signed with their names.

There are variations in the designs, but the basic system of laying the stones is fairly consistent: a single guilloche pattern of tessellated bands, incorporating a chain of large discs, runs the length of the nave; this linear chain is interrupted once or more by discs in quincunx designs, the central one often larger than those in the corners. Areas to both sides may be filled with tessellated patterns usually using triangles, squares, hexagons, and octagons. The designs do not vary much from early to late; the variations which do occur appear to result from restorations.

The *pietre dure* used are for the most part white marble, serpentine, giallo antico, and porphyry; the few pieces of

1

gray granite appear to belong to later restorations. A very few of the large discs around which the designs are organized are of serpentine; but by far the large majority is of porphyry.

We visited San Crisogono some years ago, when the cosmatesque pavement was being repaired, and noticed that the small polygonal pieces of colored marble were less than 3 cm thick, and hence were probably reused pieces of revetment from ancient buildings (a familiar example is the nymphaeum of the Domus Transitoria), while the porphyry discs were much thicker, the smaller ones 15 or 20 cm at least, and the larger ones thicker still (the idea of these observations had not yet occurred to us, and we did not take any measurements at the time). There is a practical reason for this difference in thickness, of course, since a thin but large piece of stone would more easily crack.

Dorothy S. Glass in *Studies on Cosmatesque Pavements* (British Archaeological Reports, International Series 82, Oxford 1980), has pointed out that in a cosmatesque design all measurements depend on the size of the largest porphyry disc. All the discs are treated as if their diameters were that of the largest disc or one half or one fourth of it.

In all but one of the Roman churches we noticed immediately that where the design requires uniformity of size, whether in the linear repetition of the guilloche or in the two-axis symmetry of the quincunx, the sizes of the discs vary. The variation is frequently large enough to require the insertion of one or more extra borders of the smaller polygonal pieces, since the overall patterns are always designed to accommodate the largest one of the porphyry discs.

Why did the stone-cutters of the Middle Ages, the *marmorari*, not select more uniform discs? or why did they not trim the discs and achieve uniformity that way?

It is thought that the discs in cosmatesque pavements are slices of recycled columns, since they appear at a time when Egypt, the only source of porphyry, was not accessible. Some have thought that the *marmorari* found the discs ready-cut, since porphyry pavement discs, presumably cut from columns, played a ritual role in the Byzantine period, when emperors, and perhaps their representatives, stood "on purple" to utter pronouncements of certain kinds (R. Delbrücke, *Antike Porphyrwerke*, Studien zur Spätantiken Kunstgeschichte 6, Berlin 1932). It seems unlikely, however, that the cosmatesque discs were found ready-cut. For one thing, there is in the pavements a small number of large discs of serpentine, which so far as we know had no ritual significance in the late empire. For another, many of the porphyry discs, especially those decorating bell-towers but also many in the pavements, are too small to have been used for acts performed "on purple."

We must assume that it was not possible to select specific sizes, but that the columns had to be used as they were found or allocated, though very large columns may have been reserved, only one or two really big discs being allocated to most building projects.

Except for the very largest, then, ancient columns of porphyry must have been used one at a time, each column being sawed and transferred to the building site before the next one was used. It is likely that smaller columns or fragments of columns were brought to the site and cut up there. This in fact is known to be the method used in the 1907–1937 rebuilding of Buckfast Abbey in Devon, England, where the porphyry discs in the beautiful neocosmatesque pavement were cut and pieced from a fragment of a column from the temple of Artemis at Ephesus, brought to England by Lord Elgin.

It is clear that the *marmorari* were capable of sawing columns into discs and of polishing, or at least smoothing, the cut surface. But it is equally clear that their equipment was too primitive to allow them to cut pieces with curved outlines: if they had been able to do this they surely would (like their modern successors in Sta. Maria in Trastevere and in Buckfast Abbey) have cut the discs into uniform sizes. In the very rare tessellated patterns which incorporate pieces with curved outlines, these pieces are always circles or parts of circles, clearly slices of colonnets, not bits of revetment cut into curves.

During the repairs to the pavement in San Crisogono the artisans kindly demonstrated their tools to us. They used only a pair of pincers, a small iron maul, and a chisel shaft set upright in a block of stone. They shaped their polygonal pieces from scraps of the colored stones, already in thin slices, by holding them over the chisel edge with the pincers and breaking off the unwanted bits with the maul. They did this with great accuracy, but it is clear that they could not by this method cut curved pieces.

In the church of Sto. Spirito in Sassia, among the grotesque frescos (probably dating from 1538) uncovered in a modern restoration, there are two designs which appear to refer to the tools of trades. One appears to show implements of the butchers' trade, a pick-hammer for slaughtering the beasts crossed saltire-fashion with a skinning-knife. That these are not merely the instruments of some saint's martyrdom is shown by the matching painting, where the implements crossed at the top of the design are a pair of pincers with incurved points (to prevent the marring of the object grasped) and a maul exactly like that of the modern *marmorari*. Below are two columns, again placed in a crossed design (an odd position if they are merely decorative), and below that a block of stone. This block has no embedded chisel—perhaps this is a modern refinement—

but in other respects the tools are the same as those we saw in use in S. Crisogono.

It is clear that the ancient art of working *pietre dure* into real *opus sectile* had been lost. There is no evidence in cosmatesque work of the shaping of stones beyond the sawing of blocks into thick slices and the simple breaking of thin revetment pieces into polygonal shapes. There is no sign of an ability to cut any but straight lines.

The evidence from most of the churches does support the idea that the porphyry discs were not chosen from some central supply of ready-cut pieces, but were cut on the site or elsewhere from one column at a time. The mere fact that porphyry discs are of visibly differing sizes even in designs where symmetry should have demanded uniformity makes it clear that the artists could not alter the size of the discs. Therefore we can be sure that the diameters of the discs represent the original diameters of the recycled columns, and can learn something about the number and sizes of the porphyry columns employed.

The canonical proportions for an unfluted column, from the top of the base to the bottom of the necking below the capital, are that its height should be six and a half times the base diameter and that the diameter at the top should be three quarters of the base diameter. Although both the sizes and the shapes of preserved whole porphyry columns vary, the few which we could approach to measure and photograph (all in S. Giovanni in Fonte) come close to this canon. The proportions of base diameter to height vary from six and a half to seven and a half, and the proportion of top diameter to base diameter from three quarters to seven eighths. It seems safe to say, then, that the columns in which we are interested were in height probably at least six and a half times the diameter of the largest disc.

If in fact the discs are from columns used one at a time, we would expect to find that in each church pavement their diameters would differ a little as a result of the tapering of the columns, and that the measurements would form (for each column) a continuous series without gaps. It must be borne in mind, however, that two consecutive discs will be identical in size if the top one is inverted in use. Also, columns may not taper uniformly: entasis, though not pronounced, is present in different degrees. A fragment of a porphyry column in the Antiquarium del Celio is 184.75 cm high with a 62 cm diameter at the top and a 63.75 cm diameter at the bottom, a decrease of only .01 unit in radius for each unit in height, whereas the smallest decrease in any observed whole column is .02, and in the canonical proportions is .0385. Variations in entasis will affect the degree of difference between consecutive discs.

Our research, unsponsored by any institution, was necessarily a bit hit-or-miss. We had to depend on finding a church open when it was scheduled to be, on its pavement's being unencumbered by fancy carpeting for weddings or scaffolding for restoration, and also upon the good will of sacristans and vergers to let us into roped-off areas, a very uncertain factor. Except for a serendipitous chance visit to Buckfast Abbey, we did not include churches outside of Rome.

Oddly enough, very little is known in most cases about the history of the pavements; but subsequent rearrangements of the original cosmatesque design do not affect the measurements of the porphyry discs.

There follows a list of churches in which we were able to make some observations. In each case the sizes of the discs required by the module are given, then the sizes of the actual discs, with comments on the columns from which they must have come. All measurements are in centimeters.

S. Clemente: early twelfth-century, thirteenth-century restoration. The simple guilloche design, without quincunces, needs discs all of the same size, and in fact the smaller ones have extra borders to bring them up to 54 cm. The series of diameters (30.5, 31, 31.5, 32, 44, 44.5, 45, 45, 47.25, 49, 51, 52, 52.5, 52.5, 53, 54) suggests that there may have been a 48 cm fragment of a column of more than 2 meters, cut into four 12 cm slices, from 30.5 cm to 32 cm in diameter. The larger discs could have come from a 2.5 m fragment of a 3.5 m column, cut into twelve 21 cm slices. These larger discs require a greater thickness for structural reasons, but 21 cm seems a lot; perhaps some broken discs were removed and not replaced in the eighteenth-century restoration.

Sta. Maria Maggiore: a mid-twelfth-century pavement, relaid 1740–1758, restored 1846–1878. The design requires discs 71, 35.5, and 17.75; in fact the measurements are 11, 11.5, 11.5, 11.5, 12, 12, 12, 12.5, 12.5, 12.5, 13, 13, 13, 13, 13, 13, 13, 14.5, 14.5, 14.5, 15, 15.5, 15.5, 16.5, 16.5, 16.5, 17, 17, 17, 17, 17, 17, 17, 18.5, 19, 19, 19, 19, 19, 19, 19.5, 21, 21, 21.5, 21.5, 21.5, 23.5, 26, 27, 27.5, 29, 29, 30, 30, 30, 34, 35, 38, 38.5, 39, 39.5, 39.5, 40.5, 41, 43, 43, 43, 43, 43, 43, 43, 43, 43.5, 43.5, 43.5, 43.5, 43.5, 43.5, 43.5, 43.5, 44, 44, 44, 47, 47.5, 50, 52, 52, 52.5, 52.5, 52.5, 52.5, 53, 53, 53.5, 54.5, 55, 55, 55.5, 56, 56, 56, 57, 57, 57, 59, 60, 61, 61, 61, 61, 61.5, 61.5, 61.5, 61.5, 65, 65.5, 67, 71, 71. These diameters line up in a startlingly consistent series, with no gaps. This in itself is disquieting. Since the discs cannot all be from one column, how did the *marmorari* manage to find six or more columns or fragments the top of each of which matched the bottom of the next? And why would they bother? Of course the continuity may be a coincidence: the search for columns of the required three sizes would naturally result in some overlap.

In any case the discs could have come from six columns: a colonnet nearly a meter in height, cut into twenty discs, about 5 cm thick, in diameter from 11 cm to 14.5 cm; a second a little over 1.2 m high, cut into twenty discs 6 cm thick, in diameter from 14.5 cm to 19 cm; the third a column nearly 2 m high, cut into sixteen discs 12.25 cm thick, in diameter from 19 cm to 30 cm; a fourth a little taller, cut into twenty-four discs 9.25 cm thick, in diameter from 34 cm to 43.5 cm; a fifth between 3.5 and 4 m high, cut into twenty discs 19 cm thick, in diameter from 43.5 cm to 55.5 cm; and the sixth about 4.75 m high, cut into twenty-one discs about 23 cm thick, in diameter from 56 cm to 71 cm.

These suggestions are offered only by way of example: there may, of course, have been many fragments of columns involved—after all, the one remaining porphyry column of the Basilica of Maxentius was found in four pieces— and even whole columns may not have begun and ended precisely where we have suggested. Two things are clear: it is structurally reasonable that larger discs should have been cut thicker; and if these discs are indeed from columns there must at least have been one nearly 5 m tall.

S. Lorenzo fuori le Mura: first half of the thirteenth century, restored to the original design in the last century, and again in this century after the bombardment of July 1943. The elaborate pattern requires discs of 119, 58.5, 29.25, and 14.625; the actual discs are 6.5, 7, 8, 8.5, 10, 10, 11, 11, 11.5, 13, 13.5, 13.5, 16, 16.5, 16.5, 16.5, 16.5, 17, 17, 17, 24, 24, 25, 25, 25.5, 26, 26, 26.5, 27, 27.5, 28, 28.5, 29, 30.5, 30.5, 32, 32.5, 33, 33, 33, 33.5, 33.5, 34.5, 35, 37, 37, 38, 39, 40, 40.5, 40.5, 45, 51, 56.5, 56.5, 56.5, 56.5, 60, 61, 62, 63, 63, 64, 68, 76, 85.5, 95.5, 110, 112, 119, a very satisfactory sequence except for the gaps. The four smallest discs, for example, would have to have come from a colonnet about 56 cm high, 6.5 cm at the top and 8.5 at the base, but there ought to be more of them, since there would be no point in cutting discs of this diameter into slices 14 cm thick; if they are from one column, perhaps some crumbled or were shattered in the sawing, or were destroyed in the bombardment or in one of the restorations. The rest of the series could have come (among many other possible divisions) from: a column about 87 cm high, sliced into eight discs between 10 and 11 cm thick, 10 to 13.5 cm in diameter; a piece of a column between 1.1 and 1.4 m high, in eight discs 14 cm or so in thickness and running from 16 to 17 cm in diameter; a column about 2 m high, in fourteen discs 14 cm or so thick and running from 24 cm to 30.5 cm in diameter; a column about 2.65 m high, in seventeen slices about 13 cm thick and running from 30.5 cm to 40.5 cm in diameter; a column 3.9 m high, cut into only seven discs from 56.75 cm thick and 45 to 60 cm in diameter (from here on some discs again seem to be missing); the small end of a column 5.28 m high or the large end of a column 4.94 m high, again in only seven slices, from 61 to 76 cm in diameter; and finally five discs from a larger column as much as 7.73 m in height, with diameters from 85.5 cm to 119 cm. As always, the clearly visible discrepancies are made up by the insertion of extra borders.

Sta. Croce in Gerusalemma: pavement 1144, restored 1993. The discs should all be either 129 or 32.25; they are in fact 33.5, 33.5, 34, 35, 36, 39.5, 44, 46, 46, 49, 50.5, 51, 52, 129. The series has two gaps. A possible division would be that after five discs from the top of a column about 2.9 m tall or from the base of one about 2.3 m (or somewhere in between) we have eight discs from one 3.4 m tall. The 129 cm disc must have come from a column almost 8.5 m tall.

Ss. Quattro Coronati: pavements of both the church and of the separate chapel of S. Silvestro 1111. Only some of the discs are porphyry. The design requires three sizes of disc, 139, 69.75, and 34.875; the actual measurements are 27, 28.5, 30.5, 31.5, 37, 37, 56, 68, 70, 139. The series shows several gaps: the first six discs could have come from a column about 2.4 m tall, with perhaps ten discs missing, and the next three from a column from 4.5 to 5 m tall, again with many discs missing. The 139 cm disc must have come from a column more than 9 m tall.

S. Gregorio Magno: pavement twelfth century, relaid 1729 or 1745. The complex pattern requires four sizes of disc, 141, 70.5, 35.25, and 17.625. The actual discs measure 7, 7.5, 8, 8.5, 8.5, 18.5, 22, 23, 36.5, 42, 42, 43, 46, 46.5, 48.5, 51, 52, 53, 53, 55.5, 56.5, 57, 59, 60, 65, 67, 78, 86, 141. The series shows five interruptions. The first five discs could be from a piece of a colonnet around 60 cm high, cut into discs 11 or 12 cm thick; this seems too thick for the size, so there must be some discs missing. The next three, again with discs missing, could have come from a colonnet about 1.5 m high. Although there are more discs in the next series, and 36.5 to 48.5 cm in diameter, so that they would need to be cut thicker than the smaller ones, it does not seem likely that only seven of them would be cut from a column which must have been more than 3 m high. The next thirteen discs, however, running from 51 to 67 cm, could have used up the less than 4.5 m column they could have come from, with large discs more than 33 cm thick. The next two are isolated, though they could both have come from a column at least 6 m high, and the last one must have come from a column more than 9 m high.

S. Crisogono: pavement thirteenth century, restored seventh, nineteenth, and twentieth centuries. The three sizes needed are 147, 36.75, and 18.375. We actually find discs of 13, 20, 23, 23, 25, 25, 26.5, 28, 28, 28, 28, 29.5, 35.5, 39.5, 42, 147 (two other discs were hidden under scaffolding). There is a progression, but the figures are for the most part too widely separated to suggest more than that parts of at least five columns are involved, the smallest of which must have been about 1.3 m tall and the others perhaps 1.5, 2, 3, and over 9.5 m.

Sta. Maria in Cosmedin: pavement 1123, restored eighteenth and nineteenth centuries. The design would require discs of 238, 59.5, and 29.75. Actual measurements: 28, 29.5, 31, 32, 32.5, 33, 35, 38.5, 39, 40, 40.5, 46.5, 47, 51, 51, 51, 51.5, 52.5, 59, 77, 94, 238. The sequence would allow the use of a column of around 2.4 m, cut into the first seven discs, but with considerable waste; a column of 3.4 m or so, cut into eleven discs (no waste here); and parts of three more columns to give the last four discs. One of these must have been a respectable 6 m tall, but the one from which the 238 cm disc was cut must have been a colossal 15.5 m, almost 3 m taller than the columns of the Pantheon.

Sta. Maria in Aracoeli: pavement end of the thirteenth or beginning of the fourteenth century. Much rearranged, but the original design must have been quite complex, presumably requiring discs of 245, 122.5, 61.25, 30.625, 15.312+, and 7.656+, since the discs we actually find come close to those modules. The first part of the sequence (6, 6.5, 6.5, 6.5, 6.5, 7, 7, 7, 7.5, 8, 8, 8, 8.5, 8.5, 9, 9, 9, 9.5, 9.5, 9.5, 10, 10, 10, 10, 11, 11, 11) works well as twelve slices from a 52 cm colonnet, then fifteen slices from a 72 cm one. The rest, however (14, 14.5, 17, 18, 20.5, 21, 22, 28, 31, 31, 33, 35.5, 36, 42, 58.5, 60, 65, 137, 153, 239, 245), would need the very wasteful use of eight columns, the two largest of which would have been more than 15.5 and nearly 16 m tall.

S. Giovanni in Laterano: pavement fifteenth century, much later than any of the genuine cosmatesque designs. For so large a basilica, it has very few porphyry discs, and it seems possible that those it has were brought from some other church whose pavement seemed beyond repair. The discs, all large, could all have come from two columns, the 92 and 96 cm ones from the bottom of a column 6.2 or the top of one just under 8 m tall, and the others (174.5, 177.5, 234,

235, and 235 cm) from a column of the height of about 15.25 m.

St. Alessio: pavement 1217, restored 1750. Too much was inaccessible (wedding carpet) for any useful conclusions, but the sequence of diameters which could be measured (10.5, 11, 16.5, 17, 21, 22, 23.5, 24, 25, 34, 34, 36, 37, 37.5, 37.5, 38, 42.5, 55, 105.5) does provide the kind of progression we see in other churches. Note that the largest disc must have come from a column 6.86 to 9.14 m tall.

Ss. Giovanni e Paolo: pavement, beginning of the twelfth century, restored 1718. At our visit we found most of the nave covered with carpeting for weddings, but we could observe enough to suggest that the design required two sizes of disc, 149 cm and 74.5 cm, showing the presence of at least three columns, the largest of which would have been at least 9.7 m tall.

Sta. Maria in Trastevere: original pavement before 1143. This pavement at first appeared to be an anomaly. The pattern, instead of being based on the size of the largest porphyry disc, making the others fit in by adding borders, has—much to our chagrin—all its matching porphyry discs of exactly the same size as each other. In fact, every disc is either 16, 32, 37, or 99 cm in diameter. This seemed to make nonsense of our thesis that the *marmorari* were unable to cut curves, and that the discs in any church were from the same column or columns. Investigation revealed, however, that this is not the original pavement, which had been lost at an early date (D. Kinney, *Santa Maria in Trastevere from Its Founding to 1215*, unpublished Ph.D. dissertation, NYU, Institute of Fine Arts, 1975), presumably to repairs to, or embellishments of, other churches. According to the Touring Club Italiano *Guida di Roma* (8th ed., Milano 1993), the basilica was significantly modified in restorations of 1585 and 1702, but it was probably the *restauro stilistico* of Virginio Vespignani in 1877 which produced this elegant pastiche of a cosmatesque pavement. The existing pavement, then, is probably later than the pseudo-cosmatesque design (in mosaic tesserae) of the American Church S. Paolo dentro le Mura, and only fifty-odd years earlier than that of Buckfast Abbey, where the discs are also of uniform size.

It is clearly important to the overall design of nearly every pavement that there be at least one very large disc, the one which sets the module for the whole scheme. Where did the huge columns which provided these discs come from?

It is obvious that in the churches we visited all the large discs could have come from as few as two columns, one about 8 m tall and one almost 16. Even allowing for the churches to which we could not gain access, and for the large number of pieces that must have been lost in the fall of the columns or in the cutting, or have perished over time, it is not necessary to assume that there were in the city whole colonnades of porphyry columns 8 to 16 m tall. If there had been, surely the Cosmati would have used many more of these large discs which were so important to their planning. It is perhaps more likely that these larger columns were memorial or honorary columns like the red granite column of Antoninus and Faustina at Montecitorio, or those in the Forum, like the column of Phocas, itself a little over 17 m in height.

Yet the use of colonnades of large columns is not an impossibility: the six monolithic cipollino columns of the temple of Antoninus and Faustina are 17 m tall; and the rope channels cut into their tops show that there was at least the intention of pulling them down for reuse. What appears to be the top of a porphyry column with a curious hexagonal abacus and an Egyptian-style "flower" capital lies in the Antiquarium del Celio. The column itself is badly broken, but seems to have had a radius at its top of 74 cm, suggesting a column of almost 13 m in height (without the capital). Such a column could have provided porphyry discs for Sta. Maria in Aracoeli or S. Giovanni in Laterano, and could perhaps have formed part of a propylon in the Serapaeum, not far from one of the workshops of the *marmorari*.

In the case of the smaller columns, we have seen that in ten of the churches investigated there appear to be discs missing. Were these cut and used in other churches under construction at the same time? Apparently not: if the received dating is correct, only the smaller discs from Ss. Quattro Coronati and Sta. Maria in Cosmedin could be from the same column. We must not forget, however, that there are in Rome at least ten other cosmatesque pavements which, for one reason or another, we were unable to observe.

In any case the primitive nature of the tools must have caused a great deal of waste in the creation of these porphyry discs. This stone is referred to as unusually hard but, in fact, as we can see from observing the discs which were cut too thin and have broken in their years of use, it is liable to crumble when it breaks. There must have been many discs which had to be abandoned because they cracked or crumbled in the handling. There must have been many columns which broke with oblique breaks, making them unusable for discs, when they were being salvaged. The column fragment at Buckfast Abbey must have broken in this way, since its discs are made up of segments and sectors of circles. Four centuries after the work of the cosmatesque *marmorari*, even the considerable engineering skill of Carlo Fontana could not move the granite column of Antoninus and Faustina, at Montecitorio, without breaking it into three pieces. Difficulty in moving pieces of porphyry may also explain why there are no porphyry discs in the otherwise classically cosmatesque pavement of Westminster Abbey.

There are in all these data too many variables and unknowns for definite conclusions, but we hope that we have been able to give some indication of the sizes and numbers of the porphyry columns used for cosmatesque pavements, and to throw some light on the working methods of the *marmorari* of mediaeval Rome.

Tacitus *Germania* 33.2:
The State of the Question

Herbert W. Benario
Emory University

Military service in Germany in the early nineteen fifties enabled me to visit Italy twice on furloughs. But my first *real*
experience of Italy followed in 1956, when I was fortunate
enough to attend the summer session of the American
Academy in Rome. The director, for the first year of his
quadriennium, was Paul MacKendrick, assisted by William
L. MacDonald. It was an experience that opened my eyes,
as nothing before had done, to the numerous facets of Roman civilization, the contributions offered by literature,
history, archaeology, epigraphy, and many other speciali-
ties to the understanding of the whole. Admiration for and
gratitude to both scholars developed into friendship, which
has now lasted for more than two score years, *grande
mortalis aevi spatium.*

   The opportunity, therefore, to pay tribute publicly to
Paul MacKendrick is indeed welcome, and I offer for his
pleasure a discussion of a crucial passage in a seminal work

of the Roman author who, more than any other of the early principate, probed the reality of Rome's Vergilian duty, *tu regere imperio populos, Romane, memento.*

Tacitus' second published work, following soon after the biography of his father-in-law, was an ethnographical study of the empire's great rival and enemy to the north, the Germans.[1] The *Germania* remains enigmatic in many aspects, with discussion of its precise form and purpose still very active.[2] The date of its appearance is the year 98; Tacitus had been suffect consul late in the previous year,[3] and Trajan, stationed along the Rhine in Moguntiacum as legate of Germania superior, became *princeps* after Nerva's death in late January.

In chapter 33 of the *Germania*, Tacitus reports the extirpation of a tribe, the Bructeri, at the hands of other Germans. This afforded the Romans not only advantage but delectation. He then offers the following prayer,

> maneat, quaeso, duretque gentibus, si non amor nostri, at certe odium sui, quando urgentibus imperii fatis nihil iam praestare fortuna maius potest quam hostium discordiam.

This passage has become one of the most hotly discussed and debated in the entire Tacitean corpus. And yet its presentation of a problem, if problem there is, did not engage scholars until the early years of this century. It is this debate

---

[1] I do not accept the arguments put forth by some scholars that the *Dialogus de oratoribus* was the earliest of his works.

[2] The best overall discussion, still a masterpiece, is E. Norden, *Die Germanische Urgeschichte in Tacitus' Germania* (1920, 1959[4]). Very useful are the essays in *Beiträge zum Verständnis der Germania des Tacitus* I, Eds. H. Jankuhn and D. Timpe (1989). There are recent editions, with extensive and learned commentaries, by Lund 1988 and Perl 1990.

[3] For Tacitus' career and activity, the best discussion is still that of Syme 1958, with instructive further treatment in some of the essays in Syme 1970.

which I wish to trace here, although I do not undertake to include in my discussion every scholar and every work which has alluded to the question—surely an impossibility.[4]

The huge, long-defunct and still lamented *Bursians Jahresberichte über die Fortschritte der klassischen Altertumswissenschaft* included twelve reports on Tacitus, the first appearing in 1877, the last in 1943. In none before the tenth, published in 1929 by Hans Drexler, was there any discussion of 33.2; in other words, the passage was not considered a problem nor treated as a subject of controversy. In the final report, written by Erich Koestermann, there is no discussion save in connection with Richard Heinze's book. It is strange, and a bit humbling, that a major interpretative crux of our time did not appear to exist a century or so ago.

I have not discovered in the varied collections of his papers that Theodor Mommsen wrote about this chapter of the *Germania* at all. In the recently discovered and beautifully published lecture notes made by a scrupulous listener at his *Vorlesungen* on the history of the empire, Mommsen stated, in the context of Germanicus and Arminius, "The Germans were not to make another independent appearance on the stage of Roman history until the Marcomannic Wars. The tribes fell apart and no longer posed a threat to the Roman Empire, which began to move its point of main military effort to the Danube" (138).

Yet, some ninety years later, one scholar, chosen almost at random from a host of possibilities, wrote, concerning Tacitus' phrase,

> The words convey more than anxiety; they ring out alarm. The amazement that Rome's world conquests had aroused— they were the fountainhead of Polybius' political inspira-

---

[4] See Lund 1991b, 2127–47 for fuller discussion of many of these items.

tion, Vergil's metaphysical motivation, and Livy's ethical justification—had not yet died out. But the unsettling sensation that the Roman Empire might approach its end increased alarmingly. (Storoni Mazzolani 183)

From the former understanding of Tacitus' view of Rome's condition and prospects at the end of the first century of our era to the latter is a disturbing journey. We can trace, as with modern criticism of Vergil's *Aeneid*, the everdarkening mood of modern students of Tacitus and Rome, but can it be explained?

At the beginning of the present century, Karl Müllenhoff, in his vast edition of the *Germania*, discussed the passage at considerable length and noted that some have interpreted it to forecast Rome's decline, "das ist aber ein irrtum. dergleichen in einer schrift, die im öffentlichen interesse für den kaiser geschrieben war anzusprechen, wäre ominös und unbegreiflich ungeschickt gewesen." (425) The author of the authoritative and enormous *Deutsche Altertumskunde* may properly serve as representative of *communis opinio* as the nineteenth century ended only a few years before Mommsen's life (Benario 1993–94).

Reitzenstein made the next important contribution, in a lecture delivered in early 1915 and published in the same year. Speaking of those scholars who supported the pessimistic viewpoint, he wrote, "Die düstere Stimmung, ja Trostlosigkeit, die dann in diesen Worten läge, stünde in direktem Widerspruch nicht nur zu der Stimmung des Dialogus, sondern auch zu der Stimmung jener Teile des Agricola, die sich auf die Gegenwart beziehen" (253/97). He argued vigorously for the optimistic interpretation of the passage, emphasizing Tacitus' confidence in the future of the empire.

The influential edition of Schweizer-Sidler, which, in the revision of Schwyzer, reached its eighth edition in 1923, discussed the passage from both interpretative sides and leaned rather to the negative sense. It merits citation at length.

> Es kann die Weltherrschaft oder der Untergang sein; Tac. prophezeit nichts. Aber die Berufung auf die *host. disc.* . . . macht nicht den Eindruck froher Siegeszuversicht. Dass der Zeit und auch Tac. selbst der Gedanke an ein dereinstiges Ende des Reiches, an die Ablösung des römischen Herrschervolkes durch ein andres nicht fremd war, zeigt die Ablehnung der Prophezeiungen der gallischen Druiden beim Brande Roms unter Nero immerhin. Dass eben Trajans Regierungsantritt die Herzen mit froher Zuversicht erfüllt hatte, schliesst trübe Stimmungen nicht aus. (79)

The most significant early opposition came from Heinze, in a lecture delivered in 1928 and published in the following year. He discerned the author's expression of "gloom and doom," a view which fit the contemporary mood in Germany during the Weimar Republic, a decade of hyperinflation followed after a brief interval by the Great Depression.

In his edition with translation and commentary, Fehrle expresses a view somewhere between these two extremes. He translates the last sentence of the text, "Denn dem Geschick unseres Reiches, wenn es schwer auf uns lastet, kann Gewiss das Glück nichts besseres bieten, als die Zwietracht der Feinde" (41). He comments, "Es ist zuviel gesagt, wenn man meinte, T. deute mit diesen Worten seine Ahnung vom Untergange Roms durch die Germanen an; immerhin aber zeigen sie seine Sorge um die Entwicklung des Reiches" (99).

Wolff in his influential article does not treat this passage directly. But he speaks of signs of Roman degeneracy, and the similarity of the Germans to the Romans in numerous respects, the more so as *ratio* and *disciplina* play a role among the former.

> Er begnügt sich nicht damit, den Gedanken, zu dem ihn das Nachdenken über den langen und erfolgreichen Widerstand der Germanen geführt haben mochte, einfach anzusprechen und mit billigen Hinweisen auf die kriegerische Geistesart, die Volksmenge, den Geburten-überschuss des Gegners einen "Untergang der römischen Welt durch das Germanentum" an die Wand zu malen. (286)

The great literary history of Schanz-Hosius, of the mid 1930s, recapitulates the views and mood of the pre-World War II period. Surprisingly, no mention of this passage is made in the broad sweep of their coverage. They comment that Tacitus considered the Germans "die gefährlichsten Feinde Roms" and style him "dem Pessimisten Tacitus" (624); the inevitable conclusion is that *Germ.* 33.2 would have fit this mood and spoken of the impending doom of Rome.

During the war, only a brief note by Toynbee appeared, but in the mid-fifties began a constant flow of contributions: Pöschl, Büchner, Schmid, Zanco, Häussler, Steidle, Benario, Kraft, Delpuech, Erren, Houlou, Viré. In addition, there were numerous books and other studies which at least alluded to the problem of interpretation. Since the beginning of the nineteen eighties, interest has continued at a high level: Santos Yanguas, Urban, Magno, Fornaro, Perl, Lund, Flach, Grimal, Luiselli, Timpe.

Truth cannot be approached merely by adding the views on the two sides, and declaring that the one with the greater support is that which best recognizes Tacitus' judgment But I suggest that a trend is developing, which I wish to base upon my own contribution of some thirty years ago and three subsequent comments, the last two of which appear in works whose titles effectively conceal their presence and importance.

Goodyear writes, "Tacitus does not prophesy immediately impending catastrophe, the overthrow of the empire by the Germans. The famous words *urgentibus imperii fatis* at 33.2, pregnant though they are, cannot carry all that weight, without clear corroborative evidence. Tacitus was beginning, as he would continue, as a historian, not a soothsayer" (10).

Oliver argues, in a long footnote (35), that

> The controversy over the meaning of this phrase is simply phenomenal. If one has an irresistible urge to make Tacitus prophesy the coming of Alaric, Wölfflin's emendation or Koestermann's will serve his purpose, and some such meaning could be extracted from Robinson's in spite of Robinson's own interpretation of his reading, but if there was ever an excuse for misunderstanding *urgentibus*, that excuse was based on ignorance of the parallel passages that are conveniently listed by Gudeman *ad. loc.* (*Germ.* 33) in his second edition of the *Agricola* and *Germania* (Boston 1928). Tacitus' meaning was ably demonstrated by Herbert W. Benario; his conclusions are not in the least impaired by the subsequent article by Konrad Kraft.

Chilver agrees with Oliver: "An excellent bibliography on the *Germania* passage is given by H. W. Benario in *Historia* 1968, 37ff. His ensuing discussion is surely right in attempting to interpret T. there in the light of his other writing of the year 97–8 (and especially of the optimism of the *Agricola*), rather than in submerging it in a general pool of Tacitean pessimism" (45).

I think Chilver has acutely indicated the very real difference between an overall conclusion that Tacitus' outlook was gloomy and pessimistic (who could deny that after reading the large works?) and an interpretation of pleasure and optimism in a particular instance, above all in an early work. The aura of Trajan, soon to be *optimus princeps*, is paramount here. Tacitus anticipates great events and conquests, and confidently embraces the *beatissimum saeculum*.

Works Cited and General Discussions

Africa, T. W. 1965. *Rome of the Caesars*. New York. 157–70. [pessimistic]

Alfonsi, L. 1954. "Della concezione del destino in Tacito e Stazio." *Aevum* 28:175–77. [pessimistic]

——. 1974. "Problematicità della 'Germania' tacitiana." *Mélanges de Philosophie, de Littérature et d'Histoire offerts à Pierre Boyancé*. Rome. 5–19. [pessimistic]

Alonso Nunez, J. M. 1974. "Significación de la Germania de Tácito." *Zephyrus* 25:473–78. [pessimistic]

Anderson, J. G. C. 1938. *Cornelii Taciti De origine et situ Germanorum*. Oxford. [pessimistic]

Beare, W. 1964. "Tacitus on the Germans." *G&R* 11:64–76. [pessimistic]

Benario, H. W. 1968. "Tacitus and the Fall of the Roman Empire." *Historia* 17:37–50. [optimistic]

——. 1983. "Tacitus' *Germania*—A Third of a Century of Scholarship." *Quaderni di Storia* 17:209–30.

——. 1993–94. "Theodor Mommsen—In Commemoration of the Ninetieth Anniversary of his Death." *CO* 71:73–78.

Borzsák, I. 1958. "Tacitus." *Das Altertum* 4:32–52. [optimistic]

Borzsák, St. 1968. "Tacitus." In *RE Supplementband* XI:373–512.

Büchner, K. 1960. "Hat Tacitus geglaubt, der Untergang des römischen Reiches stehe unmittelbar bevor?" In *Festschrift W.-H. Schuchhardt*. Baden-Baden. 43–48 =

Studien zur römischen Literatur. Vol. 4. Wiesbaden, 1964. 61–67. [optimistic]

Burck, E. 1974. "Grundzüge römischer Geschichts-auffassung und Geschichtsschreibung." *GWU* 25:1–40 = idem, *Vom Menschenbild in der römischen Literatur* II. Heidelberg. 72–117, particularly 107–17. [pessimistic]

Chevallier, R. 1961. "Rome et la Germanie au 1ᵉʳ siècle de notre ère. Problems de colonisation." *Latomus* 20:33–51, 266–80. [pessimistic]

Chilver, G. E. F. 1979. *A Historical Commentary on Tacitus' Histories I and II.* Oxford. [optimistic]

Delpuech, P. 1975. "Urgentibus imperii fatis: Tacite et la fin de l'Empire." *Actes du IXᵉ congrès de l'Assoc. G. Budé.* Paris. 995–1018. [pessimistic]

Drexler, H. 1929. "Bericht über Tacitus für die Jahre 1913-1927." In *Bursians Jahresbericht* 224:257–461.

Dudley, D. R. 1968. *The World of Tacitus.* Boston. [optimistic]

Erren, M. 1976. "Urgentibus imperii fatis." *LF* 99:1–30. [optimistic]

Fehrle, E. 1929. *Publius Cornelius Tacitus Germania.* Munich. [optimistic?]

Flach, D. 1989. "Die Germania des Tacitus in ihrem literaturgeschichtlichen Zusammenhang." In *Beiträge zum Verständnis der Germania des Tacitus* I. Eds. H. Jankuhn and D. Timpe. Göttingen. 27–58. [pessimistic]

———. 1995. "Der taciteische Zugang zu der Welt der Germanen." In *Arminius und die Varusschlacht.* Eds. R. Wiegels and W. Woesler. Paderborn. 143–66. [pessimistic]

Forni, G. and F. Galli. 1964. *Taciti de origine et situ Germanorum.* Rome. [pessimistic]

Goodyear, F. R. D. 1970. *Tacitus*. Greece and Rome. New Surveys in the Classics 4. Oxford. [optimistic]

Grimal, P. 1989–90. "Religion politique et sens du divin chez Tacite." *Bulletin des antiquités luxembourgeoises* 20:101–16. [optimistic]

Häussler, R. 1965. *Tacitus und das historische Bewusstsein*. Heidelberg. 264–80. [pessimistic]

Heinze, R. 1929. "*Urgentibus imperii fatis.*" In idem, *Vom Geist des Römertums* 1938, 1960². Leipzig and Berlin. 255–77. [pessimistic]

Houlou, A. 1978. "Vrgentibus imperii fatis: à propos d'un passage controversé de Tacite, Germanie, 33." In *Centre Jean Palerne: Mémoires I*. Saint-Etienne. 59–66. [optimistic]

Howald, E. 1944. *Vom Geist antiker Geschichtsschreibung*. Munich and Berlin. [pessimistic]

Koestermann, E. 1943. "Tacitus. Bericht über das Schrifttum der Jahre 1931–1938." In *Bursians Jahresbericht* 282:78–220.

Kraft, K. 1968. "Urgentibus Imperii Fatis (Tacitus, Germania 33)." *Hermes* 96:591–608. [pessimistic]

Laugier, J.-L. 1969. *Tacite*. Paris. [optimistic]

Luiselli, B. 1992. *Storia Culturale dei Rapporti tra Mondo Romano & Mondo Germanico*. Rome. [pessimistic]

Lund, A. A. 1988. *P. Cornelius Tacitus Germania*. Heidelberg. [optimistic]

———. 1991a. "Versuch einer Gesamtinterpretation der 'Germania' des Tacitus." In *ANRW* 2.33.3. Berlin and New York. 1858–1988, 2347–82. [optimistic]

———. 1991b. "Kritischer Forschungsbericht zur 'Germania' des Tacitus." In *ANRW* 2.33.3. Berlin and New York. 1989–2222, 2341–44, 2347–82.

Magno, P. 1981. "Note à propos d'un passage controversé de Tacite, *Germanie*, XXXIII: Urgentibus imperii fatis." *LEC* 49:321–25. [pessimistic]

Michel, A. 1966. *Tacite et le destin de l'Empire*. Paris. [pessimistic]

Mommsen, Th. 1996. *A History of Rome Under the Emperors*. Eds. A. Demandt and B. Demandt. London and New York. [optimistic]

Much, R. 1967³. *Die Germania des Tacitus*. Eds. W. Lange and H. Jankuhn. Heidelberg. [pessimistic]

Müllenhoff, K. 1900. *Die Germania des Tacitus*. Berlin. [optimistic]

Oliver, R. P. 1977. "Did Tacitus Finish the *Annals*?" *ICS* 2:298–314. [optimistic]

Paratore, E. 1960². *Tacito*. Rome. [pessimistic]

———. 1977. "I Germani e i loro rapporti con Roma dalla *Germania* agli *Annales* di Tacito." *Romanobarbarica* 2:149–82. [pessimistic]

Perl, G. 1982–84. "Zu zwei *loci vexati* in Tacitus' Germania (2,3 und 33,2)." *AAntHung* 30:343–51. [optimistic]

———. 1983. "Die 'Germania' des Tacitus. Historisch-politische Aktualität und ethnographische Tradition." *ACD* 19:79–89. [optimistic]

———. 1990. *Tacitus, Germania*. Berlin. [optimistic]

Pöschl, V. 1956. "Tacitus und der Untergang des römischen Reiches." *WS* 69:310–20. [pessimistic]

Reitzenstein, R. 1915. "Bemerkungen zu den kleinen Schriften des Tacitus." *Nachrichten der K ö n i g l i c h e n Gesellschaft der Wissenschaften zu Göttingen, Phil.-hist. Klasse.* 173–276 = *Tacitus und sein Werk*. Leipzig 1927. 17–120. (Rpt. as *Aufsätze zu Tacitus*. Darmstadt 1967). [optimistic]

Robinson, R. P. 1935. *The Germania of Tacitus.* Middletown, Conn. [optimistic]

Rostagni, A. 1956. "Tacito e il pensiero della decadenza dell'Impero nell'interpretazione di V. Pöschl." *RFIC* 34:441. [pessimistic]

Santos Yanguas, N. 1982. "Tácito y la decadencia del Imperio." *Emerita* 50:17–32. [pessimistic]

Schanz, M. and C. Hosius 1935⁴. "Cornelius Tacitus." In *Geschichte der römischen Literatur* II. Munich. 603–43. [pessimistic]

Schmid, W. 1961. "Urgentibus imperii fatis (Tac. *Germ.* 33)." In *Didascaliae: Studies in Honor of A. M. Albareda.* Ed. S. Prete. New York. 381–92. [optimistic]

Schweizer-Sidler, H. and E. Schwyzer 1923⁸. *Tacitus' Germania.* Halle a. d. S. [pessimistic]

Steidle, W. 1965. "Tacitusprobleme." *MH* 22:91–95. [optimistic]

Storoni Mazzolani, L. 1976. *Empire Without End.* New York. [pessimistic]

Syme, R. 1958. *Tacitus.* Oxford. [pessimistic]

——. 1970. *Ten Studies in Tacitus.* Oxford.

Timpe, D. 1993. "Die Germanen und die *fata imperii.*" In *Klassisches Altertum, Spätantike und frühes Christentum.* Eds. K. Dietz, D. Hennig, and H. Kaletsch. Würzburg. 223–45. [optimistic]

Toynbee, J. M. C. 1944. "Two Notes on Tacitus." *CR* 38:39–43. [optimistic]

Urban, R. 1982. "*Urgentibus imperii fatis.* Die Lage des römischen Reiches nach Tacitus, Germania 33,2." *Chiron* 12:145–62. [optimistic]

Viré, G. 1979. "Vrgentibus imperii fatis (Tacite, *Germanie,* XXXIII)." *LEC* 47:323–34. [pessimistic]

Wolff, E. 1934. "Das geschichtliche Verstehen in Tacitus' Germania." *Hermes* 69:121–64. [optimistic]

Zanco, B. 1962. "Nota sull'interpretazione di *urgentibus imperii fatis*, Tacito, Germania, XXXIII,3." *Aevum* 36:529–31. [optimistic]

Caesar and the Evil Eye or What to Do with "καὶ σύ, τέκνον"

CASCASCAS

Frederick E. Brenk
Pontifical Biblical Institute

In the Fitzwilliam Museum at Cambridge is a fascinating honorary stele once erected in honor of Nero. Above the main inscription are the mysterious words ΚΑΙ ΣΥ (and you).[1] The museum description does not give the Greek inscription or a translation, nor indicate the winged solar disk framing the stele at the top; and it describes the two jackals as "dogs, recumbent." In fact the words ΚΑΙΣΥ are written without a break under a winged solar disk of which the left half has broken off. Under the phrase, two jackals recline, flanking an *ankh* and sitting on a thin base line. Below them is the inscription:

---

[1] Thanks are due to Doctor Eleni Vassilika, Keeper of Antiquities, Fitzwilliam Museum, Cambridge, for providing a photograph and making available to me their information on the stele. The essentials are: #E.49.1901; Egypt, sandstone, height: 24.9 cm, width: 14.7, thickness: 3.6; acquired 1901.

31

ΥΠΕΡΤΗCΤΥΧΗC
ΝΕΡΩΝΟC ΚΛΑΥΔΙΟΥ
ΚΑΙCΑΡΟCCΕΒΑCΤΟΥ
ΓΕΡΜΑΝΙΚΟΥΑΥΤΟΚΡΑ
[ΤΟΡΟC] CΥΝΟΔ[Ο]CΛΥ
. . . . .[ΙΕΟ ?]

Ὑπὲρ τῆς τύχης
Νερῶνος Κλαυδίου
Καίσαρος Σεβαστοῦ
Γερμανικοῦ Αὐτοκρά-
[τορος] σύνοδ[ο]ς λυχο
. . . . .[ιεο].[2]

For the Tyche of
Nero Claudius
Caesar Augustus
Germanicus Imper-
ator, the Synod [of the] . . .

The description refers to an article on the inscriptions in
the museum, which offered a reconstruction. Most aston-
ishingly the author, took ΚΑΙ ΣΥ as Καί[σαρι] σύ[νοδος].[3]

---

[2] Or Λυχο in the second last line.

[3] Heichelheim 17. He lists the inscription as "X.d: Lykopolites. Dedication to Nero's Tyche. Unpublished." "Lykopolites" depends upon the
very speculative reconstruction of the last lines.

I am grateful to Professor Maria Letezia Lazzarini for looking over
the inscription of the stele. She, too, regards the reconstruction by
Heichelheim of the last lines as very hypothetical:

[τορ]ος σύνοδος Λυκο-
[πολιτῶν καὶ οἱ] νέοι ἐφ-
[ηβεικότες (?) . . . . . .]

"Synodos of the Lykopolitans" does not correspond to anything in
Dittenberger ("Exempla Sermonis Graeci") s.v. σύνοδος, 576, where we
expect something like τῶν ἐν Ἀθήναις τεχνιτᾶν (#698); see also Mason
203. However, Abydos, where many similar stelae were found, is not far

The KAI ΣΥ in the Fitzwilliam stele is startling. In similar stelae the space the words occupy is almost invariably left free of writing—either in hieroglyphs or Greek—and the words themselves seem unparalleled.[4] Moreover, the Greek formula appears in the company of some of the most venerable religious symbols of Egypt—the winged solar disk, the *ankh*, and the Anubis jackals. The jackals occupy a place usually reserved for the *uraei*, with which the Sun God strikes his enemies. The formula, then, seems to exercise a power and "prophylactic" function equal to that of the ancient Egyptian symbols.[5]

---

from Lykopolis (Assiut). A 2nd c. funerary stele from Abydos, in fact, mentions "Theon, son of Apollonides Λυκοπολείτης . . ." (Milne 69, no. 21129). For Assiut, see Beinlich 490–95. The jackals on the Fitzwilliam stele have special significance if it came from Assiut ('guardian, guard'), whose principal divinity was the jackal god Upuaut ("he who proceeds," "opens the procession"), "Lord of Assiut." This configuration seems to be reflected in the Greek name, Λύκων πόλις.

[4] See Kamal 111, 146–47, 168–77, 187–88; nos. 22128, 22152, 22161, 22181–83, 22189; pls. XXXVIII, XLIX, LIV, LVI–VII, LXIV. A very small number of the hieroglyphic stelae have hieroglyphs under the solar disk and above the heads of figures on the principal scene immediately below, which is not separated from the solar disk by a baseline (e.g., no. 22182). On one (no. 22161), hieroglyphs appear below two facing rams and above the base line, below which is the principal scene, with divinities.

[5] For the iconography, see Abdalla 99–115, esp. 99. The lunette is usually occupied by a sun disk (symbol of Horos of Behedt), with or without wings and with or without flanking *uraei*. The two jackals in animal form, indicating the power of Anubis over the dead, are very common, while the empty space between the pendent *uraei* on some stelae is occasionally occupied by a vertical hieroglyphic text, an *ankh* sign (56, no. 130, pl. 49), or by one to three sun-rays. In one case, between the two jackals there seems to be a crudely carved offering table (Milne 55–56, no. 9226, pl. VIII). Usually the lower register has the principal scene of the deceased in "presentation"—frequently with Anubis—libation and offering, adoration, etc. (101–10). The part below this was usually left undecorated, perhaps for a painted inscription, now usually lost. The prominent base line is almost universal. In the

The idea for this article, however, came a long time before seeing the Fitzwilliam stele, while looking at the mosaics of Antioch—in reproductions, not in real life.[6] The brilliant intuition was that the famous "καὶ σύ, τέκνον" (and you, [my] child [or {my} son]) addressed by the expiring Julius Caesar to Brutus might have something to do with the καὶ σύ used to ward off the evil eye. However, as with many other great insights, things suddenly began to go awry. First, the article had already been done by James Russell, an archaeologist, and done in an extraordinarily well-researched way. Russell concluded that there was a possibility Caesar with his last gasp actually uttered the (in)famous καὶ σύ, τέκνον directed at his murderer, Brutus, in an apotropaic or retributive sense—thus dying with a curse on his lips. At the same time, doubts began to grow. Russell's conclusion was not so clear. He seemed both to

---

Fitzwilliam stele, the inscription appears directly under the base line, an adaptation for its use as a dedication; cf. stele no. 9293 (Milne 29, pl. III). The inscription, too, of no. 9293 is also very similar:

Ὑπερ Αὐτοκράτορος Καίσαρος [Δο]μιτ[ιανοῦ] Σεβαστοῦ Γερμανικοῦ τύχης

"for the good fortune of Domitian and his entire house, to Hera the Greatest Goddess"—followed by the names of the dedicators, as on the Fitzwilliam stele, then the edifice they constructed, and the date (here the seventh year of Domitian), using the same names for the emperor as in the beginning).

Thanks are due to Professor Loredana Sist of the Università di Roma, "La Sapienza," now also teaching at the Pontifical Biblical Institute, for extremely valuable help with the iconography and the inscriptional material. She suggests that the two jackals may have been intended to represent Anubis and Upuaut, both worshipped at Lykopolis.

[6] The major works on the subject for the purposes of this article are: Bell; Cimok; Dickie 1990, 1991, 1995; Dubuisson; Levi 1941, 1947, 32–34, pl. XL; Norris; Russell 1980, 1982, 1987; Slane and Dickie.

J. Russell's article on the end of the *Caesar* went unnoticed for some time. I am grateful to Professor Matthew W. Dickie for bringing it to my attention in 1996, and to Professor Russell for graciously sending me a copy of it, along with some additional information.

suggest that Caesar uttered the words in a prophylactic hope the blow would not strike and also with the intention to draw down retribution on Brutus.

First, one can present some positive points in Russell's favor. The καὶ σύ phrase—not testified before the Roman period—apparently was extremely well-known and found all over the Greek and Roman world.[7] The meaning is given by Russell as "To hell with you!," but Norris and others more literally translate it, "the same to you," "may you also suffer ill;" that is, the evil influence is turned back on the evil eye, or the malicious person.[8] Caesar and his circle certainly were acquainted with Greek and would have appreciated such "trendy" and sophisticated slang. Plutarch, in fact, in his *Life of Caesar* has him using a pithy Greek phrase from popular life just before crossing the Rubicon.[9] One might argue, too, that retribution figures in the biographies of Caesar. Thus, an appropriate curse with his dying breath bringing retribution down upon the tyrannicides would be a sublimely appropriate touch, justified by later events.

[7] Russell 1980, 125–26; Norris 2366–67 (with pls. III and IV). Norris (2366) cites Waagé for the existence of the formula on some Roman "Pergamene" pottery, which Waagé dated from ca. the end of the 1st c. B.C. to ca. the beginning of the 2nd A.D. In his appended note to the off-print sent me, Russell gives two further cases of the καὶ σύ inscription: a medieval graffito on the Parthenon—citing Robert; and to the entrance of a building recently excavated at Magdala in Palestine—citing Corbo. Color plates of the "Lucky Hunchback" (Hall III, no. 3; inv. no. 1026b [85 x 85 cm]; and the "Evil Eye" (Hall III, no. 6, inv. no. 1024 [170 x 150 cm] can now be found in Cimok 54, pl. 3 and 55, pl. 6.

[8] Russell 1980, 125–26; Norris 2367; Slane and Dickie 490 with n. 44.

[9] See Dubuisson 885–86, nn. 33, 39, 40, for the ἀνερρίφθω κύβος, spoken in Greek by Caesar at the Rubicon, and testified to by the historian and eyewitness, Asinius Pollio—though textual errors seem to have caused confusion. Dubuisson (885) underscores the fact that Caesar's supposed words to Brutus in the alternate version of Suetonius constitute the only Greek phrase spoken by Caesar in that *Life*. On the expression and its use at the Rubicon, see also Brenk 1987, 324, 326–27.

But now for the problems, some of which scholars have proposed before. First, there is the strong doubt by our very sources for the words—Suetonius, *Caesar* 82.3 and Cassius Dio (Dio Cassius, Kassios Dion) 44.19.5—that they were ever said at all. The other sources for the death of Caesar are mute on the final words.[10] Suetonius says Caesar died without uttering a word—"though some related that when Marcus Brutus rushed on him he said 'καὶ σύ, τέκνον.'"[11] Cassius Dio, who seems more negative toward the formula version, is not an independent witness but used Suetonius as his source.[12] Plutarch makes a great deal out of retribution in the *Lives* both of Caesar and of Brutus. If he knew the formula version of Caesar's death, he certainly would have understood its apotropaic possibilities. He may have regarded discussions of the evil eye as inappropriate to the genre of biography (βίος) and belonging to miscellany (συμποσιακά), though he does frequently speak of superstition in the *Lives*, and sometimes discusses a particular form of it.[13]

---

[10] See, for example, Dubuisson 881. Bell (826) notes that "Appian's account (*Bell. Civ.* II, 16, 117) and Dio Cassius' (XLIV, 19) agree in every detail"; and that even earlier, those of Plutarch, *Caesar* 81–82, and Suetonius, *Caesar* 81–82, are very close (with only slight variation in the number of blows delivered). Bell apparently considers the "last words" sentimental, citing Giner Soria, who noticed this trait in Hellenistic historians. He believes details of Caesar's well-known assassination quickly became "canonical," while Pompey's death, far from Rome, under mysterious circumstances, and poorly documented, gave rise to wide variation.

[11] Suetonius, who in *Diuus Iulius* only cites authors contemporary to Caesar, probably did not use later sources; see Russell 1980, 128, n. 24, citing Weinstock 343.

[12] See, for example, Russell 1980, 123, n. 3, citing Millar 85–87, 105.

[13] Dickie (1991, 20) argues that Plutarch not only wrote on the evil eye (*Symposiaka* 680C–683B) but offered an original explanation (18); however, in Dickie 1995, 17, he argues that Plutarch somewhat dishonestly claimed to be rather alone in his opinion, since the theory of emanation was found in the medical literature.

Dubuisson—who accepts the "last words"—claimed, however, that there is a great difference between the καὶ σύ and the expression at the Rubicon, ἀνερρίφθω κύβος (Let the die be cast. [Let's give it a fling.]). The latter was a proverb, the other spontaneous, a *véritable cri du coeur.*" The moment of being riddled with wounds was no time for snobbish vaunting of language skills. Yet, Dubuisson accepts the words. He feels that they were indeed spontaneous and appropriate to Caesar's class, and observes that the conspirators themselves are not above using Greek in the pitch of the fray. Casca delivers the first blow; when Caesar wards him off, he cries out, "ἀδελφέ βοήθει" (Brother, help me.) (Plutarch, *Caesar* 66.8). According to Dubuisson—who certainly is exaggerating—the Roman upper class of Caesar's circle learned Greek from their slaves as small children and only later took Latin seriously. Greek, then, was their real "maternal" language. Both Caesar's words and Casca's cry are a return to the memories of childhood fear. Fully in possession of his senses a moment before, Caesar responds to Tillius Cimber, who aggressively seizes him by the toga, in Latin, "Ista quidem uis est."[14] But at the Rubicon, was Caesar, who speaks Greek, in full possession of his senses or not?[15]

There remain some other problems, too. The "last words," in an apotropaic sense, seem to be associated primarily with amulets or with other archaeological rather than literary material. Illuminating for the Fitzwilliam stele is the use of the phrase in colonnades, over lintels and on

---

[14] Suetonius, *Caesar* 82.1. Dubuisson seems to take Caesar's Greek words as simply a variant, given some credibility by Suetonius. But both Suetonius and Dio mostly discount it: "Caesar did not utter a cry, though some say that . . ." (Suetonius 82.3)"; "This is the most accurate account (ἀληθέστατα), but others claim . . ." (Dio 44.19.5).

[15] Or should one argue that in the heat of the moment, he returned to his childhood experience at shooting dice?

tombs to ward off evil.[16] The formula recalls other prohibitions and invocations with supernatural sanction, inscribed throughout antiquity against potential profanators and tomb-robbers.[17] However, recent authors do not cite the formula in a literary context which specifically involves retribution of the Caesar type. Perhaps, this could be inferred, though, from the archaeological material, which suggests from "the same to you," "as thou hast murdered me, so shalt thou be murdered."[18] But in most contexts, the words are directed against the possibility of the evil eye or "Envy" destroying the "excellence" of the mosaic, and the like. Presumably the formula was considered more to be good insurance against future harm than instrument of revenge for wrongs already inflicted.[19]

---

[16] See Russell 1980, 126, and n. 16; Norris, 2367; Slane and Dickie 489–91, esp. n. 43. Russell 1980, citing Levi 1947, 126, notes that a mosaic in Rome gives the fuller expression καὶ σὺ ἔρρε ("to hell with you, too!"). Slane and Dickie note the variation καὶ σοί, and the Latin version (et tibi, et tibi sit)—all of which make good sense grammatically (490 with n. 44).

[17] Both Russell and Norris refer to the very full study of Engemann; see esp. 30–35. Russell 1982, cites, for example, Palatine Anthology 9.814, where the excellence of the bath will cancel the power of envy (Phthonos) (545 with n. 21). See also Russell 1995 (two serpents, scorpion, ibis, lion and leopard attack the eye), and his long discussion of Phthonos in Russell 1987, 39, 45–47, fig. 8, pl. VIII, 11.

[18] See, for example, Slane and Dickie 490, n. 44.

[19] The formula seems particularly associated with the idea of envy. For a horrendous depiction of the punishment of Phthonos (Envy), portrayed as a youth trying to choke himself, while attacked by lions and tigers, see Dunbabin and Dickie, esp. 27–28. Evidently the image is to prevent envy causing harm to the work of art or the inhabitants of the house. This Phthonos iconography, though, seems to be relatively late and confined mainly to the eastern part of the Empire. The earliest definite dating is 79 A.D., determined by the destruction of Pompeii. The height of popularity of the Phthonos figure appears to have occurred in the middle and late Empire (28–29).

Another problem in the final words of Caesar is the address to Brutus as child (τέκνον). Most scholars have associated the phrase with the imagined paternity of Caesar. The term τέκνον in this sense is extraneous to the arguments of Russell and Dubuisson, but was central for earlier scholars who rejected the "last words." Unable to believe that even Caesar, around the age of fifteen or sixteen, could have sired Brutus on a noble Roman lady, they reluctantly pronounced the phrase apocryphal.[20]

Dubuisson, however, who sees it as a term of affection, notes the growing use of τέκνον in Hellenistic and later literature. Unfortunately, he offers no example for a person around fifty-six directing the term to one around forty-one.[21] Russell, who concentrated on the apotropaic phrase, really did not address this problem. The author of the New Testament Epistle of John likes to address his flock with the word τεκνία (my [little] children), apparently interchangeable with his other terms ἀγαπητοί (beloved) and παιδία (my

[20] Servilia was the half-sister of Cato and the sister-in-law of Lucullus; see, for example, Dubuisson 884, n. 22.

Professor John Moles graciously sent me photocopies of his unpublished commentary on Plutarch's Brutus, where he treats (78–80) Servilia's relationship with Caesar, and the "last words" of Caesar. Moles, who believes the words might have been used in the "mon fils" sense believes that both the anti-Brutus faction (charge of parricide) and the pro-Brutus faction (total disinterestedness) would have been interested in promoting the paternity legend.

[21] Dubuisson 884 and Moles 79, who describe the "mon fils" sense of τέκνον as very common, do not offer examples of adult men where the difference in age was perhaps only sixteen years. But Dickey notes that τέκνον can be used by parents to children of any age, and when used by people other than parents, that it is usually addressed to adults. The oldest addressee is over forty (Dionysios of Halikarnassos, 11.13.5). Τέκνον (vs. παῖς) is frequently used in very emotional scenes, where kinship is stressed, or by persons in loco parentis (68). Oddly, in the Septuagint, where Saul had just barely escaped being killed by David, he addresses him as Δαυιδ τέκνον, and τέκνον (1 Samuel 26.17 and 21).

[little] children). However, he is pastor to a flock and might be accentuating his age.[22] Even so, the term contrasts with the usual ἀδελφοί (brethren) and ἀγαπητοί, used in the *Epistles*. The original source behind the last words in *Caesar* might have been striving for a tragic, pathetic effect. If in a curse, the term would be contemptuous.

But as far as the Fitzwilliam stele goes, as Levi has shown, the formula need not be malignant. Such inscriptions can also be benevolent. He notes the frequent greeting to the wayfarer, on Greek and Roman tombs:

χαῖρε καὶ σύ (best wishes to you too)

or:

καὶ σύγε (and . . . especially to you).

along with Latin equivalents like *uale et tu* (best wishes to you). Sometimes the key words appear with a benevolent inscription, as on a rock relief from Thera: τοῖς φίλοις (to friends). Levi thought the same meaning could apply to the καὶ σύ written on the threshold of a house in Palermo, as well as on the lintel of Syrian houses, where one finds the expression:

ὅσα λέγεις, φίλε καὶ σοὶ δίπλα (or καὶ σοὶ ταῦτα) (whatever you say, friend, twofold to you, too [{or} the same to you]).[23]

As Levi notes, the words can work both ways, bringing a blessing to friend and benevolent passerby, a curse to the

---

[22] Bauer, Arndt, and Gingrich give τεκνία—only in the plural—in a paternalistic sense; and τέκνον (2.b) for a spiritual child or pupil; (2.c), in the plural, for the members of a church, and (2.d), for "inner spiritual similarity" (815–16). According to the CD-ROM *TLG* Plutarch uses some form of τέκνον over 200 times; but even in the (rare) vocative case, a natural child always seems to be meant.

[23] Levi (1941, 226) writes ταῦτα, but ταὐτά seems more likely.

malevolent, while also averting curses. Thus, the καὶ σύ remains ambiguous—a greeting from the dead to the living, with best wishes, or an imprecation. On the funeral monument of Flauius Iulianus at Katûrā, the formula appears ominously after a warning not to disturb the tomb in any way.[24]

Material from Egypt is especially relevant in interpreting the Fitzwilliam stele, which came from there.[25] Cosmic calamity could result from the Sun encountering the evil eye of Apopis, the primeval serpent. The countermeasure was the eye of the Sun-god or the powerful eye of Seth. The prominence of snakes in some of the evil eye representations may have something to do with this ancient iconographic association. Puzzling, too, have been the sticks in the Lucky Hunchback mosaic. In Egypt one rite apparently involved hitting a ball which evidently symbolized the eye of Apopis. Nineteen examples of this iconography have been found, depicted on various temples, where a royal figure holds a ball and stick, or thin club.[26] The evil eye is also attested for beings in the nether world. Against them, Thoth, Amun, Khons, and the eye of Re are very powerful.[27] Even so, though the Egyptian papyri refer to spells against the evil eye, as do several temple inscriptions, so far only one example has actually been found.[28] Frequently

---

[24] Levi notes another formula, καὶ τί, found at Resâs, which was placed in a *tabula ansata* on a doorpost of a home, opposite a facing doorpost with a καὶ σύ inscription in an identical frame. Dunand, who published it, thinking both came from a tomb, translated: "You and everyone [will die.]" (237 and pl. XVI, 16 and 17). But Levi takes them rather as apotropaic protection, at the entrance, against the "evil-minded" (226, with nn. 76 and 77).

[25] See Borghouts.

[26] Borghouts, esp. 122, 128; fig. 2, 3, pl. XXXIX. Perhaps the stick used to hit the ball is an antecedent of the "Lucky Hunchback's" sticks.

[27] Borghouts 143, 147–48.

[28] Berlin wooden tablet 23308; see Borghouts 148.

$w\underline{d}_3t$-eyes appear on magical papyri, amulets, sarcophagi, doors, false doors, stelae, tomb walls, and model boats. Presumably, the winged solar disk on the Fitzwilliam stele serves as the solar eye. The Anubis-type jackals are protective deities, and might have been thought to protect against the evil eye, like some other gods. Naturally, the *ankh* is a powerful protective force. In any case the καὶ σύ has been ennobled through its association with the awesome, auspicious symbols of Egyptian religious tradition from time immemorial.

The very idea of wide diffusion of the superstition of the evil eye in ancient Near Eastern civilizations, though, has recently been seriously questioned. Apparently, early Assyriologists greatly exaggerated its importance and diffusion, calling it a "wide-spread belief." [29] At the present time seven incantations against the evil eye have come to light. Though it seems associated with witchcraft and sorcery, the results appear to be natural accidents: too little rain, a tool breaking, cheese going wrong, clothes torn, and so forth. Outside of the evil eye in one text causing a nurse to lose her hold on a baby, there is nothing about babies being particularly affected.[30] Eye imitations seem to have been used as protection in the ancient Near East, but in the literature there are other remedies. Some involve strands of wool, or binding black and white wool around the head; tying on something mixed with a certain oil; placing bread on the head. The only known ritual instructions are fragmentary and do not look like special weapons: libation with beer, prayers, throwing an incense burner into the river.[31] The

---

[29] Thomsen. Burkert relates the evil eye to animal activity, where it denotes aggression—especially on the part of predators—while the contrary (avoiding eye contact) denotes submission (43, and n. 19, p. 198, with many references, including Schlesier 33–64, 86).

[30] Thomsen 20–23. For the nurse's hold see line 10 of text (TCL 16.89:3–12(A) = BL, no. 443, 3–9 (B) Thomsen 23).

[31] Thomsen 26–27; ritual: BAM 374 obv. 3'–8'.

superstition is attested already in the third millennium B.C., but the relatively small number of references would apparently rule out speaking of "wide-spread belief." With few exceptions the evil eye belongs to Sumerian literature, while witchcraft is Akkadian. But even witches are rarely accused of looking at their victims.[32]

One possible explanation offered for the difference between the Sumerian and Akkadian material is chronological, the existence of a very early strand of religion. But a counter-argument is that incantations and ritual texts were the work of highly trained specialists. The evil eye, like witchcraft, was the work of humans, and not really dangerous, since it usually did not affect the health of the person. It was not important enough, like demons, witchcraft, and diseases, to require an important ritual. Thus, the evil eye may have been very important, but the written sources give a different impression.[33] Some recent general books on Graeco-Roman magical papyri and amulets also suggest that the belief was not so important, and that the καὶ σύ formula was relatively infrequent.[34] Oddly enough, we have apparently only one ancient Greek or Latin description of

---

[32] For the exceptions, Borghouts 147 and n. 8, cites *Oracular Amuletic Decrees*: 'irt rmt in L. 2 rt. 83; vs. 28.

[33] Thomsen 27–28.

[34] See the cautious assessment of Slane and Dickie 502, who suggest chronological and geographical differences. Kotansky 1994, with sixty-six texts, does not mention the καὶ σύ phrase. There are two references to the evil eye (32.31 and 52.103)—oddly both in Jewish spells; see commentary, 145, 298. He states (145) that the evil eye is not found often in the magical papyri, but cites Bonner 96–98, for its frequent occurrence on amulets. Betz lacks an index. However, none of the over 140 titles of spells, etc., mentions the evil eye. Kotansky 1991 mentions a silver amulet with a somewhat generic protection formula, including that against the evil eye, but without the καὶ σύ (119). Similar is the dream ritual directed to Bes, again, without the καὶ σύ formula; see Eitrem 178 in the same volume.

someone putting the evil eye on another—if it can be called
that—and this is of the mythical Medeia bewitching Talos.[35]

Where does this get us with Caesar and Brutus? A number of possibilities are open. First, Plutarch and other authors who omitted the "final phrase" might not have found
them in their sources. Second, they might have considered
them out of place, for example, feeling uncomfortable with
Caesar calling Brutus, "son." Extraneous elements would
blur the thematic line, for example, of retribution in
Plutarch. Introduction of the evil eye at this time would
only confuse the issue. On the other hand, one need not
take the phrase as a curse. A pathetic note of tragic irony,
inspired by connotations of benevolence toward Brutus in
the past, would be perfectly suitable for Caesar's death.

The words were not in the best sources. There need not
have been behind them a reference to the evil eye, and no
author explicitly states that there was. But there are other
considerations. First, envy, which seems most characteristic
of evil eye contexts, appears irrelevant here. If Plutarch and
others who omitted the last words did know of them, they
had no compelling reason to take them in the superstitious
sense. But let us suppose they did. They might still have regarded them as unsuitable for the death of a great man. Or
they might have believed that both Caesar and Brutus by
character would have disdained magic and superstitious
practices. Stoics and Epicureans, for example, attacked
paradoxography, a genre to which the evil eye belonged.
Many philosophers believed in the principle "*actio in
distans repugnat*"—something cannot produce physical effects without contact.[36] Purely literary reasons, however,

[35] Apollonios of Rhodes, *Argonautika* 4.1669–70; see Dunbabin and
Dickie 11.

[36] On disdain for magic and the like among the upper classes, see
Aune, esp. 1515 (with nn. 29–31) and 1521; Dickie 1995, 9, 14, (citing

could have suggested the intrusion of the belief in the evil eye, since the hero of Plutarch's parallel life, Alexander, collapses before superstition at the end. But the sources which Plutarch followed apparently were working in just the opposite direction: if Caesar had been more superstitious, he might have saved his life.

In general the words καὶ σύ need a rather precise context. And even when they possess one, they may be polysemic or ambivalent. Suetonius and Cassius Dio were right to cast doubt on the words ever having been spoken. Nor do they suggest they alluded to the evil eye, and not to simply a close relationship between Caesar and Brutus. But these authors, as so often in classical literature, liked to have their cake and eat it too. They claim to discount the final words but cannot bear giving them up.

Now for a number of "ifs." Those six letters, however, would have carried enormous weight. In the past, Caesar had called blessings down upon Brutus; in the present tragically ironic circumstances of betrayal, affection would turn into hatred and blessings into a curse. If—unlikely as it may seem—Caesar did say them, and if they were a curse, then the proof of the pudding is in the eating. They brought upon Brutus a tragic end, ushered in the Triumvirate, and then Augustus and the Roman Empire, Constantine and Christianity, the Middle Ages, the Renaissance and Reformation, and eventually our own ultra-technological modern world, which—as no one can deny—affects our lives in every possible way.[37]

Plutarch, *Symposiaka* 680C, and Heliodoros, 3.7.2), 16, 19, 24, but also 9, 31–33, for implicit belief; Brenk 1986, 2140–43.

[37] I am very grateful to Professor James Russell of the University of British Columbia, and Matthew Dickie of the University of Illinois, Chicago, for generously looking over the manuscript of the article and offering many helpful corrections and suggestions.

Works Cited

Abdalla, A. 1992. *Graeco-Roman Funerary Stelae from Upper Egypt*. LMAOS. Liverpool.

Aune, D. E. 1980. "Magic in Early Christianity." *ANRW* II.23.2:1507-57.

Bauer, W., W. F. Arndt, and F. W. Gingrich. 1957. *A Greek-English Lexikon of the New Testament and Other Early Christian Literature*. Chicago.

Beinlich, H. 1975. "Assiut." In *Lexikon der Ägyptologie* I. Eds. W. Helck and E. Otto. Wiesbaden. 490-95.

Bell, A. A. 1994. "Fact and Exemplum in Accounts of the Deaths of Pompey and Caesar." *Latomus* 53:824-36.

Betz, H. D., ed. 1986. *The Greek Magical Papyri in Translation*. Chicago.

Bonner, C. 1950. *Studies in Magical Amulets*. Ann Arbor.

Borghouts, J. F. 1973. "The Evil Eye of Apopis." *The Journal of Egyptian Archaeology* 59:114-50.

Brenk, F. E. 1986. "In the Light of the Moon: Demonology in the Early Imperial Period." *ANRW* II.16.1:2068-2145. (Indices *ANRW* II.36.2 [1987] 1283-99).

———. "An Imperial Heritage: The Religious Spirit of Plutarch of Chaironeia." *ANRW* II.36.1:249-349. (Indices *ANRW* II.36.2 [1987] 1300-22).

Burkert, W. 1996. *Creation of the Sacred. Tracks of Biology in Early Religions*. Cambridge, Mass.

Cimok, F. ed. 1995. *Antioch Mosaics*. Istanbul.

Corbo, V. 1978. "Piazza e villa urbana a Magdala." *Liber Annuus* 28:232-40.

Dickey, E. 1996. *Greek Forms of Address. From Herodotus to Lucian*. Oxford.

Dickie, M. W. 1990. "Talos Bewitched: Magic, Atomic Theory and Paraoxography in Apollonius, *Argonautica*

4.1638–88." In *Roman Poetry and Drama. Greek Epic, Comedy, Rhetoric.* Eds. F. Cairns ad H. Malcolm. Leeds. 267–96.

——. 1991. "Heliodorus and Plutarch on the Evil Eye." *CP* 86:17–29.

——. 1995. "The Fathers of the Church and the Evil Eye." In *Byzantine Magic.* Ed. H. Maguire. Dumbarton Oaks. 9–34.

Dittenberger, W. 1924. *Sylloge Inscriptionum Graecarum* IV.1. 3rd ed. Leipzig.

Dubuisson, M. 1980. "'Toi aussi, mon fils!'" *Latomus* 39:881–90.

Dunand, M. 1933. "Nouvelles inscriptions du Djebel Druze et du Hauran (Suite)." *Revue Biblique* 42:235–54.

Dunbabin, K. M. C., and M. W. Dickie. 1983. "*Invidia rumpantur pectora.* The Iconography of Phthonos/Invidia in Graeco-Roman Art." *Jahrbuch für Antike und Christentum* 26:7–37.

Eitrem, S. 1991. "Dreams and Divination in Magical Ritual." In *Magika Hiera. Ancient Greek Magic and Religion.* Eds. C. A. Faraone and D. Obbink. New York and Oxford. 174–87.

Engemann, J. 1975. "Zur Verbreitung magischer Übelabwehr in der nichtchristlichen und christlichen Spätantike." *Jahrbuch für Antike und Christentum* 18:22–48.

Giner Soria, M. C. 1983. "Elementos del finis vitae." *Helmantica* 34:229–48.

Heichelheim, F. M. 1942. "The Greek Inscriptions in the Fitzwilliam Museum." *JHS* 62:14–20.

Kamal, A. B. 1905. *Catalogue Général des Antiquités Égyptiennes du Musée du Caire. Stèles ptolémaiques et romaines* I–II. Cairo.

Kotansky, R. 1991. "Incantations and Prayers for Salvation on Inscribed Greek Amulets." In *Magika Hiera. Ancient Greek Magic and Religion.* Eds. C. A. Faraone and D. Obbink. New York and Oxford. 107–38.

——.1994. *Greek Magical Amulets.* I. *The Inscribed Gold, Silver, Copper, and Bronze Lamellae.* Part I. *Published Texts of Known Provenance.* Opladen.

Levi, D. 1941. "The Evil Eye and the Lucky Hunchback." In *Antioch-on-the-Orontes.* III. *The Excavations 1937-39.* Ed. R. Stillwell. Princeton. 220–32.

——. 1947. *Antioch Mosaic Pavements* I. Princeton.

Mason, H. J. 1974. *Greek Terms for Roman Institutions.* Toronto.

Millar, F. 1964. *A Study of Dio Cassius.* Oxford.

Milne, J. G. 1905. *Catalogue Général des Antiquités Égyptiennes du Musée du Caire. Greek Inscriptions.* Oxford.

Norris, F. W. 1990. "Antioch as a Religious Center. Paganism before Constantine." *ANRW* II.18.4:2322–79.

Robert L. 1978. "Des Carpathes à la Propontide." *Dacia* 22:325–29.

Russell, J. 1980. "Julius Caesar's Last Words." In *Vindex Humanitatis. Essays in Honour of John Huntly Bishop.* Ed. B. Marshall. Armidale, Australia. 123–28.

——. 1982. "The Evil Eye in Early Byzantine Society. Archaeological Evidence from Anemurium in Isauria." In XVI. *Internationaler Byzantinistenkongress (Wien 1981) Akten* II.3. Jahrbuch der österreichischen Byzantinistik. Eds. W. Hörander, et al. Vienna 1982. 539–48.

——. 1987. *The Mosaic Inscriptions of Anemurium.* ÖAW Phil.-Hist. Kl. Denkschr. 190. Vienna.

——.1995. "The Archaeological Context of Magic in the Early Byzantine Period." In *Byzantine Magic.* Ed. H. Maguire. Dumbarton Oaks. 35-50 (41, fig. 5).

Schlesier, R. 1994. *Kulte, Mythen und Gelehrte.* Frankfurt.

Slane K. W., and M. W. Dickie. 1993. "A Knidian Phallic Vase from Corinth." *Hesperia* 62:483–505.

Thomsen, M.-L. 1992. "The Evil Eye in Mesopotamia." *Journal of Near Eastern Studies* 51:19–32.

Waagé, F. 1948. "Hellenistic and Roman Tableware of North Syria." *AO* 4:32–38.

Weinstock S. 1971. *Divus Julius.* Oxford.

Honorary Stele in Cambridge

Linear A on Trojan Spindlewhorls, Luvian-Based FANAΞ at Cnossus*

Edwin L. Brown
University of North Carolina at Chapel Hill

When the distinguished Indo-Europeanist Emmanuel Laroche ventured in 1970 his considered opinion on the Late Bronze Age language current in Northwest Anatolia, he said, "There is not the slightest indication . . . what the group of people who formed the background of the Homeric lay belonged to."[1] By 1984 Calvert Watkins, concluding his Bryn Mawr College lecture on "The Language

---

* This paper may be said to have begun its long incubation under the MacKendricks' benign eyes when I was a Junior Fulbright scholar at the American School of Classical Studies at Athens, and they were in residence also in the Visiting Professor's apartment in Loring Hall. It was then, after indelible days on Crete at the winter solstice, that I came to the determination one day to work on the Linear A script, and so to the realization that my graduate work must focus on philology, no longer archaeology. Only thus could I hope eventually to join in making those mute signs speak, knowing that Paul was eliciting eloquence from the stones.

[1] Laroche 1972, 126.

51

of the Trojans," could fairly state, on the basis of the evidence in favor of Luvian dialect which he there brought forward, "Perhaps we are, after all, a little closer to the unknowable language of the Trojans."[2]

Then in 1990 the island of Samothrace, within sight of the mound of Hissarlik, yielded the first signs of Minoan presence or influence in the Northeastern Aegean: an early second millennium (late 18th c.?) roundel stamped with Linear A or Minoan hieroglyphic.[3] Four years later Louis Godart republished two clay spindlewhorls which Schliemann had excavated at Troy in 1873 and which the world effectively forgot after the philologues' efforts to read Greek into the five (fully?) corresponding signs on each had failed.[4] Since none would deny Godart "son étonnante perspicacité" in the reading and editing of the written documents of Minoan Crete, his assertion that these two whorls are inscribed with Linear A syllabograms encourages me to return to the study of their inscriptions. This time, though, I propose to read them not as Greek inscriptions, but as Luvian—on the strength, first, of the case that has been made by Palmer, Huxley, and others for detecting Hittite's sister dialect in the Linear A documents of Crete.[5] At the same time, this choice of language is newly supported by Manfred Korfmann's ongoing Trojan finds,

[2] Watkins 62.

[3] Matsas 170–72.

[4] Godart 1994a, 457–60, Schliemann 363–68. Though even without autopsy I concur with Godart's judgment that each whorl bears five signs (not the six assumed in the early attempts to read them by M. Haug and T. Gomperz on the basis of the then-newly-deciphered Classical Cypriote Syllabary), I cannot as readily accept that they erred in regarding the inscriptions as identical (whereas Godart distinguishes AB51 on the second whorl [inv. no. 2445] from AB39 on the first [inv. no. 2444]).

[5] Bibliography on these early proponents of Luvian-in-Linear-A, cited in Brown 1990, 226, was intended as exemplary only.

which now include a bit of undoubted Luvian writing, on a Troy VII biconvex seal inscribed with Luvian hieroglyphs (such as were once called Hieroglyphic Hittite).[6]

But to focus on the spindlewhorls: we may read the Linear A syllabic signs on both whorls as two words, PI-MI-D/TA PU-RIA, by adopting the sound values established by Ventris for their Linear B counterparts.[7] This reading retains the left-to-right order of the signs, with the same word-beginning and -end as was assumed by Godart. Let us also adopt the spelling rules that apply generally in Linear B (though in Linear A voiced and unvoiced dentals alike are represented by the *T*+vowel signs of Linear B), and assume too the word-order and syntax of all the Indo-European tongues—Hittite, Luvian, Palaic—attested in Bronze Age Anatolia. Then one may transliterate PI-MI-D/TA as a compound personal name, *Pimidas*, and PU-RIA as a common noun, *puri(y)as* in the nominative singular or *puria* in the nominative plural.

For the meaning of this *puriyas*, though the lexicon of Luvian words so far assembled appears to be deficient here, the far richer stores of Hittite words may furnish the relevant cognate: the reduplicated *purpura-* means 'clod' or 'lump'; preceded by the bread ideogram NINDA, *purpura-* means 'dumpling' or again 'lump'.[8] On spindlewhorls *puriyas* should mean the clay whorl itself, clay being the most usual substance of which whorls have immemorially been made.[9]

[6] Hawkins and Eastman 1996, 111–16.

[7] These phonetic values for the Linear A signs in question are essentially those presented by Packard in his grid, Fig. 5, except that his *TA* appears here as *D/TA*, since I have sought to show (1995, 25–54) that the voiced and unvoiced forms of each of the stop consonants—*d/t* as well as *g/k* and *b/p*—is represented by the same sign.

[8] See Hoffner 178f and 207.

[9] Barber 37.

Our two whorls' biconvex shape may provide the clue to an Indo-European root for *purpura-*, and for *PU-RIA as well. **puro-* in its suffixed form **pur-en-* is thought to have yielded Greek, 'stone' of a pitted fruit.[10] I would propose, then, that Hittite *purpura-* was related in sense to our *PURIA- much as Spanish *nuez* 'nut' has the extended meaning 'whorl', or as Italian *nocciolino* 'spindle-whorl' is derived from '*nocciolo* '(fruit) stone', 'pit'. For 'spindle-whorl' the Greeks themselves employed, and still make metaphorical use of, σφόνδυλος or 'vertebra'.

It would be satisfying to find this term for 'whorl' inscribed upon the surfaces of spinners' whorls that have been retrieved from digs in Classical Greek lands. But though many surviving whorls have been written on or painted on—not as many whorls as loomweights, to be sure—, the proprietary formula used in these inscriptions seldom named the object itself, as an early 7th-century aryballos from Cumae, reading "I am Tataie's lekythos," does, or the mid-7th-century skyphos from the Athenian Agora, announcing "I am Tharios' cup." More often the object merely states, "I am Isodice's," say, to cite an inscription on a late archaic loomweight from Siris.[11]

As for **Pimid/tas* taken as a Luvian personal name in the possessive genitive, it would, when construed with a nominative *puriyas, form either a nominal sentence, "The spindlewhorl is Pimida's," in the way that Greek too may omit forms of the verb 'to be', or else simply the phrase "Pimida's spindlewhorl." Now, cuneiform Luvian replaces the genitive case of the noun by a genitival adjective, and it would probably have been rash to suppose, without written proof, that an insular Luvian dialect became established on

[10] Watkins (1969, 1536) may most readily be consulted, 1536 *s.v. puro-*.

[11] These inscriptions are all included in Jeffery 45 and 240, *3*; 69 and 76, *4*; 286 and 288, *1*.

Crete before this adjectival usage emerged in Asia Minor itself. Fortunately, we have the witness of hieroglyphic Luvian from its 16th-century inception till its demise at the end of the 8th that the genitive case was alive and well in Luvian spoken on the Anatolian mainland.

At all events, the first element , *Pi-* or *Piya-* meaning 'gift' or 'given', of this compound name could not be more characteristic; it is the initial term to be studied by Laroche in the chapter on Hittite and Luvian compounds of his *Noms des hittites*, and remains current as a first or second element of compound names through every later period of Anatolian Indo-European literacy.[12] The uncontracted form *Piya-* predominates, as in 'Piyamaradu', the name of a notorious troublemaker for that New Kingdom Hittite king who wrote the so-called Tawagalawas Letter. But the syncopated *Pi-* of **Pimidas*, or, again, of Pissilis, king of Carchemish, is also found,[13] earlier than Laroche could demonstrate in 1966.

The second element **-MID/TA* might on the basis of parallels signify either a toponym or a personal name, human or divine. In fact, both the placename Mita/Mida (a town in the district of the Anatolian cult center Zippalanda)[14] and the royal name Mita—identical with that of Phrygian Midas, who may in turn be equated with Mita of Mushki, the formidable foe of Sargon II[15]—are well attested in the Hittite documents and Assyrian annals, respectively. And finally, the common noun *mi-ta₄-* in hieroglyphic Luvian conventionally means 'servant', but from the context has a connotation closer to 'vassal'[16] or 'slave' of the god in the

---

[12] Laroche 1966, 317–19.

[13] Güterbock 136.

[14] Haas 588.

[15] For a recent summary account see Sams 1149 and cf. Macqueen 1101–2.

[16] See Hawkins 1975, 149, following Bossert.

sense that *do-e-ro* sometimes has in the Mycenaean archives: 'devoted servant', then, may best convey the meaning of our *Pimid/tas*.

It has seemed worthwhile thus to rescue from oblivion an expatriate Minoan spinster who would be the earliest female personnage of possibly European origin to whom a name can tentatively be attached. It may even be speculated that the pair of whorls have both survived because they were together retired from use, and it is certain that spinsters did often possess sets of whorls, since thread would be consumed in weaving far faster than it was prepared by spinning. At Troy such a pair of whorls—and thousands of votive weights and whorls have similarly been excavated at ancient sanctuaries, such as Athena's at Lindos[17]—would most fittingly have been deposited in that temple on the height of Hissarlik whose deity Homer called Athena.

The Luvian analog to Athena, however, as we now know from the records of Lydia, Lycia, and other formerly Luvian lands, was *Maliya*, who according to Lebrun attained outstanding importance among Luvo-Hittite goddesses.[18] Her association with Athena has till now been thought to depend solely on the fact that both were city-guardians.[19] But an even more significant link can be forged between the two if we consider the semantics implied in Maliya's name when its apparent Indo-European etymon is examined. For, without in any way having the divine name in mind, Watkins well proposed a decade ago that Hittite *mal-* is 'inner strength' < *'mental force' from a root noun to PIE *men-* (cf. CLuv. *mali(ya)-* 'think' and *mali-* 'thought').[20]

---

[17] See, e.g., Blinkenberg 130–35.

[18] Lebrun 126–28; cf. Demargne 97 for first confirmation of the Maliya/Athena correspondence.

[19] Lebrun 124, 129.

[20] Watkins 1985, 617 n. 2.

So long as our pair of inscribed whorls remain the only evidence of Linear A in Northwest Anatolia, it is most natural to suppose that whoever wrote upon these two clay objects hailed from Crete, where till now all but a handful of Linear A documents have been unearthed.[21] Thus, it may be of significance that, among the toponyms listed in a treaty of Hellenistic date between Lato and Olus, a place called Mita (?, dat. MITOIΣ) shows up.[22] One must wonder, therefore, whether *PIMID/TA may even have reached the Troad from her native Crete, a literal 'gift of Mita' township there. After all, we provisionally accept that the 'women of Milatos', 'of Knidos', and 'of Lamnos' mentioned in Linear B tablets from Pylos do actually document a similar but East-to-West transfer of skilled as well as unskilled workers (spinners included) from Miletus, Cnidus, and Lemnos to the Southwest Peloponnese.[23]

But if we are to hypothesize that our inscribed whorls indeed represent Luvian dialect in a Linear A guise returning to the West Anatolian mainland from Crete, it is desirable now to find ways, short of furnishing a full decipherment of Linear A script, to strengthen the case for its Luvian character. The approach I have mainly pursued until now has been to assume that the creators of Linear A script relied on the principle of acrophony in choosing the shapes

[21] It gives pause, nevertheless, to note that the Troy IV date (2050–1900) which Godart 459 accepts for the whorls corresponds with that of the earliest writing yet known from Crete itself, from Archanes. Eighty years of digging at Mycenae passed before its Bronze Age literacy was demonstrated. But a 500-year blank in the evidence of writing in Western Anatolia from, say, 1900 to 1400 is striking, though not unparalleled, as witness the dearth of Phoenician documents in the homeland of alphabetic writing from 10th to 5th century.

[22] This town's location, of course, should be sought in light of its companion-sites, in that East Cretan area where pre-Greek traditions long survived; see Guarducci 119, line 54.

[23] Chadwick 80.

of their syllabograms. Thus I have observed the match between the sound value of each Linear A sign identifiable
with some object inspiring its shape and the first syllable of
that object's Luvian name. Not all the schematized signs
are recognizable now, and not always do we know the
Luvian word for the given object , even when the schematic
form is still recognizable. Such acrophonic equations between object's name in Luvian and Linear sign's sound
value continue to accumulate since the report on about
three dozen signs which I have presented earlier[24]—for example, the matching of sign L28/AB40 to the Luvian
name for a chariot-box: it was only with Neumann's recent
discovery of 'chariot box' as the meaning of Hittite *widuli-*
that I recognized in L28 the contours and main elements of
the Bronze Age chariot's superstructure as rendered in
Mycenaean and Minoan depictions.[25]

But Thomas Palaima has opened up a third promising
means of getting at the linguistic bearings of Linear A. By
cogent synthesis of his own with others' research he has established more firmly than anyone till now the priestly
character of the Mycenaean *wanax*, for Palaima the central
figure of authority in the palatial society of mainland
Greece.[26] Moreover, along with emblems of royal and religious ideology, both the term *wanax* and its bearer's func-
tions have been derived by him from Minoan Crete.
Palaima assumed, to be sure, in his "Nature of the
Mycenaean Wanax" that, because the speakers of Linear A
dialect were non-Greek, their language was accordingly
non-Indo-European. Such a supposition is traceable at least
as early as 1932 when Meillet reasoned that, if ϝάναξ were

[24] This report, first made at the A.P.A. meeting in Atlanta, is now
published in Brown 1995, 25–54.
[25] Neumann 234–38; cf. the drawing there of a chariot-box engraved
on a seal from Laconia.
[26] Palaima 119–41, esp. 125–34.

borrowed from a substrate tongue then current in the Aegean, it must be non-Indo-European.[27]

Now, the pre-forms of Greek γυνή and Luvian *wana-* with its extended form *wanatti-* (syncopated *unatti-*), whose meaning is 'woman' or 'lady', have a common Indo-European root.[28] That this gender-specific term or a derivative could have been borrowed into Mycenaean dialect and used by patriarchal proto-Greeks to signify 'lord' may at first appear improbable enough. Still, arguments of linguistic and general cultural character combine to make a derivation of Mycenaean *wa-na-ka* / /*wanax*/ from Luvian *wana-* appealing:

[27] Meillet 587–89.

[28] For the Luvian preforms, PIE and Proto-Anatolian (*$g^w \eta éh_2$-, *$g^w eneh_2$-, *$g^w ón \bar{a}$-), see Melchert 1994, 264, and 1992, 36–37 with bibliography there. The very meaning of *wana-* has been known only since Starke 74–86. Curiously, the ideogram which stands for 'woman' in Linear B tablets, and which famously led A. E. Cowley to read the signs now transliterated as *ko-wo* 'boy' rather as 'girl' or, logographically, as 'child, female', may conceivably have here its phonetic application. If the sign's syllabic value *wo*—which Linear B retains—was first adopted by Mycenaean scribes when the sign in question may already have become vestigial in the donor signary, C. J. Ruijgh 386–87 was right in supposing that the sign was drawn from a word signifying 'woman', though not from his pre-form of ὄαρ.

The very notion that we might one day succeed in showing Linear A to have been created at a stage in the evolution of Luvian when the initial voiced labiovelar of Proto-Anatolian *$g^w ona$- had become /w/ but before /o/ had become /a:/ in *wana-* must be relegated to a footnote. Yet the idea that Mycenaeans must have borrowed their signary at a substantially earlier date than their first preserved writings is not new and helps explain the still unschematized form in which some of the Linear B signs became fixed, forms more archaic in fact than their Linear A counterparts.

It exceeds even a speculative footnote to pursue the further implication that Luvian successors of those who created a five-vowel signary adjusted the original -*e* and -*o* signs suitable for proto-Anatolian to represent short *a* and *u* in their own three-vowel phonology.

1) The derivation need not have been direct. All students of Minoan civilization acknowledge to some degree the remarkable prominence of women in its art, nowhere more strikingly than in the great Cnossian complex now called the Palace of Minos. Sara Immerwahr following Helga Reusch refers to the goddess/priestess who sat upon the chair of state in the famed Throne Room of the palace.[29]

2) For her part, Nanno Marinatos regards the elite group of ladies whom she distinguishes in the frescoes of the Cnossian palace as a harem.[30] This term, of course, from signifying a house or section of a house reserved for the women in a Moslem household came to mean the women occupying such a household. Similarly I propose that ἄναξ may have been backformed from ᾿Ανάκειον, which was (wrongly) taken to mean 'sovrans' abode', though actually compounded of Luvian *wana(tti)-*, or *wanassa/i-* 'woman's' 'women's', plus *-aya-* (conventionally transliterated *-eya*), the best identified Linear A suffix. Here *(u)wana-*'s pre-form **(u)wanah-* with the PIE laryngeal surviving between vowels—thus **uwanahaya-* or the like—may be posited.[31]

3) Historically, the shift of meaning has often gone from architectural feature to personal title: by the time of Akhenaton the Egyptian word for 'Great House' signified 'Pharaoh' as we employ the word; the Sublime Porte eventually designated also the head of the Otto-

[29] Immerwahr 96–97.

[30] Marinatos, esp. 36–46.

[31] Without the need to build on any prehistoric component, recourse to the genitival adjective *wanassa/i-*, plus the *-aya-* suffix as before, may be thought to account for ᾿Ανάκειον. But while the *ss* of the Luvian *-assa/i- > h* (CLuv. *massanassa/i- >* Lyc. *mahanahe/i-*) in Iron Age Lycian, whose speakers had reputedly emigrated from Late Bronze Age Crete, the surviving pre-Greek toponyms in *-ssos* on Crete all tend to put this option out of court.

man government; and Mikado or 'exalted gate', initially said of the imperial court, came to be applied to the Emperor himself.[32] The latter instances are alike in that the transferred meanings were brought about by outsiders, and I think it possible that *wanakteros* or *wanaktoron* 'palace' 'temple,' which is attested already in Linear B, may have led to *wanax, wanaktos* by back-formation.[33] Such a sequence—whereby the Mycenaeans' adoption of Minoan sacred ideology, materially expressed in palace, throne, and other symbols of politico-religious authority, included the taking over of the Cretan palace designation in acceptably Mycenaean form—would have two important results. It would both account for the shape of the back-formed stem *wanakt-* and explain the remarkable fact that the etymon for *wanax* 'lord' was *wana-* 'lady', no less.

Towards the end of that seminal study by Palaima, he introduces "one final point . . . from palaeography," the Linear B sign for the vowel *o*, which is L80/AB61 in Linear A.[34] To this sign, which Sir Arthur Evans termed "the throne and sceptre," I had earlier contented myself to give the sound value short *u,* on the basis that its variant took the shape of a bovine head, 'cow' being in Luvian *uwawi-/wawi-*. But the far more frequent throne-and-scepter sign combines the seat of power with the authority of its scep-

---

[32] Gardiner 75.

[33] Rather than assume back-formation and other means of accounting for the *-k-* of Myc. *wa-na-ka,* it is tempting to see in the Cretan pre-form of ἄναξ preservation of final laryngeal before a consonant-initial suffix (cf. the attested *-ti-* of (*u*)*wanatti-*). A case for such preservation in Palaic at least among the Anatolian I-E dialects has been made by Watkins 1973, 358–78. (For the evolution within Greek of the relevant consonant cluster, see Lejeune 69, 103 n. 2, and 108 n. 4, but cf. Del Freo, esp. 171–72.)

[34] Palaima 135–37 and Plate XLIIf.

tered occupant—a good symbolic shorthand for the palace or *uwanahaya-, the approximate form of the word which, I believe, stands behind the acrophonic sign L80 in its usual form.

This proposal for the word inspiring L80 does not have to be accepted or even correct in order for my identification of Luvian wana- (wanassa-) as the etymon behind Mycenaean wa-na-ka /wanax/ to be valid. Neither do the relevant words in Luvian need to be identified in the Linear A documents; as Palaima concluded in light of their overwhelmingly domainal character, "it would be more surprising to find the word for Minoan ruler in the Linear A texts . . . than it is not to find it."[35] Were I to alter his conclusion in any respect, it would be merely to substitute "Minoan cognate for wanax" in place of his "word for Minoan ruler."

So far I have spoken as if Troyland and Crete were a binary system of which Troy and Cnossus formed the sole significant foci. Yet Paul Faure among others has demonstrated, partly through shared toponyms such as their respective Mt. Idas, that strong early links must have existed between northwest Anatolia and the great South Aegean island.[36] As for the actual name of Crete, I have proposed[37] that a Luvian derivation for it, referring to the strip of land shorn off the continental mass, lies close at hand in the abstract kursattar/kursattn- 'cutting' or 'sliver', from *kursa(i)- 'cut off' or 'separate', attested in the borrowed Hitt. 2nd sg. imv. kursai.[38] One may compare 'Skerry', and other island names, all based like kuratt(i)- itself on the PIE root * (s)ker. Frank Starke, indeed, had earlier shown that the related

[35] Palaima 128.

[36] Faure 427–29.

[37] Paper read (October 1991) at ACOR in Amman and at II Congresso Internaz. di Micenologia in Rome.

[38] Melchert 1993, 112.

kursawar, which shares the same Luvian base as *kur(s)att(i)-*, signifies 'island',[39] so that **Kursatta* > > Κρήτη should denote 'the island *par excellence*'.

Cnossus itself, settled more than 8000 years ago and continuously occupied since then, is highly likely to have inherited its name from long before Luvian speakers arrived in Crete. A decade ago, however, I noted that the town name Itanos, which hovered round the northeast tip of Crete till the end of antiquity, would form the natural rendering in Greek of Istanuwa, the name of the renowned Sun City of Luvian and Hittite documents.[40] It was the cult center Istanuwa, as the Hattusan archives inform us, that produced the Luvian epic incipit, "When the hero from steep Wilusa came."[41] Meanwhile the Cretan placename Itanos may be a mere namesake, if not an accidental look-alike to the Istanuwa to which Hittite scribes traced the finest remains of Luvian literary art. Yet as years elapse and the Bronze Age typology of Asia Minor advances steadily, the continuing absence of evidence for Istanuwa as a mainland site should at least serve to keep the Cretan option open.

Be that as it may, I venture here a fresh view of a final Cretan toponym, which simultaneously recalls the substantial role that placenames played in the decipherment of Linear B, draws upon nomenclature of the Luvian pantheon, and possibly ties back to Troy and the Trojan artifacts from which this paper began. Just as divine Leto (Doric Lato) is widely thought to have given her name to the Cretan city of Lato, so Maliya, I submit, gave her name to the city of Malia,[42] whose palatial culture in Middle

[39] Starke 1981, 141–52.

[40] Paper read (August 1987) at the 6th Internat. Colloquium on Aegean Prehistory, in Athens, and published [1992], 228–29.

[41] Watkins 1986, 58–62.

[42] Though this Minoan site combining palace with polis has been dubbed Malia (often misspelled Mallia) simply because the modern vil-

Minoan times must have approached that of Cnossus itself. Such a correlation between a town's name and that of its tutelary deity, further, adds to the ways in which Maliya and Athena resemble each other.

Bearing in mind these points of likeness between the two goddesses, I find Maliya to be the more natural candidate to fill the lacuna in the Alaksandus Treaty at the point where Sommer sought a mention of the main Wilusian goddess, and where Güterbock (having Aphrodite in view) restored "[ISTAR-*li-is*]" with a question mark.[43] But we know that Maliya repeatedly alternates with ISTAR-*li-is* in Luvo-Hittite texts,[44] and that a goddesss often syncretized with Athena would play the part of city guardian better than Aphrodite in a solemn compact such as the Alaksandus Treaty was.

To end on an avowedly speculative note: the claim that a Linear-A-reading and Luvian-speaking spinster named *Pimidas once possessed spindlewhorls so labelled, which she may eventually have deposited in the temple on the Trojan citadel, provides a plausible scenario to account for Schliemann's finds of 123 years ago. The passage of but a few years more may be required before such a scenario is

---

lage in its neighborhood possessed that name, the extraordinary tenacity of place-names on Crete creates a real possibility that the Bronze Age city was already called Mali(y)a.

[43] It is in this treaty (KUB XXI.1.IV.27) that the earliest preserved occurrence of Apollo's name, in *A]-ap-pa-li-u-na-as*, was recognized by Emil Forrer as that of one among three named deities of Wilusa. Accepted by Kretschmer, Nilsson, and (provisionally) Laroche, but rejected by Sommer, Goetze, and others, the identification has now been positively entertained on various grounds by Watkins, Güterbock, and Mellink, and defended linguistically ('The One of Entrapping') as well as epigraphically in my "Leto the 'Benign'," presented at the CAMWS meeting in Richmond, October 1992. For his own views and others' see Güterbock 1986, 42, where earlier bibliography is cited.

[44] Haas 850.

either validated or disproved, now that the hope is being held out of finding archives in the lower city. Meanwhile, the Trojan whorls, like the name ϝάναξ itself, and the other bright pebbles lying on the shore of the Linear unknown, are offered as indicators keeping the possibility open that Luvian was written in Linear A. At least from the 16th century Luvians were developing their own writing system, called now Luvian Hieroglyphic, on the Anatolian mainland, where their descendants and kinfolk would one day devise the Lydian, Carian, and Lycian alphabets; these many and various strivings after literacy must count in favor of their creating Linear A as well in Bronze Age Crete.[45]

Works Cited

Barber, E. J. W. 1993. *Women's Work*. New York.

Blinkenberg, Chr. 1931. *Lindos: Fouilles de l'acropole (1902–1914) I*. Berlin.

Brown, Edwin. 1990 [1992]. "Traces of Luvian Dialect in Cretan Script and Toponym." *SMEA* 28:225–37.

———. 1992–93 [1995]. "The Linear A Signary: Tokens of Luvian Dialect in Bronze Age Crete." *Minos* 25:27–54.

Chadwick, John. 1976. *The Mycenaean World*. Cambridge.

[45] I want to record warm thanks to my Indo-Europeanist colleague Michael Weiss, who generously lends his exquisitely trained ear to those less practiced in the expression of linguistic detail. Further, Lora Holland, current member of our graduate program, has reminded me that Ebeling's *Lexicon Homericum* I s.v. ἄναξ contains these prophetic words: "Legerlotz, miscell. et crit. Halle 1858 ϝάναξ pro γϝάναξ skr. janaka gr. γυναικ- quod non omnino improbat Ebel (<*KZ*> 8, 381). . . ."

Finally, I am indebted to my colleague David Ganz for knowledge of Gallo-Latin comparanda in the form of inscribed spindle-whorls; see, e.g., Wolfgang Meid, *Gallisch oder Lateinisch?* (Innsbruck 1980) 13–38. Of far later period than the Trojan ones, and of distinctly Gallic spirit, these 3rd-to-5th-century messages of donor swains to their lady-loves suggest the potential range of sentiments to be deciphered on whorls.

Cowley, A. E. 1927. "A Note on Minoan Writing." In *Essays on Aegean Archaeology*. Ed. S. Casson. Oxford.

Del Freo, Maurizio. 1989. "*Pa-sa-ro, wa-na-so-i* e il valore dei sillabogrammi <*s*-> e <*z*-> in miceneo." *SMEA* 20:151–89.

Demargne, Pierre. 1979. "Athina, les dynastes lyciens et les héros grecs." In *Florilegium Anatolicum: mélanges. Laroche*. Paris.

Faure, Paul. 1965. "Noms de montagnes cretoises." *BAGB* Ser. 4:427–29.

Gardiner, Sir Alan. 1957. *Egyptian Grammar*. 3rd ed. London.

Godart, Louis. 1994a. "La Scrittura di Troia." *Rend. Mor. Acc. Lincei* Ser. 9, vol. 5, fasc. 3:457–60.

——. 1994b. "Les écritures cretoises et le bassin méditerranéen." *CRAI* fasc 3:707–31.

Guarducci, Margarita. 1935. *Inscriptiones Creticae I*. Rome.

Güterbock, H. G. 1956. "Notes on Luvian Studies." *Orientalia* 25:114–40.

——. 1986. "Troy in Hittite Texts? Wilusa, Ahhiyawa, and Hittite History." In *Troy and the Trojan War*. A symposium held at Bryn Mawr College, October 1984. Ed. M. T. Mellink. Bryn Mawr. 33–44.

Haas, Volkert. 1994. *Geschichte der hethitischen Religion*. Leiden, New York, and Köln.

Hawkins, J. David. 1975. "The Negatives in Hieroglyphic Luvian." *An. St.* 25:119–56.

——, and Donald F. Easton. 1996. "A Hieroglyphic Seal from Troia." *Studia Troica* 6:111–16.

Hoffner, Harry, Jr. 1974. *Alimenta Hethaeorum*. New Haven: AOS.

Immerwahr, Sara I. 1990. *Aegean Painting in the Bronze Age*. University Park, Pa. and London.

Jeffery, L. H. 1961. *The Local Scripts of Archaic Greece*. Oxford.

Laroche, Emmanuel. 1966. *Les noms des hittites*. Paris.

——. 1972. "Linguistique asianique." *Minos* 11:112–35.

Lebrun, René. 1982. "Maliya, une divinité anat. malconnue." In *Studia Paulo Naster oblata* II. Ed. J. Quaegebeur. Leuven. 123–30.

Lejeune, Michel. 1972. *Phonétique historique du mycénien et du grec ancien*. Paris.

Marinatos, Nanno. 1989. "The Minoan Harem: The Role of Eminent Women and the Knossos Frescoes." *DHA* 15, 2:33–62.

Meillet, Antoine. 1932. "Les noms des chefs en grec." In *Mélanges G. Glotz* II. Paris. 587-89.

Melchert, Craig. 1994. *Anatolian Historical Phonology*. Amsterdam and Atlanta.

——. 1993. *Cuneiform Luvian Lexicon*. Chapel Hill.

Neumann, Günter. 1990. "Hethitisch *widul(i)*-'Wagenkorb'." *Orientalia* 59, 2:234–38.

Packard, David. 1974. *Minoan Linear A*. Berkeley, Los Angeles, and London.

Palaima, Thomas G. 1995. "The Nature of the Mycenaean Wanax." In *The Role of the Ruler in the Prehistoric Aegean*. Aegaeum 11. 119–41.

Puhvel, Jaan. 1981. "'Spider' and 'Mole' in Hittite." In *Bono Homini Donum Kerns I*. Eds. Y. L. Arbeitman and A. R. Bomhard. Amsterdam. 237–42.

Ruijgh, C. J. 1967. *Études sur la grammaire et le vocabulaire du grec mycénien*. Amsterdam.

Sams, G. Kenneth. 1995. "Midas of Gordion and the Anatolian Kingdoms of Phrygia." In *Civilizations of the*

Ancient Near East. Vol. II. Eds. J. M. Sasson et al. New York. 1147–59.

Schliemann, Heinrich. 1875. *Troy and its Remains: A Narrative of Researches and Discoveries Made on the Site of Ilium and in the Trojan Plain.* London.

Starke, Frank. 1980. "Das luwische Wort fur 'Frau'." *KZ* (now *HZ*) 94:74–86.

———. 1981. "Die keilschrift-luwischen Wörter fur 'Insel' und 'Lampe'." *KZ* 95, 1:141–52.

Watkins, Calvert. 1969. "Indo-European Roots." Appendix to *The American Heritage Dictionary of the English Language.* Boston.

———. 1975. "Die Vertreten der Laryngale in gewissen morphol. Kategorien in den indogerm. Sprachen Anatoliens." In *Flexion und Wortbildung.* Akten der V. Fachtagung der Indo-germanischen Gesellschaft. Ed. H. Rix. Wiesbaden. 358–78 .

———. 1985. "Greek *menoináai*: A Dead Metaphor." *Internat. J. of Am. Ling.* 51, 4:614–18.

———. 1986. "The Language of the Trojans." In *Troy and the Trojan War.* A Symposium held at Bryn Mawr College, October 1984. Ed. M. T. Mellink. Bryn Mawr. 45–62.

From *Clementia Caesaris* to *La Clemenza di Tito*

Jeffrey L. Buller
Georgia Southern University

The forced marches and fortified camps of Caesar's Gaul seem a world away from the graceful minuets and polished manners of Mozart's Vienna. Nevertheless, rulers such as Francis I and Joseph II attached great importance to the title of "Holy Roman Emperor" and drew much of their inspiration from the Rome of the Caesars.[1] Thus authors and composers who sought parallels between the great figures of the past and the political leaders of the present could win considerable acclaim. Perhaps for this reason, *La Clemenza di Tito*, a neo-classical libretto written by the Italian poet Pietro Metastasio (1698–1782), had been set to music *nearly sixty times* before it was assigned to Mozart for Leopold II's coronation as King of Bohemia.[2] Unlike his

---

[1] See Beales 258-60.

[2] Among the most important of these precursors to Mozart's opera were versions by Antonio Caldara (1670-1736) in Vienna, 1734;

predecessors, however, Mozart created an opera that was soon recognized as a masterpiece.[3] So closely, in fact, did *La Clemenza di Tito* reflect the neo-classical values of the eighteenth century that it is still possible to identify Metastasio's ancient sources in the work and to see how the opera's classical values passed, largely unchanged, from the age of Augustus to the Augustan Age.

In 45 B.C., among the honors granted to Julius Caesar for his victory in Spain, the Senate decreed that a temple of *clementia Caesaris* be built.[4] This temple was apparently never completed,[5] although both Plutarch (*Caesar* 57.3) and Appian (*Bella Civilia* 2.106) mention plans for the structure. The virtue honored by the Senate's decree was one that Cicero defined as a quality "through which passions,

---

Leonardo Leo (1694–1744) in Venice, 1735; Johann Adolf Hasse (1699–1783) in Pesaro, 1735 (renamed *Tito Vespasiano*; revised for Dresden in 1738 and further revised for Naples in 1759); Georg Christoph Wagenseil (1715–1777) in Vienna, 1746; Antonio Gaetano Pampani (1705–1775) in Venice 1748; Christoph Willibald Gluck (1714–1787) in Naples, 1752; Nicolò Jommelli (1714–1774) in Stuttgart, 1753; Giuseppe Scarlatti (1718–1777) in Venice, 1757; Ignaz Holzbauer (1711–1783) in Mannheim, 1757; Baldassare Galuppi (1706–1785) in Turin, 1760; Andrea Bernasconi (1706–1784) in Munich, 1786; Johann Gottlieb Naumann (1741–1801) in Dresden, 1769; Giuseppe Sarti (1729–1802) in Padua, 1771; and Johann Peter Salomon (1745–1815) in Rheinsberg, 1774 (renamed *Titus*).

[3] Heartz 339–40.

[4] Dio Cassius 44.6. "The immediate occasion of the vote was Caesar's generosity in granting to his opponents in the Civil War life, citizenship, and the retention of their property . . ." Coulter 513. See also Rambaud 284, Dahlman 17, Volkmann 154–57, and Leggewie 17–36.

[5] Only *apparently* never built because a denarius struck by P. Sepullius Macer in 44 B.C. depicts the front of a tetrastyle temple bearing the inscription *clementia Caesaris*. See Babelon vol. 2, 29 no. 52 and Weinstock 43 n. 9.

though rashly stirred to hatred against others, are restrained by civility" (*per quam animi temere in odium alicuius
concitati comitate retinentur. De Inventione* 2.164). In Cicero's
definition, there are three essential characteristics of
clementia: the triumph of reason over an impulse to act
rashly (*temere*), gentleness (*comitate*) in the treatment of
one's opponents and, most importantly of all, the ability to
delay action until passion and anger are restrained
(*retinentur*).

Caesar, whom the Senate regarded as the personification
of this virtue, is the same individual who, according to his
own admission in the *Gallic Wars*, had six thousand men of
the canton Verbigenus executed for escaping after they had
surrendered (1.27.4–28.2). More than sixty thousand
Nervii (2.28.2) and four thousand Atuatuci (2.33.5) were
similarly killed, while fifty-three thousand others were sold
into slavery (2.33.7). The Senators among the Veneti were
slaughtered outright and the rest reduced to slavery
(3.16.4). The villages and farms of the Morini and Menapii
a were burned (3.29.3 and 4.38.3), as were the towns of the
Sugambri (4.19.1). Women and children of the Tencteri
and Usipetes were murdered (4.18.5). The leaders
Dumnorix (5.7.9) and Indutiomarus (5.58.6) were slain.
The farms of the Menapii were burned on three separate
occasions (6.6.1). The food supply of the Ubii was reduced
in the belief that, *should* they ever revolt, they would do so
at a great disadvantage (6.10.2). The Eburones were reduced to starvation (6.43.3) and the conspirator Acco was
executed *more maiorum* (6.44.2). Cenabum was burned and
its population taken prisoner (7.11.8). When Avaricum was
captured, nearly forty thousand of its residents were killed,
including women, children, and the aged (7.28.4). No food
was given to the Mandubii who were turned out of Alesia
(7.78.5). The rearguard of the Gauls was almost annihi-

lated (7.88.6–7) and Gallic prisoners were distributed as slaves to the Roman army (7.89.5). Those defending Uxellodunum had their hands cut off (8.44.2).

Throughout the *Gallic Wars*, in other words, Caesar demonstrates, not clemency, but overt cruelty towards his enemies. At the same time, however, that his actions are at their most brutal, he attempts to surround himself with an *illusion* of compassion. On many occasions in the *Gallic Wars* Caesar mentions proof of his own clemency precisely when he is about to commit an act of vindictiveness or hostility. The Aeduan leader Dumnorix is thus spared (1.20.5–6) shortly before six thousand Verbigenians are killed. Immediately afterwards, the Helvetii are given food (1.28.4) and Caesar tries to end the outrages of Ariovistus without violence (1.33.1; 34.1–2). Vercingetorix's cruelty is contrasted to Caesar's alleged clemency (7.4.9–10) which leads him to spare the Aedui (7.41.1: *quos iure belli interficere potuisset*) and allow both Viridomarus and Eporedorix to go free (7.54.2). Ironically, these acts are part of the very campaign that saw Cenabum destroyed, the inhabitants of Avaricum slaughtered, food refused to the Mandubii, and Gallic prisoners distributed as booty to Caesar's troops.

Similar acts of "clemency" continue to be chronicled in *Bellum Civile*. Lucius Pupius is pardoned (1.13.4–5) and Attius the Paelignian is allowed to go free (1.18.4). Caesar's efforts to protect his enemies during the fraternization is contrasted to the treachery of Pompey's supporters (1.77). When the Battle of Lerida is over, Caesar pardons the opposing army (1.86.1). He advises Trebonius to restrain the solders at Marseille (2.13.3) and later spares the city (2.22.6). Lucius Vibullius Rufus, that "experienced prisoner," is released by Caesar three different times (described at 1.34.1 and 3.10.1). Lucius Torquatus is spared (3.10.3–4). Those who survive the wreck of the Rhodian ships are sent home unharmed (3.27.2). Caesar's generosity is distinguished from the savage treatment that Bibulus (3.14.3) and Labienus (3.71.4) give their prisoners. Finally, a climactic display of Caesarian *clementia* appears in the general amnesty that the dictator offers after the Battle of Pharsalus (3.98.2 where Caesar speaks to the troops *de lenitate sua*).

For Caesar, public acts of *clementia* were intended to divert his readers' attention from the grimmer realities of war. *Clementia*, as a *reasoned* and *deliberate* surrender of the right to punish inferiors, became for Caesar a calculated, even a cynical, attempt to win public support. Moreover, because this policy *did* win Caesar a large measure of popular acclaim, a reputation for clemency quickly became a goal to be pursued by his successors. In *De Clementia* (1.9), for instance, Seneca recounts a story that later generations would cite as evidence of the clemency of Augustus. L. Cinna, described by Seneca as both "dull-witted"—*stolidi ingenii virum*—and a grandson of Pompey the Great (not at all mutually exclusive categories), conspired to seize control of the government. When Augustus learned of this plot, he could not decide whether to punish Cinna or forgive him for his previously blameless conduct. Only when Livia (who is described by Seneca as utterly unlike the harridan appearing in the novels of Robert Graves) speaks to the emperor, does Augustus decide to forego vengeance. In light of Caesar's own propagandistic use of *clementia* in the *Gallic Wars*, the tack taken by Livia is particularly interesting. Cinna is in custody, she tells Augustus; he cannot do any harm. On the other hand, an act of generosity could enhance the emperor's reputation (*Deprehensus est. Iam nocere tibi non potest. Prodesse famae tuae potest*: 1.9.59). Satisfied with this advice, Augustus pardons Cinna, later granting him a consulship. The former conspirator became a strong supporter of Augustus and (perhaps not so dull-wittedly after all) named the emperor as his sole heir. In fairy-tale

fashion, Seneca concludes his story with the words "And after this no one ever plotted against Augustus again" (*Nullis
amplius insidiis ab ullo petitus est*: 1.9.60).

In succeeding generations, emperors continued to make
a show of their alleged *clementia*. Stephan Weinstock has
summarized the ways in which political forbearance became a stock attribute of the emperors.

> Tiberius issued a coin in A.D. 22/3 with the legend
> 'Clementiae,' and the Senate erected an altar to [*clementia*]
> in 28. . . . An annual festival was instituted in 39 in honour
> of the Clementia of Caligula. . . . In 66 the Arvals included
> Clementia in a sacrifice made in honour of Nero on the oc-
> casion of a thanksgiving. The personification [of *clementia*]
> . . . first appears on a coin of Vitellius in 69, and for the sec-
> ond time . . . on many coins of Hadrian.[6]

Then, during the Flavian dynasty, Suetonius makes Titus'
clementia a central theme in his brief life of that emperor.
Suetonius recounts, for instance, the story of two patricians
who had been found guilty of conspiring against Titus
(*Divus Titus* 5.1–2). Rather than punishing the traitors,
Titus merely announces that power is a gift of the gods and
offers to provide them with anything else they desire. He
informs the mother of one of the conspirators that her son
is safe. Then, inviting both men to dinner, he has them
seated near him at a gladiatorial combat, boldly allowing
them to inspect the swords of the contestants.

Clementia became so firmly entrenched with the concept
of Roman imperial rule that, even a millenium and a half
later, the French playwright Pierre Corneille celebrated it
as a distinct quality of the early emperors. In his tragedy
Cinna (1641), subtitled *La Clémence d'Auguste*, Corneille
elaborated upon the story of how Augustus forgave L.

---

[6] Weinstock 240.

Cinna as told by Seneca in *De Clementia*.[7] In keeping with the dramatic expectations of his time, however, Corneille also added a love interest to the story. A fictitious young noblewoman, Amelia (whose father, we learn, had been proscribed under the triumvirate), becomes the motivating force in the conspiracy. The playwright also supplies Cinna with a friend named "Maximus" who joins the conspiracy and with whom Cinna discusses his moral dilemma. Most important of all, however, Cinna is transformed from the dim-witted figure described by Seneca to a hero . . . or, perhaps, to a heroic failure, a noble imitation of the younger Brutus. Though he is the pawn of Amelia, Cinna truly believes that, by assassinating Augustus, he will be ridding Rome of a tyrant.[8]

In the eighteenth century, *clementia* continued to be a virtue associated with Julius Caesar and his successors. In Händel's opera *Giulio Cesare* (1724), with a libretto by Nicola Francesco Haym, these words are assigned to Caesar in act 1: "The virtue of great men is to pardon offenses" (*Virtù de' grandi è il perdonar le offense*). Several years later, when Pietro Metastasio drafted his libretto for *La Clemenza di Tito*, he drew upon *all* these earlier discussions of *clementia*, beginning with Caesar and Seneca and continuing through Corneille and Händel. In Mozart's opera, which was completed precisely three months before the composer's death in 1791, critics have seen everything from Baroque absolutism[9] to the humanitarian values of

---

[7] Corneille's direct source was probably Montaigne 1.24 where Seneca's account is both translated and discussed.

[8] Augustus' tyranny, and the hollowness of his *clémence*, are consistently depicted throughout the play. "Is it not the ultimate ruse of a tyrant to make one's subjects happy, to give them a sense of their subjectivity as inseparable from the repressions of his Law, and to have them articulate this repression as their supreme pleasure?" Greenberg 117.

[9] Brophy 70, 231, 268.

the Enlightenment.[10] More important than either of these influences, however, is the resemblance that Titus' *clemenza* bears to Caesar's *clementia*. Despite the passage of time, imperial clemency remained for the Habsburgs precisely what it had been for the Julio-Claudians: a reasoned surrender of the right to punish inferiors; a virtue to be exploited more for its propaganda value than for its humanitarian intent; a triumph of the will rather than a victory of the heart.

Metastasio had originally written *La Clemenza di Tito* in 1743 in honor of Emperor Karl IV. By the late 1700s, however, his libretto's antiquated style—with its pattern of recitative/aria/recitative in endless succession—seemed dated and quaint. Mozart insisted that the text be modified extensely before beginning his composition.[11] As a result, nearly a third of Metastasio's original libretto was discarded, including eighteen entire arias. With the text pared down from three acts to two, the Saxon court poet Caterino Mazzolà (1745-1806) then began the process of expanding the work once again, adding four new arias, two duets, three trios, and finale ensembles for both acts.[12] With these changes, Mozart's *La Clemenza di Tito* seems closer in style to the neo-classical operas then popular in France and Germany—with their austere vocal lines and more compact numbers—than to the *opere serie* of Metastasio's day.[13] Pleased with the modifications that Mazzolà had made, Mozart wrote in his "catalogue of all my works" on September 5, 1791, that the libretto had

[10] Till 261-63.

[11] The degree of Mozart's involvement in the revision of the libretto has been keenly debated. The most reliable account may be found at Robbins Landon 96-97.

[12] Downs 545 and Sadie 162.

[13] Sadie 162.

been "reduced to real opera" (*ridotto a vera opera*) for the first time.

Volkmar Braunbehrens has said that "Mazzolà's libretto was well suited to a coronation, for it expressed the expectation that a good ruler would subordinate his personal inclinations to the interests of the state, exercise moderation, and let reason and justice prevail as the highest virtues of a sovereign."[14] As with ancient *clementia*, the emperor's cool rationality must win out over his instinct. To make this point, Metastasio derived much of his plot from Corneille's *Cinna*. In addition, he combined that story with Suetonius' account of the two anonymous patricians plotting against Titus. *Mutatis mutandis*, Corneille's Augustus becomes Metastasio's Titus, Cinna becomes Sextus (Sesto), and Amelia becomes Vitellia.

One of Metastasio's most important changes was to transform Sextus into a less noble character than Cinna. Sextus lacks Cinna's republican spirit and is motivated solely by his love for Vitellia. For her part, Vitellia hates Titus with a blind rage—not because her father had been proscribed under the triumvirate, as was true for Amelia—but because Vespasian, Titus' father, had deposed her own father, Vitellius. To make matters worse, Vitellia's hatred for Titus' family is confused with her own love for the emperor himself. Her filial anger mingles with jealousy when Titus passes her over *twice* in the opera, becoming romantically involved first with Berenice and then with Servilia.

Though superficially drawn from classical sources, the plot of *La Clemenza di Tito* actually derives from a stock eighteenth-century love triangle, as did nearly all of Mozart's operas on Roman themes. For this reason, *La Clemenza di Tito* is not a work that contains a historically recognizable image of ancient Rome, but a drama of rela-

[14] Braunbehrens 390.

tionships, a moral tale containing characters who embody specific qualities and emotions (clemency, jealousy, passion, and the like) rather than reflecting the full range of human experience. As Braunbehrens suggests, Metastasio's Titus "is frozen into an embodiment of good, a lifeless statue with no possibility of showing any human characteristics, such as emotion, shock, or doubt. He is denied passions by the author's enlightened rationalist conception of the story."[15] Titus, in other words, is not so much a person as he is a personification. And what Titus personifies is imperial *clementia* as it was understood in the eighteenth century.

Metastasio begins his libretto by depicting Titus straight out of the pages of Suetonius. Reflecting that author's description of the emperor as "the darling and delight of the human race" (*amor ac deliciae generis humani: Divus Titus* 1.1), Metastasio's Sextus addresses Titus as "the darling of the world, the father of Rome" (*la sua delizia al mondo, il Padre a Roma*": beginning of act 1). Later, in No. 5,[16] Publius reports that the Senate has bestowed upon Titus the title of "father of his country" (*della patria il Padre*) because of his self-sacrifice in repudiating Berenice. Though the plot of Metastasio's libretto has little in common with the history of ancient Rome, the *clementia* displayed by its central character is precisely the virtue described by classical authors. The emperor's *clementia* is derived from his superiority of position, his rationality, and his restraint. In the recitative section of No. 1, Annius concludes that "Titus has control both of the world and of himself" (*Tito ha l'impero del mondo, e di se*). In No. 4, Titus mentions his decision to exile Berenice by saying "Enough. I mastered myself. She left." (*Basta; ho vinto; partì*).

[15] Braunbehrens 390.

[16] To avoid confusion with other settings of Metastasio's libretto, all numbers cited refer to Mozart's opera.

The coolness of Titus' rationality does not mean, however, that his *clementia* lacks the gentleness or civility (*comitas*) that was central to Cicero's definition. In No. 5, for instance, Titus refuses the tribute offered him for the building of a temple dedicated to *il Nume di Tito*; instead, the emperor insists that these funds be used to help the victims of Vesuvius. Learning of this plan, Annius calls Titus a "true hero" (*vero Eroe*). Later, in No. 7, Titus says that there is only one real fruit of supreme power: the ability to help the poor and reward outstanding merit.

Perhaps the clearest example of the continuity between Caesarian *clementia* and Metastasian *clemenza* occurs in No. 25 when Titus learns of the treachery of Sextus and Vitellia. Betrayed by his closest friends, he declares, "I know all, forgive all, forget all" (*Io tutto so, tutti assolvo, e tutto oblio*). This phrase, with its conscious echo of *Veni. Vidi. Vici.*, provides a direct link between the libretto's Titus and the historical Julius Caesar. The parallels drawn between the emperor and the great figures of Roman history are now complete. Like Aeneas, Titus places the welfare of the state above his own emotional needs. Like Caesar, he forgoes the punishment of his opponents for a greater political good. Like Augustus, he pardons an avowed enemy, restoring him to a position of responsibility and trust. The lesson for eighteenth-century kings and emperors must have been obvious: enlightened rulers are those whose reason controls their anger and who do not punish their subjects when such generosity is to the benefit of the state.

Braunbehrens questions, however, the impropriety of the thirty-five-year-old Mozart offering such a lesson to Leopold II at his coronation.[17] As Braunbehrens states, Leopold was no young and inexperienced monarch. He had already served for twenty-five years as ruler of Tuscany

[17] Braunbehrens 392.

and had a reputation for making enlightened progress to-
wards a constitutional state. So liberal were many of
Leopold's actions that C. A. Macartney concluded that
"Perhaps alone of all the Habsburgs who ever reigned,
[Leopold II] was a genuine constitutionalist. He approved
Montesquieux's [sic] doctrine of the division of powers, believed in the right of the people to fix taxation and to be
protected against arbitrary rule, and...[held that] force only
'estranged hearts and spirits without altering views'..."[18] *La
Clemenza di Tito* can thus hardly be viewed as a serious attempt to instruct the new king of Bohemia in how to be a
successful monarch. But if that is not what it was, what was
it?

The answer to this question may be found in the history
of the libretto itself. Mozart did not choose the text and
does not seem to have been particularly interested in setting it. Throughout the eighteenth century, texts for oper-
atic commissions were either chosen by the royal patrons
themselves or by the individual who was producing the
event. In the case of Mozart's *La Clemenza di Tito*, the text
had been suggested by the impresario Domenico
Guardasoni (1731–1806), director of the Bondini opera
company, with the approval of Leopold's own agents.
There were two reasons why *La Clemenza di Tito* was a suitable subject for Leopold's coronation. To begin with, the
opera had to be completed quickly. Guardasoni arrived in
Vienna to discuss the project with Mozart only on July 14,
and the coronation had already been set for early September. Modifying an established text, especially one familiar
to Guardasoni's royal patrons, would occupy far less time
than obtaining approval of both emperor and composer
for a new libretto.[19] More importantly, however, *La*

18 Macartney 134.
19 "I agree to have the libretto caused to be written, either on the
two subjects given to me by H. E. the Count of the Castle, and to cause

Clemenza di Tito contained symbolism that the Habsburgs wished to convey at Leopold's coronation.[20] The new king was, after all, the son of Maria Theresa; his brother was Joseph II. Both of these rulers had cast themselves as social reformers, enlightened monarchs who guided the state for the benefit of their people. Their reforms had been widely celebrated. Either individually or together, Maria Theresa and Joseph II had abolished the death penalty, expanded literacy, relaxed censorship, limited serfdom, and ended the clergy's exemption from taxation. It is not at all surprising, therefore, that Metastasio's *La Clemenza di Tito* was produced so frequently during Joseph's reign. The libretto celebrated precisely those values that the emperor wished to embody. Under the Habsburgs, the opera seemed to be saying, there would be no need for the sort of social upheaval still convulsing France: like the emperor Titus, the Habsburgs represented something infinitely more important than *liberté, egalité, fraternité*; they represented *clementia*.

As was the case with Julius Caesar, however, the *reality* of Joseph II was somewhat different from the public image he wished to convey. For all of his reforms, Joseph remained "an ardent and inveterate militarist"[21] who greatly ex-

---

it to be set to music by a celebrated master; but in case it will prove to be impossible to do this because the time is so short, I obligate myself to procure an opera newly composed on the subject of *Tito* by Metastasio." From Guardasoni's contract with the High Estates of Bohemia, as cited and translated by Robbins Landon 88.

[20] ". . . the subject matter —an emperor forgiving his potenial assassins, and showing mildness and goodness—was considered suitable not only for the character of Leopold II (who had abolished torture in Tuscany) but for the Age of Enlightenment in general. *La Clemenza di Tito* in Prague was to express the ideal, the Enlightenment, which should be in stark contrast to the alarming events in France." Robbins Landon 100.

[21] Macartney 130.

panded the size of his army through conscription.[22] The empire's increased military force was involved in several misguided attempts at adventurism.[23] While it is true that Joseph II abolished the death penalty, he did so only because he believed that long periods of forced labor were more effective as punishments.[24] As Paul B. Bernard has noted, "the conditions of prisoners pulling barges on the Danube or, even worse, being galley slaves on old derelict men-of-war tied up on the river, amounted to a living death."[25] The emperor increased the funding available to state charities, but did so by dissolving more than six hundred monasteries and confiscating their property.[26] While taking steps to improve basic literacy throughout the empire, Joseph II greatly reduced the number of gymnasia and humanistic high schools.[27] Though eliminating several layers of bureaucracy, he also established a secret police to inform on the activities of his civil servants and officers.[28] As C. A. Macartney concludes, "Joseph II is perhaps the completest enlightened despot in European history, and the noun in the phrase is quite as fully operative as the adjective."[29]

The early Habsburgs thus viewed reform and tolerance—the central values of the Enlightenment—in much the same way that Caesar viewed *clementia*. These were virtues to be meted out deliberately and on select occasions. They were

---

[22] Tapié 233–34.

[23] Kann 162–68 and Tapié 235–36.

[24] Beales 234–36.

[25] Bernard 100. See also Macartney 126.

[26] Macartney 121, Kann 191, and Tapié 220–21.

[27] Macartney 125. and Kann 194 Joseph's support of education did not extend to *higher* education. Even his mother's pet project, the Theresianum (a Viennese academy for the sons of the nobility), was closed.

[28] Macartney 125.

[29] Macartney 119.

triumphs to be celebrated with great fanfare so that they might divert attention from the increasing absolutism of the monarchy. By reinforcing imagined parallels between present-day rulers and a highly idealized image of the past, operas like *La Clemenza di Tito* conveyed upon the Habsburgs an aura of forgiveness, tolerance, and the triumph of reason over passion . . . the same attributes that had been associated with *clementia* since the time of Julius Caesar. That this virtue had also, from its inception, been more a matter of appearance than reality was an irony that seems to have gone unnoticed.

At the premiere of Mozart's *La Clemenza di Tito*, Leopold II demonstrated something of the Habsburg temperament. In what was said to be a calculated insult to both the composer and Mazzolà (neither of whom enjoyed favor with the royal family), Leopold and his entourage arrived more than an hour late. The festivities in honor of the coronation competed with the opera for attendance and, as a result, its initial audience was quite small.[30] Maria Luisa, Leopold's Italian-born wife, dismissed the work as "typical German hogwash" (*una porcheria tedesca*),[31] and her contempt for the opera became common knowledge.[32] Aristocrats did not attend the work's repeat performances, making the opera so unsuccessful initially that Guardasoni petitioned the Bohemian estates for compensation. Soon, however, as performances continued and members of the bourgeoisie replaced the aristocracy as the opera's primary audience, the fortunes of the work began to change and *La Clemenza di Tito* enjoyed a popularity that continued for the next fifty

[30] Solomon 486–87.

[31] Brauehrens 387, Solomon 486, and Clive 97–98.

[32] In addition to describing the work as a *porcheria*, Maria Luisa also "wrote to her daughter-in-law Maria Theresia (the wife of Archduke Franz, the future emperor Francis II) that the music had been so bad that 'almost all of us fell asleep.'" Clive 98.

years. While the Habsburg dynasty remained in power for another half century, it preserved to the end the same preference for the *appearance* of *clementia* over its reality that had originated nearly two millenia earlier in the pages of Caesar's *Gallic Wars*.

Works Cited

Babelon, E. 1886. *Description des monnaies de la république romaine*. Rollin et Feuardet.

Beales, Derek. 1987. *Joseph II*. Cambridge University.

Bernard, Paul P. 1968. *Joseph II*. Twayne.

Braunbehrens, Volkmar. 1990. *Mozart in Vienna, 1781–1791*. Tr. Timothy Bell. Harper.

Brophy, Brigid. 1988. *Mozart the Dramatist*. Da Capo.

Clive, Peter. 1993. *Mozart and his Circle*. Yale University.

Coulter, C. C. 1931. "Caesar's Clemency." *CJ* 26: 513–24.

Dahlmann, H. 1934. "Clementia Caesaris." *Neue Jahrbücher für Wissenschaft und Jugendbildung*. 10:17–26.

Downs, Philip G. 1992. *Classical Music*. Norton.

Greenberg, Mitchell. 1986. *Corneille, Classicism, and the Ruses of Symmetry*. Cambridge University Press.

Heartz, Daniel. 1990. *Mozart's Operas*. University of California.

Kann, Robert A. 1974. *A History of the Habsburg Empire, 1526–1918*. University of California.

Leggewie, O. 1958. "Clementia Caesaris." *Gymnasium*. 65:17–36.

Macartney, C. A. 1969. *The Habsburg Empire: 1790–1918*. Macmillan.

Rambaud, M. 1966. *L'art de la déformation historique dans les Commentaires de César.* Société d'Edition Les Belles Lettres.

Robbins Landon, H. C. 1988. *1791: Mozart's Last Year.* Schirmer.

Sadie, Stanley. 1983. *The New Grove Mozart.* Norton.

Solomon, Maynard. 1995. *Mozart: A Life.* Harper Collins.

Tapié, Victor-Louis. 1971. *The Rise and Fall of the Habsburg Monarchy.* Tr. Stephen Hardman. Praeger.

Till, Nicholas. 1992. *Mozart and the Enlightenment.* Faber & Faber.

Volkmann, H. 1952. "Zur Amnestiepolitik Julius Caesars." *GWU* 3:154–57.

Weinstock, Stephan. 1971. *Divus Julius.* Clarendon.

"Tripe and Garbage:" William Abbott Oldfather on the Limits of Research

William M. Calder III
University of Illinois

I. Introduction

The nineties have seen an extraordinary revival of interest in William Abbott Oldfather (1880–1945),[1] along with Basil Lanneau Gildersleeve (1831–1924) and Paul Shorey (1857–1934), one of the three American *patres philologiae*, founder

---

[1] I draw attention to two fundamental biographical studies: Michael Armstrong, "A German Scholar and Socialist in America: The Career of William Abbott Oldfather," *CJ* 88 (1992/93) 235–53 [henceforth cited: Armstrong] and John Buckler, "William Abbott Oldfather," *Classical Scholarship: A Biographcal Encyclopedia*, ed. Ward W. Briggs and William M. Calder III (New York 1990) 346–52. For a concise bio-bibliography see Michael Armstrong in *Biographical Dictionary of North American Classicists*, ed. Ward W. Briggs, Jr. (Westport 1994) 459–61. Best on Oldfather the man is C. A. Forbes, "William Abbott Oldfather 1880–1945," *CJ* 41 (1945/46) 8–11.

of a productive and cohesive school.[2] No complete bibliography of his work exists.[3] What he wrote lasts: indices, bibliographies, editions, informed reviews and some 500 Pauly-Wissowa articles. He bravely defended the Germanic in American scholarship against English dilettantism. On 31 October 1917 he was "accused by Federal agents of Socialist and pro-German sentiments and disloyalty to the United States."[4] Following World War I he allied himself with Gildersleeve to defend the German tradition against Shorey, whom he never approved, and the fundamentalist, John Adams Scott (1867–1947).[5] His success was abiding and his cause was unexpectedly supported by the influx of some twenty outstanding classical scholars, the victims of national socialist persecution, Jews, husbands of Jews, and Kurt von Fritz.[6] The productive devotion of Oldfather to solid, mainline scholarship requires no documentation. A glance at even a partial list of his publications makes that clear. Therefore, all the more interesting because unexpected is an impassioned protest against positivism. We find it in a letter of 5 April 1939, here published for the first time, to one of his most distinguished students, the nonagenarian, Levi Robert Lind (b. 29 July 1906), now University Distinguished Professor of Classics emeritus at the Univer-

[2] See S. N. Griffiths, "Doctoral Dissertations Completed at the University of Illinois under William Abbott Oldfather," *CJ* 74 (1978/79) 149–53. She lists forty-six dissertations written between 1920 and 1945.

[3] Professor Michael Armstrong has completed one which I hope will soon see publication as part of a volume containing selected *Kleine Schriften*.

[4] See Armstrong 237.

[5] See William M. Calder III, "William Abbott Oldfather and the Preservation of German Influence in American Classics 1919–1933," *Altertumswissenschaft in den 20er Jahren: Neue Fragen und Impulse*, ed. Hellmut Flashar (Stuttgart 1995) 403–21.

[6] See William M. Calder III, "The Refugee Classical Scholars in the USA: An Evaluation of their Contribution," *ICS* 17 (1992) 153–73.

sity of Kansas.[7] I owe the text and permission to publish it to the kindness of Professor Lind.[8]

II. The New Text

University of Illinois
108 Lincoln Hall
Urbana, Illinois
April 5, 1939

Mr. L. R. Lind
114 Central Avenue
Crawfordsville, Indiana[9]

Dear Bob:

Much obliged for the interesting offprint.[10] Of course I was very glad to sponsor your request.[11] But the more "research" which I attempt to do, the more I feel doubt about its relative importance in the total scheme of cultural values. Treated as beautiful, stimulating, + meaningful for life and joy, Greek literature, thought and fine art are of transcendent value;[12] but treated as mere materials for scientific re-

[7] For his life and a bibliography of his extensive publications see William Whallon, *Levi Robert Lind: A Bibliography* (East Lansing 1988).

[8] Professor Lind has generously given Calder the letters of Oldfather to him. They will shortly be added to the Oldfather Collection at the University of Illinois in Urbana/Champaign.

[9] L. R. Lind taught from 1929 to 1940 at Wabash College, a private liberal arts college for men with a strong tradition until this day in Classics.

[10] For Lind's publications in 1939 see *Bibliography*, 6–7. It is uncertain to which of them Oldfather refers.

[11] Presumably Oldfather supported his former student for an ACLS fellowship: see n. 17 *infra*.

[12] Conviction of the transcendent value of Greek culture which Oldfather was able to reconcile with his passionate historicism he owed to his Munich mentor, Otto Crusius (1857–1918): see E. Christian Kopff

search, and by that I mean linguistics,[13] and grammatical statistics, studies of drain-pipes,[14] shoestrings, door knobs, locations,[15] trivial forms of social and political organization,[16] and all the rest of the tripe and garbage that are dignified by the term "research," they seem hardly more important than mineralogy, or comparative anatomy, or even educational statistics—than which what can be more banal? Of course some knowledge of the material setting is useful as background and proportion and emphasis to the appreciation of better things. But I sometimes feel that too much attention to the sauce is apt to lose us the rabbit. When our subject ceases to mean anything important for our daily living, then it will go, and it ought to go, the way of all flesh. Of course these melancholy remarks are particularly inappropriate in your case, because among all the students I have ever had you seem to possess the most truly humanistic attitude. But then that's the way with most preaching; we exhort the already saved, because the others wouldn't listen to us anyway.

---

in *Wilamowitz nach 50 Jahren*, ed. William M. Calder III, Hellmut Flashar, and Theodor Lindken (Darmstadt 1985) 548.

[13] Oldfather uses the word to denote arid grammatical studies, epitomized in Oldfather's America by the epigoni of scholars like Gildersleeve, Goodwin and Smyth.

[14] Oldfather had been visiting professor at the American School of Classical Studies in Athens 1937–1938 (first semester): see Louis E. Lord, *A History of the American School of Classical Studies at Athens 1882–1942 An Intercollegiate Project* (Cambridge 1947) 360. Oldfather had learned art history under Adolf Furtwängler (1853–1907) at Munich and expectedly found the "dirt archaeology" of the agora trivial.

[15] Many of his own *RE* entries on place-names in Lokris he might place under this very rubric.

[16] This certainly reflects Oldfather's impatience with the work of William Lee Westerman (1873–1954) at Columbia where Oldfather had been guest-professor spring semester 1938. See William M. Calder III, "*Nuda Veritas*: William Abbott Oldfather on Classics at Columbia," *ICS* 18 (1993) 359–78, esp. 370–71 (cited *infra*).

I did not know that you belonged to the A.C.L.S.,[17] but presume it was in some capacity connected with your medieval studies.

Looking forward to seeing the whole family next summer,[18]

Sincerely yours,
WAO
W. A. Oldfather

WAO/ck

III. What Have We Learned?

The view is fundamentally Wilamowitzian.[19] The abiding value of research cannot be overestimated; but there is research and there is research. One must see the forest and the trees.[20] There is a context for what he writes. Oldfather by 1939 was over extended. At his sudden death in 1944 he left some eleven projects unfinished.[21] This may have caused moments of dispair or doubt. In 1939 the contrast between German and American research was easily apparent. Americans went on doing their dissertations on grammar, syntax, metric or palaeography. But Germans chose topics of central interest to the time in which they wrote: *Aristoteles über*

---

[17] Lind was a Fellow of the American Council of Learned Societies in 1940. He worked under C. H. Beeson (1870-1949) at the University of Chicago in Medieval Latin: see *Bibliography*, 1.

[18] Lind married Elena Marchant y Riquelme in 1929. The union yielded one daughter Rosa. Oldfather refers to these three.

[19] For Oldfather and Wilamowitz see William M. Calder III, "Ulrich von Wilamowitz-Moellendorff to William Abbott Oldfather: Three Unpublished Letters," *CJ* 72 (1976/77) 115-27 = Ulrich von Wilamowitz-Moellendorff, "Selected Correspondence 1869-1931," *Antiqua* 23 (Naples 1983) 243-55; 308-9.

[20] See William M. Calder III, "How did Ulrich von Wilamowitz-Moellendorff Read a Text?," *CJ* 86 (1990/91) 344-52.

[21] Armstrong 248 with n. 72.

Diktatur und Demokratie, Das Führerideal bei Polybius, Das Bild des Herrschers in der griechischen Dichtung.[22] The German tradition has at last affected American publications with endless books on the plight of women, homosexuality, cripples, obscenity and racial prejudice in antiquity. All reflect contemporary liberal concerns. But this sort of use of the past was unknown in the American positivism of 1939.

Finally, his visiting professorships at the American School and at Columbia University in spring semester 1938 contrived only to discourage him. The Columbia Department was controlled by a narrow-minded papyrologist incapable of distinguishing the lasting and important from the trivial. Oldfather's *damnatio* of Westermann provides the context for his letter to Lind:[23]

> ". . . W. L. Westermann, a competent historian indeed, but only in an extremely narrow and unimportant aspect of ancient history, he is utterly without understanding of or taste for the aesthetic, literary, philosophical, and linguistic aspects of Greek and Roman culture. He systematically decries and belittles those humanistic values, which alone justify the continued existence of the Classics at all, in comparison with the trivial minutiae of the price of pigs, and the methods of writing fractions, or the barbarous bookkeeping in some wholly obscure and damnable village in decadent Egypt. Such narrow-visioned specialists there must be, & of course, they must be fanatical about the value of their own work, or else nothing could possibly induce them to do it, but to allow a man of such domineering temper and such utter lack of cultural interests to control the entire future of the Classics, whose values are surely cultural if they possess any values at all, is just a kind of tragedy."

[22] See Armstrong 240 with n. 24 and esp. W. A. Oldfather, *CW* 35 (1941/42) 53–55.

[23] I cite from *ICS* 18 (1993) 370–71.

Oldfather's warnings have a peculiar cogency today. The value of specialized research cannot be denied. With Warburg "Der liebe Gott steckt im Detail." But no specialist can afford to lose sight of what is important, what is "beautiful, stimulating and meaningful." The *exemplum virtutis* is our *honorandus*, whose contributions to exact scholarship endure but who has also done so much to confirm the enduring value of our legacy for those who are not specialists.

Some Names on a Cup
by Makron:
Etymology and Louvre G 148

ಌ

Robert Cromey
Virginia Commonwealth University

If the etymology of Greek personal names helps to explain the history of words, so the study of personal names scattered on vases helps to organize Athenian art and its chronology, and serves, when text and image combine, as an index to the values of Athenian society over more than two hundred years—years when other primary texts are rarest. The following essay presents prosopographical readings taken afresh in 1993 from a cup by Makron in the Louvre.[1] "Early, and crude" Makron, according to Beazley, the cup was found broken and still lacks its foot and about seven fragments of the design. Nevertheless, with the names of eight men or boys inscribed wholly or partially, it is respectably complex in a prosopographical way, and provides a

[1] I thank Dr. Martine Denoyelle for help under difficult circumstances.

good lesson how vase inscriptions make even philology a part of the enjoyment of the Greek spirit. For as Ernst Curtius wrote long ago, "Their sense of the beautiful and good is stamped upon their names as upon their art."[2]

Transliteration of vase inscriptions into standard modern Greek can be a somewhat deceptive "leveling" practice, sometimes creating forced readings. Letter-forms therefore are included here as written on the cup, but without attempting to show original spacing between letters or their correct size. Louvre G 148 may even add something to the chapter on courting scenes and how they relate to sexual mores, but despite the erotic nature of the interior and both sides, there are no kalos-inscriptions, only personal names.[3]

Louvre G 148 + CP 11290.[4]

8 inscriptions, 7 identifiable names, 5 legible: Antomenes (sic) > Automenes. Aristarchos. Asopokles. Stomios. Timokritos. *Fragmentary:* Lys[.2–3.]ides. -]orides. sal[–3?–] (name?).

---

[2] E. Curtius, "Personnenamen," *Gesammelte Abhandlungen*, vol. 1 (Berlin 1894 = *Berr. der Berl. Akad.* [1870] 517).

[3] On the published vases, Makron uses the certain kalos or kale-names Polydemos (Makron, *ARV* pp. 458–80: #108), Rhodopis (118), Antiphanes (146), Hippodamas (196, 336, 337, *Para.* 313 *bis*), Melitta (336), and the uncertain kalos-names Aristagoras (186; *ARV* 1566), Hik[etes] (*Para.* 506), Eury[pt]olemos, Eukrates (Metropolitan Museum of Art, New York 1979. 11.8, Bothmer, "Makron," 33), and ".....]as," which may be Hippodamas, Aristagoras, or another. But since sure kalos-names are found on only six out of over 600 known vases (Makron is the most profuse of cup-painters: are these therefore bespoke pieces?), one hardly admits him to the ranks of compulsive kalos-admirers like Oltos, Euphronios, Onesimos, Skythes, Douris, the Achilles Painter and so many others.

[4] *ARV* 470.180, 1560, 1566 (+ 470.183 = Cp 11290); *Add.*

Rf kylix. Restored from several dozen fragments. It lacks its foot and fragments of tondo and both sides, chiefly of [*B*] which was cleaned in 1994, and new fragments added.
Painter: Makron (attr. Beazley; *ARV* 470.180, 183, 1560, 1566; *Add.*[5])
Date: 495–90. Louvre: 490–80.[6] "Early," Beazley, *ARV.* "Early" Makron generally is set c. 500–495.
Lettering: Three-bar sigma, untailed rho.[7] Inscriptions, like other details painted in light red (wreaths, plants), are much faded.
Provenance: Ex Campana collection, acquired 1863 by the Louvre.[8]

[5] *Add.* p. 245, under the mistaken number "469.148."

[6] The Louvre's date of 490–80 presumably is that followed by *Lex*, "490–80," in its only entries from G 148, s.v. *Lex.* Α(ὐ)τομένης 80.3, Asopokles 77.2, Timokritos 432. In matters of prosopography, vase dates are important. Outside specific Panathenaic prize amphorae with archon names, numerical dates for pottery are estimates. More secure than numerical dates is the system of ranking vases by ceramic sequence, artist development and interrelation with other artists, workshop, groups and so forth, a methodology where the science of attribution developed by Beazley, and continued by many others, still has its place. For the major artists and groups, including Makron, and for a great number of the lesser, this comparative structure still is reasonably secure, although individual artists or vases of lesser rank will always require readjustment. It is possible that some early red-figure ware will need to be revised downward very slightly; but generally see J. C. Waldbaum, J. Magness, "The Chronology of Early Greek Pottery: New Evidence from Seventh-century B.C. Destruction Levels in Israel," *AJA* 101 (1997) 25, 40, quite supportive of traditional dating.

[7] Makron was not consistent in letter-form: *AS* 90.

[8] Found in Italy, inventoried as a fragment in the purchase of the Campana collection and later recomposed from other fragments in the same purchase (Pottier 181). Provenance happens to be important since stray fragments from the Campana collection exist in so many private and public collections, including the Louvre, that pieces still may surface to complete side [*B*] and its inscriptions, just as several have been added since Pottier's publication in 1922. On the Campana collection and its sale see D. von Bothmer, "Les vases de la collection

Figures are described from left to right. Enumeration applies to the inscriptions, not to figures. Women wear the Doric peplos and himation, men a himation, most garments carrying an embattled border.

[*I*] *(Fig. 1)* A man L with lyre leans on his staff, speaks to boy R, who clutches a piriform object to his chest (purse or fruit). Both are garlanded.
—At L border tondo facing inw.:

(1)   Ἀντομένης   ΑΝΤοΜιΕΝΕ$

—From the boy's mouth (presumably speaking), letters very faint, retrograde from R-L:

(2)   Τιμόκριτος   ; ⅄ Ι ੧ Ӿ ∨ Ⲙ ⁛ ⁄

[*A*] *(Fig. 2)* Three pairs of courting males who face each other. All names are those of the boys.
—First pair: An anonymous man holding a plant-sprig before his face leans on a staff.
—A boy holds a sprig in each hand, one before him. Over the boy's head:

(3)   Λυσ[.1–2.]ίδης   Ⳑ ∨ $ ⅃ ⁄ Δ ⴹ $

—An anonymous man on a staff offers a hare to a boy.
—A boy lifts his hand as if speaking. Over his head, apparently complete at its start:

Campana," *Revue du Louvre* 4 (1977) 213–21; G. Nadalini, "Le Musée Campana: origine et formation des collections," *L'Anticomanie. La collection d'antiquités aux 18e et 19e siècles*, eds. Annie-France Laurens, Krzysztof Pomian (Paris 1992) 111–21; E. Gran-Aymerich, J. Gran-Aymerich, "La collection Campana dans les musées de Province et la politique archéologique française," *L'Anticomanie* 128–30. See *Cataloghi del Museo Campana. Museo Campana Classe I. Vasi dipinti etruschi ed italo-greci* (Rome 1857) 195 (page numbers are hand-written into the Louvre copy; the catalog was unpaginated). The letter forms are untrustworthy and inscriptions illiterately given. There were vases sold from this collection which do not appear in the printed list but are hand-written into appendices in the Louvre copy without description other than shape and item number.

Fig. 1. Louvre G 148, Interior

Fig. 2. Louvre G 148, Side [A]

Fig. 3. Louvre G 148, Side [B]

(4)   Στομ[.1-2.]ς   *s* T *o* Λ*λ*   *ξ*

—Youth leans on staff, left hand held open as if explaining.

—A boy sniffs a sprig. Over his head:

(5)   'Αρίσταρχ[ο]ς   *A* P I*ɟ* T *ʌ* *ʌ* *L* *ξ*

[B] *(Fig. 3)* Three pairs of males facing females. All names are those of the males.

—A male leans on a staff (head lost).

—A woman holds a sprig toward her face. Over her head (probably continued from the male's head):

(6)   ]ΟΡ.ΙΔΗΣ   *ш* P I *Δ* *Є* *੫*

—A man extends a purse.

—A woman lifts her hand holding a sprig. Extending from his face, across and between the two:

(7)   ΣΑΛ (σαλ[.3.])   *ξ* *Λ* *L*

—A young woman raises her arms to kiss a youth to R (he in shoes).

— Under the R handle, next to the youth in this pair, probably applying to him:

(8)   'Ασωποκλῆς   *A* *ξ* *o* Γ *ʌ* *Ⱶ* *L* *Є* *ξ*

Notes on the inscriptions:

[*I*] (1) 'Αντομένης. Epic ἄντομαι means 'meet face to face' in a hostile or friendly way, and (trag.) 'to beseech'. Homer (*Il.* 11.237) gives the Epic form ἀντομένη, from which it is clear that "Antomenes" is possible as a personal name, not necessarily Athenian. Such a name would mean something like 'Pleasant to Meet', but also 'He who is Requesting', and in what here seems a courting scene[9] it may appear to be a 'telling name', con-

---

[9] For the lyre-gift in courting, see e.g. the unmistakable meaning of side [A] (lyre gift) and side [B] (money gift) on a pelike by the Tyszkiewicz P., Kopenhagen Natl. Mus. 3634 (*ARV* 293.51), Carola Reinsberg, *Ehe, Hetärentum und Knabenliebe im antiken Griechenland* (Munich 1994) 174, fig. 94; Gundel Koch-Harnack, *Knabenliebe und*

structed by the artist to illustrate the action shown. Such names certainly give something of a control over deciding whether a scene represents real or fictional characters. But this reading is unlikely because (1) on the cup Munich 2656 Makron also makes a mistake when using a nu (retrograde) in writing "Aristagons kalos" (sic) for "Aristagoras"[10]; (2) according to H. Immerwahr, Makron is prone to making more orthographic errors than the Panaitios Painter, Onesimos, or Douris—the latter two prolific artists like Makron[11]; (3) names beginning 'Αντο- are almost nonexistent[12]; and (4), on the whole, if the artist intends a true personal

---

Tiergeschenke (Berlin 1983) 166–67, figs. 84–85; the theme seems repeated on a pelike by the Orpheus P.: man offers purse, youth with lyre, Athens, National Museum 1418, *ARV* 1104.11: M. Meyer, "Männer mit Geld," *JdI* 103 (1988) 112, fig. 26; n. a., *Le Corps et L'Esprit* (Lausanne 1990) 111.

[10] Munich, Museum antiker Kleinkunst 2656, *ARV* 471.186, a cup carrying an unusual number of kalos-inscriptions for the artist. See G. Nachbauer, "Unbekanntes von Makron aus der Werkstatt des Hieron," *JOEAI* 54 (1983) Hauptblatt, pp. 34, 38, figs. 5–7; *AS* 90. On Munich 2656 Makron, probably copying an exemplar, seems to have read the rho and alpha as one letter, leaving the loop off the rho, the hasta off the alpha.

[11] *AS* 89–90. Although the Panaitios P. is usually thought an early phase of Onesimos, Immerwahr prefers to keep them separate on orthographic grounds.

[12] Pape-Benseler and Bechtel list no real example, nor does *Lex.* 1; *Lex.* 2 lists only 'Αντόξενος, 'Hostile to Strangers' (not a true name) on a fragmentary neck-amphora lately reattributed to Euphronios: Louvre G 106, above a figure previously assumed to be an Amazon, but which M. Denoyelle demonstrates is a Scythian bowman (in I. Wehgartner et al., *Euphronios der Maler* [Berlin 1991] 148–50); this name suits the martial figure shown, and alteration into (Π)αντόξενος therefore is unnecessary (suggested by Immerwahr, *AS* 70), a name itself rare, with a single parallel in *Lex.* 359, Παντοξένα καλά, found on two skyphoi by the Pantoxena Painter (*ARV* 1050.1–2), probably a Corinthian hetaira with her own *nom de guerre*, 'Entirely a Guest/Host'.

name, "Antomenes" seems less likely than two alternatives:

(1) 'Αντ(ι)μένης, from ἀντάω, 'to meet with, to take part in', as e.g. a youth kalos c. 525-20 on a hydria by the bf. Antimenes Painter (Leiden PC 63, *ABV* 266.1). Here on Makron's cup, twenty to thirty years later,[13] this conceivably may name the same person, now adult and c. 50 years of age. This is not a common name (*Lex.*

[13] The real age intended by the word "kalos" seems deliberately imprecise. To explain this generalizing term one perhaps may use a general rule: adolescents are "kalos" after puberty, approximately from 14–18, preferably at the upper end of those dates. At eighteen, or at whatever age young men enter the citizen corps as adult males, to receive gifts from admirers would be thought at best childish and unmanly, at worst prostitution obliging loss of citizenship if brought to court, as it well might be. On pottery—as presumably in life—the term easily is extended in age for athletes who momentarily perform well ("Bravo!"), or for men who have a fit form; and there are other technical uses of "kalos" on pottery which do not apply to humans. Examples of older men titled "kalos," cited in David M. Robinson, Edward J. Fluck, *A Study of the Greek Love-names* (Baltimore 1937) 9, involve Sokratic irony precisely because they do not fit the accepted limits of "kalos." There seems always to be a moral as well as physical implication (as, e.g., good athletic form took self-disciplined training, and only those from the proper class had leisure to train), but the weight of meaning leans toward the physical. See further: John Boardman, "Kaloi and other Names on Euphronios' Vases," in *Euphronios. Atti del Seminario Internazionale di Studi,* eds. Mario Cygielman et al. (Arezzo 1990) 45–50; Kenneth J. Dover, *Greek Homosexuality* (Cambridge, Mass. 1978) 115–22; Oddeliese Fuchs, *Der attische Adel im Spiegel der "Kalosinschriften" (480–410),* Diss. der philosophischen Fakultät der Universität Wien, 1974 (unpublished) 13–26; Karl Schefold, "T. B. L. Webster: *Potter and Patron in Classical Athens,*" *Erasmus* 25 (1973) 369–72; Konrad Schauenburg, "ΑΙΝΕΑΣ ΚΑΛΟΣ," *Gymnasium* 76 (1969) 42–53; Theodore Panofka, "Die griechischen Eigennamen mit ΚΑΛΟΣ im Zusammenhang mit dem Bilderschmuck auf bemalten Gefässen," *Kön. Akad. Wiss., Berlin,* Phil.–hist. Kl., Abh. 1849 (1851) 37–126, pls. 1–4; Secondiano Campanari, *Intorno i vasi fittili dipinto rinvinuti ne' sepolcri dell' Etruria* (Rome 1836) 73, not useless.

36.1–16), and after Louvre 148 is not afterward attested until a casualty list of 459.[14]

(2) Α(ὐ)τομένης, the likely solution, accepted by *Lex.* 80.3, means 'Self-sufficient', 'Freisleben' (Pape-Benseler). Although the name is even less common than "Antimenes," "Automenes" (*Lex.* 80.1–12) is a name kalos on a bf. hydria near the Lysippides P. (Boulogne 417, *ABV* 260.32), and perhaps on a bf. hydria near the Mastos P. (Rimini, *ABV* 261.36), both dating c. 525–20, probably the same youth as the "Automenes kalos" on a rf. cup by Oltos c. 520 (Florence 80601, *ARV* 64.96, 1568). A new fragment added to the well-known "self-portrait" symposion stamnos by Smikros (Brussels A 717) now supplies the name of the male to the far right on side [A], "Automenes."[15] The Brussels stamnos dates c. 520–10, and its adult Automenes may be associated in some manner with the adult A(u)tomenes of Louvre G 148 here, c. 30 years later. In ceramic art bearded males unfortunately look alike with only the truly aged given white hair and beard; the name Automenes is quite uncommon; the

---

[14] *IG* I³ 1147.38. The advantages of homonymity recede as dates lower and population increases. The errors possible in merging two homonomous individuals into one are seldom acknowledged, exceeded in hazard only by the practice of conjuring two persons out of one name, common in Kirchner's stemmata: *Quod nomina attinet, tot Atheniensibus idem nomen erat, ut nihil exinde colligere possimus*: Hugh J. Rose, *Inscriptiones Graecae vetustissimae* (Cambridge 1825) 112 (*non vidi*), cited by Wesley E. Thompson, "Tot Atheniensibus idem nomen erat. . . .," in *ΦΟΡΟΣ. Tribute to Benjamin Dean Meritt*, eds. D. W. Bradeen, and M. F. McGregor (Locust Valley, N.Y. 1974) 144–49. Names that are *hapax* also require caution.

[15] Stamnos Brussels, Musées Royaux A 717: *ARV* 20.1; *Add.*; completed by the fr. New York, Metropolitan Museum of Art 1985. 60.1 (not in *Lex.*), D. von Bothmer, *GMJ* 14 (1986) 18 n. 22; D. Kurtz, ed., *Greek Vases. Lectures by J. D. Beazley* (Oxford 1984) 47, pls. 25.3–4.

population of archaic Athens smaller; and the social circle therefore may be much the same as that which, a generation earlier or less, had involved Smikros, his friends and "kaloi" Antias, Pheidiades, Diodoros, Eukleides, Diomnestos, Mousokles, Antiphanes, Delphis, Gnathon, Philokydes, Aristaichmos, Melas, Leagros, Egerthos, Andriskos, Ambrosios, Euphronios and others. If, on the other hand, c. 520–10 the youth "kalos" on the three pieces above (by Oltos and the Lysippides and Mastos painters) is the adult Automenes of Louvre G 148 (Smikros' Automenes then being someone else, perhaps a relative), he would be an adult aged at least c. 18 in 520, and aged c. 45–50 on Louvre G 148 of c. 490. After G 148 one must wait until 422 for the next attested "Automenes" (Ar. *Vesp.* 1275).

(2) Τιμόκριτος. *Lex.* 432.1; Pottier.[16] From τιμή 'reward', 'honor', 'price', and κρίνω, 'estimating' (or as a verb. adj. κριτός, 'chosen, choice'), "Judged Worthy, Judged Honorable; Judging Worth," uncommon: *Lex.* 432.1–8, not another until the 4th c. B.C. Since there is no "kalos," evidently we are to understand that the youth gives the older man his name, "I'm Timokritos." Contrary to expectation, in the word-play of naming-patterns inside Athenian families a "Timokritos" seems linked only once to a family of similar name, one which often employed the much more common name Timokrates: Timokritos Timokratous, born by 371.[17]

Side [A] (3) Λυσ[.1–2.]ίδης. ΛΥΣΙΠΙΔΕΣ (sic), Hartwig, Klein, Hoppin, who present the name as if complete; and per-

[16] Pottier's plate 118 shows the final sigma facing right, not boustrophedon with the rest of the inscription, now almost illegible. I thank Prof. H. Giroux for confirming Pottier's reading with an alcohol wash.

[17] John K. Davies, *Athenian Propertied Families* (Oxford 1971) 513: 13768; *Lex.* 431.1–133: 55.

haps once it was. Λυσ[ιππ]ίδης, Pottier (text). The modern artist who reinscribes onto Pottier's plates the otherwise near-invisible inscriptions, occasionally more accurate than Pottier's text, offers Λυσι[..]ιδες: the first iota is no longer visible, if in modern times it ever was. Although names compounded with "hippo-, -hippos" were so common that they sometimes seem to escape all meaning (e.g., Ἀμύδριππος, Ἀισχύλιππος; "Στρούθ(ο)-ιππος," unless referring to a brand: *IG* XII 9 no 241.38), "Lysippides" on its face means something like "Son of Freed Horse," and is not a common name (*Lex.* 1–8), all other examples beyond Louvre G 148 coming from the 4th c. B.C. except the namesake "kalos" of Beazley's bf. Lysippides Painter c. 530–20 (*ABV* 670). The name "Lysippides" may take the form of a patronymic, but not all personal names with this suffix were true patronymics (i.e., with a father "Lysippos"), the implication rather being that of gentilic aristocracy, as if belonging to a large genos or oikos named "Lysippidai," or even generally "eupatridai."[18] Although the individual on G 148, a boy, is not the bf. Lysippides, c. 490 he is at least of age to be the son of a father himself once an admired "Lysippides kalos," now 30–40 years old.

Alternative readings that follow Pottier's plate, rather than text, open the door to other names: Λυσι[κλε]ίδης (*Lex.* 291.1–13, from Λυσικλῆς), Λυσι[θε]-ίδης (*Lex.* 290.1–14, as if from Λυσίθεος). Based on what is visible on the cup now, one may propose Λυσ[ων]ίδης, known from mid-5th c. B.C., *Lex.* 295.1–2: Λύσων (not a popular name, *Lex.* 295.1–13) appears c. 560 on an

[18] On the formation of this type of patronymic see, e.g., *Formation* 362–63. We seldom know a wife's ancestry or even her name, and in a society where it was thought proper to marry one's first cousin in alternate generations use of patronymics may depend on the name of a maternal rather than paternal grandfather.

unattributed bf. kylix,[19] and on Louvre G 148 a nu would suit what may be the remnant of a letter to the right of the break. But see also Λυσ[αρχ]ίδης (*Lex.* 289, c. 259–50 B.C., *hapax*) from Λύσαρχος, itself rare: there is only a 5th c. B.C. Eubioan (?), *Lex.* 1.292, together with a hellenistic Athenian Λάσαρχος, *Lex.* 289). Other names use more letters. Λυσ[ιπ]ίδης (sic) is better than other restorations, but scarcely certain.

(4) Στομ[.1–2.]ς. Στόμ[ιο]ς, Pottier; "...ΣTOME..Σ," Klein.

No letters are visible before sigma, and Pottier's "Stomios," 'Little Mouth', is acceptable. Cf. the Athenian Olympionikos of 644 Στόμας (*Lex.* 405, *hapax*), hypocoristic for Στόμαργος *vel sim*,[20] the 5th c. B.C. Athenian Στόμης (Pand. *Lex.* 405, *hapax*), Στομίλος, "(Dear) Little Mouth," in 5th c. B.C. Euboian Styria (*Lex.* 1.413, *hapax*), the Troizenians Δερίας Στομᾶ ('Neck son of Mouth'[21]), and Στομῆς on 2nd c. B.C. Tenos (*Lex.* 1.413, *hapax*). Compare also the name ΧΙΛΟΝ on two vases by Oltos: Χίλων, from χεῖλος, 'lip', not from χιλιάς, 'thousand'.[22]

Given the historical parallels, "Stomios" therefore is a true name, not a nickname whose bearer officially

---

[19] Toulouse, Musée de Ste. Raymond 347, *ABV* 165, its upsilon upside-down; *AS* 244.

[20] Bechtel, "Spitznamen," 29, 64.

[21] 4th c. B.C., *IG* IV 764 II 3, Bechtel 481, "Spitznamen," 30.

[22] London, British Museum E 19; Florence, Museo Archeologico 81601, *ARV* 63.95, 64.96; cf. *Lex.* Χίλων 478.1–3, to be taken with Χείλων 478.1–6. Further, Bechtel, "Spitznamen," 29. The few anthroponyms based on numbers derive from the cardinals, not ordinal numbers, and an anthroponym from χιλίας should have the root χιλιοστ-; there are none. The main "numerical" exceptions, rarely used, are a few calendar-day names, for the obvious reason that these were the birth-days. See A. Fick, Fritz Bechtel, *Die griechische Personennamen*[2] (Göttingen 1894) 295–97, and generally W. Havers, "Neuere Literatur zum Sprachtabu," *SAWW* Phil.-hist. Kl., Abh. (1946) 223:5.

carried an altogether different personal name: someone's baby had an unusual (large?) mouth. With reasonable certainty, it may be restored here.

Hoppin, Klein, Hartwig read "...ΣΤΟΜΕ..Σ," and restore as ['Αρι]στομέ[νη]ς, recalling the youth kalos c. 480–70 (*Lex.* 58.3, *ARV* 535.1 foot, Syracuse 21130): this is not supported by evidence on the cup.

(5) 'Αρίσταρχ[ο]ς. A new reading, from secure traces. ΑΡΙΣΤ[ΑΓΟΡΑΣ], Hartwig. ΑΡΙΣΤ..., Klein, nevertheless restoring both this and (4) as 'Αριστομένης. Aristarchos: 'Best in Command', 'Werthold' (Pape-Benseler). An Aristarchos is kalos on a cup by Onesimos of c. 480;[23] on several by the Antiphon Painter c. 485, whose style is similar to that of the later Onesimos;[24] and on a lost cup, ex Canino (*ARV* 1566.3). Therefore the Aristarchos of G 148 well may be the same as the Aristarchos elsewhere "kalos." Not a seldom name, however: *Lex.* 51.1–61.

Side [B] (6)]ΟΡΙΔΕΣ. ['Ακεστ]ο[ρ]ίδης, Hoppin, Pottier. ΑκεσΤΟΡΙΔΕΣ ΚΑΛος (sic), Klein, incorrectly, drawing his kalos from (7). According to Beazley, "if [ΑΚΕΣΤ]ΟΡΙΔΕΣ is read as the name of one of the persons on the cup Louvre G 148 . . . it must be an earlier Akestorides" than the Akestorides kalos of *ARV* 1560, about 470–60.[25]

[23] Schwerin, Museum 725 (1307), *ARV* 325.73.

[24] Baltimore, Walters Art Gallery 48.2115, *ARV* 336.16; U. Ill., Urbana KAM 70.8.7, *CVA* US 24: Krannert Mus. 1 (1989) 19–20: 25, *Add.*, p. 293; N. Schimmel, King's Point, N.Y., in Oscar Muscarella, *The Norbert Schimmel Collection* (Mainz 1974) #61.

[25] On the later Akestorides, Oddeliese Fuchs (above, n. 13) 71–72. This later Akestorides is interlocked with other individuals called "kalos" on ware by the Timokrates, Oinonokles and Nikon painters, all conventionally dated c. 470–60: for the date see Gisela M. A. Richter, *Red-figured Athenian Vases*, vol. I (New Haven 1936) 55, #33. This date

The letter before -o- requires Δ, Ν, Τ, or Φ: *Lex.* 494, "Reverse Index," lists seven different names ending in -δωριδης, four in -νοριδης, four in -τοριδης, one in -φοριδης: "Akestorides" therefore is a reading far from certain.

(7) ΣΑΛ[.3.]. Traces of at least three more letters are very faint. "ΣΑΛΝΕΣ (?)," Pottier. ΣΑΛV.., Louvre entry (computer). Not [κ]αλ[ος] with the -]οριδες of #6 (as Klein, Hoppin). Possible restorations would be the bf. potter's name Σάλαχς c. 500 B.C.;[26] Σάλιος, 4th/3rd C. B.C., *Lex.* 393; Σάλαγος, *hapax*, heroic, Chios, *Lex.* 1. 400; Σάλακος, *hapax*, 6th c. B.C., Thera, *Lex.* 1.400; and perhaps a few others, all from σάλακος, σαλάκων, 'boast', itself from σαλάσσω, 'cram full, stuff', cf. Engl. 'bombast'.[27] Such a name need not be foreign.[28]

(8) Ἀσωποκλῆς. Extending vertically under the R handle,

---

(470) is certainly too late for "early" Makron. According to Beazley Makron's work disappears about 480; D. von Bothmer states that there are "no vases by him that can safely be dated after 480 B.C." ("Makron," 49), though some would stretch to 470, e.g. "480/470," Bertild Gossel-Raeck, *Kunst der Schale, Kultur des Trinkens* (Munich 1990) 482, fig. 36.3; "bald nach 480" for London, British Museum E 140, *ARV* 459.3, Erika Simon, *Die griechischen Vasen* (Munich 1976 [1981]) 121, #167.

[26] Salax: plate, Agora Museum P 1386, *ABV* 351, *Agora* 23 #1407, *AS* 74 #435.

[27] Salax: for etymology (most recently), see Olivier Masson, "L'apport de l'anthroponymie grecque à l'étymologie et à l'histoire des mots," *La Langue et les textes en grec ancien. Actes du colloque Pierre Chantraine, Grenoble–5–8 sept. 1989*, ed. Françoise Letoublon (Amsterdam 1992) 263.

[28] Anton Scherer, "Fremdsprachige Personennamen im alten Griechenland," *Symbolae linguisticae in honorem Georgii Kurylowicz* (Warsaw 1965), most recent in suggesting that the potter's name Salax is Illyrian, citing Illyrian inscriptions bearing the name Σαλλας, but this name may not differ from, e.g., the Theraian's name given above, derived from σαλάσσω, also cited by Scherer; and see the note by Olivier Masson, *Onomastica Graeca Selecta* I (Université de Paris X-Nanterre 1990) 92 = "Quelques noms grecs rare," *Philologus* 110 (1966) 257, with further bibliography, minimizing foreign origin.

the name applies to the leaning youth on this side, who is drawn too near the handle to inscribe his name above.

Ἀσοπόκλης, Pottier (sic), *Lex.* 77.2. 'Glory of Asopos', probably the same person as the athlete found on a Proto-Panaitian kylix akin to early Onesimos (Cab. Méd. 523, *ARV* 316.4, *Add.*, *Lex.* 77.1). Dating the Proto-Panaitian cup 500–490 —although some of its names are "early" according to Beazley—and Louvre G 148 to c. 490–80, *Lex.* perhaps unnecessarily here distinguishes two individuals as Asopokles 1–2: on the Proto-Panaitian cup [*I*], Asopokles appears as a ephebic-age "trainer" for two wrestlers, and there seems little reason why these two cups cannot both date c. 490.

"Asopokles" is not a name derived from alpha-privative and σῶς ⟩ σωτ- ⟩ ἄσωτος, 'destroyer' (of his genos, Aesch. *Ag.* 1597), 'beyond salvation, tosspot, wastrel', 'medically beyond hope', and so on (lexica, e.g., Hesych.). A toponym "Asopos," usually belonging to rivers, river-plains and moors, in turn gave rise to the theonym Ἀσωπός from which personal names are derived, and clearly the word (probably first meaning 'marsh' or 'moor') originated among the several pre-Hellenic ethnica with root -οπ-, -ωπ-, like Dolopes, Meropes, Aeropes, Dryopes, and in Boiotia of Ἀσώπιοι, Her. 9.15, or Παρασώπιοι, Strab. 9.404, 408, those living along the river Asopos, "Morländer" (Pape-Benseler).[29]

The lad shown here thus ultimately draws his name from a toponym; and as for those, there was a locale Ἀσώπιον in Athens (attested only in Hesych., s.v. ἀσωτεῖον); and as with several versions of the anthroponym, there were also several rivers named Ἀσωπός in the lower-central Greek mainland, but note:

---

[29] Prehellenic: *Formation* 259–60.

(1) a river and plain of Sikyon (Paus. 2.5.2), whose "ancient name" was Asopia (Ath. 11.491c).

(2) in the context of 550–490 one may count the river Asopos between Theban and Attic territory which, perhaps c. 517, following yet another border-battle with Thebes, successfully made an enclave of Plataia (Hdt. 6.108.6), a good occasion for naming a son Asopokles, "Glory of Asopos," aged c. 27 in 490. This toponym probably also yields the names of the Plataian individual "Asopolaos" (Thuc. 3.52), and—perhaps after transformation into a theonym—the Theban "Asopodoros" (Hdt. 9.69.2).

(3) a river of Euboian Chalkis (Σ *Il.* 2.535). In 507 Athens' new democracy defeated Chalkis and confiscated prime land there for 4000 Athenian settlers (Hdt. 5.77), an apt moment to name an infant "Asopokles," who would appear aged about 17 on a cup drawn c. 490.

Thus in Attica the names "Asopokles" (*Lex.* 77.1–14) and "Asopodoros" (*Lex.* 77.1–13) are first attested c. 500–480 (following *Lex.* dates, and without multiplying otherwise unattested individuals), and historically there seems little reason why we should look for them any earlier.

* * *

A part of the value of vase inscriptions is that they very often are attached to depictions of an individual's age, something usually quite lacking in stone epigraphy unless listed as "*paides*" or "*epheboi*," particularly rare in the archaic period. Given their visual clue, these names then may be linked to other vases with different names, or with the same painter or groups of painters in a workshop. This happy circumstance helps distinguish the "telling name" from reality—and from the overwhelming world of pseudomythological fantasy that, by c. 425 with the hard victory of democratic ideology and art, had usurped vase illustration and diminished a market for depictions carrying the values of a discredited "aristocratic" class. Louvre G 148 may offer a general and rewarding introduction to prosopography on vases and its problems; but given the adjectival nature of Greek personal names, the rare or well-attested nature of its inscribed names clearly places us in the midst of gentlemen of leisure and their enviable pastimes, soon to be engulfed in intense wars with barbarian invaders.

Abbreviations

ABV = Beazley, J. D. 1956. *Attic Black-figure Vase-painters.* Oxford.

ARV = Beazley, J. D. 1963. *Attic Red-figure Vase-painters.* 2nd ed. Oxford.

Para. = Beazley, J. D. 1971. *Paralipomena.* Oxford.

Add. = Carpenter, T. H. 1989. *Beazley Addenda.* 2nd ed. Oxford. [Consult using Beazley page and vase numbers.]

AS = Immerwahr, H. R. 1990. *Attic Script.* Oxford.

Bechtel = Bechtel, F. 1917. *Die historischen Personennamen des Griechischen.* Halle.

Formation = Chantraine, Pierre. 1933 [1979]. *La Formation des noms en Grec ancien.* Paris.

Hartwig = Hartwig, Paul. 1893. *Die griechischen Meisterschalen.* Stuttgart. 294, pp. ll.30, 31.

Hoppin = Hoppin, Joseph. 1919 [1973]. *A Handbook of Attic Red-figured Vases.* Cambridge, Mass. 2, 104.

Klein = Klein, Wilhelm. 1898. *Die griechischen Vasen mit Lieblingsinschriften.* 2nd ed. Leipzig. 153.

Lex. 1 = Fraser, Peter M., and Elaine Matthews. 1987. *A Lexicon of Greek Personal Names.* Vol. I. *The Aegean Islands,*

Cyprus, Cyrenaica. Oxford. Cited in the form: Ἐπίγονος 1.155.19 = vol. 1, p. 155, individual number 19 of that name.

Lex. = Osborne, Michael, and Steven Byrne. 1994. *A Lexicon of Greek Personal Names. Volume II. Attica.* Oxford.

"Makron" = von Bothmer, Dietrich. 1982. "Notes on Makron." *The Eye of Greece.* Eds. Donna Kurtz and Brian Sparkes. Cambridge. 29–52.

Pape-Benseler = Pape, Walter, and Georg Benseler. 1911. *Wörterbuch der griechischen Eigenname.* 2 vols. 3rd. ed. Braunschweig.

Pottier = Pottier, Edmond. 1922. *Vases antiques du Louvre.3e série, Salle G.* Paris. 180–81, pls. 118 [*I*], 119 [*A*]; side [*B*] is not reproduced.

"Spitznamen" = F. Bechtel. 1898. "Die einstämmigen männlichen Personennamen des Griechischen, die aus Spitznamen hervorgegangen sind." *Königl. Akad. Wiss. zu Göttingen*, phil.-hist. Kl., Abh., NF 2:6:1–83.

Norbert Kunisch, *Makron*, 2 vols. (Mainz 1997). (*Kerameus* 10) was published as this article was in proof stage. Louvre G 148 = Kunisch p. 168, #74, pl. 29. This article provides readings that Kunisch omits; note also the slight difference in the photograph of side [*B*], here including the face of the young woman to far right.

Reconsidering the Riddle of the Sphinx in *Oedipus at Colonus* and *I'm Not Rappaport*

corocrocro

Judith de Luce
Miami University

What is that which has one voice and yet becomes four-footed and two-footed and three-footed?

(Apollodorus III.v.8)

"The very old, they are miracles like the just-born; close to the end is precious like close to the beginning."

(Nat, in *I'm Not Rappaport*)

I do not intend to provide here a definitive interpretation of Sophocles' *Oedipus at Colonus*[1] or of Herb Gardner's *I'm Not Rappaport*, nor is it my intention to present a full picture of growing old in fifth-century Athens or in late twentieth century America.[2] Rather, I want to use these two

[1] For a range of scholarly reflections on *Oedipus at Colonus* which have informed my perspective, see: Bowra, Cole, Datan, Falkner 1993, 1995, Knox, Whitman.

[2] For specific information about aging in antiquity as well as broader discussions about old age, see: Cole, Van Tassel, and Kastenbaum, de

115

pieces of dramatic literature as case studies to reconsider a question which has occupied my attention for some time now: whether the riddle of the Sphinx is a persuasive metaphor for human experience.

If there is any point to reading literature, surely it is in finding expressions of and opportunities for reflection upon the most central aspects of human experience. Glenn Gould's reflections on the impact of music apply to literature as well and to this essay in particular. Gould explored art's ". . . capacity to serve as a mirror to those who contemplate it." The pianist concluded that "perhaps what one discovers . . . is nothing less than one's own real self, revealed in its weaknesses and strengths, its simplicity and complexity" (Payzant 64).

Keeping Gould's perspective in mind, let me turn to the riddle of the Sphinx. One interpretation of the riddle might argue that from birth as a vulnerable, dependent child requiring constant care, we follow a circular course which brings us back to vulnerability and dependency, unable to care for ourselves. But couldn't we also say that the route of our lives is circular only in the sense that it is continuous, that what is important is not that we return to vulnerability, but that we remain throughout our lives what we were at the start?[3]

Recent studies in gerontology have reflected on the nature of the life course and the relationship between aging parents and adult children, a relationship clearly connected with the implications of the riddle. I include myself among those gerontologists who are unwilling to pass off that relationship as one of role reversal (Blenkner, Brody 1990,

---

Luce 1993, 1996, Falkner 1995, Falkner and de Luce 1989, 1992.

[3] Cicero's Cato argues for continuity across the lifespan. For a multidisciplinary discussion of Cicero's *De Senectute*, see: de Luce 1993.

Jarvis, Rautman, Seltzer). To be sure, caring for a frail, elderly parent may include activities associated with the care
of young children, as indeed is attending to anyone unable
to care for her/himself, regardless of age. (Archbold,
Gadow, Horowitz, Matthews). Nevertheless, although infant
and old person share a liminal status, the unique position
of being very close to the threshold of life, we regard that
proximity quite differently. The child increases the distance
between her/himself and the threshold even as that child
grows increasingly independent, but the old person inexo-
rably narrows that distance (Archbold, Brody 1985, 1990).
As caregivers we respond with enthusiasm and optimism to
the one, with profound grief and dread to the other. In addition, since we see our own fates in our parents', our dread
is as much for ourselves as for them. Finally, caring for an
aging parent forces us to grow up, to assume an adulthood
which often seems elusive until our parents' deaths. Caring
for a child may not significantly alter our own status but
caring for a parent surely does.

More importantly, the relationship between caregiver and
recipient is not the same with child and aging parent. With
a young child, there is no past relationship, only the possibility of a future one. The aging adult, on the other hand,
has a past which includes the caregiver. Authority, wisdom,
and approval once resided in the parent (Seltzer). A
parent's weakness and need for care frustrate our expectations that our parents should care for us, our own maturity
notwithstanding (Brody 1985). For their part, our parents
may become frustrated by their inability to exercise the authority and independence befitting their parental status
(Blenkner, Brody 1990, Hayes). The roles do not reverse
because the parent does not cease to be a parent, does not
relinquish a past rich with experience and action, does not
revert to the infinite potential and utter history-less condi-

tion of the child. No matter how old or how impaired, the aging parent can never revert in fact to the condition of a child.

The popular press, however, has seldom shared this scholarly perspective. The September, 1989 *Lear's*, for example, included a feature on "Our Parents" which addressed intelligently and humanely, for the most part, the complexity of this relationship. The article concluded that the loss of power is "what is so troubling about this reversal of parent and child . . . this turnabout." The obligation of the caregivers is ". . . very like the responsibility we feel towards our own children." This tendency to equate parent care with child care extends even to suggesting that we need a Dr. Spock for geriatric care: "We like the assurance of our graphs and texts. Why not know as much about caring for the aged as about raising our kids? Dr. Spock gave us the baby bible in 1946, during the first baby boom, when folk and family wisdom needed the correction of sensible science. We have come to such a moment toward the end of the century—Methuselen Age, Era of the Elderly, whatever we may eventually call it. . . ."

We may very well like "the assurance of our graphs and texts," but I would add that we also like the safe distance they afford. I have chosen two case studies which may help us reduce the distance between the graphs and texts and the human experience of growing old. In dramatic literature in particular, whether read or performed, there is no safety in the statistics and refined analysis of the scholar. Rather, drama confronts us directly with issues of profound human concern, couched in language and action which we cannot avoid.[4] To take a page from Aristotle, for example, drama requires us to enter into the action ourselves, to ex-

[4] For an enlightening examination of what takes place at a dramatic performance, see States.

perience firsthand what it means to be both adult child and aging parent.

An experience on my own campus underscores this peculiar power of drama. I recently attended a student performance of Caryl Churchill's *Vinegar Tom*, a play in which women alleged to be witches are tortured and hanged onstage. I knew perfectly well that I was watching red dye staining the women's costumes and that the administration of Miami would never condone the torture or hanging of its students, but that is not the point. The tension between reality—this is just a play—and the deception of the stage—that is real blood—was palpable. I found myself reacting to the torture scene as if it were real in spite of knowing that it was not actually happening, and that reaction was essential to the performance.

The theater audience agrees to attend to the play and to apply its imagination and intelligence to the performance. In that sense the audience completes the performance (—after all, a performance without an audience is a rehearsal); it is not only present at the creation of a particular work of art, but it is itself a performer in that work. Indeed, the theater audience assumes an active role at the very start when it agrees to a number of conditions as it enters the theater—to abide by the conventions of dramatic performance; to believe that whatever occurs onstage is virtually true. Indeed, as a character in Robertson Davies' *Lyre of Orpheus* observes: "We are deceived because we will our own deception. It is somehow necessary to us" (248). The excitement of the stage relies on the very fact that we know that what is onstage is not true, that we know these are actually actors, and that the actors know we know it.

Moreover, theater is a community experience. Our physical presence is part of the performance and affects the performance as a whole for actors and other audience members. Wendy Lesser sees the experience of theater within the context of a group ritual: "Part of what theater gives us—at its best, and its audience's best—is a sense of community, a feeling of shared if unspoken response" (198–99). Athenian tragedy, of course, provided the ultimate community experience since a fifth-century audience member would have attended the tragic performances during a public festival.

I selected these plays for several reasons. Granted, these plays reflect two very different cultures, Athens in the fifth century B.C.E. and New York in the late twentieth century C.E. They represent different genres of drama, one classically tragic, the other sardonically comic. Their profound differences require that we study them cautiously and that we try not to force onto one play the cultural assumptions and expectations of the other.

In spite of the enormous differences, however, I was struck by the even greater correspondences between the two plays. Both Sophocles and Gardner represent the experience of growing old through the eyes of old persons. Both remind us that growing old, needing care, and providing care are all aspects of human experience which transcend space and time. Both are written by male authors who give voice primarily to the experiences of old men, but the plays share a breadth of vision which transcends gender and class.

The protagonists in each play share limited mobility, impaired vision, poverty, threats to their dignity, and attempts to reduce them to the status of children. They also share pasts filled with actions and relationships, and none of them is willing to deny those pasts or to act as if aging and ill health nullify the experiences which shaped them as individuals.

Oedipus both affirms and defies in *Oedipus at Colonus* the very riddle which he had answered. At first this Oedipus seems to bear little resemblance to the clever, dogmatic man of *Oedipus Tyrannus*. That man had been supremely confident, hot-tempered, arrogant. That Oedipus had pushed and probed until he discovered that he was the source of the pollution in Thebes, that the unspeakable destiny he had sought so carefully to avoid had in fact pursued him.

In *Oedipus at Colonus*, we first see the exiled king in rags, dependent on his daughters' physical strength as well as their counsel. He is frightened and as burdened by the rigors of exile and the memories of his past as by the physical realities of old age. He seems to embody the chorus' predictably pessimistic vision of old age (de Luce 1996, Falkner 1987, Falkner and de Luce 1992):

> The endless hours pile up a drift of pain
> More unrelieved each day; and as for pleasure,
> when he is sunken in excessive age, You will not see his pleasure anywhere. (1214–17; tr. E. Wyckoff)
> . . .
> Not to be born surpasses thought and speech. The second best is to have seen the light
> and then to go back quickly whence we came. (1224–26)
> . . .
> And in the end he comes to strengthless age.
> abhorred by all [people], without company,
> unfriended in that uttermost twilight
> where he must live with every bitter thing. (1235–38)

But if the chorus assumes old age is a time of deprivation, hardship, and loneliness, it also attributes to old age wisdom born from experience. When the chorus first sees him in the sacred grove of the Eumenides and fails to recognize him in spite of the disfiguring scars on his eyes, Oedipus gives an eloquent account of himself to which the chorus responds: "Old man. This argument of yours compels our wonder. It was not feebly worded" (295). The chorus, Creon, Theseus all remark at some point on the difference between being old and being witless.

Oedipus' strength of mind is not matched by his bodily strength, however. He needs care, and he expects that care from his children. Oedipus' brutal dismissal of his sons for their failure to care for him would not have surprised Sophocles' audience. A politician could be expelled from office were it proven that he had failed to provide care for his aging parents (Schaps). Sons, rather than daughters, would naturally have been in the best financial position to be caregivers. Oedipus' harsh criticisms of his sons for failing to provide this care, then, reflect reasonable expectations on his part. One may label this gender reversal, that it is the daughters who provide care for their father, but this is no role reversal. The original relationship between Oedipus and his children does not give way in the face of age and physical infirmity.

Creon, sent by Eteocles to persuade Oedipus to return to Thebes, preys on a father's love for his daughters and his commitment to paternal obligations. Referring to Antigone, Creon insists

> "I never thought she'd fall to such indignity,
> poor child! And yet she has;
> forever tending you, leading a beggar's life
> with you; a grown-up girl who knows nothing of marriage...
> is this not a disgrace?" (749–53)

The sisters do not regard as disgraceful the care they give their father nor the hardships they have endured on his behalf. Oedipus openly concedes his physical disabilities and his need for help, but his daughters never regard him as anything less than their father, with all that that implies.

Just as his daughters never treat him as any less than their father, Oedipus does not relinquish the role of father, either, as we see when Antigone tries to persuade him to speak to Polynices. She does not condescend or patronize the old man, but instead argues carefully and passionately with the man whose temper and confidence informed *Oedipus Tyrannus*:

> "Father: listen to me, even if I am young . . .
> Don't be afraid: he will not throw you off your resolve, nor
> speak offensively.
> What is the harm in hearing what he ways?"
> Her words recall the entire past of her father:
> "Reflect not on the present, but on the past,
> think of your mother's and your father's fate and what you
> suffered through them!" (1181-97)

> Oedipus listens but has no sympathy for the tale Polynices
> tells: ". . . you drove me into exile;
> me, your own father: made me a homeless man,
> insuring me these rags you blubber over
> when you behold them now—now that you, too, have fallen
> on evil days and are in exile . . . (1356-59)
> I have begged my daily bread from other men.
> If I had not these children to sustain me,
> I might have lived or died for all your interest. . . . (1365-66)
> As for you two, you are no sons of mine!" (1369)

And so Oedipus, powerful in his weakness, curses his sons, rejects Polynices and sends him away to his death.

It would be easy to see in this play little more than the "strengthless age" of an old man who must depend on these daughters for his very survival, but even as he leans on Antigone for support, we recognize in Oedipus the man who answered the riddle of the Sphinx. Blind and lame, he may remind us of the crippled child exposed on the mountainside, but this Oedipus is no child; in fact he is not so very different from that younger man in *Oedipus*

Tyrannus. Oedipus is still a persuasive speaker, still a formidable intellect, and as stubborn as he was as a young man.
In the end, the Oedipus who was smart enough to answer
the riddle of the Sphinx but could not evade his destiny,
who has wandered through his exile, blind, feeble, unable
to walk without the physical support and sight of Antigone,
leads his daughters and Theseus deeper into the grove of
the Eumenides to meet his death. Most significantly, he
leads them unaided.

Oedipus at Colonus is "about" many things—power, vulnerability, independence, necessity, expectations, family, old
age. *I'm Not Rappaport* continues those themes and does so
in language which echoes provocatively the language and
imagery of Sophocles' tragedy.[5]

The play revolves around two friends who meet daily on a
bench in Central Park and the individuals whom they confront there. Midge is 81, African American, nearly blind
with cataracts and in danger of losing his job as super of a
building about to go coop. We know considerably less
about Nat, also 81, who apparently never tells the truth
about himself but instead spins elaborate yarns about his
adventures. Both old men respond to the challenges of
New York with their own particular brand of courage and
determination—Nat with daring ingenuity and verbal bra-
vado, Midge with more caution but no less grit.

---

[5] The origin of this essay must be traced to my search for a paper
topic for the annual meeting of the Classical Association of the Middle
West and South. I had been thinking of writing something about parent
care in *Oedipus at Colonus* when I headed for the Cincinnati Playhouse
to see *I'm Not Rappaport.* Halfway through the first act I whispered to
my companion, "Gardner has written *Oedipus at Colonus* with a New
York accent." While I have not tried here to argue that claim with any
comprehensiveness, I am never far from wanting to, and I have left that
challenge for another time.

Instead of relying on what a choral ode might tell us, we see what it is to be old directly through these men's eyes, a vision at first specific to their class, races, and the city in which they live. Nat and Midge understand what it means to be old men in a city not famous for its gentle treatment of the poor, the old, or the vulnerable. The two men compare survival tactics, from procuring day-old rolls from the Plaza Hotel to trying to make do on Social Security checks.

At the start of the play, both men are afraid of failing eyesight, of falling, of losing their independence, of the violence of the City. The motif of sight pervades the contemporary as much as the ancient play. Here, Nat and Midge grapple most often with the issue not of seeing but of being seen. Nat claims to be a spy in "deep cover": "They figure an old man, nobody'll pay attention. Could wander through the world like a ghost, pick up some tidbits" (6).

The two men cope with visibility differently. Midge says that he has survived by not making trouble, by becoming "the wise old invisible man" (14). But Nat counters with, "What do you know? What does a ghost know? People see me; they see me! I make them see me!" Midge thinks Nat is kidding himself: "Old fool, crazy old fool; they can't see you. They can hear ya, but they sure can't see ya . . . both of us ghosts only you ain't noticed. We old and not rich and done the sin of leavin' slow." (15) Nonetheless, after the two have compared notes on their failing eyesight, Nat prophetically announces in a line reminiscent of the blind Teiresias in *Oedipus Tyrannus*: "Who needs sight when we have vision" (19).[6]

The blindness of Oedipus is here, so is the lameness. If Midge is nearly blind, Nat at various times walks with a cane and a walker, and both men are beaten and fall in the

---

[6] Teiresias charges Oedipus in *OT*: "You have your eyes but see not . . ." (412–14).

course of the play. When his companion has fallen trying to slug him, Nat reassures Midge: "It's nothing; I fall down every morning. I get up, I have a cup of coffee, I fall down. That's the system; two years old you stand up and then, boom, seventy years later you fall down again" (10). Nat continues with what sounds suspiciously like one interpretation of the Sphinx's riddle: "The very old, they are miracles like the just-born; close to the end is precious like close to the beginning" (47).

Oedipus' past was always with him in part because his scars identified him and served as reminder of who he was and what he had done. Nat and Midge, on the other hand, establish and maintain their individual identities in part by recalling their pasts themselves. Midge often reflects upon his success as a boxer and on his amatory adventures. Nat, not unlike that inveterate liar Odysseus, creates so many different pasts for himself, and does so with such exuberance, that it is not until the very end of the play that we find out who he actually is.

Oedipus may have expected care from his family, but these men are anxious to live independently. Midge confesses that he is ". . . scared of goin' foolish. My daddy went foolish five years before he died, didn't know his own name" (25). Although he refers to receiving some help from his family, it does not appear that they are anxious to impose care on him. Midge rejects the suggestion that he move to the Amsterdam Hotel. "Amsterdam's ninety percent foolish people. . . . Only way you can tell the live ones from the dead ones is how old their newspapers are. . ." (41).

Nat resists care absolutely. At various points in the play Nat has equated old age with childhood, but faced with his own child, Nat drops those equations and bullies his daughter by inventing an entirely fictitious daughter who is coming to take him back with her to Israel. Clara's intentions seem sincere and probably are, but in the face of his resistance, she slips into speaking as if to a very young person: "You have to be watched. I'm not letting you out of my sight, Dad" (68). Nat says that Clara embarrasses him when she tries to keep him quiet, "shushing me like I was a babbling child. . . ." asking, "[T]he test questions to see if I'm too old . . . One wrong answer you'll wrap me in a deck chair and mail me to Florida; *two* mistakes you'll put me in a home for the forgettable. I know this. My greatest fear is that someday soon I will wake up silly, that time will take my brain and you will take me. That you will put me in a place, a home—or worse, *your* house. Siberia in Great Neck. Very little frightens me, as you know; just that. Only what you will do" (70–71).

Clara gives Nat three choices: live with her family on Long Island, in Great Neck; live in a senior residence near her; live in his own place in the city and go to the senior citizen's center for lunch and daily activities. But these are hardly choices to Nat: "We got exile in Great Neck, we got Devil's Island, we got kindergarten" (Gardner 81). In exasperation, Clara threatens to take him to court to have him declared incompetent.[7]

Finally, these two irascible, irrepressible old men, like Oedipus frail physically but not emotionally or intellectually, conceive a plan to help a young woman who owes money to

[7] The question of competence recalls the story of Sophocles and his son. Tradition preserved by Plutarch (*Moralia*, "Whether an Old Man Should Engage in Public Affairs"), Lucian (*Octogenarians*), Cicero (*On Old Age*) says that his son took Sophocles to court arguing that his father suffered from dementia; that Sophocles was squandering the family property, and should be declared incompetent and put in his son's care. In his defense, Sophocles read from the *Oedipus at Colonus* which he had been writing, and so moved the jury that he was acquitted of the charge. The jury agreed that no one capable of writing with such power could be regarded as incompetent; Lucian says that the jury found the son guilty of insanity instead.

a drug dealer called the Cowboy. Their plan is in most respects absurd and hardly likely to succeed since it requires Nat to assume the persona of an underworld don and Midge, that of his enforcer. It is also a plan which requires enormous courage.

As the final scene opens, the two men appear to have exchanged roles. Nat is no longer the ebullient, outrageous storyteller of the previous scenes; he is now subdued, insisting that "I have retired my mouth" (107). He has also capitulated to Clara's insistence that he join in the activities at the local senior citizens' center.

Nat may be dispirited, but Midge has emerged from the confrontation with the Cowboy and hospitalization after the drug dealer's attack on him more vigorous than he has been at any point in the play. He flourishes a souvenir of the fight, a small piece of the dealer's coat, and recalls with relish the Cowboy's shock when Midge brandished a knife at him. In words reminiscent of Nat's own earlier: "Yeah, yeah, he seen me, all right—he seen me. . ." (108).

Nat listlessly prepares to go to the center, but before leaving, he admits his true identity: ". . . I was, and am now, no one. No one at all" (110). But Midge, who has complained throughout the play about Nat's garrulity, refuses to accept the truth, insisting that Nat is even now spinning a tale. The curtain falls as Nat slowly returns to the bench and begins to tell another story.

In each play the old men are physically weak; all have imperfect sight and like Teiresias himself see beyond the limitations of physical vision. None of the old men pretends to be what he is not. They concede their infirmities; they acknowledge their reliance on the help of others, whether that help is the sight of Antigone or the advice of Ismene or the rolls from the Plaza. Each one acts with courage and vision, however, and at the same time that he grants a superficial resemblance to the dependency of a child, insists on his adulthood, on his role as a parent, on his dignity, on his freedom to be foolish or belligerent or wise. Oedipus needs and wants care, but strictly on his own terms. Midge and Nat do not welcome care, no matter how well intentioned, which would interfere with their independence or deny them the opportunity to be active participants in the life of the City.

These plays encourage us to move beyond our graphs and texts to confront directly, through the vivid language and action of the stage, the human experience of growing old. Both plays remind us that the consequence of interpreting the riddle too simply is to deny the rich pasts of our elders, to take the easy way out and to choose a convenient characterization which oversimplifies the relationship between elder and other. We do not really come full circle. To insist on that simpler, literal interpretation of the riddle is to deny the opportunity for a Nat or a Midge to confront with outrageous creativity the challenges of living in New York, or for a blind Oedipus to walk unaided to his death.

Epilogue

While I began studying gerontology in part to understand the experiences of my parents as they grew older,[8] I have not forgotten Glenn Gould's observations about art as a mirror on ourselves. It seems appropriate to conclude with

[8] I have a special interest in this topic. When I began working on the question of elder care several years ago, I became embroiled in a lively on-going discussion about role reversal and parent care with Mildred Seltzer, of Miami University's Scripps Gerontology Center. In recent months I have lived our discussions, caring for my very ill father and often finding my intellectual convictions of the impossibility of role reversal borne out by my own experience. This essay is in a very real sense an act of filial devotion: to my mentor Millie Seltzer, this is the final project for which she served as my muse before her death, and to Hollinshead de Luce, who died as I was completing the essay.

Gardner's reflection of ourselves by way of a reminder to take the lessons of these plays seriously. As Nat warns, "You collect old furniture, old cars, old pictures, everything old but old people. Bad souvenirs, they talk too much. Even quiet, they tell you too much; they look like the future and you don't want to know. . . . One day you too will join this race."

Works Cited

Apollodorus. 1976. *The Library*. Tr. J. G. Frazier. Cambridge, Mass.

Archbold, P. G. 1983. "Impact of Parent-caring on Women." *Family Relations* 32:39–45.

Blenkner, M. 1965. " Social Work and Family Relationships in Late Life." In *Social Structure and the Family: Generational Relationships*. Eds. E. Shanas and G. Streib. Englewood Cliffs, NJ.

Bowra, C. M. 1944. *Sophoclean Tragedy*. Oxford.

Brody, E. M. 1990. "Role Reversal: An Inaccurate and Destructive Concept." *Journal of Gerontological Social Work* 15:15–22.

——. 1985. "Parent Care as a Normative Family Stress." *The Gerontologist* 25:19–29.

Cole, T. 1987. "Oedipus and the Meaning of Aging: Personal Reflections and Historical Perspectives." Paper read at the annual meeting of the American Academy of Religion, Boston, Mass.

Datan, N. 1985. "The Oedipus Cycle: Developmental Mythology, Greek Tragedy, and the Sociology of Knowledge." Paper read at the annual meeting of the Gerontological Society of America, New Orleans, La.

Davies, R. 1988. *The Lyre of Orpheus*. New York.

de Luce, J., ed. 1993. "Reading Cicero on Aging." *Journal of Aging Studies* 7:335-81.

——. 1996. "Mythology and Aging." In *Encyclopedia of Gerontology*. Ed. J. Birren. Orlando, Fla.

Falkner, T. 1987. "Strengthless, Friendless, Loveless: the Chorus and the Cultural Construction of Old Age in Sophocles' *Oedipus at Colonus*." In *From the Bard to Broadway*. Ed. K. Hartigan. Lanham, Md. 51-59.

——. 1995. *The Poetics of Old Age in Greek Epic, Lyric, and Tragedy*. Norman, Okla.

Falkner, T., and de Luce, J. 1992. "A View from Antiquity: Greece, Rome, and Elders." In *Handbook of Aging and the Humanities*. Eds. T. Cole, D. Van Tassel, and R. Kastenbaum. New York.

——. 1989. *Old Age in Greek and Latin Literature*. Albany, NY.

Finley, M. I. 1989. "The Elderly in Classical Antiquity." In *Old Age in Greek and Latin Literature*. Eds. T. Falkner and J. de Luce. Albany, NY.

Gadow, S. 1983. "Frailty and Strength: The Dialectic in Aging." *The Gerontologist* 23:144-47.

Gardner, H. 1986. *I'm Not Rappaport*. New York.

Hayes, R. 1993. "Life, Death, and Reconstructive Self." *Journal of Humanistic Education and Development* 32:85-88.

Horowitz, A. "Sons and Daughters as Caregivers to Older Parents: Differences in Role Performance and Consequences." *The Gerontologist* 25:612-17.

Jarvis, L. F. 1990. "Role Reversal: Implications for Therapeutic Intervention." *Journal of Gerontological Social Work* 15:23-34.

Knox, B. W. 1966 *The Heroic Temper: Studies in Sophoclean Tragedy*. Berkeley.

Lesser, W. 1993. *Pictures at an Execution: An Inquiry into the Subject of Murder.* Cambridge, Mass.

Matthews, S. 1988. "The Burdens of Care: A Critical Evaluation of Recent Findings." *Journal of Aging Studies* 2:157–65.

Payzant, G. 1978. *Glenn Gould: Music and Mind.* Toronto.

Rautman, A. L. 1962. "Role Reversal." *Geriatrics Mental Hygiene* 46:116–20.

Schaps, D. 1979. *Economic Rights of Women in Ancient Greece.* Edinburgh.

Segal, C. 1981. *Tragedy and Civilization: An Interpretation of Sophocles.* Cambridge, Mass.

Seltzer, M. M. 1990. "Role Reversal: You Don't Go Home Again." *Journal of Gerontological Social Work* 15:5–14.

Sophocles. 1967. *Sophocles I: Oedipus the King, Oedipus at Colonus, Antigone.* Eds. D. Grene and R. Lattimore. New York. *Oedipus the King.* Tr. D. Grene. *Oedipus At Colonus.* Tr. E. Wyckoff.

States, B. O. 1985. *Great Reckonings in Little Rooms: On the Phenomenology of Theater.* Berkeley.

Whitman, C. H. 1966. *Sophocles: A Study of Heroic Humanism.* Cambridge, Mass.

Firmicus Maternus
and the Politics of Conversion

H. A. Drake
University of California, Santa Barbara

It would be only a slight exaggeration to identify Julius Firmicus Maternus as the poster child of Christian intolerance. His English translator tactfully described Firmicus' call for coercion in *De errore profanarum religionum* as "a new note in Christian literature."[1] More succinctly, Gaston Boissier called the book "un manuel d'intolérance."[2] Franz Boll found the work filled with "Fanatismus" and "leidenschaflichen Hasse," a judgment echoed by the Budé editor, Robert Turcan ("un pamphlet encore plus fanatique et assurement plus hargneux que ceux de Tertullien ou d'Arnobe").[3] To Leslie Barnard, it signified "un' intoll-

---

[1] Forbes 1970, 15; cf. Forbes 1959–60, 148: "This was the first appearance of the doctrine that enforced conversion is desirable, justifiable and indeed imperative."

[2] Boissier I:68.

[3] Boll col. 2378; Turcan 23.

eranza totale."[4] Scholar after scholar, the judgment is the
same; only the language differs.

Such judgments are well deserved. In *De errore*, Firmicus
not only took Christian anti-pagan rhetoric to a new level by
demanding that the emperors destroy the temples and melt
down the idols, but he also went beyond any previous author by calling for the forcible conversion of pagans. To do
so he exploited a medical analogy that was well known from
pagan literature. Just as "those who are ill crave what is not
good for them," Firmicus argued, so too, "There are those
who refuse and reject [a religious cure] and are led by cupid-
ity to desire their own death."[5] But Firmicus improved on
his classical exemplars, which can be found as far back as
Plato.[6] Where they were content with the point that cures
can require bitter medicine, Firmicus argued for a sort of
preventative medicine: Just as the good physician must give
bitter medication to the sick, so it is better for the emperors
"that you free the unwilling than that you allow the willing
to be ruined."[7] Christians were familiar with the medical
analogy, but prior to Firmicus they had used it only for sick
Christians, that is, heretics. In the second century, Ignatius
recommended treating troublesome Christians as if they
were diseased, and more recently Constantine had tasked
heretics with infecting healthy souls. Later in the century,
Bishop Epiphanius of Salamis would call his catalogue of
heresies a "Medicine Chest" (*Panarion*).[8] In extending the

---

[4] Barnard 509.

[5] *Error* 16.5 (Turcan 115): Aegrotantes contraria delectant; 16.4:
Nolunt quidam et repugnant et exitium suum prona cupiditate
desiderant.

[6] See, e.g., *Gorgias* 464d, 467c.

[7] *Error* 16.4 (Turcan 113): melius est ut liberetis inuitos quam ut
uolentibus concedatis exitium.

[8] Irenaeus, *Ep. ad Polycarp*. 2.1. Constantine's "Edict to the Heretics"
is in Eusebius, *De vita Constantini* 3.64. See further Dvornik, II:629;

analogy to pagans, Firmicus innovated, opening a door to particularly dangerous consequences. Sick pagans could be left alone if all they harmed were themselves; but the medical analogy carried with it the notion of infection, meaning they were not a danger just to themselves. Drawing on the stern cadences of the *Book of Exodus*, Firmicus warned that their sacrilege would bring God's wrath upon the entire community if it were not suppressed.[9]

It is not Firmicus' intolerance that makes him an apt subject for this volume, but the challenge he presents. Paul MacKendrick's students range throughout antiquity in their interests, but the one thing he gave all of us was the pleasure of testing received opinion. Here is where Firmicus becomes a challenge. According to a traditional view, Christians exploited Constantine's conversion by taking reprisals on their sworn adversaries. Driven by the internal logic of their faith, they shared the belief in a life-and-death struggle with paganism from which there could emerge only one victor.[10] Firmicus seems to fit comfortably into this design. He wrote *De errore* approximately a decade after writing *Mathesis*, the most complete tract on astrology to survive from the ancient world.[11] Although Christians were known to dabble in astrology despite the anathemas of the Church, references to "the gods" in *Mathesis* indicate that Firmicus was still a polytheist when he wrote it.[12] Presumably, he con-

---

Wilken 117: "The metaphor of disease was common among the rhetors, both pagan and Christian."

[9] *Error* 28.10.

[10] Classically stated by Momigliano 79–80: "The winners became conscious of their victory in a mood of resentment and vengeance. A voice shrill with implacable hatred announced to the world the victory of the Milvian Bridge: Lactantius' *De mortibus persecutorum*. . . . If there were men who recommended tolerance and peaceful coexistence of Christians and pagans, they were rapidly crowded out."

[11] Monet 11.

[12] Boll 2365; Turcan 16. On Christians and astrology, cf. Lifshitz.

verted to Christianity in the interim between the two works. The stridency of *De errore*, therefore, would be the product of Christian intolerance combined with the zeal of a convert, both of which made Firmicus "plus royaliste que le roi," in the words of Turcan, who doubts this explanation for the virulence of *De errore*, as for different reasons do I.[13]

The assumption that coercion was a natural result of Christian intolerance is doubly flawed, first by a failure to distinguish properly between the meanings of intolerance and coercion, and second by its failure to take into account a strong Christian tradition that true belief must be freely given.[14] The foundation for the traditional scholarly assumption of a virulent Christian-pagan hatred during this period is equally shaky. Newer scholarship has developed a more nuanced understanding of the differences between Christianity and paganism in the fourth century, and I have argued elsewhere that Constantine himself envisioned a Church that could coexist peacefully with at least the more refined types of late pagan beliefs.[15] Ironically, Firmicus himself is proof of this policy. Constantine's last years are generally agreed to be the most overtly Christian of his thirty-year reign, and are also assumed to be the ones in which he took his most aggressive steps against pagan "superstition."[16] Yet in these very years Firmicus, who had friends in high places and may have been himself a Senator,[17] evidently felt confident enough to publish a work on

[13] Turcan 23.

[14] Drake 1996.

[15] Drake 1995; See, e.g., the perceptive remarks of Lifshitz; Bagnall 272; Salzman 194–95, 223; Bowersock 44; Brown 47.

[16] Hunt 145. For the policy of Constantine's last years: Alföldi 30.

[17] The manuscript of *De errore* adds the initials "V. C." to Firmicus' name, indicating that he held the *clarissimate*, a rank ordinarily reserved for members of the Senate. However, André Chastagnol has concluded that it also was awarded to non-senators. See Turcan 12.

the always touchy subject of astrology. It is not enough to say that Firmicus was simply foolish or out of touch, for he tells us that he wrote at the urging of the proconsul Lollianus Mavortius, who was sufficiently in Constantine's good graces to be designated for the consulship.[18]

The problem with the conflict model is that it uses a very narrow band to scan what was quite a broad spectrum of pagan and Christian sentiment. By tuning out nuances, it hears only extremes and comes dangerously close to transmitting stereotype. Much may be learned, for instance, by discarding assumptions about Christian conversion and looking at continuities between Firmicus' two writings.[19] As others have observed, Firmicus does not attack astrology in *De errore*, and the pagan Firmicus set just as high a standard for personal morality in the *Mathesis* as the Christian Firmicus would do in *De errore*.[20] Firmicus enjoined those

[18] *Math.* 1.Pr.7–8. In the same place, Firmicus refers to Lollianus' appointment as governor of East by Constantine, and addresses him as "Proconsul and designated consul ordinarius." Lollianus did not actually become consul until 355. *PLRE* I, 512–14. However, other references—to the consuls of 334 and to Constantine as the emperor, led Mommsen to conclude that it was written between 334 and 337, and his judgment has been generally accepted, although Thorndike 419, n. 2, worried that Lollianus' high rank in 336 would have meant he was quite old by 355. At 1.10.13 (Monet I:88), most manuscripts identify the current emperor's father as "Constantine," raising the possibility that the Constantine mentioned at this point was not Constantine I, despite the appellation "Magnus," but his son, Constantine II. However, the text goes on to identify this emperor's place of birth as Naissus, which is correct for Constantine I but not for Constantine II, who was born at Arles: *PLRE* I:223. Monet has therefore bracketed the final "n" in the father's name ("Constanti[n]i").

[19] The argument that these two works were produced by different authors was disproved by Moore on the basis of vocabulary and style.

[20] Astrology: Thorndike, 418–19; on morals, idem, 429: "It is interesting to observe that in the *De errore* Firmicus criticizes the immoral ritual of pagan cults in the same phrases that he employs in predicting vice in the *Mathesis*."

who would practice astrology to "Be virtuous, honest, sober,
content with modest food and goods, lest the desire of base
fortune bring into disrepute the renown of this divine science," and he urged them to "Take pains that in your way of
life and purpose you surpass the way of life and purpose of
good priests."[21] Among other things, he advised practitioners of the art never to give false witness, lend money at
interest or attend the games, "For the high priest of the gods
must be above and a stranger to the corrupt lure of enter-
tainments."[22] Such strictures would not have been out of
place in instructions to a Christian priest. The pagan
Firmicus could conceive of a God who was above the dic-
tates of astrology, and he also recognized the power exor-
cists held over demons, though in other ways his description
of this type of person was hardly flattering.[23]

There is another important way in which these books are
alike: in both, Firmicus catered to known proclivities of the
emperor. *Mathesis* is larded with Constantinian themes,
from avowals of the emperor's closeness to a tutelary deity
to echoes of his frustration with injustice and corruption in
the courts. These are themes that stayed constant throughout Constantine's reign; they can be found in orations delivered in his presence by both pagan and Christian orators.[24]

---

[21] *Math.* 2.30.2 (Monat I:140): . . . Esto pudicus, integer, sobrius,
paruo uictu, paruis opibus contentus, ne istius diuinae scientiae gloriam
ignobilis pecuniae cupiditas infamet. Dato operam ut, instituto ac pro-
posito tuo bonorum, institutum ac propositum uincas sacerdotum. . . .

[22] *Math.* 2.30.12 (Monat I:143): antistes enim deorum separatus et
alienus esse debet a prauis illecebris uoluptatum. Cf. 2.30.1-2, 8-9.

[23] He describes such persons as ones who "faciet diis terribiles, et
qui omnia periuriorum genera contemnant." *Math.* 3.4.27 (Monat II:49).

[24] For Constantine's closeness to deity: see PL IX (XII).26.1 of 313
(next note); Eusebius of Caesarea, *laus Constantini* II (Richardson 583-
84) and Constantine's famous "pagan vision" of 310 in *PL* VI (VII).21.3-
5 (Mynors 201-2). For the courts: see n. 31 below. Constantine's preference for a general definition of monotheism is expressed most suc-

Particularly striking are parallels with the panegyric delivered to Constantine by a Gallic orator in 313: like that
speaker, Firmicus invoked a god of uncertain provenance
and prayed for eternal rule of Constantine and his house.[25]

The connection of *De errore* to policies of Constantius II
and Constans is a bit less straightforward. In 341,
Constantine's sons ruled that "the madness of sacrifices
shall be abolished." This decision was confirmed the follow-

cinctly in his letter to Bishop Alexander and Arius, *VC* 2.71 (Richardson
517–18): "As far, then, as regards the Divine Providence, let there be
one faith, and one understanding among you, one united judgment in
reference to God. But as to your subtle disputations on questions of
little or no significance, though you may be unable to harmonize in
sentiment, such differences should be consigned to the secret custody
of your own minds and thoughts."

[25] *Mathesis* is replete with such terms as *numen* (1.5.6) *fabricator deus*
(4.1.3), *deus summus* [2.30.5] and the ever-popular *divina mens* [1.5.10,
3.1.9]. Cf *Math.* 5.Pr.3 (Monat II:218): Quicumque es deus . . . cui tota
potestas numinum seruit, cuius uoluntas perfecti operis substantia est,
cuius incorruptis legibus conuenta, natura concta substantia
perpetuitatis ornauit, tu, omnium pater pariter ac mater, tu tibi pater
ac filius, uno uinculo necessitudinis obligatus, tibi supplices manus
tendimus, te trepida cum supplicatione ueneramur and *Math.* 1.10.14
(Monat I:89): "Sol Optime Maxime . . . Constantinum maximum
principem et huius inuictissimos liberos, dominos et Caesares nostros,
consensu uestrae moderationis et dei summi obsecuti iudicio perpetua
his decernentis imperia. . ." with *PL* IX (XII).26.1 (Mynors 289):
Quamobrem te, summe rerum sator, cuius tot nomina sunt quot gentium
linguas esse uoluisti (quem enim te ipse dici uelis, scire non possumus);
siue tute quaedam uis mensque diuina es, quae toto infusa mundo omnibus miscearis elementis, et sine ullo extrinsecus accedente uigoris
impulsu per te ipsa mouearis, siue aliqua supra omne caelum potestas
es quae hoc opus tuum ex altiore Naturae arce despicias: te, inquam,
oramus et quaesumus ut hunc in omnia saecula principem serues. Compare both with the language of the "Edict of Milan" in Lactantius, *De
Mortibus Persecutorum* 48.2 (Creed 71): quo quicquid <est> diuinitatis in
sede caelesti, nobis atque omnibus qui sub potestate nostra sunt
constituti, placatum and propitium possit existere. On this language,
see Ando 188–89.

ing year with a ruling that at the same time spared from destruction temples "outside the walls" or those used for public amusements. A third law ordering that "the temples shall be immediately closed . . . so as to deny to all abandoned men the opportunity to commit sin" was given in either 346, 354 or 356.[26] These are precisely the steps Firmicus urged in *De errore*, leading some to conclude that the emperors' increased militancy was a response to this work. However, from internal references it is clear that Firmicus could not have written this book before 343, and probably did not write it until after 346.[27] Only the last of these laws, then, could possibly have been influenced by *De errore*, and then only if the earliest of its suggested dates is not the correct one. In this case, one might argue that Firmicus wrote after the second law and in protest of its apparent retreat from the war against the temples; the third law, the most vigorous of the three in both language and intent, was a response to the fervor of Firmicus' eloquence. In support of this argument is the third law's reference to "abandoned men" (*perditi*), since *perditi* is one of Firmicus' favorite aphorisms in *De errore*.[28] But the influence might just as easily have flowed in the opposite direction, as is certainly the case with the verbal parallels in *Mathesis*.[29]

[26] *CTh* 16.10.2, 16.10.3, 16.10.4, tr. Pharr 472.

[27] *De errore* addresses Constantius II and Constans, two of the three sons who succeeded Constantine on his death in 337. The absence of Constantine II, who died in 340 during an abortive invasion of Italy, and reference to Constans' military successes in Britain mean it cannot have been written before 343, while a fulsome promise that God would never fail to aid the emperors seems inappropriate to any date after the bloody Battle of Singara in 348. In any case, it would have to have been written before Constans' death at the hands of the usurper Magnentius at the start of 350. Jones I:112–13; Turcan 25–26. For suggestion that *De errore* provoked laws: Jones I:92, n. 32.

[28] Forbes 1959–60, 149.

[29] Turcan 19, 25–26, accepted the date of 346 for the third law and

There is a paradox in these similarities. The continuity in religious sentiments suggests a gradual and easy conversion, such as we know to have been the case for other pagan intellectuals in this period, not the type of rabid ferocity exhibited in *De errore*.[30] Turcan thought that the zeal of *De errore* might have been necessary to atone for the publication of *Mathesis*, a sensible explanation that has the added value of calling attention to the precarious situation a convert like Firmicus might have found himself in. It is an important part of the puzzle. But it should first be noted that this explanation does not follow from the religious similarities that tie the two works, but from the other set of similarities, those indicating that Firmicus was eager to align himself with the known desires of the ruling power. It is, in other words, an explanation that points in a political direction, and suggests that Firmicus wrote *Mathesis*, and possibly also *De errore*, with the traditional motive of currying favor with those important to his career. It must be admitted that his claim in the former work to have abandoned all interest in public life has a funny ring to it: isolated by his honesty in a sea of corruption, fighting tirelessly to protect those who were being victimized by greed and mischief-makers, with nothing to support him but his "steadfast faith in the right"—this was a resumé crafted to win its author a favorable reputation in the court of an emperor whose impatience with legal shenanigans still leaps out from the law codes.[31]

---

noticed an additional parallel between "gladius uindex," *De errore* 29.2 and "gladius ultor" in the third law.

[30] See Markus 28–29.

[31] *Math.* 4.Pr.1. For Constantine's concern with judicial corruption see, e.g., *CTh* 1.16.7: "The rapacious hands of the apparitors shall immediately cease, they shall cease, I say, for if after due warning they do not cease, they shall be cut off by the sword" (Pharr 28). At *vita Constantini* 4.29, Eusebius describes the speeches Constantine gave chiding his court officials. Firmicus' comments suggest he may have held the post of *defensor civitatis*, a sort of public defender office that does

To put it bluntly, the real similarity between these two books is that in both Firmicus appears to have been angling for a job.[32] Just as Constantine's laws against corruption in the courts inspired Firmicus to position himself as a defender of the poor in *Mathesis*, so too did his sons' laws against pagan practices inspire the furious zeal of *De errore*. Constantine had removed all the disabilities against Christian participation in public life, and even taken steps to favor Christians in appointments. His sons are believed to have accelerated this trend.[33] The antennae of Romans like Firmicus were perennially tuned to pick up, and adjust to, such shifts in the tastes of those who had jobs to offer. Such carefully attuned political antennae are what led Turcan to identify Firmicus as the type of opportunistic convert whose extremism reflects their need for credibility: "Ils se font donc extrémistes pour être crus. Ils deviennent terroristes parce qu'ils sont terrorisés."[34]

To be believed by whom? *De errore* is addressed to the emperors, but emperors typically handed out jobs through intermediaries like Lollianus.[35] Despite the address, then, Firmicus should have had a more immediate audience in mind. A detailed study of an author with whom Firmicus is frequently compared, and from whom he almost certainly drew inspiration, Arnobius of Sicca, suggests who that audience is likely to have been. Although scholars have usually assumed that Arnobius, like Firmicus a convert, wrote

---

not appear in the *Codex Theodosianus* until a law of Valentinian in 364. See Jones, *LRE* I, 144–45; Frakes.

[32] Heather 18–19 estimates that there were "something like 3000 very good jobs in each half of the empire by c. 400 A.D.," a good job being defined as one which "provided the holder with top equestrian status (the *perfectissimate*) or, as increasingly became the case through the fourth century, senatorial rank."

[33] Barnes 1990, 321; cf. Barnes 1995.

[34] Turcan 24, 30.

[35] Wallace-Hadrill 80–81.

Adversus nationes half a century earlier in order to bring his skills as a rhetor to play in the fierce war between pagans and Christians, Michael Simmons has suggested that his real purpose was to prove to his bishop, who found him suspect as a former Neoplatonist, that his conversion was sincere.[36] If there was reason to doubt the sincerity of a convert like Arnobius at the turn of the fourth century, when there were as yet no political or social advantages to be gained from becoming Christian, then there would have been even more reason to do so when Firmicus wrote, and as the author of a work on astrology, Firmicus would have been under at least as much a cloud as a former Neoplatonist like Arnobius.

Here, then, is the central question. Assuming that converts like Firmicus and Arnobius were under some pressure to demonstrate the sincerity of their beliefs, why did they respond by launching an offensive against the old gods? To say that their responses are merely proof of the inherent intolerance of Christianity is insufficient, because the central tenet of that faith is to return hatred with love, to endure but not inflict harm. The search for an explanation must be redirected, away from theories of Christian belief and toward the dynamics of social movements. It is a given of political science that the more secure a community is, the more willing it will be to tolerate variant behavior. Conversely, the more insecure, the more steps it will take to demand conformity. It is a small step from this premise to the proposition that large numbers of newcomers can pose a threat to a host community that, like Christianity, defined membership ac-

---

[36] Simmons, ch. 3. A key text is Jerome's *Chronicon*, sub anno 326–27, where Arnobius is identified as a famous rhetor who was initially spurned by the bishop because of his prior hostility, but later gained admission after writing an attack on his former beliefs, which books "tamen velus quibusdam obsidibus pietatis foedus impetravit." For the text and discussion of chronological difficulties, see Simmons 47–53. For Arnobius' influence on Firmicus, see Forbes 1970, 30.

cording to a set of acquired principles or beliefs, rather than hereditary or traditional affinities.[37] There is some contemporary evidence that converts posed just this sort of threat in the fourth century. No sooner was Constantine dead than his biographer lamented "the scandalous hypocrisy of those who crept into the Church, and assumed the name and character of Christians." At the turn of the next century, the crusading Bishop Porphyry of Gaza had to reassure his flock that the pagans coming into the church as the result of his success in gaining imperial support posed no threat to them.[38]

What disturbed Porphyry's flock was not that these pagans were converting—a cause for rejoicing—but that they were converting "out of fear" (διὰ φόβον), a sentiment that confirms the long-standing Christian principle that true belief cannot be coerced.[39] The Antiochene rhetor Libanius played on this Christian sentiment with great skill in his oration to Theodosius I on behalf of the temples some twenty years earlier, when he warned the emperor that those who were advising him to coerce belief were speaking "utter nonsense." Persons converted in this way, Libanius pointed out, "have not really been changed—they only say they have . . . . They go to their ceremonies, join their crowds, go everywhere where these do, but when they adopt an attitude of prayer, they either invoke no god at all or else they invoke the gods."[40] Real conversion, Libanius explained, only comes through persuasion: "If persuasion fails and constraint is employed, nothing has been accomplished, though you think it has." In taking this tack before a Christian em-

[37] Drake 1996.

[38] Marcus Diaconus, *vit. Porph.* 72–73 (Grégoire-Kugener 57–58). See further Fowden 78. For Eusebius of Caesarea's comment, see *De vita Constantini* 4.54 (Richardson 554).

[39] *vit. Porph.* 73 (Grégoire-Kugener 57).

[40] Oration 30 *pro templis* 28 (Norman II:125–27).

peror, Libanius was not asserting pagan toleration in the face of Christian intolerance. To the contrary, he was adopting arguments from his adversaries' own rule book in order to strengthen his case, as he himself noted:

> It is said that in their very own rules it [coercion] does not appear, but that persuasion meets with approval and compulsion is deplored. Then why these frantic attacks on the temples, if you cannot persuade and must needs resort to force? In this way you would obviously be breaking your own rules.[41]

Presumably, Libanius was not the first to confront Christians with this blatant contradiction between their beliefs and their actions. Logically, in the face of such arguments Christians should have rethought the readiness with which they resorted to coercion as the century progressed; instead, they resolved the problem by demanding evidence of *bona fides* from suspect converts.

Such considerations might explain why converts like Firmicus and Arnobius produced written proofs of their faith, but they do not explain why those proofs consisted of hatred, scorn and calls for repression, instead of, say, a reasoned exposition of the way their old beliefs had gradually led them to the truth of Christianity. Convenience was certainly part of the reason. In Firmicus' case, the continuities between *Mathesis* and *De errore* suggest that he had always shared Christian distaste for the baser aspects of traditional belief, and his training in forensic oratory would naturally have inclined him to acquit himself by attacking and discrediting the old faith. Moreover, if, as seems to be the case, Firmicus converted at a time when the number and nature of converts were creating insecurities in the Christian community, *De errore* would also have been an easier and more

---

[41] Ibid. 30 (Norman II:129).

acceptable way to purge himself of suspicion. It represents not so much the intolerance that comes with Christian belief as a tactical decision: the best defense is a good offense.

The explanation of Christian preference for coercion is not a simple one; it involves a redefinition of Christian belief and responsibility that was taking place on many levels during the course of this century. As part of this process, Christians who favored coercive measures came increasingly to be seen as more genuine Christians: when Porphyry won permission to destroy the temple of Marnas in Gaza, he asked the empress to entrust the order to "a zealous Christian" (ζηλωτὴ Χριστιανὸν), for fear of having the project betrayed, as it has been once before, by officials "who only pretended to believe" (προσποιήτως εἶχον τὴν πίστιν).[42]

A complete study of Christian coercion in the fourth century would have to account for this growing militancy. Here it is sufficient to notice that the role converts have to play in the growing willingness of Christians to use the coercive mechanisms of the state to compel belief is not as clear-cut as usually believed. If erudite converts like Firmicus and Arnobius wrote their polemics for tactical rather than ideological reasons, then the prospect opens that at least some of what we now identify as evidence for Christian intolerance was the result of a different process that is primarily social and political in nature, and to which Christian hatred of the ancient gods is, at best, tangential. In that case, Firmicus Maternus' *De errore* is not proof of the intolerant nature of Christianity; rather, it opens another window onto a political and social process that over the course of the fourth century allowed militant Christians to impose their views on the entire community.

---

[42] *vit. Porph.* 51 (Grégoire-Kugener 42).

Works Cited

Alföldi, A. 1948. *The Conversion of Constantine and Pagan Rome*. Tr. H. Mattingly. Oxford.

Ando, Clifford. 1996. "Pagan Apologetics and Christian Intolerance in the Ages of Themistius and Augustine." *Journal of Early Christian Studies* 4:171-207.

Bagnall, Roger. 1993. *Egypt in Late Antiquity*. Princeton.

Barnard, L. W. 1990. "L'intolleranza negli apologisti cristiani con speciale riguardo a Firmico Materno." *Cristianesimo nella storia* 11:505-22.

Barnes, T. D. 1990. "Christians and Pagans in the Reign of Constantius." In A. Dihle, ed., *L'Église et l'Empire au IVe siècle*. Fondation Hardt, Entretiens sur l'antiquité classique 34:301-44.

———. 1995. "Statistics and the Conversion of the Roman Aristocracy." *JRS* 85:135-47.

Boissier, G. 1903. *La fin du paganisme. Étude sur les dernières luttes religieuses en Occident au quatrième siècle*. 2 vols. Paris.

Boll, F. 1909. "Firmicus." *RE* 6.2:2365-79.

Bowersock, G. 1990. *Hellenism in Late Antiquity*. Ann Arbor.

Brown, Peter. 1995. *Authority and the Sacred. Aspects of the Christianisation of the Roman World*. Cambridge.

Creed, J. L., ed. and tr. 1984. *Lactantius, De mortibus persecutorum*. Oxford.

Drake, H. A. 1995. "Constantine and Consensus." *Church History* 64:1-15.

———. 1996. "Lambs Into Lions: Explaining Early Christian Intolerance." *Past and Present* 153:3-36.

Dvornik, F. 1966. *Early Christian and Byzantine Political Philosophy*. 2 vols. Washington, D.C.

Forbes, C. A., tr. 1970. *Firmicus Maternus, The Error of the Pagan Religions*. Ancient Christian Writers. New York.

Forbes, C. A. 1959–60. "Firmicus Maternus and the Secular Arm." *CJ* 55:146–50.

Fowden, G. 1978. "Bishops and Temples in the Eastern Roman Empire, A.D. 320–435." *JTS*, ser. 2, 29:53–78.

Frakes, R. M. 1994. "Late Roman Social Justice and the Origin of the Defensor Civitatis." *CJ* 89:337–48.

Garnsey, P. 1984. "Religious Toleration in Classical Antiquity." In W. J. Shiels, ed., *Persecution and Toleration*, Studies in Church History 21:1–27.

Grégoire-Kugener. 1930. *Marc le Diacre, Vie de Porphyre, éveque de Gaza*. Ed. and tr. H. Grégoire and M.-A. Kugener. Paris.

Heather, P. J. 1994. "New Men for New Constantines: Creating an Imperial Elite in the Eastern Mediterranean." In P. Magdalino, ed., *The Rhythm of Imperial Renewal in the East from Constantine the Great to Michael Palaiologos*. Society for the Promotion of Byzantine Studies, Publications 2. Leiden. 11–33.

Hunt, David. 1993. "Christianising the Roman Empire: the evidence of the Code." In Jill Harries and Ian Wood, eds., *The Theodosian Code: Studies in the Imperial Law of Late Antiquity*. London. 143–58.

Jones, A. H. M. 1964. *The Later Roman Empire: A Social, Economic and Administrative Survey*. 2 vols. Norman, Okla.

Lifshitz, F. 1993. "Review of The Relationship Between Neoplatonism and Christianity." *Bryn Mawr Classical Review* 4.4.22.

Markus, R. A. 1990. *The End of Ancient Christianity*. Cambridge.

Momigliano, A. 1963. "Pagan and Christian Historiography in the Fourth Century A.D." In idem, ed., *The Conflict*

Between Paganism and Christianity in the Fourth Century. Oxford. 79–99.

Mommsen, Theodore. 1894. "Firmicus Maternus." *Hermes* 29:468–72.

Monat, P., ed. and tr. 1992-94. *Firmicus Maternus, Mathesis*. Budé ed. 2 vols. Paris.

Moore, Clifford H. 1897. "Julius Firmicus Maternus der Heide und der Christ." Diss. München.

Mynors, R. A., ed. 1964. *XII Panegyrici Latini*. Oxford.

Norman, A. F., tr. 1977. *Libanius, Selected Works*, II. Loeb Classical Library. Cambridge, Mass.

Pharr, Clyde, tr. 1952. *The Theodosian Code and Novels and the Sirmondian Constitutions*. Princeton.

Richardson, E. C., tr. 1890. *Eusebius of Caesarea, The Life of Constantine*. In P. Schaff and H. Wace, eds., *A Select Library of Nicene and Post-Nicene Fathers of the Christian Church*. 2 ser, I. New York. 471–559.

Salzman, Michele. 1990. *On Roman Time: The Codex-Calendar of 354 and the Rhythms of Urban Life in Late Antiquity*. Berkeley.

Simmons, Michael. 1995. *Arnobius of Sicca: Religious Conflict and Competition in the Age of Diocletian*. Oxford.

Thorndike, L. 1913. "A Roman Astrologer as a Historical Source: Julius Firmicus Maternus." *CP* 8:415–35.

Turcan, Robert, ed. and tr. 1982. *Firmicus Maternus, L'Erreur des religions païennes*. Paris.

Wallace-Hadrill, A. 1989. "Patronage in Roman Society: From Republic to Empire." In idem ed., *Patronage in Ancient Society*. New York. 63–87.

Wilken, R. A. 1983. *John Chrysostom and the Jews: Rhetoric and Reality in the Late Fourth Century*. Berkeley.

Cicero The Dramaturge: Verisimilitude and Consistency of Characterization in Some of His Dialogues[1]

Andrew R. Dyck
University of California, Los Angeles

If poetry is an imitation of life,[2] the characters depicted in poetry can be expected to conform to the behavior expected of such a person in life. Such a congruent relationship was described by the Greeks as πρέπον, and τὸ πρέπον became for ancient critics of literature a criterion of quality and, where quality could be assumed, authenticity.[3] Accordingly careful authors, such as Cicero, tried to maintain τὸ πρέπον in their characterizations and avoid falling into any depiction that was παρὰ τὸ πρέπον. Cicero cites examples of

---

[1] I am pleased to offer these reflections on such a happy occasion to a *vir Ciceronianus par excellence*, Paul L. MacKendrick, as a modest token of appreciation for the generous counsel and kind support he gave a University of Wisconsin undergraduate almost thirty years ago.

[2] Cf., after Plato, Arist. *Poet.* 1447a13ff.

[3] Cf. Dyck 1996b: ad *Off.* 1.97 and 97–98 with literature.

τὸ πρέπον (= *decorum*) in characterization at *Off.* 1.97: such wicked statements as *oderint dum metuant* or *natis sepulchro ipse est parens* (= Acc. *trag.* 203 and 226) would be inappropriate on the lips of a good character like Aeacus or Minos but quite apt for the wicked Atreus. Cicero himself once had to admit having represented characters παρὰ τὸ πρέπον in the first edition of the *Academica* (*Att.* 13.16.1). Prodded by Atticus (ibid. 13.13.1; cf. 13.19.5), he came to see that Catulus, Lucullus, and Hortensius were far too inexperienced in such matters to be represented discussing problems of epistemology in such nuance and detail, and he transferred their parts accordingly to Atticus, Varro, and himself. Cicero wanted, on the one hand, to honor certain famous Romans and, on the other hand, to expound certain doctrines. Never did the two sets of agenda clash so sharply as in the *Academica priora*.

This example should alert us to the possibility of a tension of matter and speaker elsewhere in Cicero's dialogues on rhetoric and philosophy. Robert Epes Jones has collected a set of passages useful for studying the problem of Cicero's characterizations, but he proceeds from the premise that "Cicero's dialogues can . . . be trusted for the biographical details of the characters," accepts the existence—as most did at the time—of a historical Scipionic circle as described by Cicero in *De Republica* and *De Amicitia*, and generally tries to harmonize the historical facts with Cicero's depictions by such reasoning as "the personal integrity of Scipio and Laelius would lead one to think that they accepted the opinions that Cicero attributed to them,"[4] viz., because Cicero has assigned them honorable opinions. This approach is not satisfying, because it affirms the correspondence of Cicero's construct to reality on a priori grounds without examining the probable goals

---

[4] Jones 308, 315, and 314 respectively.

or basis of the construct or its relation to evidence available to Cicero. Hermann Strasburger has studied the Scipionic circle on the basis of the sober premise that Cicero, too, had to form an impression of the second century largely through written sources and that his constructs always need to be checked against such other written sources as we have. I would add that Cicero himself was too young to socialize as an equal with L. Licinius Crassus, C. Antonius, et al., and his own impressions from boyhood are not likely to have carried him very far in reconstructing the attitudes and social relations of an earlier generation (see below à propos De Orat. 2.1–4), so that his picture of Crassus' circle will be based on written sources, reminiscences of some younger associated figures such as Cotta or Hortensius, and extrapolation from his own social relations.[5] We thus need to rebuild our concept of Cicero's characterizations from the ground up, with Cicero's own imagination receiving a larger, historical reality a smaller share in the final product. This paper aims to produce a more realistic picture of the way Cicero went about conceiving and deploying the characters in the dialogues set prior to his adulthood (viz., De Orat., Rep., Sen., and Amic.).

After Cicero had written a draft of the first two books De Republica, his friend Sallustius mooted a similar change of speakers to that later effected in the Academica, a change that Cicero seriously contemplated, as he indicates in a letter from the end of October or beginning of November, 54 (QF 3.5.1–2). At the time of writing Cicero planned to transfer the discussion from Scipio, Laelius, et al. to himself and Quintus; the advantages alleged were a gain in

[5] In contrast to Strasburger 72, I do not see the "Scipionic circle" as modeled on the circle of Crassus but rather both of the earlier "circles" as modeled primarily on Cicero's own circle of friends. Strasburger plays down the role of oral tradition, but cf. Horsfall 229.

auctoritas for the doctrines put forward[6] and the ability to comment on recent events. Sallustius' proposal was couched in terms bound to flatter Cicero's ego (. . . *admonitus sum ab illo multo maiore auctoritate illis de rebus dici posse si ipse loquerer de re publica, praesertim cum essem non Heraclides Ponticus sed consularis et is qui in maximis versatus in re publica rebus essem*) and buttressed by Aristotelian precedent (*Aristotelem denique quae de re publica et praesenti viro scribat ipsum loqui*).[7] But Scipio, too, was, of course, a *consularis*, indeed twice consul and a former censor to boot; he also had the other qualifications for speaking on the topics of this dialogue indicated by Laelius at *Rep.* 1.71; and Plato had written about the state through the mouths of other characters, rather than in his own person. Viewed soberly, Sallustius' proposal could not really claim greater *auctoritas*.[8] Another consideration was that the historical framework would preclude his touching on major political events of his own time (*QF* 3.5.2). Perhaps in the end Cicero decided he ought rather to content himself with ominous hints, such as the one placed in Laelius' mouth at *Rep.* 3.41. He did, however, change, presumably in the interest of greater perspicuousness, from a nine- to a three-day format.[9]

Cicero's readiness to contemplate Sallustius' proposed change, whereby, presumably, the part assigned to Scipio would have been taken over by himself, once again reminds us that the content was not specially geared to the speaker.

---

[6] For *hominum veterum auctoritas* as an advantage of a historical setting cf. *Amic.* 4.

[7] *QF* 3.5.1.

[8] Cf. Levine 12–13. On the other hand, Cicero could and did claim greater *auctoritas* for the speaker in *Sen.*, namely the elder Cato, as compared with Tithonus, the speaker in a work on the subject by Aristo Ceus (for the identification cf. Powell app. 2); cf. *Sen.* 3.

[9] For the interpretation of this letter cf. further Zetzel 1995, 4 n. 11.

Indeed, even in the text that survives some features clearly
fit Cicero and not Scipio. Thus at the very beginning of the
drama, when his nephew Tubero meets Scipio in his bedroom and a conversation is struck up about the appearance
of a second sun (*parhelion*) in the sky, Scipio expresses the
wish that the Stoic philosopher Panaetius were on hand to
participate; yet he also voices a reservation: . . . *non nimis
assentior in omni isto genere nostro illi familiari, qui quae vix
coniectura qualia sint possumus suspicari, sic affirmat ut oculis
ea cernere videatur aut tractare plane manu* (*Rep.* 1.15.4).
Though the commentators are silent on this point, this cri-
tique is typical of the skeptics' view of the dogmatic schools
of philosophy generally: they treat mere theories as if they
were palpable facts. Cicero explains his own skeptical strategy for avoiding the *adfirmandi adrogantia* at *Off.* 2.7–8 and
in greater detail at *Luc.* 99.[10] There is, however, no evidence linking Scipio with the Academy; the reservation fits
Cicero[11] but not what we know of Scipio. Similarly when at
1.38 Scipio insists on a definition of terms at the outset of
the discussion of the state and as preliminary to a consideration of the *quale sit*, he is following Socrates' procedure in
Plato's dialogues and also replicating what was evidently
Academic teaching of Cicero's day[12]—and that in spite of
Scipio's wish to avoid a didactic tone (*Rep.* 1.38.4 and
70.1).[13] Rather than argue that "the personal integrity of
Scipio and Laelius would lead one to think that they ac-

[10] See Dyck 1996b: ad *Off.* loc. cit.; Görler 185ff., esp. 188–90.

[11] His lifelong affiliation with the Academy has been challenged of
late, unsuccessfully I think; see Dyck 1996a, 340.

[12] Cf. *Part.* 66 on the *quale sit* presupposing and going beyond the
quid sit in that it implies a comparison of qualities: *non enim simpliciter
solum quaeritur quid honestum sit . . . sed etiam ex comparatione quid
honestius . . .* For the Academic provenance cf. *Part.* 139.

[13] At *De Orat.* 2.109 Antonius recommends omission of definitions
(in courtroom speeches) as too pedantic and too easily controverted.

cepted the opinions that Cicero attributed to them,"[14] we should recognize the unlikelihood that the positions just discussed, or indeed the doctrine of the mixed constitution itself, would have been put forward by Scipio.[15]

A similar instance involving another character of *De Republica* is the characterization of L. Furius Philus by C. Laelius at 3.8 as one who made a practice of arguing opposite sides of a question in order to get at the truth.[16] The Peripatetic method of *in utramque partem disputari* so that the truth may become apparent was, of course, well known to Cicero.[17] One may doubt, however, that Philus practiced it; the notion serves, however, to help motivate the following exchange of speeches between Philus and Laelius.

De Oratore posed a different problem of characterization in that there were those still alive at the time of composition who remembered the eloquence of the characters, so that Cicero could indulge—or so he claims—in no wholesale invention about their type of eloquence (. . . *non de Ser. Galbae aut C. Carbonis eloquentia scribo aliquid, in quo liceat mihi fingere, si quid velim, nullius memoria iam refellente, sed edo haec iis cognoscenda, qui eos ipsos de quibus loquor saepe audierunt . . .* , *De Orat.* 2.9). In fact, however, suspicion is roused by Cicero's protesting too much about his creations, Antonius and Crassus. Thus at *De Orat.* 2.1–4 he is at pains to refute, based on impressions of his relations and of him-

---

[14] Jones 314.

[15] Against Scullard's view that the theory of the mixed constitution was a guiding principle of Scipio's political activity after the fall of Carthage cf. Astin 285ff.—The doctrines discussed in the text would not, of course, be consistent with the degree of learning Scipio claims for himself at *Rep.* 1.36.2, but εἰρωνεία is not excluded (on the historical Scipio as an εἴρων cf. C. Fannius, *hist.* fr. 7).

[16] (Laelius is the speaker): . . . *nec sit ignota consuetudo tua contrarias in partis disserendi, quod ita facillume verum inveniri putes.*

[17] Cf. Dyck 1996b: ad *Off.* 2.8.

self in boyhood, the notion that Antonius was unlearned. He reinforces the notion of Antonius' *dissimulatio* of his own learning through Crassus' remarks at 2.350 and returns for good measure for a repudiation of the notion that Antonius was *ieiunior*, Crassus *plenior* than as depicted in *De Orat.* (3.16). It seems very likely that Cicero has rather created both orators, in learning and style, in his own image. In addition, the details of Crassus' oratorical training were probably inaccessible to Cicero; nevertheless he describes it in detail at *De Orat.* 1.154ff. Compared to Cicero, Crassus was clearly limited in experience of various kinds—in what he had heard, read, and written (ibid. 1.95, clearly an oblique reference to Cicero). Although he does not claim that Crassus, like himself (*Brut.* 310), declaimed in Greek or that as an *adulescens* Crassus had studied with Greek teachers, Cicero's Crassus speaks of reading and expounding Greek orators and composing Latin versions of his Greek reading (*De Orat.* 1.155).[18] One suspects that the Greek component in Crassus' education is overstated. Crassus' remark at the conclusion of his description of his training, *quae fortasse, quemcumque patrem familias adripuissetis ex aliquo circulo, eadem vobis percontantibus respondisset* (ibid. 1.159), is a broad hint that Crassus' "autobiography" should be seen as a general picture of rhetorical training of the time—probably Cicero's own time—, not history.[19]

One of the surprises of *De Oratore* is that in the second day's discussion Antonius takes a quite different tack, echoing rather than contradicting Crassus' exaltation of the orator, when he says that nothing is more splendid than a complete orator, there is no subject that is not the orator's own, etc. (2.33ff.). Crassus cannot, of course, fail to notice

---

[18] As Cicero did (or planned to do) if *Opt. Gen.* is genuine; for the problem cf. Dyck 1996b: ad *Off.* 2.67.

[19] It is taken to be historical, e.g., by Häpke 254.22ff.

and comment on the difference: *nox te nobis, Antoni, expolivit hominemque reddidit. nam hesterno sermone unius cuiusdam 'operis' ut ait Caecilius 'remigem' aliquem aut baiulum nobis oratorem descripseras, inopem quendam humanitatis atque inurbanum* (ibid. 2.40; *com.* Caecil. inc. 274). Antonius' excuse is that his change of emphasis is conditioned by the change of audience: *heri enim hoc mihi proposueram ut, si te refellissem, hos a te discipulos abducerem; nunc Catulo audiente et Caesare, videor debere non tam pugnare tecum quam quid ipse sentiam dicere* (ibid.). The younger participants Sulpicius and Cotta are, however, still present, so that Antonius could still attempt to win them over as students; hence that part of his rationale is hard to credit. It is true that Scaevola has been replaced by Catulus and Caesar, but Antonius might have been thought to be at least as interested in impressing that most senior member of the circle as Catulus and Caesar. Antonius' altered approach is, then, implausible on its own terms. Nevertheless the problem of consistency is trivial. Antonius' stance in the first day's discussion is dramatically satisfying in itself; he takes on the task of relieving and supplementing the arguments of the aged Scaevola[20] against Crassus' exalted conception of the orator. The result is an example of *in utramque partem disputare* that conjures up the famous rivalry of Crassus and Antonius in the courts. On the other hand, in Book 2 Cicero wanted, for variety's sake, to change the main speaker and so assigned to Antonius the exposition of the topics *inventio, dispositio,* and *memoria,* according to one of the traditional divisions of rhetorical handbooks.[21] Thus Antonius' position in Book 1 is revealed *ex post facto*

[20] On Scaevola's role here, which Cicero consciously modeled on the aged Cephalus in Pl. *Rep.* 1, cf. *Att.* 4.16.3, especially the comment *credo Platonem vix putasse satis commodum fore si hominem id aetatis in tam longo sermone diutius retinuisset.*

[21] For details of the organization of this Book see Leeman et al.

as an assumption of the role of devil's advocate. The awkwardness lies only in his attempted rationalization.[22]

A propos the characterization of Laelius in *De Amicitia* Jones contrasts the figure of Cato in *De Senectute* and finds that "the known opponent of Greek culture is represented as versed in Greek literature and philosophy, while in the *De Amicitia* . . . there is no direct statement of Laelius' interest in Greek learning, and the few references to Greek literature and philosophy are couched in indefinite terms."[23] This is, however, a false antithesis. Cato is made to explain his use of Greek examples as based on the study of Greek he undertook in old age (*Sen.* 26; cf. 3) because this feature would otherwise have seemed quite implausible. No such rationale was needed, however, for Laelius, since his association with learned men like Terence was well known (cf. *Amic.* 89: *familiaris meus*). "Direct statement" or no, Laelius' speech is sprinkled with allusions to Greek history and thought, some of them, it is true, left vague, but others quite explicit: note mention of Empedocles (*Agrigentinum . . . doctum quendam virum*, §24), Themistocles (§42), the "wise men" of Greece (§45), including quotation of a saying of Bias (§59), Timon of Athens (§87), and quotation of Archytas of Tarentum (§88); Pythagoras' famous characterization of friendship is twice cited without attribution (§§81 and 92). Jones' hypothesis that the portrayal of Cato drew criticism that caused Cicero to avoid indication of Laelius' learning in the later dialogue is thus superfluous.[24]

The Laelius of *Rep.* 1 is different, however. There, like the practical Antonius of *De Oratore*, Laelius endorses the anti-

---

[22] His announcement that his previous remarks did not represent his real opinion would not in itself necessarily have been "a lame device," as Clarke 52 called it, but the contradiction, if discussed, should have been better motivated.

[23] Jones 316.

[24] Ibid.

intellectual tone of the Ennian Neoptolemus (*philosophari velle, sed paucis; nam omnino haud placere*: *Rep.* 1.30.4 = *trag.* 340 = *scen.* 376 = 95 Jocelyn; cf. *De Orat.* 2.156)[25] and grows impatient with the astronomical topic of discussion (i.e., the recently observed *parhelion*) introduced by Q. Aelius Tubero (*Rep.* 1.19 and 31). The role of Laelius in steering the conversation from astronomy to politics in *Rep.* 1 has, perhaps, a deeper sense. A famous Ciceronian passage (*Tusc.* 5.10) describes the presocratic philosophers (rather one-sidedly) as wholly devoted to astronomical concerns: . . . *numeri motusque tractabantur, et unde omnia orerentur quove reciderent, studioseque ab is siderum magnitudines intervalla cursus anquirebantur et cuncta caelestia.* By contrast Socrates *primus philosophiam devocavit e caelo et in urbibus conlocavit et in domus etiam introduxit et coegit de vita et moribus rebusque bonis et malis quaerere.*[26] This role corresponds precisely to that of Laelius in *Rep.* 1: he calls the discussion down from the heavens and gets the interlocutors to focus on politics, of which, for the ancients, ethics was a branch (Arist. *EN* 1094a18ff.). This role, analogous to that of Socrates, probably suggested itself to Cicero from the oracle that told Chaerephon that no one was wiser than Socrates (Pl. *Ap.* 21a) together with Laelius' cognomen *Sapiens.* Cicero later made the connection explicit at *Amic.* 6–7 (Fannius to Laelius): *te autem alio quodam modo . . . studio et doctrina esse sapientem nec sicut vulgus, sed ut eruditi solent appellare sapientem, qualem in reliqua Graecia neminem . . . , Athenis unum accepimus et eum quidem etiam Apollinis oraculo sapientissimum iudicatum . . .*

In *Rep.* 3, on the other hand, speaking in a Stoic vein as the champion of justice, Laelius develops a lofty concep-

[25] For the parallelism of roles of Laelius and Antonius cf. also Zetzel 1995: ad *Rep.* 2.21–22.

[26] For Greek parallels cf. Boyancé 23, n. 4 *bis.*

tion of natural law (§33), which he supplements with a theory of Peripatetic type of "fitness to govern" (§§36–37),[27] his advocacy of "philosophy in moderation" apparently forgotten. As with Antonius in *De Orat.* 1–2 it is a case of a different mask for different needs. In Book 1 Laelius' position as the special friend of Scipio (cf. *Rep.* 1.18.1–3) qualifies him to introduce the topic of the state, an obvious one in view of the current state crisis. He can thus serve as the catalyst for the change of topic from astronomy (which will be combined with politics only in the *Somnium*).[28] In Book 3, on the other hand, Carneades' lectures for and against justice are divided between two speakers and presented in reverse order, with, as in a court of law, the prosecution followed by the defense.[29] Variety of speakers seems, as in *De Orat.*, a likely factor in the choice of Laelius as defender of justice, since the obvious choice, Scipio, has already spoken at such length in Books 1–2 and will be the main speaker again in Books 4–6; but it is also inherently appropriate that the "Roman Socrates" should defend justice, just as Socrates himself had done in Plato's *Republic*. In this role Laelius must needs expound philosophical doctrine and does so with eloquence,[30] whereas in Book 1 he had expressed surprise at the discussion of astronomy, remote from everyday concerns (§19.4). The extant text gives no evidence that Cicero highlighted the difference; perhaps since *De Orat.* he had learned not to call attention to such points.

. . . *Ipse mea legens sic adficior interdum ut Catonem, non me, loqui existimem* (*Amic.* 4; Cicero speaking in his own person about *Sen.*); so greatly did Cicero's literary creations be-

[27] For Peripatetic background cf. Büchner ad *Rep.* 3.36.

[28] Cf. the change of subject from historiography to law prompted by Atticus' query at *Leg.* 1.13.

[29] Cf. Zetzel 1996, 300–1.

[30] For the reconstruction cf. Ferrary.

guile their own author, or rather such was Cicero's power
to imagine himself in other rôles. For, though he had read
widely in Cato's speeches (*Brut.* 65), Cicero had never
heard him speak, and indeed *Sen.* is the only dialogue that
lacks even a fictive modality of transmission to Cicero himself. Cicero has to a degree sought historical verisimilitude
in his creations, but he has not been obsessed with this aspect. Indeed, he has not hesitated, as we have seen, to trick
out the younger Scipio and L. Furius Philus with features
borrowed from his own biography, L. Licinius Crassus with
a course of studies typical of Cicero's day, C. Antonius with
a far greater erudition than he ever possessed, and both
Crassus and Antonius with a style closer to his own mature
style than to their own. For each dialogue he has chosen
his cast of characters economically, in *Sen.* and *Amic.* con-
tenting himself with three each—the older main speaker
and two admiring junior interlocutors. *De Orat.* presents a
complication of this technique: the junior members Cotta
and Sulpicius are the catalyst for the prolonged discussion
(1.100ff.), with main speeches divided among the elder
statesmen present on topics related to their special interests
or achievements, with occasional interventions by the
philhellene Catulus. *Rep.* similarly includes junior and senior participants with the main speeches reserved for the
seniors. In view of the limited circle of characters of the
major dialogues and in the interest of variety of main
speakers Cicero does not hesitate to "double" roles: in *De
Orat.* Antonius is both the antagonist of Crassus' oratorical
ideal in Book 1 and his partner in the exposition of the system of rhetoric in Book 2; in *Rep.* Laelius is both doubtful
of the value of abstruse speculations in Book 1 and an ex-
pounder of philosophical doctrines in Book 3. Like the
stage dramatist,[31] Cicero is evidently counting on a convinc-

---

[31] Cf. Wilamowitz-Moellendorff with Lloyd-Jones; Dawe.

ing overall effect mitigating any problems of consistency in detail.[32]

Works Cited

Astin, A. E. 1967. *Scipio Aemilianus.* Oxford.

Boyancé, Pierre. 1975. "L'éloge de la philosophie dans le *De legibus* 1, 58–62." *Ciceroniana* n.s. 2:21–40.

Büchner, Karl. 1984. *M. Tullius Cicero. De re publica. Kommentar.* Heidelberg.

Clarke, M. L. 1953. *Rhetoric at Rome: A Historical Survey.* London.

Dawe, R. D. 1963. "Inconsistency of Plot and Character in Aeschylus." *PCPS* 9:21–62.

Dyck, Andrew R. 1996a. Review of J. G. F. Powell, ed. *Cicero the Philosopher. BMCR* 7:333–42.

———. 1996b. *A Commentary on Cicero, De Officiis.* Ann Arbor.

Ferrary, J.-L. 1974. "Le discours de Laelius dans le troisième livre du *de re publica* de Cicéron." *MEFRA* 86:745–71.

Görler, Woldemar. 1974. *Untersuchungen zu Ciceros Philosophie.* Heidelberg.

Häpke, N. 1926. "L. Licinius Crassus" (Licinius no. 55). *RE* 13.1:252.28ff.

Horsfall, Nicholas. 1989. Review of Powell. *CR* 39:227–29.

Jones, Robert Epes. 1939. "Cicero's Accuracy of Characterization in His Dialogues." *AJP* 60:307–25.

Leeman, Anton D., et al. 1981–. *M. Tullius Cicero. De Oratore libri III. Kommentar.* Heidelberg.

[32] I would like to thank my colleague David Blank for helpful comments on an earlier version of this paper.

Levine, Philip. 1957. "The Original Design and the Publication of the *De Natura Deorum*." *HSCP* 62:7–36.

Lloyd-Jones, H. 1972. "Tycho von Wilamowitz-Moellendorff on the Dramatic Technique of Sophocles." *CQ* 21:214–28.

Powell, J. G. F., ed. 1988. *Cicero, Cato maior de Senectute*. Cambridge.

Scullard, H. H. 1960. "Scipio Aemilianus and Roman Politics." *JRS* 50:59–74.

Strasburger, Hermann. 1966. "Der 'Scipionenkreis'." *Hermes* 94:60–72.

Wilamowitz-Moellendorff, Tycho von. 1917. *Die dramatische Technik des Sophokles*. Ed. Ernst Kapp. Berlin.

Zetzel, James E. G., ed. 1995. *Cicero, De Republica. Selections*. Cambridge.

———. 1996. "Natural Law and Poetic Justice: A Carneadean Debate in Cicero and Virgil." *CP* 91:297–319.

Aulus Vettius Caprasius Felix
of Ancient Pompeii

James L. Franklin, Jr.
Indiana University

Although candidate for both aedile and duovir in Pompeii's last years, Aulus Vettius Caprasius Felix has drawn little modern, scholarly attention. The main development of his life, his adoption into a major Pompeian family, has been only cursorily examined, its importance for understanding social forces in the ancient city unexplored. Yet there is substantial evidence still extant to document this life; at issue is a confusing tangle of evidence that can fairly easily be undone to allow for reconstruction of an interesting and illustrative career.

We can trace Vettii back to Augustan times when P. Vettius Celer served as duovir, although the exact date of his incumbency is unknown.[1] In A.D. 3 an Agathemeros,

---

[1] *CIL* X. 907, 908. Both lack consular dating, but Celer's colleague as duovir, D. Alfidius Hypsaeus, had been aedile in A.D. 2-3 (*EphEp* 8, 316), and their duovirates should have followed within a few years. On the Vettii in general, see Castrén 239-40, to which now add Varone 3

slave of a Vettius—likely of Celer the most prominent
Vettius of the time—was named *minister Fortunae Augustae*.[2]
Later, Celer's probable son P. Vettius Syrticus stood for
aedile.[3] Lucii Vettii, Quinti Vettii, and even one Gaius
Vettius are attested in the fifties and sixties A.C.,[4] but in
these last generations of Pompeii's existence, the Auli
Vettii came to the forefront.

Probably in Claudian, perhaps in Neronian, days,[5] A.
Vettius Firmus stood for aedile and was warmly supported
in a notice posted by his neighbors in general and by
Caprasia and Nymphius in particular.

> *CIL* IV. 171:
>
> A(ulum) Vettium Firmum
>
> aed(ilem) o(rat) v(os) f(aciatis) dign(us) est
>
> Caprasia cum Nymphio rog(at)
>
> una et vicini o(rant) v(os) f(aciatis)

(94–95), a programma supporting Vettius Caprasius Felix with no office specified.

[2] *CIL* X. 824.

[3] *CIL* IV. 568, 935*g*, and possibly 9936.

[4] L. Vettius Aethon, L. Vettius Auctus, and L. Vettius Valens are
known from the wax tablets of Caecilius Iucundus (tablets 38, 88, and
26 and 35 respectively). Named in graffiti were Q. Vettius Q. l.
Barniaeus (*CIL* IV. 1865), Q. Vettius Hemeros (*CIL* IV. 1109) and C.
Vettius Firmus (*CIL* IV. 6851, 6852). With two exceptions, the dated of
the tablets of Caecilius Iucundus belong to the years A.D. 52–62, and
the men named in them clearly belong to the the fifties and sixties A.C.
(Andreau 27).

[5] Castrén thought Vettius Firmus a Flavian candidate, but several of
the programmata supporting him were clearly older (*CIL* IV. 7143:
antiquior; 7930: *antiquioris vestigia*; 7504: *antiquior*; 7738: *antiquior*;
7911: *supersunt reliquiae delapso tectorio*; 7964: *superest antiquioris linea
prima*; 7971: *antiquior*), and he belongs to earlier days.

"Along with Nymphius, Caprasia asks that you elect A. Vettius Firmus aedile. He is worthy. Together with their neighbors they ask that you elect him."

Firmus lived in the Casa del Centauro, a grand, double atrium house fronting on the Via di Mercurio at VI.9.3–5, while Caprasia and Nymphius ran the *caupona* and lived just down the street at VI.10.2–4.[6] To us, the best known poster supporting Firmus is one written between scenes of felters at work in their shop along the Via dell' Abbondanza at IX.7.7,[7] but he also sought the support of the apple-dealers (*pomari*)[8] and was supported by ball-players (*pilicrepi*) at the Praedia of Julia Felix,[9] as well as by his neighbors to the south, the inhabitants of the handsome Casa dei Dioscuri, Nigidius Fuscus and Nigidius Vaccula.[10]

CIL IV. 175:
A(ulum) Vettium Firmum aed(ilem) o(rat) v(os) f(aciatis)

Fuscus cum Vaccula facit

"Together with Vaccula, Fuscus supports A. Vettius Firmus for aedile; he asks that you elect him."

It was Vaccula, a bronze merchant, who had given to both the Forum and the Stabian Baths bronze furniture deco-

[6] On the identification of the house of A. Vettius Firmus, see Della Corte 40–41; on Caprasia, Nymphius, and their *caupona*, Della Corte 53.

[7] *CIL* IV. 7838.

[8] *CIL* IV. 183.

[9] *CIL* IV. 1147.

[10] So Richardson 1955, 80–93, although the case for Fuscus, who also supported Firmus separately in *CIL* IV. 176 immediately adjacent, is weak; he may well be simply another neighbor (Della Corte 44).

rated with calves' heads and legs and plaques of heifers (*vacculae*) in an obvious play on his name.[11]

There is no further information on Firmus' political career, although we do know that he failed to produce an heir, so that he was forced to the expedient of adoption. His choice to inherit his wealth and connections was D. Caprasius Felix, an obvious relation to the Caprasia of the first of these notices supporting Firmus for aedile, and when adopted, Caprasius became our A. Vettius Caprasius Felix. It is uncertain when the adoption actually took place, although another notice found on the façade of the house of Firmus suggests that it had been completed when Firmus stood for aedile, for in that notice he was supported by a Felix, presumably his adopted son A. Vettius Caprasius Felix.

> *CIL* IV. 174:
>
> A(ulum) Vettium Firmum
>
> aed(ilem) v(irum) b(onum) o(rat) v(os) f(aciatis) Felix cupit
>
> "Felix wants and asks that you elect Aulus Vettius Firmus, a good man, aedile."

Other evidence, however, suggests that the situation may not have been so straightforward. In fact, it seems more likely that the posters of Felix and Caprasia and Nymphius reflect rather their own campaign for the adoption of Caprasius than their support for Firmus.

Oddly, although Caprasius (then adopted) was supported by Firmus' neighbors along the Via di Mercurio when he later stood for office, it was not so enthusiastically: only

---

[11] On three benches in the Forum Baths was repeated *CIL* X. 818: *M(arcus) Nigidius Vaccula p(ecunia) s(ua)*; on a brazier in the Stabian Baths was *CIL* X. 8071.48: *M(arcus) Nigidius* (the image of a heifer) *p(ecunia) s(ua)*.

two programmata were posted in his favor along the street, while Firmus had been supported by five.[12]

CIL IV. 204:
      A(ulum) Vettium C[ap]r[as]ium Felicem aed(ilem)
         o(rant) v(os) f(aciatis) vicini

"The neighbors ask that you make Aulus Vettius Caprasius Felix aedile."

As we shall see, his neighbors' apparent lack of enthusiasm for his candidacy was probably owed to Caprasius' late association with this part of town; otherwise we would expect more posters to remain from his than from Firmus' earlier campaign. The key to the problem is Caprasius' age at adoption: he will have been adopted late, only after he had reached manhood and when Firmus was an old man, sometime after his stand for aedile.

Across town near his original house at IX.7.20,[13] in contrast to that of his adoptive father, Caprasius was warmly supported—again even by his united neighbors.[14]

CIL IV. 3687:
             A(ulum) Vettium Caprasium

  Felicem aed(ilem) v(iis) a(edibus) sacr(is) p(ublicisque)
         p(rocurandis) vicini rogant

---

[12] For Vettius Caprasius Felix, CIL IV. 204, 205; for Vettius Firmus, CIL IV. 171, 174, 175, 176, 183. CIL IV. 222 supported four men, of whom Vettius Caprasius Felix was one, but it is impossible to trace the individual enthusiasm that presumably underlay the poster.

[13] For the identification of the house, see Della Corte 426–27.

[14] CIL IV. 3687 was posted in the next block at IX.3.20. Also in this street were CIL IV. 2985, 2986 (west side of IX. 7), 3685 (east side of IX. 3), and 3701 (west side of IX. 6); any notices found along the east side of IX.1 went unrecorded. On the notices posted for Caprasius by Bruttius Balbus around the corner along the Via di Balbo, see below.

"The neighbors ask Aulus Vettius Caprasius Felix for aedile for overseeing the streets and sacred and public buildings."

Unfortunately, Pompeii's most famous prosopographer, Matteo Della Corte, failed to understand that D. Caprasius Felix and A. Vettius Caprasius Felix were one and the same man and consequently muddied the picture by trying to explain how Vettius could be supported by the neighbors here at the house of Caprasius while his true neighbors supported him, albeit without enthusiasm, across town.[15] Once the late adoption is understood, no such problem exists; Caprasius had grown up and lived for years in this his original house, and the neighbors here always accepted him more readily than those near the Casa del Centauro. It is, besides, from a graffito found here that we know the personal detail that Caprasius Felix was apparently married to a Fortunata, who was saluted along with him in a room to the south of the atrium.

CIL IV. 5375:

Suc(ces)sus Fel[i]ci salutem

et Fortunatae

"Successus (wishes) health to Felix and Fortunata."

In their Lararium was a statue of the goddess Fortuna sitting on a richly ornamented throne,[16] and Felix and Fortunata were indeed lucky and blessed by Fortuna in the adoption of Felix by Vettius. However, Della Corte's confusion about this adoption, based on the campaign posters found around this house, was not without reason.

---

[15] Della Corte 427 postulated so close a relationship between the two that Vettius Caprasius Felix was taken by the neighbors as an effective inhabitant (effettivamente abitante) of the house of Caprasius Felix.

[16] Boyce 439; illustrated at Plate 5,1.

Q. Bruttius Balbus lived just around the corner from the house of Caprasius at IX.2.16.[17] In posters found on his house façade and on the long stretch of blank wall across from it Balbus had advertised himself as an eager (*cupidus*) supporter of Vettius Firmus and with P. Vettius Syrticus had himself been supported for office by his neighbor Caprasius.[18] Then, when Caprasius stood for office, Balbus' support was requested in turn.

CIL IV. 935*i*:

A(ulum) Vettium Caprasium

Felicem aed(ilem) Balbe rogamus

"We ask, Balbus, Aulus Vettius Caprasius Felix for aedile."

Balbus' response was a poster supporting Vettius Caprasius and a second candidate for the year, P. Paquius Proculus. Perhaps limited by space, his poster recognized Caprasius' adoption by employing his correct, adopted praenomen, but knowing his friend of old, Balbus gave him only his best known gentilicial, Caprasius.[19]

CIL IV. 935*h*:
A(ulum) Caprasium et Paquium Proculum IIvir(os)
i(ure) d(icundo) Balbus facit

"Balbus is electing Aulus Caprasius and Paquius Proculus duovirs for speaking law."

Although officially a Vettius, Caprasius nevertheless remained a Caprasius in the minds of many, like Balbus. This

---

[17] On the house and its inhabitants, see Della Corte 428.

[18] *CIL* IV. 935*b* and 935*g* respectively.

[19] *CIL* IV. 935*e* and 935*k*, presumably also posted by Balbus, carried both gentilicials.

double identity, obvious to his contemporaries, was certain to confuse later scholars, as it did first Della Corte and then Jean Andreau, who invented a homonymous son to serve as our adoptee.[20]

In fact, Caprasius' name is itself indication that he was adopted late. It was normal practice to include an adjectival form of the adoptee's original gentilical in his name, as for example, with one of Pompeii's best known citizens, M. Lucretius Decidianus Rufus. When the adoptee was an adult, however, the original gentilicial itself was retained, as with D. Lucretius Satrius Valens[21] and the lesser known Q. Coelius Caltilius Iustus.

Indeed, Coelius Caltilius Iustus, who had served as duovir in A.D. 52-53[22] perfectly illustrates the sort of name confusion that plagues also study of Vettius Caprasius Felix. Apparently born L. Caltilius Iustus, son of L. Caltilius Pamphilus a freedman and new arrival in Pompeii,[23] he was adopted by a Q. Coelius after he had already reached manhood and begun his public career,[24] so that he became Q. Coelius Caltilius Iustus. After this adoption, he signed two of the wax tablets of Caecilius Iucundus. In A.D. 53 on tablet 138, written when he was duovir, his full name Q. Coelius Caltilius Iustus appeared in the formal date to the document, while a second, clear

---

[20] Andreau 201.

[21] On the career and adoption of Lucretius Satrius Valens *flamen Neronis Caesaris Augusti filii perpetuus*, see Franklin.

[22] Attested in tablet 138 of Caecilius Iucundus. On the Caltilii at Pompeii, see Castrén 147.

[23] Pamphilus is known only from the inscription of the tomb of his wife, found in six fragments and apparently belonging to the large tomb 34N outside the Porta di Ercolano: *CIL* X. 1046: *L(ucius) Caltilius L(uci) l(ibertus) / Coll(ina tribu) / [P]amphilus / [—]ae uxori / [—]mo.*

[24] Nothing more is known (*pace* Della Corte 456-67) of Q. Coelius, who may have lived at VIII.3.7-9; on the Coelii at Pompeii, see Castrén 155-56.

reference to him was to Caltilius Iustus, and as sitting magistrate he signed yet a third variation of his name, Coelius Iustus. Then, three years later he signed as a witness to tablet 19 the name Caltilius Iustus. Nothing could be more confusing to the modern student: Q. Coelius Caltilius Iustus, Coelius Iustus, and Catilius Iustus were one and the same man.

A. Vettius Caprasius Felix has caused us less confusion, to be sure. Yet armed with his correct lineage, we can now begin to make sense of his life. He must have early on been known to Vettius Firmus, probably through business connections—although in this small town a variety of means of acquaintance could be postulated—and to have caught the older and wealthier man's eye. Likewise, the details of Firmus' life will have been equally well known to Caprasius, for he and his kin saw the longterm advantage of warmly supporting the childless candidate for aedile, with the strategically located campaign posters that began our study. In the meantime, the men lived their separate lives, Firmus in the Casa del Centauro, Caprasius in his much more modest house at IX.7.20. In the case of Caprasius especially, graffiti and campaign posters attest an active, developing life. Mutual knowledge and respect eventually paid off for Caprasius, for he was in fact adopted by Firmus, probably very near the end of the older man's life, since no posters in support of Caprasius were signed by Firmus, so that he must have died before he could publicly endorse his adopted son. The recent adoption, too, explains the neighbors' lukewarm support of this new, somewhat intrusive inhabitant of the Casa del Centauro when he did stand for office.

A. Vettius Caprasius Felix was thus still owner of two urban properties when Pompeii was destroyed, and from that simple fact arose all the confusion surrounding the man. Along with property, he will have inherited the clientela and connections of Vettius Firmus, including Pompeii's best known Vettii, A. Vettius Restitutus and A. Vettius Conviva, inhabitants of the famous Casa dei Vettii at VI.15.1.[25] As famous today, in fact, for its *cabina d' amore* as for its legendary dining room decorated with the charming friezes of the Cupids, the house is the goal of nearly every tourist. They and we may well wonder at relations between that property, residence of obviously successful and powerful freedmen—Conviva was even an augustalis[26]—and the Casa del Centauro, seat of a new patron still to prove himself even to his neighbors. But those and other connections among the Vettii must wait to be traced in a study of the *gens* at large. In that study, A. Vettius Caprasius Felix can now firmly take his place.

Works Cited

Andreau, J. 1974. *Les affaires de Monsieur Jucundus. CEFR* 19. Rome.

Boyce, G. K. 1937. *Corpus of the Lararia of Pompeii. MAAR* 14. Rome. (Unless otherwise specified, references are to entry numbers, not pages.)

Castrén, P. 1975. *Ordo Populusque Pompeianus: Polity and Society in Roman Pompeii. ActaInstRomFin* 8. Rome.

Della Corte, M. 1965. *Case ed abitanti di Pompei.* 3rd ed. by P. Soprano. Naples. (Unless otherwise specified, references are to entry numbers, not pages.)

Franklin, J. L., Jr. 1979. "Notes on Pompeian Prosopography: Two Non-Existent Ancients and the DD. Lucretii Valentes." *PP* 34:405–14.

[25] Most recently on the house, see Richardson 1988; 324–29. On its inhabitants, see Della Corte 89–93.

[26] *CIL* IV. 3509: *Vetti[i] Co[nvi]va august[al]i[s]* (found painted on the house façade).

Richardson, L. jr. 1955. *The Casa dei Dioscuri and Its Painters. MAAR* 23. Rome.

———. 1988. *Pompeii: An Architectural History.* Baltimore and London.

Varone, A. 1987. "Nuovi *tituli picti* pompeiani." *RStPomp* 1:91–106. (References are to entry numbers, followed by page numbers in parentheses.)

Alexander and Olympias

E. A. Fredricksmeyer
University of Colorado

The importance of Alexander the Great as one of the most influential men in history is undisputed. Most briefly stated, through his conquests Alexander enabled Greek civilization, hitherto limited in influence no matter how brilliant, to become a world civilization, the Hellenistic, and this, through its adoption by the Romans, along with the native Roman contribution, provided the foundation of Western civilization. But Alexander's career did not occur in a vacuum. While allowance must be made for the uniqueness of Alexander's personality and achievements, he was also the product of his environment, and in this the early influence of his mother Olympias no doubt was primary.

Olympias was an extraordinarily complex person, ruthless, domineering, and above all ambitious for herself and for Alexander as heir-apparent to the throne.[1] We hear that

[1] Cf. Green 30: "Our sources, while admitting Olympias' beauty, describe her variously as sullen, jealous, bloody-minded, arro-

177

after Philip's murder, in which Olympias may have been involved, she took advantage of a brief absence of Alexander
from the capital to engineer the murder of Philip's new
wife Cleopatra and her infant-daughter by Philip. On his return, Alexander expressed shock, but beyond this did nothing (Just. 9.7.12; Plut. *Alex.* 10; Paus. 8.7.7). This set a pattern for the future. Alexander was never able, or willing, to
cross his mother.[2] So while on campaign in the East,
Alexander received frequent complaints from Olympias
about his deputy in Europe, Antipater,[3] while for his part
Antipater lodged a number of protests, no doubt justified,
against Olympias' constant "meddling" in the performance
of his tasks (Arr. 7.12.6; Just. 12.4.3; Diod. 17.117.1). On
one occasion, on the receipt of yet another complaint from
Antipater, Alexander exclaimed that Antipater "did not understand that one tear from a mother wiped out ten thousand letters" such as this (Plut. *Alex.* 39). We are not surprised to hear, then, that Alexander later expressed a desire to secure posthumous divine honors for Olympias
(Curt. 9.6.26; cf. 10.5.30). In the light of such life-long devotion we should expect that during Alexander's formative
years (Philip was away on campaign much of the time)
Olympias came to exercise a lasting influence on
Alexander.

In what ways? I should like to suggest two of some conse-
quence. One concerns Alexander's attitude toward women.
We know that in the age following Alexander, the lot of
Graeco-Macedonian women improved and their status in

---

gant, headstrong and meddlesome." Olympias has an almost universally bad reputation with both ancients and moderns. But see now
Carney 1987 and 1993.

   [2] E.g., Diod. 17.118.1: τοῦ βασιλέως διὰ τὸ πρὸς τὸ θεῖον εὐσεβὲς
πάντα βουλομένου τῇ μητρὶ χαρίζεσθαι.

   [3] Plutarch, *Mor.* 180D, calls them διαβολάς; cf. Arr. 7.12.5.

society rose considerably.[4] Apart from the fact that women
in Macedonia had always been less confined than were
their sisters in the Greek *poleis*, perhaps we can see here
also (among other factors) the influence, by the authority
of personal example, of Alexander, to whom the Hellenistic rulers, setting an example for their people, looked as
their role model and ultimate source of legitimacy. Be that
as it may, throughout his career Alexander treated women,
at any rate aristocratic women with whom he dealt on a
personal basis, with more than common respect.[5] Ordinary

[4] Blundell 199: "In general it can be said that there was an ero-
sion in the asymmetry between the sexes during the Hellenistic age,
and a consequent improvement in the status of women." See further,
e.g., Grant 194–214 and Pomeroy.

[5] E.g., Arr. 3.12.5 (Persian women); 4.20.1–4 (Statira and
Roxane); Aristobulus *ap*. Plut. *Mor*. 259D–260D, and *Alex*. 12
(Timoclea); *Alex*. 22 (Ada); 21 (captive women); 22 (Darius' wife); 30
(grief at death of Darius' wife); Curt. 3.11.3 (Darius' wife, mother, children); 3.12.12 (Darius' wife and mother); 3.12.18–23 (Darius' women);
3.12.17, 25 (Darius' mother); 3.12.21–26 (royal women); 4.10.18–34
(grief at death of Darius' wife); 4.11.3 (Darius' women); 10.5.19–25
(suicide of Darius' mother at news of Alexander's death); Diod.
17.38.4–7 (Darius' women); 17.37.6 (Darius' mother); 17.38.1 (Persian
women); 17.54.7 (death of Darius' wife); 17.118.3 (suicide of Darius'
mother at news of Alexander's death); Just. 11.9.12–16 (Darius'
women); 11.12.6–7 (Darius' women); 13.1.5–6 (suicide of Darius'
mother at news of Alexander's death). See also Berve nos. 206, 688,
711, 722.

In my opinion Carney 1996 overestimates the extent to which
in his treatment of Asian women Alexander was motivated by political
self-interest, to wit a desire to make himself acceptable to the Persians
as Darius' legitimate successor. This does not accord with Alexander's
destruction of Persepolis, the high citadel of Achaemenid kingship.
Our sources attribute Alexander's conduct to his *humanitas*. E.g., Arr.
2.12.3–8; Diod. 17.37.3–38.4; Curt. 3.11.3–12.26; 8.4.23; Plut. *Mor*.
259D–260D and *Alex*. 12; *Mor*. 329E–F; 338D–E; Just. 11.12.6–7. Surely
Alexander could have viewed his self-interest in quite different ways,
which would not involve such kind treatment of these women. Certainly
it came as a great surprise to them. Carney herself observes appropri-

women have left scarcely a trace in our tradition, but perhaps Alexander's respect was not limited to the elite. We hear of one case when on being informed of the rape of the wives of some mercenaries by Macedonian soldiers, Alexander sent word to the officer in charge to put the men on trial and, if convicted, to put them to death "like wild beasts born for the destruction of mankind" (Plut. *Alex*. 22). Likewise, when at the capture of Thebes a woman named Timoclea, the sister of a bitter enemy of his, was brought before him on the charge of murdering a Macedonian officer who had raped her, he pardoned and released her together with her family (Aristobulus *ap*. Plut. *Mor*. 259D–260D; Plut. *Alex*. 12). And at the sack of Persepolis, we are told, Alexander gave orders that "the women were not to be touched" (Curt. 5.6.8).[6] Can we see here the influence of Olympias? We know that Olympias was a devotee of the Dionysiac and Orphic mystery cults (Plut. *Alex*. 2; Duris *ap*. Athen. 13.560F; cf. 14.659F) which regarded men and women as of equal worth, and even tended to blur the distinction between the sexes (Dionysus himself was sometimes viewed as androgynous).[7] Surely a commitment to these cults could not fail to enhance the sense of self-worth of a woman like Olympias, and it is reasonable to speculate that she in turn instilled in Alexander a more than usual respect, or sympathy, for women in general.

---

ately (1996, 579): "The [eventual] sad fate of all the royal Asian women speaks to the views of the Macedonian elite when they no longer had to cope with Alexander."

[6] Note also the story (Plut. *Mor*. 179E) that on one occasion a girl was brought to his bedroom to spend the night with him, and when he asked her why she came so late, she replied that she had to wait until her husband had gone to bed. At this, Alexander bitterly rebuked his servants since because of them "he had almost become an adulterer."

[7] See Kraemer; Henrichs 1978 and 1984.

We can identify another important, and less elusive, influence of Olympias on Alexander. At the royal court in Pella Olympias probably was a lonely figure. Her marriage to Philip had gone sour almost at the beginning, and because of her imperious temperament and foreign (Epirote) birth, albeit of royal blood, she seems to have been quite unpopular. But in addition to being the mother of the heir-apparent she held one major trump card, her acknowledged descent from the brilliant hero of the *Iliad*, Achilles (Plut. *Alex.* 2; *Pyrrh.* 1; Paus. 1.11.1; Arr. 1.11.8; 4.6.29; 4.11.6; Just. 7.3.1). For most Greeks, at any rate the Macedonians still in the fourth century, the heroic past was essentially history. In Macedonia, more than in the sophisticated city-states to the south, there still prevailed a code of honor, as it was exemplified by the Homeric heroes, which placed the highest premium on valor, honor and glory. The education of the nobleman, and a fortiori of Alexander, focused on the *paradeigma* of the great heroes of the past, and among them Achilles was preeminent.[8] The *Iliad* was central in Alexander's course of studies. No doubt Olympias encouraged this concentration with its emphasis on Achilles, as we know that she was influential in Alexander's education also in other respects.[9] We may be sure that Olympias made the most to Alexander of her descent from the great hero of the *Iliad*, and Alexander adopted him as his personal exemplar (Arr. 1.12.1; 7.14.4; Plut. *Alex* 5, 8, 15; Diod. 17.4.1; 17.17.3. Cf. Philostr. *Her*. 326).

Now while Achilles was the son of a goddess, Heracles, hero par excellence and Alexander's ancestor on Philip's side, was a son of Zeus (Arr. 2.5.9; 3.3.2; 4.10.6; 4.11.6;

[8] Fredricksmeyer 1990, 304–5.

[9] The appointment of Leonidas, a relative of Olympias and thus not a Macedonian, as Alexander's head teacher and mentor (probably before Aristotle) no doubt was due to the influence of Olympias (Plut. *Alex*. 5).

5.26.5; 6.3.2; Curt. 4.2.3; Diod. 17.4.1; Isoc. 5.109–15). Surely, for the religious faithful like Olympias, what had happened in the past could happen again. There is some evidence that Olympias came to believe that Alexander's father was not Philip (whom she came to loathe) but a god, either Dionysus, or possibly Zeus himself.[10] No less an authority than Eratosthenes informs us that as Alexander set out on his conquest of Asia, Olympias told him "the secret of his begetting, and charged him to prove himself worthy of it" (ap. Plut. Alex. 3). Later, at his visit to the oracle of Zeus Ammon in Libya, the priest identified Alexander as son of Zeus, Alexander accepted the identification, and for the remainder of his life believed in it.[11] After his visit to the oracle Alexander wrote to his mother that "he had received certain secret oracular responses (τινὰς αὐτῷ μαντείας ἀπορρήτους) which he would tell her alone after his return" (Plut. Alex. 27). It is not unlikely that these revelations concerned details of Alexander's begetting. Of course, Alexander never did return to Macedonia and never did see his mother again. But he stayed in touch with her by correspondence (e.g., Athen. 4.659F), and he remained devoted to her to the end of his life.

Olympias' influence on Alexander almost certainly went far beyond what is recorded in our spotty tradition, which on the whole paid scant attention to women. Even so, we have seen that there are enough traces in it for us to recognize, with some plausibility, two important ways in which Olympias influenced Alexander: one, his more than traditional regard for women, and the other, his acceptance of the binding force of his descent from Achilles and his faith in the paternity of Zeus. By virtue of his divine descent and

[10] Hamilton 4–5; Fredricksmeyer 1991, 199–200.
[11] Fredricksmeyer 1991, 199–200.

the magnitude of his achievements, Alexander came to believe that he deserved honors as a god in his lifetime.[12]

Works Cited

Berve, H. 1926. *Das Alexanderreich auf prosopographischer Grundlage*. Vol. 2. Munich.

Blundell, S. 1995. *Women in Ancient Greece*. Cambridge, Mass.

Carney, E. D. 1987. "Olympias." *Anc. Soc.* 18:35–62.

———. 1993. "Olympias and the Image of the Virago." *Phoenix* 47:29–55.

———. 1996. "Alexander and Persian Women." *AJP* 117:563–83.

Fredricksmeyer, E. A. 1990. "Alexander and Philip: Emulation and Resentment." *CJ* 85:300–15.

———. 1991. "Alexander, Zeus Ammon, and the Conquest of Asia." *TAPA* 121:199–214.

Grant, M. 1982. *From Alexander to Cleopatra. The Hellenistic World*. New York.

Green, P. 1991. *Alexander of Macedon*. Berkeley.

Henrichs, A. 1978. "Greek Maenaedism from Olympias to Messalina." *HSCP* 82:121–52.

———. 1984. "Male Intruders among the Maenads: The So-Called Male Celebrant." In *Mnemai. Classical Studies in Memory of Karl K. Hulley*. Ed. H. D. Evjen. Chico. 69–91.

Kraemer, R. S. 1979. "Ecstasy and Possession. The Attraction of Women to the Cult of Dionysus." *HThR* 72:55–80.

Pomeroy, S. B. 1990. *Women in Hellenistic Egypt*. Detroit.

---

[12] Fredricksmeyer 1991, 213–14.

Crawford's *Cecilia:*
Conversions on the Janiculum

cononon

Katherine A. Geffcken
Wellesley College

When I think of Paul MacKendrick, I immediately place
him in Rome, on the Janiculum, in the Library at the
American Academy or eating Sunday night supper at the
neighborhood *Vascello*. I see him in a circle of friends who
all found Rome irresistibly alluring, more than twenty or
even thirty years ago. Of course, his own Roman days
stretch much further back, but my memories are most vivid
of those times when Italy had emerged from her postwar
recovery into a spectacular season of high style and excitement. With nostalgia for those days on the Janiculum, I offer him this essay on an American novelist who understood
changing Rome in an earlier, significant era.

As F. Marion Crawford's novel *Cecilia* (1902) opens, two
young men sit quietly talking in the Bosco Parrasio on the

* For my copy of *Cecilia* I am grateful to Virginia Payne Ahrens,
whose nine volumes of Crawford came into my possession through the
thoughtfulness of her daughter Marion Ahrens Allen.

185

eastern slope of the Janiculum. The pale, thoughtful man is Guido d'Este, the younger son of a deceased ex-sovereign who lost his small European kingdom in a nineteenth-century revolution. Guido's social position is ambiguous because his mother was a commoner, the king's second, morganatic wife. But his paternal aunt, Princess Anatolie, a relic of this royal past, presides imperiously over her Roman villa and threatens to ruin her nephew. The old Princess has a weakness for financial advice supplied her in séances by a malicious medium. Acting on this foolish advice, she forced her nephew, despite his resistance, to invest a million francs of her fortune in a speculative venture. The money was lost, and now the Princess demands he return her million francs. Guido, however, has only an adequate, if not overly generous allowance from his father's Estate; he cannot repay the money and thus faces social disgrace or must disappear from Rome.

The other young man sitting in the Bosco Parrasio contrasts strikingly with the dark, pensive Guido. Rugged, red haired and red bearded, Lamberto Lamberti is an officer in the Italian Navy with ten years' service at sea and in battle. On hearing Guido's troubles Lamberto regrets that the day of mediaeval poisons has passed ("we should have poisoned the old woman," 12). The conversation ranges over other possible ways to solve Guido's problem—marriage to an heiress (at this stage both men reject such a crass idea), escape to South America (intolerable to Guido), and finally suicide, proposed as an honorable step by Guido and totally rejected by Lamberto. The visit to the Bosco ends with nothing solved, only ominous days ahead for Guido.

Why did Crawford choose the Bosco Parrasio for the first scene of this novel? Though both men know the garden (2), it is Guido who brought Lamberto there for serious, uninterrupted conversation. In fact, Guido and the Bosco with its literary associations have much in common. He knows literature, ancient and modern. He cherishes books, prints, and paintings, especially his own beloved Andrea del Sarto, and he keeps up with Giacomo Boni's excavations in the Forum (78–80). Crawford describes him as a cultivated man of leisure: "Guido d'Este was one of those Italians who are content to survive from a very beautiful past without joining the frantic rush for a very problematic future . . . he was a dreamer" (3–4). Guido feels at home in the Bosco and looks around with sensitive interest, recording in his mind the "neglected old garden with a stone-pine in the middle, clearly cut out against the sky" (17). The stone-pine is still there in the Bosco, one of the most distinctive trees on the Janiculum.

Crawford evokes romantic nostalgia in describing this "forgotten garden of the Arcadian Society" (1). To convey the bygone world that the Bosco stands for, he sets the scene not only with topographical details but also with full description of a lush, almost decaying *locus amoenus*:

> Few people, Romans or strangers, ever find their way to that lonely and beautiful spot beyond the Tiber, niched in a hollow of the Janiculum below San Pietro in Montorio, where Beatrice Cenci sleeps. The Arcadians were men and women who loved poetry in an artificial time, took names of shepherds and shepherdesses, rhymed as best they could, met in pleasant places to recite their verses, and played that the world was young, and gentle, and sweet, and unpoisoned, just when it had declined to one of its recurring periods of vicious old age. The Society did not die with its times, and it still exists, less sprightly, less ready to mask in pastorals, but rhyming, meeting, and reciting verses now and then, in the old manner, though rarely in the old haunts. Even now fresh inscriptions in honour of the Arcadians are set into the stuccoed walls of the little terraced garden under the hill.

It is very peaceful there. Above, the concave wall of the small house of meeting looks down upon circular tiers of brick seats, and beyond these there are bushes and a little fountain. To the right and left, symmetrical walks lead down in two wide curves to the lower levels, where the water falls again into a basin in a shaded grotto, and rises the third time in another fountain. An ancient stone-pine tree springs straight upwards, spreading out lovely branches. There are bushes again and a magnolia, and a Japanese medlar, and there is moss. The stone mouldings of the fountains are rich with the green tints of time. The air is softly damp, smelling of leaves and flowers; there are corners into which the sunlight never shines, little mysteries of perpetual shade that are full of sadness in winter, but in summer repeat the fanciful confidences of a delicious and imaginary past. (1–2)

The reference to Beatrice Cenci, the description of moss, dampness and shade undercut the idyllic with potentially sinister tones.

The society called the Arcadia was founded in 1690 by fourteen *soci* or *pastori* who had frequented the circle around the late Queen Christina of Sweden (d. 1689). Led by Giovan Mario Crescimbeni, the Arcadia aimed to restore good taste in poetry. Until 1724 the society met in various parts of Rome for its seven sessions a year, to hear its members recite their poetry. Then in 1724 the king of Portugal, João V, gave 4000 *scudi* to purchase the property on the Janiculum, a sloping wedge of land lying between the Aurelian Wall and the old Via Aurelia. The first stone of the *casino* at the top of the Bosco was laid October 5, 1725, and the *casino* inaugurated May 1, 1730. The architect of the Bosco was Antonio Canevari, assisted by Nicolò Salvi, who was soon to become famous as the designer of the Trevi Fountain.

Although seldom used today, the formal entrance to the garden is a large gate standing above an ascending curve in Via Garibaldi. It opens onto the first, lowest level, followed by semicircular ramps (as Crawford describes) up to the second level, which features a fountain and grotto "of Alcaeus." Then further stairs, each formed almost like a ninety-degree angle, lead up to the small theater. Here the circle of seats rises in four rows (Crawford shows Guido and Lamberto sitting here where poets listened to their colleagues' verses). The concave façade of the *casino*, articulated by engaged columns and niches, serves as a *scaenae frons* for the theater. Everywhere in sculpture and inscriptions are reminders of pastoral themes: Pan and Syrinx, Pallas and Mercury, Pegasus, and tablets with the rules of the Arcadia. Most important, the name Bosco Parrasio refers to a region of Greek Arcadia and evokes Vergil's and Ovid's adjective *Parrhasius* (e.g., *Aen.* 8.344, and *Fasti* 1.618). As Crawford mentions, the members took pastoral names: for example, Crescimbeni became Alfesibeo Cario, the poet Pietro Metastasio (actually born Trapassi) became Artino Corasio, and Pope Leo XIII took the name Neandro Aracleo. The theater provided a setting also for musical performances and in 1781 even for a wedding. But as the Arcadians' poetry went out of style, the property fell into disrepair. In 1850 the architect Giovanni Azzurri restored the *casino*, and in the 1930s the property was again cleaned and repaired. In 1925 the society had been reorganized as the Accademia degli Arcadi (Belli Barsali 427, Brigante Colonna 553–60, Gigli 120, 122).

Today the Bosco remains an almost secret garden of the Janiculum, entered only by appointment. The nuns there in Crawford's account are no longer present, but we can identify with Guido and Lamberto's departure onto the street through an iron door that "closed with a rusty clang" and with their descent along "the steep way that leads down from the Porta San Pancrazio to the Via Garibaldi" (19). One senses that Crawford, who knew Rome from childhood, had also sat one early spring afternoon in the Bosco and departed down this steep street.

These best friends Guido d'Este and Lamberto Lamberti establish the polarities between the old and the new in *Cecilia: A Story of Modern Rome*. In many previous novels, Crawford had shown his concern for changing Rome, from the sleepy Papal City to burgeoning national capital. He documented the enormous transformation of social structure and landscape especially in his *Saracinesca* trilogy (*Saracinesca* 1887, *Sant' Ilario* 1888, and *Don Orsino* 1891). Now, in *Cecilia*, he traces the relationship of his heroine to the two friends. An only child, Cecilia Palladio is herself a symbol of Italy after the reunification. While "Cecilia" points back to the ancient Caecilii Metelli (137–38), her surname is not Roman, but rather suggests the Veneto and the famous architect of that name (22). Her father Count Palladio fought in 1860 with Garibaldi and then became involved in South American railroads, the Suez Canal, and the perfection of a new kind of machine gun. Her late stepfather Count Fortiguerra bore a meaningful name: he was a professional soldier, who rose to be Italian ambassador at Madrid. Thus, most of Cecilia's life has been spent outside of Italy. From her travels she knows cosmopolitan culture, from study in Paris she knows philosophy, and from her childhood she remembers her father's tales of early Roman kings and Vestals.

As the novel begins, this strong-minded heiress Cecilia and her rather helpless mother have just returned to Italy. They take an apartment in the Palazzo Massimo alle Colonne, and Cecilia buys and tastefully restores the Villa Madama (Crawford must have enjoyed giving her ownership of this notable structure, in fact acquired by the Italian government!).[1] But Cecilia also has a secret inner life. She indulges in self-hypnotic trances, in which she sees herself in a previous form, as the last Vestal living in the Atrium Vestae, which Giacomo Boni was then bringing to light.[2] When she meets Guido, she enjoys his company. He is a cultivated, attractive man with a romantic name, and he sympathizes with her interests in learning. Old Princess Anatolie, of course, sees Cecilia as an heiress whose fortune through a marriage settlement would provide the lost million francs. And so, Cecilia becomes engaged to Guido. But in her trances and dreams, she sees not Guido but Lamberto. As she becomes caught between her affection for Guido and her obsession for Lamberto, Guido's world falls apart. He battles influenza, delirium, and suicidal depression, confined for weeks to his flat in the Palazzo Farnese. Facing her feelings honestly, Cecilia breaks the engagement, but worse is to come for Guido when an evil dependent of Princess Anatolie sabotages Guido's honor with malicious innuendo in the Paris *Figaro*. As Crawford repeatedly calls Guido "the personification of honor," (e.g., 399),

---

[1] See Vance 243 on Crawford's amusing choice of this villa. Designed by Raphael and decorated with wall paintings by Giulio Romano, this sixteenth century villa stands on the eastern slope of Monte Mario, with a more distant view of Rome than the Janiculum offers. Three important scenes in *Cecilia* take place at Villa Madama: 149–68, 263–66 (note especially the description of Rome and the hills in the distance 264), and 417–21 (the last scene in the novel).

[2] The many references in *Cecilia* to the Vestals and the scenes at their area in the Forum (e.g., 80–85, 326–37) show current excitement in Rome about Boni's excavations (1899–1902). Note that the heroine Cecilia "had followed Giacomo Boni's astonishing discoveries with breathless interest" (193). It is also possible that Crawford had read Rodolfo Lanciani's accounts of the last Vestals (e.g., Lanciani 1888, 168–77; 1897, 230). Did Crawford pick the name "Cecilia" for its similarity to Coelia Concordia, whom Lanciani emphasizes as one of the last *Vestales Maximae* (1888, 169–70; 1897, 230)? Lanciani himself excavated in the Vestals' area from October 1883 to early 1884.

this slander almost effects a death blow. But fortunately the Princess dies unexpectedly, and naturally the strong and loyal Lamberto outmaneuvers the perpetrator of slander. Though desperately ill, Guido survives.

Almost at the end of the novel, while Guido is still convalescing, the two friends drive up one still, hot August afternoon to the Janiculum, not back to the Bosco but to the other, northern end of the hill. Just where the Janiculum ends in a sharp slope, on the side facing Rome, is a small outdoor theater, the site nowadays of rollicking performances of Plautus. Crawford recalls the opening sentence of the novel as he writes:

> The two men were sitting on the brick steps of the miniature Roman theatre close to the oak which is still called Tasso's, a few yards from the new road that leads over the Janiculum through what was once the Villa Corsini. It was shady there, and Rome lay at their feet in the still afternoon. The waiting carriage was out of sight, and there was no sound but the rustling of leaves stirred by the summer breeze. It was nearly the middle of August. (408)

As the men look out over "the deep city towards the hills to eastward" (409), Lamberto tells Guido that he, Lamberto, and Cecilia will marry, but that no engagement will be announced until Guido hears all that happened, none of it dishonorable. The bond between the men survives this news, however painful to Guido.

After long conversation, Guido reaffirms their friendship and says,

> ". . . Shall we go home? I feel a little tired."
> Lamberti helped him to the carriage and drew the light cover over his knees before getting in himself. Then they drove down towards the city, by the long and beautiful drive, past the Acqua Paola and San Pietro in Montorio.
>
> (415–16)

Their carriage thus departs toward the Villa Aurelia, leaving the park by the Passeggiata Margherita, named for the Queen of Italy and inaugurated in 1887. This stretch of the Passeggiata (now called simply Passeggiata del Gianicolo) emerges from the park just below the Villa Aurelia and opposite the Villa Sforza Cesarini. Their ride, in fact, takes them within a few feet of the precipitous stairway down to the Bosco Parrasio.

At the northern end of the park from which they came, we now know well the curving loops of the road down to Piazza della Rovere and the Lungotevere. Unlike the southern stretch, this northern branch, passing close by S. Onofrio and the hospital Bambin Gesù, was inaugurated in this century, on October 28, 1939 (Gigli 146, 148). Today, because of this street and the hospital that almost encircles S. Onofrio, we do not think of the theater and the church as part of the same property. But, originally, Tasso's oak, now a dead trunk teetering near the street, and the theater were both located in the *vigna* of S. Onofrio.

Again, in this scene Crawford evokes old Rome, but this time old spots transformed by new Rome. The gardens no longer belong to the Corsini but are named instead for a queen of the House of Savoy. In 1898 Crawford published his two-volume *Ave Roma Immortalis*, subtitled *Studies from the Chronicles of Rome*. His pages about S. Onofrio could serve as a commentary on our chapter in *Cecilia*. He approaches the church from the Vatican side, up the steep, straight Salita di S. Onofrio:

> If one comes from the Borgo by the Lungara, and if one turns up the steep hill to the right, there is the place where Tasso died. . . . The small monastery of Sant' Onofrio, where he spent the last short month of his life, used to be a lonely and beautiful place, and is remembered only for his sake, though it has treasures of its own . . . as well as memories of Saint Philip Neri. . . . It was far from the streets and

thoroughfares in older times, and the quiet sadness of its
garden called up the infinite melancholy of the poor poet
who drew his last breath of the fresh open air under the old
tree at the corner, and saw Rome the last time, as he turned
and walked painfully back to the little room where he was
to die. . . .

   There died the man who had sung, and wandered, and
loved; who had been slighted, and imprisoned for a mad-
man; who had escaped and hidden himself, and had yet
been glorious; who had come to Rome at last to receive the
laureate's crown. . . . Everything in Tasso's life was contradictory, everything in his works was harmonious. (*Ave* 147–
49)

Just as Torquato Tasso was "torn and harassed" (*Ave* 148),
so too Guido d'Este has raved in delirium, and is now
"painfully thin" with "hollow eyes" (409).[3] At the same time,
Guido possesses an inner harmony, and he will return to
his books and prints. Unlike Tasso, he will doubtless live on
for some years, in his familiar surroundings and quiet com-
fort.

   If by recalling the Renaissance poet of lost loves and epic
heroes, Crawford characterizes Guido, where does his
friend Lamberto fit? The analogy is not intended to be exact, but I suggest the two men sit in this theater because
Crawford indirectly refers to St. Philip Neri, the joyous
Roman saint, who assembled his followers on this slope for
their exercises. On nice afternoons Philip developed the
practice of moving his "Oratory" outside to a garden. Accompanied by his Oratorians and often by large crowds,

---

[3] On the "masochistic, languid renunciation of life" in Tasso's *rime
amorose*, see Brand 146–48. Crawford was also probably influenced by
the "legend" that developed about Tasso (that Tasso went mad from his
love for Leonora d'Este—note Crawford's use of this princely name of
Ferrara for Guido!). In English, the most prominent treatment of this
"legend" is Lord Byron's *Lament of Tasso*. See Brand 205–25.

Philip walked through the city and settled in a cool spot for sermons and musical interludes (*laudi*). Dominant in these religious exercises was a buoyant, recreational tone. In 1590 the Oratorians rented the slope on the Janiculum from the monastery of S. Onofrio. Fabrizio dei Massimi was the guarantor; indeed, over the years Philip was closely associated with the princely family at Palazzo Massimo.[4] In a short time, this *vigna* of S. Onofrio became one of Philip's favorite places. The city spread out below like a stage, the Alban and Sabine Hills in the distance like a backdrop. The whole setting provided a magnificent theater. Philip loved the crowd singing together; he also liked to withdraw alone to the highest spot for meditation and prayer (Ponnelle and Bordet 397–98).

Different as they were, Tasso and Filippo Neri are linked both by this close association of place and by their time of death. They died in 1595 within a few weeks of one another, Tasso at S. Onofrio on April 25th and Philip in his bed at the Chiesa Nuova on May 26th. After Philip's death, his Congregation purchased the slope on the Janiculum,

---

[4] Fabrizio dei Massimi in particular ardently supported Philip Neri for decades, but in fact the saint was confessor to many members of the Massimi family and visited the palazzo frequently until his health declined. The most famous incident linking Philip to the Massimi was his raising Fabrizio's son Paolo briefly from the dead, on March 16, 1583, at Palazzo Massimo alle Colonne (Ponnelle and Bordet 163–64, 504). The room where this incident occurred is still open to the public every March 16th. By locating Cecilia's residence at this palazzo and Guido's at Palazzo Farnese, Crawford places his characters within Philip Neri's daily world (before moving to the Chiesa Nuova, the saint lived for years at San Girolamo, one block from Piazza Farnese). Of course, Philip Neri was a far more complex person than indicated in this essay. Besides his laughter, Ponnelle and Bordet stress his uncommon sensitivity (especially as a confessor), his emotional response to the Mass (during which he frequently wept), the extraordinary palpitations of his enlarged heart, and his concern for the spiritual nurturing of young men but often stern treatment of women (Ponnelle and Bordet *passim*).

where in 1619 they entrusted Marsilio Onorati with constructing the outdoor theater immediately next to Tasso's oak. Crawford calls the theater "Roman" (408) because the *cavea* rests against a gentle hollow in the hillside in the manner of ancient structures, but in Italian terms it is also a *scalinata*, or monumental kind of staircase. Like the ramps, stairs, and seating in the Bosco Parrasio, it shows the Italian gift for converting a natural slope into a graceful structure. And so, for over two hundred years, lovers of poetry made pilgrimages to Tasso's oak and the Oratorians used the theater, but in the nineteenth century change came to this lovely spot. On September 22, 1843, the oak suffered a devastating strike of lightning, and in the second half of the century the theater was expropriated, becoming part of the new public *passeggiata* (Gigli 156). Thus, in *Cecilia* Romans like Guido and Lamberto can drive at leisure in the park. But even so, when they sit together on the steps of the *scalinata*, Crawford surely juxtaposes the melancholy and joy evoked by memories of Torquato Tasso and San Filippo Neri. And here, as at the opening of the novel, a theater on the Janiculum provides a place for undisturbed conversation, for viewing the intense life of downtown Rome from a garden on the City's periphery.

Works Cited

Belli Barsali, Isa. 1970. *Ville di Roma: Lazio I*. Milan.

Brand, C. P. 1965. *Torquato Tasso: A Study of the Poet and of His Contribution to English Literature*. Cambridge.

Brigante Colonna, G. 1938. "Il *Bosco Parrasio*." *Capitolium* 13:553–60.

Crawford, F. Marion. 1898. *Ave Roma Immortalis: Studies from the Chronicles of Rome. Vol. II*. New York. [cited as *Ave*.]

———. 1902. *Cecilia: A Story of Modern Rome*. New York. [cited by page number alone, e.g., (1–2)]

Gigli, Laura. 1977. *Rione XIII: Trastevere*. Parte I. *Guide Rionali di Roma* 28. Rome.

Lanciani, Rodolfo. 1888. *Ancient Rome in the Light of Recent Discoveries*. Boston.

———. 1897. *The Ruins and Excavations of Ancient Rome*. London.

Ponnelle, Louis and Louis Bordet. 1932. *St. Philip Neri and the Roman Society of His Times*. Tr. Ralph Francis Kerr. London.

Vance, William L. 1989. *America's Rome*. Vol. II. New Haven.

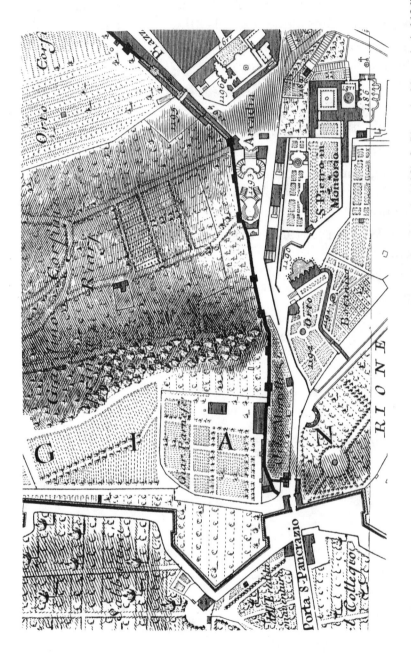

Fig. 1. Section of G. Nolli's plan of Rome (1748) showing the Arcadia in right center (#1193), S. Pietro in Montorio (#1186), the Aqua Paola (#1190). Porta S. Pancrazio to left, the Giardino Farnese (= Villa Aurelia), and above, the Giardino Corsini.

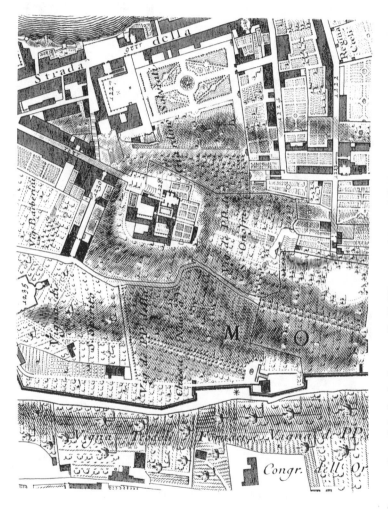

Fig. 2. *The northern section of the Janiculum on G. Nolli's map of Rome (1748). The Scalinata of the Oratorians, shown here as six steps, appears in the lower center (#1229) at the edge of the Vigna of S. Onofrio. The church of S. Onofrio itself is #1228. The trunk of Tasso's oak now stands just to the north of the theater.*

Erotodidaxis: *Iucunda Voluptas* in Lucretius 2.3 and Propertius 1.10.3[1]

cononono

Joy King

The *praeceptor naturae*, Lucretius, in 2.3, and the *praeceptor amoris*, Propertius, in 1.10.3, each uniquely, employ the phrase *iucunda voluptas*, a fact noted without discussion by W. A. Merrill in his edition of Lucretius and by P. J. Enk in his edition of Propertius' *Monobiblos*.[2] In the proem to *DRN*

---

[1] The author wishes to acknowledge a personal debt of gratitude to Professor Paul MacKendrick because of 1) his demonstration of effective teaching techniques especially by providing extensive bibliography, inclusive course outlines and well-organized lectures, 2) his elucidation of the meaning, as well as the form, of classical works, through attention to structure, *leitmotif,* and the use of key words, and 3) his encouragement of discussion linking ancient theory with socio-political issues. For me, he was truly an "eye-opener" and model.

[2] Merrill ad loc. Enk ad loc. Texts cited are those of Bailey for Lucretius and Barber for Propertius (where v is substituted for u). Scodel and Thomas remark on Vergil's use on three occasions of a key Callimachean word, the Euphrates, in a place the same number of lines

201

2, Lucretius uses the phrase to teach his addressee Memmius that ἡδονή, the *summum bonum* of Epicurean philosophy, is the absence of *malis* (4), defined here as *dolor* (18), *cura* (19), and *metu* (19), faced by humans engaged in *laborem* (1–2) on the high seas and in *belli certamina* (5) for the purpose of acquiring power and wealth. Elsewhere, in 3.984–94 and in 4.1037–1287, the passions of love are characterized also as *mala*, to be avoided if the reader would achieve personal happiness. Propertius, on the other hand, in 1.10, observes his addressee Gallus in love, exclaims in approval (*o . . . iucunda voluptas!*), and proceeds to give instructions to the lover so that he will remain forever *humilis* and *subiectus* (27), *numquam . . . liber* (30), suffering the *ultima mala* of love (1.5.4). To the reader mindful of Lucretius' attitude to love, the two passages appear contradictory. It is the purpose of this essay, however, to show that Propertius' use of *iucunda voluptas* in 1.10.3 is not only inspired by *DRN* 2.3 but pivotal in pointing to the way Propertius, virtually throughout his poetry, owes phraseology, motifs, and especially the poet's role as *praeceptor* to his predecessor in didactic.[3]

(six) from the end of the poem as Callimachus in his "programmatic" use of the word in *H.* 2.108. Here Propertius uses *iucunda voluptas* at the end of line 3, the same position as Lucretius in *DRN* 2.

[3] Lucretius' role as an intermediary between Propertius (and the other love-elegists) and the archaic, classical and hellenistic Greeks has not regularly been discussed in studies about the development of Latin love-elegy, e.g., by Wheeler or by Day, doubtless because of the apparent differences in genre (didactic *epos* and "subjective" elegy) and subject-matter (philosophy, love) in these poets' work. Conte, although including Lucretius and love-elegy in the same study of didacticism in Latin poetry, says little of Propertius, directing attention rather to Ovid. Allen 259–60 mentions briefly Lucretius' definition of love in connection with Propertius' treatment in 1.1. Brown 142 notes the lack of a definitive study but recognizes that Propertius implicitly accepts Lucretius' view of love's devastating power and irrationality.

For Lucretius, *voluptas* is a key word appearing twenty-five times in the poem, but only at 2.3 with *iucunda*. In the proem to Book 1 (1–148), it frames the introduction to the poem with an address to *Venus genetrix* (1), symbol of the generative power or sexual energy producing all things, as *hominum divomque voluptas* (1), along with a reminder that *sperata voluptas suavis amicitiae* (140), the pleasure in his poetry that will generate the approval of his reader, inspires this work of enlightenment (140–45). In brief, *voluptas* in 1.1 and 140 signifies the true happiness that can come to a man through understanding the ways of nature when he is instructed in the truth of Lucretius' poetry. Similarly, *iucunda* modifying *voluptas* in 2.3 and *sensu* in 2.19, a variation of *voluptas*, frames the introduction to the proem of Book 2 (1–19) with an emphasis on the sensation of happiness to be enjoyed by a mind free of care and fear, the Epicurean view of the essential need faced by humankind (16–19), to be achieved through *naturae species ratioque* (61). The concept is repeated at 29–33 where enlightened individuals care for their simple needs *iucunde* (31) in an atmosphere of quietude and withdrawal to a pastoral (as opposed to an urban Roman) scene:

> Suave, mari magno turbantibus aequora ventis,
> e terra magnum alterius spectare laborem,
> non quia vexari quemquamst iucunda voluptas,
> sed quibus ipse malis careas quia cernere suave est;
> 5 suave etiam belli certamina magna tueri
> per campos instructa tua sine parte pericli,
> sed nil dulcius est. bene quam munita tenere
> edita doctrina sapientum templa serena,
> despicere unde queas alios passimque videre
> 10 errare atque viam palantis quaerere vitae
> certare ingenio, contendere nobilitate,
> noctes atque dies niti praestante labore
> ad summas emergere opes rerumque potiri.

o miseras hominum mentis, o pectora caeca!
15 qualibus in tenebris vitae quantisque periclis
degitur hoc aevi quodcumquest! nonne videre
nil aliud sibi naturam latrare, nisi utqui
corpore seiunctus dolor absit, mente fruatur
iucundo sensu cura semota metuque?
20 ergo corpoream ad naturam pauca videmus
esse opus omnino, quae demant cumque dolorem,
delicias quoque uti multas substernere possint;
gratius interdum neque natura ipsa requirit,
si non aurea sunt iuvenum simulacra per aedes
25 lampadas igniferas manibus retinentia dextris,
lumina nocturnis epulis ut suppeditentur,
nec domus argento fulget auroque renidet
nec citharae reboant laqueata aurataque templa,
cum tamen inter se prostrati in gramine molli
30 propter aquae rivum sub ramis arboris altae
non magnis opibus iucunde corpora curant,
praesertim cum tempestas arridet et anni
tempora conspergunt viridantis floribus herbas.
nec calidae citius decedunt corpore febres,
35 textilibus si in picturis ostroque rubenti
iacteris, quam si in plebeia veste cubandum est.
quapropter quoniam nil nostro in corpore gazae
proficiunt neque nobilitas nec gloria regni
quod superest, animo quoque nil prodesse putandum;
40 si non forte tuas legiones per loca campi
fervere cum videas belli simulacra cientis,
[43] ornatas\<que\> armis statuas pariterque animatas,
[42] subsidiis magnis et ecum vi constabilitas,
[43a] fervere cum videas classem lateque vagari,]
his tibi tum rebus timefactae religiones
45 effugiunt animo pavidae; mortisque timores
tum vacuum pectus linquunt curaque solutum.
quod si ridicula haec ludibriaque esse videmus,
re veraque metus hominum curaeque sequaces
nec metuunt sonitus armorum nec fera tela
50 audacterque inter reges rerumque potentis

versantur neque fulgorem reverentur ab auro
nec clarum vestis splendorem purpureai,
quid dubitas quin omni' sit haec rationi' potestas?
omnis cum in tenebris praesertim vita laboret.
55 nam veluti pueri trepidant atque omnia caecis
in tenebris metuunt, sic nos in luce timemus
interdum, nilo quae sunt metuenda magis quam
quae pueri in tenebris pavitant finguntque futura.
hunc igitur terrorem animi tenebrasque necessest
60 non radii solis neque lucida tela diei
discutiant, sed naturae species ratioque. (*DRN* 2.1-61)

Appropriately as a teacher Lucretius defines his terms
and underlines their importance through repetition (*suave
. . . iucunda voluptas . . . suave est; suave etiam . . . dulcius*, 1,
3, 4, 5, 7), facilitating his readers' understanding of the
problem by use of pastoral-idyllic imagery symbolic of their
withdrawal from the rigors of "normal" Roman patrician
life to view objectively, helped by the *doctrina sapientum* (8),
a way of life that guarantees freedom from *dolor, cura, metus*
and allows enjoyment of *mente . . . iucundo sensu* (18-19).[4]
By "honeying the cup"—*suave* (1) . . . *suave* (4) . . . *suave* (5)
. . . *dulcius* (7) also evoke the famous passage in 1.921-50
where, with *suaviloquenti carmine* (945-46), Lucretius
teaches important subjects (*magnis doceo de rebus*, 931) and
touches all *quasi musaeo dulci . . . melle* (947)—and treating
his readers gently as small boys (cf. 2.55-58 cited above), he

---

[4] Elder 89 comments on the didactic effect of repetition. Other repeated key words in this passage will be discussed later: *laborem* (2), *labore* (12), *laboret* (54); wealth and its trappings (*opes* [13], *aurea* [24], *argento* [27], *auroque* [27], *aurataque* [28], *ostroque rubenti* [35], *gazae* [37], *auro* [51], *vestis purpureai* [52]); *dolor* (18), *dolorem* (21); fear (*metuque* [19], *timefactae* [44], *timores* [45], *metus* [48], *metuunt* [49], *metuunt . . . timemus* [56], *metuenda* [57]); *cura* (19), *curaque* [46], *curaeque* [48]); noble birth, power (*nobilitate* [11], *rerumque potiri* [13], *nobilitas . . . gloria regni* [38], *reges rerumque potentis* [50]).

shows the benefits of learning the "truth"—no easy task in view of the fact that his "students," educated Romans of "reading" families, are of the very class whose normal activities (war, politics, family honor) are to be renounced if they are to benefit from the lessons Lucretius teaches here (cf. 2.1–2, 5–6, 9–13 above).[5] The lure is *iucunda voluptas* (3), *iucundo sensu* (19), enjoyed *iucunde* (31).

Lucretius' characterization of *voluptas* as *iucunda* and the repetition of *suave* (1, 4, 5) and *dulcius* (7) also recall the opening lines of Theocritus *Id.* 1 ('Αδύ τι τὸ ψιθύρισμα . . . ἀδύ δὲ καὶ τύ συρίσδες . . . ἄδιον, ὦ ποιμήν,τὸ τεὸν μέλος . . .) and underline the pastoral-idyllic quality and import of his message.[6] The contrast between the pastoral-idyllic "approved" life-style enjoyed by those who "dwell in calm heights well-secured by the teachings of the wise" (7–8) and those who pursue "epic" ways (*errare . . . viam palantis quaerere vitae . . . certare . . . contendere . . . niti . . . emergere . . . rerumque potiri* [9–13] evoke Odysseus' struggles; cf. also 40–43) establishes both a philosophical position, withdrawal from the political scene in order to view objectively life's real goals (17–19), and a poetic one, his determination to honey the cup of didactic with the "sweetness" of pastoral.[7]

----

[5] I take the addressee of the *DRN*, Memmius, to be the *nobilis* Gaius Memmius: see Bailey ad loc. 1.26. His career suggests the hazards of political life alluded to in the proem of Book 2 and later at 3.995–1002. He was praetor in 58 B.C., ran for the consulship in 54, lost in the election, and was sent into exile in 52. Ovid reports (*Tr.* 2.433) that he wrote erotic poems, perhaps a reason for Lucretius' inclusion of the diatribe on love. Whatever his character, he was an aristocrat and intellectual (i.e. he engaged in war, politics, and could read). Such an individual would typify Lucretius' (other) readers.

[6] Rosenmeyer 42–44 comments upon the strong affinities between Greek pastoral poetry and many aspects of Epicureanism. Betensky studies the pastoral element in Lucretius *DRN* 2.

[7] Cameron 458 notes that the bucolic poet rejects the traditional themes of epic, war and death.

Propertius in 1.10 acknowledges his stance as *praeceptor amoris* in these lines:

> possum ego diversos iterum coniungere amantis
> et dominae tardas possum aperire fores;
> et possum alterius curas sanare recentis,
> nec levis in verbis est medicina meis. (15–18)

The occasion for the poem is the poet's witnessing of the addressee's first encounter with his beloved, an event that has so entranced Propertius he cannot take his eyes away and is inspired to write this poem in response in order to advise the lover, Gallus, on appropriate courting behavior so that he may enjoy with greater frequency the benefits of love, such as they are (1.10.27–98):

> at quo sis humilis magis et subiectus amori,
> hoc magis effectu saepe fruare bono.

> (Cf. *ut qui . . . mente fruatur / iucundo sensu cura semota metuque* [*DRN* 2.17–19].)

Several features of the introductory passage evoke *DRN* 2.1–19:

> o iucunda quies, primo cum testis amori
> affueram vestris conscius in lacrimis!
> o noctem meminisse mihi iucunda voluptas,
> o quotiens votis illa vocanda meis,
> 5 cum te complexa morientem, Galle, puella
> vidimus et longa ducere verba mora!
> quamvis labentis premeret mihi somnus ocellos
> et mediis caelo Luna ruberet equis,
> non tamen a vestro potui secedere lusu:
> 10 tantus in alternis vocibus ardor erat. (1.10.1–10)

First of all, the triple repetition (*o iucunda quies . . . o . . .*

iucunda voluptas . . . o quotiens . . . vocanda, 1, 3, 4) evokes
Lucretius' *suave . . . iucunda voluptas . . . suave . . . suave*,
DRN 2.1, 3, 4, 5) as well as the exclamatory *o miseras
hominum mentis, o pectora caeca*! (2.14). Although Propertius'
scene is not pastoral like Lucretius' and *iucunda* suggests a
sexual element that is not of primary importance in *DRN*
2.1–19, 29–33, *iucunda quies* (1) and *iucunda voluptas* (3) do
evoke the pleasure of idyllic quietude affected by Lucretius
in 2.1–6, and, like *suave, iucunda*, and *dulcius* in the
Lucretius passage imply a similar allegiance to pastoral poetry (that is, here, poetry that eschews war and politics and
encourages *amicitia* on the part of the participants).[8] Benjamin has shown, too, that 1.10 appears to resemble
Catullus 50, where one poet "sees" (i.e., reads about it in
poetry on the subject: Scott) the *amores* of another poet and
cannot take away his eyes. As he reads the other's poetry,
he is inspired to stay up all night himself writing his own
poem in response, a scene resembling that involving the
cognoscenti in *DRN* 1.140–45, united in *sperata voluptas
suavis amicitiae*. Elsewhere it has been suggested that the
lover of the piece, Gallus, is meant to evoke the poet
Cornelius Gallus.[9] If so, the complimentary adjective,
iucunda, suggests approval not only of Gallus' new venture
in love but also of his love poetry, appropriate camaraderie
between two *amici* who are poets.

More important is the treatment of love that is suggested
by the evocation of *DRN* 2.3 in 1.10.3. For Lucretius
iucunda voluptas is the pleasure to be derived from observ-

[8] Propertius is known as a poet of the city where his mistress lives.
However, he does use pastoral motifs at various places in his work. 1.14
is a notable example where the river, trees, love theme, and general re-
pose evoke pastoral poetry. 1.5, also to Gallus, emphasizes the *amicitia*
of poet-lovers linked in the camaraderie of fellow sufferers, also a pastoral theme.

[9] King 1980 and Ross 83; contra, Fedeli 235.

ing from afar "the other man's trouble" (*alterius . . . laborem*, 2) and enjoying the scene *mente . . . iucundo sensu* (19) because you are not involved. *Miseras hominum mentes* (14) are the wretched politicians and strivers for wealth who are to be pitied. For Propertius *iucunda voluptas* derives from observing from the side-lines the *mala* of love: *lacrimis* (2), the victim "dying" (*morientem*, 5; cf. *DRN* 2.45), suffering speech impediments (*longa ducere verba mora*, 6), *dolores* (13; cf. *DRN* 2.18, 21), *curas* (17; cf. *DRN* 2.19, 46, 48), needing *medicina* (18), being *humilis, subiectus* (27), and never feeling free (*numquam vacuo pectore liber*, 30), that is, the *servitium amoris* that, like the role of *praeceptor*, is a distinctive feature of elegy.[10]

This impression of love as *dolor*, the condition Lucretius wants his reader(s) to avoid, is reinforced by another poem to Gallus, 1.5, where Propertius is even more outspoken on the miseries of love as he claims to have experienced it himself. Gallus, here a prospective rival for Cynthia's love, is addressed as *insane* (3), Propertius' love is characterized as *meos furores* (3), *ultima mala* (4; cf. *DRN* 2.4); the lover is *miser* (5; cf. *DRN* 2.14), walks through *ignis* (5), drinks *e tota toxica Thessalia* (6); the beloved causes *curarum milia quanta* (10; cf. *DRN* 2.19), described in more detail in 11–18 and including no sleep (11), no free use of one's eyes (11), sobs (14), *tremulus horror* with tears (15), *timor* (16; cf. *DRN* 2.45, 48, 56, 57, 59), and inability to speak (17). Worst of all, the lover loses his identity (18) and social status, since *servitium* (19) is the result for which *nobilitas* and *priscis imaginibus* (23–24) help not at all (cf. *DRN* 2.37–38). As a lover him-

---

[10] Copley 291 emphasizes the poetic significance attached to the motif and notes that it is a veritable "doctrine" of love omnipresent in Roman elegy that he ascribes to the elegists themselves (300). He sees no similar usage in Greek literature or in common Greek or Roman speech. He does cite a number of Alexandrian references to love as a "pain" (290 n. 19).

self, he is happy to embrace sympathetically a fellow suf-
ferer (*alter in alterius mutua flere sinu,* 30). Additional horrors of love are portrayed in 1.13, also to Gallus.[11]

The point is that Propertius takes up Lucretius' serious
attitude about the *mala* to be avoided in life by Epicurean
quietism and withdrawal and applies the *iucunda quies* to
love, the very *malum* theorically to be avoided—an attitude
that seems contrary to the very positive value he assigns to
love in 1.14,

>   Tu licet abiectus Tiberina molliter unda
>   Lesbia Mentoreo vina bibas opere,
>   et modo tam celeres mireris currere lintres
>   et modo tam tardas funibus ire ratis;
> 5 et nemus omne satas intendat vertice silvas,
>   urgetur quantis Caucasus arboribus;
>   non tamen ista meo valeant contendere amori:
>   nescit Amor magnis cedere divitiis.
>   nam sive optatam mecum trahit illa quietem,
> 10   seu facili totum ducit amore diem
>   tum mihi Pactoli veniunt sub tecta liquores,
>   et legitur Rubris gemma sub aequoribus;
>   tum mihi cessuros spondent mea gaudia reges:
>   quae maneant, dum me fata perire volent!
> 15 nam quis divitiis adverso gaudet Amore?
>   nulla mihi tristi praemia sint Venere!
>   illa potest magnas heroum infringere vires,
>   illa etiam duris mentibus esse dolor:
>   illa neque Arabium metuit transcendere limen
> 20   nec timet ostrino, Tulle, subire toro,
>   et miserum toto iuvenem versare cubili:
>   quid relevant variis serica textilibus?
>   quae mihi dum placata aderit, non ulla verebor
>   regna vel Alcinoi munera despicere.

---

[11] The *dolor* of love in 1.13: *nostro casu* (1), *perditus* (7), *tardis pallescere curis* (7), *toto vinctum . . . collo* (15), *demens . . . furor* (20), *periturus* (773).

Here, in a poem to the *nobilis* Tullus, a figure reminiscent of Lucretius' addressee Memmius, Propertius, as in 1.10, alters the pastoral tradition to suit his own purpose in the sense that he pictures an urban-"pastoral" landscape (1–6) as the place to appropriate for love (by contrast with Epicurean friendship) the epic power and value of wealth and employs Odyssean epic allusions (2, 24) to note, like Lucretius (*DRN* 2.9–13, elaborated in 2.20–28, 34–54), that riches alone fail to offer relief to the man in misery.[12] For Propertius, love can "break the great strength of heroes (*magnas heroum infringere vires*, 17), cause *dolor* to *duris mentibus* (18), has no fear (*neque . . . metuit*, 19) to cross an Arabian threshold, no dread (*nec timet*, 70) of climbing into the wealthy man's bed and under "the purple coverlet" (*ostrino . . . toro*, 70). No matter how rich he is, the victim becomes "poor," a *miserum iuvenem* (21). *Serica* (22), silk sheets, do not help at all. The ills suffered by the lover thus resemble greatly those endured by Lucretius' rich and famous (*DRN* 2.24–28, 34–52).[13] The poor man who devotes

[12] King 1982 on 1.14. Tullus is probably the nephew of L. Volcacius Tullus, consul with Octavian in 33 B.C. and proconsul of Asia in 30–29 B.C. (cf. 1.6.19–20). Poems to Tullus frame the book as a whole (1.1, 22) as well as the central panels (1.6, 14) with an emphasis on Propertius' own dedication to Cynthia (1) and the reason for his adoption of a life devoted to love alone, revulsion at the consequences of the civil war (22), an attitude that contrasts dramatically with Tullus' traditionally honorable career of provincial civil servant (6) and way of life befitting ancestral wealth (14). See King 1975–76, 1982, Nethercut, and Putnam.

[13] Much in 1.14 evokes *DRN* 2.1–61: the *locus amoenus: abiectus Tiberina molliter unda* (1.14.1); cf. *prostrati in gramine molli / propter aquae rivum* (*DRN* 2.29–30); *et nemus omne satas intendat vertice silvas / urgetur quantis Caucasus arboribus* (1.14.5–6; cf.*sub ramis arboris altae* (*DRN* 2.30); Love breaks the strength of great heroes (1.14.17); cf. fear does not surrender to kings and the lords of the world (*DRN* 2.48–50); without love, who can rejoice in wealth? (1.14.15); cf. jewels, noble rank, power have nothing to do with the well-being of the body or soul

his life to love at least enjoys the "wealth" that comes to him when love is "kind" (11–13). His conclusion is repudiation of material wealth exemplified by "the gifts of Alcinoüs," Homer's epic symbol of kingly power and the riches that come from commerce, a neatly contrived reminiscence of Tullus' interests in 1.14.3–4, where he watches the river traffic on the Tiber, a chief source of Rome's wealth. We may note as well Propertius' option for love in 1.19.25–26:

> quare, dum licet, inter nos laetemur amantes:
> non satis est ullo tempore longus amor.

and the reasons implied in 1.21–22 for a "career" in love/ love-poetry in the face of civil war.[14]

We must note that the horrors of love that Propertius pictures in 1.5, 10, and 13 to Gallus (and in 1.14 to Tullus) resemble in many details Lucretius' portrayal in Books 3 and 4. For example, in 3.992–94, Tityos, devoured by vultures, is the man *in amore iacentem* (992), eaten by *anxius angor* (993), and torn by *quavis cuppedine curae* (994), a picture supplemented by the famous diatribe on love and the *remedia amoris* in 4.1058–1191, where Lucretius gives full details about lovers who are never satisfied, essentially Propertius' picture as well of frustration and dissatisfaction but inability to withdraw from the situation, the thought behind the concluding advice in 1.10:

(*DRN* 2.37–39); *ostrino . . . toro, variis serica textilibus* (1.14.20, 22); cf. *fulgorem . . . ab auro / nec clarum vestis splendorem purpureai* (*DRN* 2.51–52).

[14] Nethercut 470–72, Putnam 107, 122–23; cf. Prop. 2.1.17–38. This topic becomes the chief theme of Latin love-elegy as practiced by Tibullus and Ovid in the *Amores*: see Conte 42–43 and his discussion of how Ovid ends the practice in his *Remedia Amoris*, also derived from Lucretius' treatment of the subject in 4.1063–77.

at quo sis humilis magis et subiectus amori
  hoc magis effectu saepe fruare bono.
is poterit felix una remanere puella,
  qui numquam vacuo pectore liber erit. (1.10.27-30)

The sad picture of the lover in *DRN* 3.992-94 is juxta-
posed to that of the politician who, as *alter Sisyphos*, is always seeking power that is never attained and endures always *durum laborem* (999), the very picture the poet op-
poses to *iucunda voluptas* in 2.2, 5, 9-13 (and in more detail
in 37-46).[15] Lucretius thus in his work pictures both the
lover and the politician in a Hell on earth and opts for a
policy of withdrawal from such pursuits as the way to happiness. By acknowledging the hell love imposes on a man at
the same time that he makes it of first importance in his
own life—and despite the irony seen throughout the
Monobiblos, this is the net result of the book as a whole,
summarized in such passages as 1.14.8, 13, 23-24 and
1.19.25-26, cited above—Propertius shows, through the depiction of the utter misery of his choice, the depth of the
personal necessity that occasioned it, the need for close
personal relationships in an atmosphere of *quies* to offset
the effects of the civil war (1.21-22) and for a kind of poetry suited to this subject-matter.[16] Similarly Lucretius plays
on the sexual implications of *voluptas* in 1.29-40 when

[15] Political ambition is the butt of Lucretius' attack also at 3.59-64
and 5.1120-35.

[16] King 1975-76, 119-23. These ideas are also expressed and reaf-
firmed in the explicit and programmatic introduction to Book 2, where
the mistress is his *maxima historia* (2.1.5-16) and preferable to *Mutinam
aut civilia busta Philippos* (97). Here Propertius argues that *amores* are a
reasonable alternative to epic poetry, which he refuses to write, because
it represents a life-style that is itself *dura*, a literary key-word for epic
poetry and the way of life it represents. See also Wiggers and Kühn on
2.1. Commager 37-77 shows the antipolitical nature of Propertius' poetry.

Venus Genetrix, symbolic mother of the Roman race, *hominum divumque voluptas* (1.1), is urged to seduce Mars, god of war, in order that an enduring peace for Rome might be effected (*fera moenera militiai . . . sopita quiescant,* 1.29–30), an emphatic appeal by the poet for peace (= personal happiness) as a social ideal (1.1, 2.3).

Quinn 144–47 briefly asserts that Lucretius killed the Catullan tradition of "serious" love poetry by reducing the whole experience to a form of insanity, thereby undercutting the concept of love as a *foedus* expected to grow through mutual understanding and fidelity.[17] Propertius, however, picks up the challenge of treating love as a serious subject for poetry. He accepts Lucretius' *dicta* on the subject and chooses love anyway, acknowledging its madness (*nullo vivere consilio,* 1.1.6), for reasons implicit at least in 1.21–22, aversion to the life-style that has brought death and destruction to Italy. And not only does he choose love as his "career," he also becomes its *praeceptor,* like Lucretius, in his description of love and the *mala* it entails. *Dolor* though it can be, *amor* is, nevertheless, his recipe for happiness.

The following general conclusions may be reached. Lucretius' evident sincerity and serious attitude about the efficacy of Epicureanism in providing *voluptas* to his student-reader(s) lends an aura of utilitarianism and serious purpose to Propertius' admittedly anti-political and, therefore, by Roman standards, counter-cultural and even frivolous approach to poetry. He is following in the footsteps of a great predecessor, the *praeceptor naturae.* As *praeceptor amoris* he elaborates upon, and modifies somewhat, but does not radically change, attitudes towards love presented by Lucretius, only the advice concerning it. The message is

---

[17] Dalzell 1973, 98 remarks on the difficulty of deciding whether Lucretius borrowed from Catullus or vice versa. Both poets had an important influence on later poetry.

clear: love is degrading, a form of madness, involving pain, mental anguish, loss of wealth and reputation, a state of degradation akin to *servitium*. Even though Lucretius does not use the word *servitium* in connection with love, the picture of slavery in love (e.g., in 1.5) may well have been developed by Propertius from *DRN* 4.1063–67, where, set on one love, the lover insists on *servare sibi curam certumque dolorem* (1067).

Lucretius' use of a specific addressee, Memmius, needing instruction in Epicureanism and the virtues of a life-style apart from politics may well have been the inspiration for Propertius' use of addressees like Tullus, a civil servant (1.1, 6, 14, 22, 3.22), Gallus, love-poet and civil servant (1.5, 10, 13, 20, 21), Ponticus, epic poet (1.7, 9), and Bassus, iambic poet (1.4), to illustrate attitudes opposed to his own.[18] Antagonistic addressees personalize the message, affording opportunities for instruction and example, all in the name of *amicitia*, Lucretius' rationale for "spreading (his) bright light" (*DRN* 1.141, 144).

Lucretius' inclusion of love as a topic on which he gives specific instruction in his teaching on how to achieve happiness may very well have served to influence Propertius to take up the idea and use it as the foundation for his own original discourse on *voluptas*, which features love, with all its *curae, dolores, furor, ignis, labores*, and *mala*, as man's alternative to the quality of life suffered in the preceding period of civil war, a point of view that echoes Lucretius' advice to Memmius in 2.1–61 and elsewhere. For Propertius to respond to Lucretius' challenge by choosing love despite its pitfalls only underlines for his readers the desperate quality

[18] For Gallus, see King 1980. Tullus and Ponticus are as described in the poetry about them. Suits accepts the identification of Bassus with the iambic poet mentioned by Ovid at *Tr.* 4.10.47–48 and remarks on the iambic nature of 1.4. Abel discusses the antagonistic purpose of the addressees.

of his decision. We must keep in mind, too, that for
Lucretius Love (*Venus Genetrix*) makes the world go round
and brings *voluptas* to men and gods (1.1).[19] On a practical
human level long-term love (*consuetudo*) is no deterrent to
happiness and may even benefit (*quod superest, consuetudo
concinnat amorem, DRN* 4.1283-87). Propertius, for his part,
recommends keeping to one love: *sua quemque moretur/cura,
neque assueto mutet amore locum* (1.1.35-36).

Lucretius, the great amagalmator of literary sources from
Homer to Catullus and observer of life around him, system-
atized the language of love and the picture of physical pain,
mental anguish, and degradation suffered by the lover.[20]
Thus in the development of love elegy from its Hellenic/
Hellenistic antecedents to Propertius, Lucretius must be
seen as an important and influential intermediary.

We do not see Catullus acting as *praeceptor*, although we do
see him in the role of lover suffering the *mala* and *dolores*
described by Lucretius. There is no hint that Gallus played
such a role either. We do have Propertius' full-scale presentation of *praecepta*, especially in the *Monobiblos* but reflected throughout the corpus, based in large part on those
outlined by Lucretius. These become the foundation of
"personal love-elegy."

Propertius shows his debt to Lucretius through the use of
specific key words and phrases.[21] In addition, Lucretius'

---

[19] For *voluptas* in love: *DRN* 4.1075, 4.1081, 4.1085, 4.1201, 4.1208;
cf. Prop. 1.10.3; for *gaudia* in love: *DRN* 4.1106, 1206; cf. 1.4.14,
1.8B.29, 1.12.18, 1.13.24, 1.14.13. Brown 196-97 discusses Lucretius'
attitude.

[20] Lucretius' poetic sources have been collected extensively in the
editions of Leonard and Smith and Merrill and discussed by Kenney
1977, 10-16, who cites especially Homer, Hesiod, Aratus, Callimachus,
Empedocles, Cicero, Euripides, Hellenistic epigram (especially
Meleager), and Ennius. Wormell notes Lucretius' reactions to contemporary society and love poetry (e.g., Catullus).

[21] Definitions for love shared by Lucretius (*DRN* 3.984-94, 4.1058-

forceful picture of the lover as a veritable Tityos lying prostrate in Hell, tortured by vultures (*DRN* 3.984, 992) is reflected in Propertius' poetry (cf. *inter Tityi volucres mea poena vagetur*, 2.20.31) as is the use of *iacere* to signify the lover's degradation.[22] In 1.1 alone, Propertius' program poem, many key words evoke their use by Lucretius and make very clear Propertius' acceptance of Lucretius' position that love is *amara, cura, furor, ignis, labor*, etc. and the lover is "wounded" by it but is enchained and must remain faithful to Venus regardless of these circumstances.[23]

1287 and Propertius (in the *Monobiblos*) include the following: *ardor*: *DRN* 4.1077, 4.1086, 4.1116, 4.1216/1.3.13, 1.7.94, 1.10.10, 1.13.28; *cupido*: *DRN* 4.1090, 4.1138, 4.1153/1.1.2: *curae*: *DRN* 3.994, 4.1060/ 1.1.36, 1.5.10, 1.10.17, 1.13.7, 1.18.23 et.al.; *dolores*: *DRN* 3.990, 4.1067, 4.1079/1.7.7, 1.9.7, 1.10.13 et al.; *furor*: *DRN* 4.1069, 4.1117/1.1.7, 1. 4.11, 1.5.3, 1.13.20; *ignis*: *DRN* 4.1138/1.5.5, 1.6.7, 1.9.17, 1.11.7; *labores*: *DRN* 4.1121/1.6.23; *mala*: *DRN* 4.1119, 4.1141, 4.1159/1.1.35, 1.5.4, 1.5.28, 1.7.14. Their lovers are *miseri*: *DRN* 4.1076/1.5.5, 18 et al., suffer wounds in/for love (*vulnus*): *DRN* 4.1120/1.1.13, 2.12.12; they perish (*pereo*): *DRN* 4.1121, 4.1136/1.6.27, 1.9.34, 1.13.33, 1.15.41.

[22] The key words in Lucretius' description (*volucres, iacere, perferre, dolorem*) figure as well in Propertius 1.6.25, 1.9.3, 1.16.23, 1.18.25–26, 2.17.5–10. In 3.3.31 Lucretius' birds become *Veneris dominae volucres, mea turba, columbae.*

[23] *Capere, oculi, sani/miseri*: 1.1.1: Cynthia prima suis miserum me cepit ocellis . . .
1.1.26: quaerite non sani pectoris auxilia.
cf. *DRN* 4.1075–76: nam certe purast sanis magis inde
voluptas / quam miseris.
4.1078: nec constat quid primum oculis manibusque fruantur.
4.1090: tam magis ardescit dira cuppedine pectus.
4.1147–48: non ita difficile est quam captum retibus ipsis
exire et validos Veneris perrumpere nodos.
cf. 4.1159, 1179
cura, cupido; contingere: 1.1.2: (me) contactum nullis ante cupidinibus.
1.1.35–36: . . . sua quemque moretur
cura, neque assueto mutet amore locum.
cf. *DRN* 3.994: aut alia quavis scindunt cuppedine curae; cf. 4.1090

Add to these parallels the number of poems, or parts of
poems that appear to be inspired by suggestions made by

4.1057: namque voluptatem praesagit muta cupido; cf. 4.1138,
    4.1153
4.1060: stillavit gutta et successit frigida cura; cf. 4.1067
4.1118: cum sibi quid cupiant ipsi contingere quaerunt . . . .
furor: 1.1.7: et mihi iam toto furor hic non deficit anno . . . .
cf. *DRN* 4.1069: inque dies gliscit furor atque aerumna gravescit . . .
    4.1117: inde redit rabies eadem et furor ille revisit . . . .
adverso: 1.1.8: adversos cogor habere deos.
cf. *DRN* 4.1142–44: in adverso vero atque inopi sunt,
                prendere quae possis oculorum lumine operto,
                innumerabilia;
labor: 1.1.9–10: Milanion nullos fugiendo, Tulle, labores
           saevitiam durae contudit Iasidos.
cf. *DRN* 4.1099: sed laticum simulacra petit frustraque laborat . . .
    1121: Adde quod absumunt viris pereuntque labore . . . .
saucius, vulnus: 1.1.13–14: ille etiam Hylaei percussus vulnere rami
    saucius . . . ingemuit.
cf. *DRN* 4.1048: idque petit corpus, mens unde est saucia amore.
    1049: namque omnes plerumque cadunt in vulnus . . . .;
    cf. 1070, 1120
noscere: 1.1.18: nec meminit notas, ut prius, ire vias.
cf. *DRN* 4.1206: quod facerent numquam nisi mutua gaudia nossent
    . . . .
convertere mentem, alio, alia (as remedy for love):
    1.1.21–22: en agedum dominae mentem convertite nostrae. . . . ;
cf. *DRN* 4.1064: . . . . (decet) alio convertere mentem . . . .
ignis: 1.1.27: fortiter et ferrum saevos patiemur et ignes . . . .;
cf. *DRN* 4.1138: quod cupido adfixum cordi vivescit ut ignis . . . .
amarus, Venus nobis, nostra Venus: 1.1.33: in me nostra Venus noctes
    exercet amaras . . . .
cf. *DRN* 4.1058: Haec Venus est nobis; hinc / autemst nomen amoris
    . . .
    4.1133–34: . . . quoniam medio de fonte leporum
            surgit amari aliquid quod in ipsis floribus angat . . .
    4.1185: nec Veneres nostras hoc fallit.
malum: 1.1.35: hoc, moneo, vitate malum.
cf. *DRN* 4.1119: nec reperire malum id possunt quae machina
    vincat:

Lucretius. I mention the following, but the list is not exhaustive (and influences other than Lucretius' may also be present in these same poems):

1.1.9–16: Milanion, the *saucius amator* (cf. *DRN* 4.1048: *idque petit corpus, mens unde est saucia amore*)

1.3: sensation, enjoyment from eyes, hands (cf. *DRN* 4.1078: *nec constat quid primum oculis manibusque fruantur*)

1.4: no *vagae puellae* for Propertius (cf. *DRN* 4.1070–79: si non prima novis conturbes vulnera plagis vulgivagaque vagus Venere ante recentia cures aut alio possis animi traducere motus)

1.5: *servitium amoris* (as discussed above on *DRN* 4.1063–67)

1.6: public service vs. love (cf. *DRN* 2.1–61, the advice to Memmius to seek *iucunda voluptas* elsewhere than in politics, war)

1.10: *iucunda voluptas* (cf. *DRN* 2.1–61)

1.13: enslavement to one only (cf. *DRN* 4.1066–67)

4.1141–42: Atque in amore mala haec proprio summeque secundo / inveniuntur:
4.1159: nec sua respiciunt miseri mala maxima saepe.
frui amore / vitare amorem: 1.1.35–36: hoc, moneo, vitate malum.
cf. *DRN* 4.1073: nec Veneris fructu caret is qui vitat amorem . . . .
4.1146: nam vitare, plagas in amoris ne iaciamur . . . .
unus amor: 1.1.35–36: . . . . sua quemque moretur
cura, neque assueto mutet amore locum.
cf. *DRN* 4.1066–67: nec retinere, semel conversum unius amore,
et servare sibi curam certumque dolorem.
dolor: 1.1.38: heu referet quanto verba dolore mea!
cf. *DRN* 4.1067: et servare sibi curam certumque dolorem;
cf. 1079
These parallels are multiplied throughout Books 1–3.

1.14: *liquores*, the "waters" of love (e.g., 1.14.11: *tum mihi Pactoli veniunt sub tecta liquores*) (cf. *DRN* 4.1113–14: usque adeo cupide in Veneris compagibus haerent, membra voluptatis dum vi labefacta liquescunt)

1.15: misinterpretation of words and actions (cf. *DRN* 4.1137–40)

1.16: *exclusus amator* (cf. *DRN* 4.1177–79)

2.9: suspicion of beloved (cf. *DRN* 4. 1139–40)

2.12: the wounds of love (cf. *DRN* 4.1048–50)

2.15: constancy of the lover (cf. *DRN* 4.1063–67)

2.17: the lover's pains compared with Tantalus', Sisyphus' (cf. *DRN* 3.980–83, 995–1002)

2.20: Propertius' infidelity should be punished with Tityos' penalty (cf. *DRN* 3.992–94)

2.23: Propertius, the *vulgivagus* (cf. *DRN* 4.1070–72)

3.5: Love, god of peace (cf. *DRN* 1.1–49)

Propertius tells us in 3.5.23–48 that, when old age has put a stop to love (*Venerem . . . interceperit*, 23), then he will "learn the ways of Nature" (25) as an alternative to participation in war. The *Monobiblos* suggests considerable previous familiarity with Lucretius' version of the subject.

Works Cited

Abel, W. 1930. *Die Anredeformen bei den römischen Elegikern.* Berlin.

Allen, A. W. 1950. "Elegy and the Classical Attitude Toward Love: Propertius I,1." *YCS* 11:255–77.

Bailey, C. 1947. *Titi Lucreti Cari De Rerum Natura Libri Sex.* 3 vols. Oxford.

Barber, E. A. 1960². *Sexti Properti Carmina*. Oxford.

Benjamin, A. S. 1965. "A Note on Propertius 1.10: *O Iucunda Quies*." *CP* 60:178.

Betensky, A. 1976. "A Lucretian Version of Pastoral." *Ramus* 5:45–58.

Brown, R. D. 1987. *Lucretius on Love and Sex*. Leiden, New York, København and Köln.

Cameron, A. 1995. *Callimachus and His Critics*. Princeton.

Commager, S. 1974. *A Prolegomenon to Propertius*. Cincinnati.

Conte, G. B. 1994. *Genres and Readers: Lucretius, Love Elegy, Pliny's Encyclopedia*. Tr. G. Most. Baltimore and London.

Copley, F. O. 1947. "*Servitium Amoris* in the Roman Elegists." *TAPA* 78:285–300.

Dalzell, A. 1973. "A Bibliography of Work on Lucretius, 1945–1972." *CW* 66:389–427; 67:65–112.

Day, A. A. 1938. *The Origins of Latin Love-Elegy*. Oxford.

Elder, J. P. 1954. "Lucretius 1.1–49." *TAPA* 85:88–120.

Enk, P. J. 1946. *Sex. Propertii Elegiarum Liber 1 (Monobiblos)*. 2 vols. Leiden.

Fedeli, P. 1981. "Elegy and Literary Polemic in Propertius' *Monobiblos*." *PLLS* 3:227–42.

Kenney, E. J. 1970. "Doctus Lucretius." *Mnemosyne* 23:366–92.

———. 1977. *Lucretius*. Greece and Rome. New Surveys in the Classics 11. Oxford.

King, J. K. 1975–1976. "Propertius' Programmatic Poetry and the Unity of the *Monobiblos*." *CJ* 71:108–24.

———. 1980. "The Two Galluses of Propertius' *Monobiblos*." *Philologus* 124:212–30.

———. 1982. "Propertius 1.14: The Epic Power and Value of Love." *CW* 75:329–39.

Kühn, J. H. 1961. "Die Prooimion-Elegie des zweiten Properz-Buches." *Hermes* 89:84–105.

Leonard, W. E. and S. B. Smith. 1942. *T. Lucreti Cari: De Rerum Natura: Libri Sex.* Madison.

Merrill, W. A. 1907. *T. Lucreti Cari De Rerum Natura Libri Sex.* New York, Cincinnati and Chicago.

Nethercut, W. R. 1971. "The ΣΦΡΑΓΙΣ of the *Monobiblos*." *AJP* 92:464–72.

Putnam, M. C. J. 1976. "Propertius 1.22: A Poet's Self-Definition." *QUCC* 23:93–123.

Quinn, K. 1963. *Latin Explorations: Critical Studies in Roman Literature.* London.

Ross, D. O., Jr. 1975. *Backgrounds to Augustan Poetry: Gallus, Elegy and Rome.* Cambridge, London, New York and Melbourne.

Scodel, R. S. and R. F. Thomas. 1984. "Virgil and the Euphrates," *AJP* 105:339.

Scott, W. C. 1969. "Catullus and Calvus (Cat. 50)." *CP* 64:169–73.

Suits, T. A. 1976. "The Iambic Character of Propertius 1.4." *Philologus* 120:86–91.

Wheeler, A. L. 1910. "Propertius as *Praeceptor Amoris*." *CP* 5:28–40.

———. 1910–1911. "Erotic Teaching in Roman Elegy and the Greek Sources." *CP* 5:440–50; 6:56–77.

Wiggers, N. 1977. "Reconsideration of Propertius II.2." *CJ* 72:334–41.

Wormell, D. E. W. 1965. "The Personal World of Lucretius." In *Lucretius.* Ed. D. R. Dudley. London. 35–67.

Domitianic Construction at Cumae (Campania)

Alexander G. McKay

"The shoreline and waving forests are stirring, the din travels far and wide through the communities that lie between . . . and grape-bearing Massicus throws back to Gaurus the echo that is splintered on every side. Relaxed Cumae marvels at the noise, so does the marsh at Liternum and the sluggish Savo."

. . .

"But whom do I see, white-haired and white-ribboned, at the far end of the new road, where Apollo shows antique Cumae? Does my vision deceive me, or is the Sibyl bringing out Chalcidic bayleaves from her sacred grottoes?"

Statius, *Silvae* 4.3.61–66; 114–18

Before the Flavians turned their attention to Cumae and the Campi Phlegraei, Rome had already witnessed the power and glory of their grandiose buildings, massive reconstructions and repairs, and had great expectations for what was to come: the Colosseum, Forum Transitorium, Temple of Peace, Baths of Titus, and Temple to the Deified

223

Vespasian were first and foremost; Domitian's personal projects included the lavishly reconstructed Temple of Jupiter Optimus Maximus on the Capitoline, the Temple of Jupiter Tonans, the Temple of the Gens Flavia on the Esquiline, Forum Transitorium and Temples of Minerva, restored Temple of Isis and Serapis, and a completely rebuilt Forum of Julius Caesar, a rebuilt Curia, Porticus Divorum, Stadium and Odeum in the Campus Martius, the reconstructed Domus Tiberiana on the Palatine, and his own Domus Augustiana, overlooking the Circus Maximus and the Forum Romanum. Its public space offered a basilica, reception hall, triclinium and shrine to the Lares, an extensive courtyard with garden pool and a state dining hall paved in marble. For visitors and sightseers approaching from the Forum Romanum and the Velia, the palace facade, ennobled by a pediment and columns, marked superior housing for a divinity, and *Dominus et Deus* was not incidentally a preferred designation for Domitian. All of these, and many others, challenged the scale and diversity of the Augustan program.[1] A constant influx of masters and craftsmen from the Eastern Mediterranean must have serviced the Flavian programs which verged on pharaonic proportions. Rabirius was Domitian's architect, but the emperor doubtless influenced the overall design and "Greek architectural forms . . . suited Domitian's view of his position as emperor, colored as it was with the tints of Hellenistic kingship."[2]

Flavian buildings in Campania and in the Campi Phlegraei were equally impressive and diversified.[3] The eruption of Vesuvius in A.D. 79 was the occasion for an out-

---

[1] On Flavian Rome and Domitian's projects, consult: Robathan 130–44; MacKendrick 224–50; Anderson 1981, 41–48; 1983, 93–105; and 1984; Jones 82–96 (a list of buildings).

[2] Stambaugh 74.

[3] Cf. D'Arms 99–103.

pouring of imperial largesse, spirited compensatory measures, and personal intervention. Titus came twice to survey the ravaged cities under Vesuvius and spent his energy in Naples supervising the activities of a specially appointed commission: *curatores restituendae Campaniae.*[4] Domitian followed suit with massive public works programs and religious and secular building. Motives were no doubt diverse and complex. Economic recovery and a quick-start to depressed communities, damaged by the eruption of A.D. 79, must have been involved. But there were emotional, propagandistic aspects, too. The Flaming Fields enshrined the legendary zone of the Gigantomachy, in its Italian dispensation, a locale where the Olympians with the help of Hercules scotched the Giants' attempt to displace them, where thunderbolts rained on the powers of barbarity, of darkness and chaos and left steaming, sulphurous craters as memorials. [5] Domitian's alliance with Jupiter, Juno, and Minerva enabled him to assume the role of Jupiter's viceregent on earth, with the Cyclopean thunderbolt as hallmark,[6] particularly after the defeat of the villainous Chatti and Geti . A new mythology was impressed on the popular mind.[7] Apollo had been Octavian's saviour; but Jupiter was the Flavian redeemer and protector of the New Order, a reawakened golden age of peace and prosperity. The charismatic emperor saw himself as Jove's viceroy; his reconstruction of Rome's Capitolium and the institution of quadrennial Capitoline Games (Suet. *Dom.* 4), featuring competitions in music, public speaking, horsemanship and gymnastics, (Statius, *Silvae* 5, 2, 23) were token of his pious

---

[4] Suet. *Titus* 8.3.4; Dio 66.23; 24.3.

[5] For the topography: Diod. Sic. 4.21.5–7; Sil. Ital. *Punica* 12.133–46; for political implications of the Gigantomachy, consult Hardie.

[6] For numismatic evidence and the implications of Jove's thunderbolt as Domitian's weapon, see: Fears 1981, "The Cult of Jupiter."

[7] Cf. Fears 1975, 8.

allegiance. When Apollo's Sibyl salutes the completion of the Via Domitiana and its terminus at Cumae, she extols the Emperor's supernatural, viceregal, beneficent power over Mankind and Nature:

> "See! a god is he, by Jupiter's command he rules the happy lands in his stead; none worthier than he has taken up these reins since under my guidance Aeneas, eager to know the future, entered the prescient groves of Avernus and left them again. He is a friend to peace and fearsome in arms, more bountiful than Nature and more powerful." (Statius, *Silvae* 4.3.128-35)

Statius' verses surely echo the proletariate's enthusiasm in the Sibyl's encomium, particularly in the Flaming Fields and notably at Cumae. *Si monumenta requiris, circumspice:* a magnificent new Temple of the Capitoline Triad, a triumphal arch and fountain house, a Temple of Deified Vespasian and Titus, a Basilica, a Curia, renovated Central Baths, an enhanced Crypta Romana, an updated Isis Temple complex, improved harbour facilities, an urban renewal program with new streets and porticoes, Curia and civic offices, city gates, a new highway with a grandiose arch (Arco Felice), an enlarged amphitheatre, and new Temple alongside.[8] Augustus attuned his patronage and energies to Cumae's acropolis and defenses, redesigning the Apollo Temple on the lower terrace to accommodate the Palatine triad of Latona, Apollo and Diana, and reviving the Portus Cumanus and providing a tunnel through the acropolis which would cope with traffic to and from the harbor, with another tunnel driven through Mons Grillus to Lake Avernus, both designed to guarantee the security and efficacy of Cumae's havens on the Tyrrhenian and the

---

[8] Cf. Caputo 148-63, 168-76.

grandiose new facility of Portus Julius.[9] Domitian's programme no doubt included repairs and reconditioning on the acropolis and in the Cumaean port, but generally speaking the Forum area below was favored. The triumviral Crypta Romana was monumentalised with an eye-catching vestibule, furnished with four overhead niches doubtless to accommodate Flavian worthies: Vespasian, Titus, Domitian and Domitilla.

Completion of the Via Domitiana on the eve of Domitian's death was integrated with the building program at Cumae. Statius' daytime travel through the Campanian landscape, orchestrated with the cacophany of construction work, differs markedly from Vergil's magical night voyage from Cumae to the Tiber, a haunting barcarole, with a complex of night effects and an eerie transition into dawn as the ships of the Aeneadae approach the Tiber and the landing below Ostia. Domitian's Highway was a welcome alternative to the often tempest-tossed passage by sea, or the bruising trials of the passage by land along the Via Appia, the mosquito-ridden passage through the Pomptine Marshes, and the trek from Sinuessa to Cumae through the sand dunes and swamps of the coastal route.

The new highway signalled Flavian concern, paternalistic and commercial, for the antique territory of the Flaming Fields, and for the venerable communities whose prosperity had suffered somewhat with the eruption of Vesuvius in A.D. 79. Damage from the volcanic fallout, dislocations and ruined properties, lost markets and loss of life, abandoned homes and markets, and interrupted trade, called for emergency aid and decisive response by the imperial house.

[9] For the acropolis temples, Portus Julius, Octavian, Agrippa and architect engineer L. Cocceius Auctus: Paget 166–69; Frederiksen 333–36; Caputo 87–92. For the tunnels, Crypta Romana and "Grotto of Cocceius": Amalfitano 294–98; Caputo 132–38, 169–71.

Titus[10] adopted serious relief measures: the administrators designated to meet the emergency undertook to resettle displaced homeowners on the properties of lost, intestate citizens, and provided cash subventions to individuals and corporations to restart their trades and professional activities. Naples probably saw Titus at least twice during A.D. 79 and 80 when the major recovery operations were under way. The populace and the institutions of the Campi Phlegraei communities, Cumae, Misenum, Puteoli, and Baiae were all indebted to the Imperial largesse. Misenum's Shrine of the Augustales signals the popularity of the dynasty: a yield of marble statues, heroized versions of Vespasian and Titus, and a spectacular charging equestrian bronze of Domitian, "reconditioned" after Domitian's *damnatio memoriae* to resemble Nerva.[11]

Cumae's prosperity and prestige, concerns of Augustus and Agrippa in time past, were obviously Flavian priorities. The arterial support was the Highway. Statius' fervor for Domitian's achievement in the peacetime, ravaged and undernourished confines of the Phlegraean Fields, matches the emperor's role as victor over a resistant, sometimes personified Nature with that of the conqueror of foreign foes. The Campanian Gigantomachy, the Herculean role of Domitian as Jove's ally, and his dedication to Campania's recovery after the volcanic onslaught, must have been closely allied in the popular imagination.

The new highway, linking Sinuessa (Mondragone) with Puteoli, was opened in A.D. 95. Before this, Rome's contact by highway with Puteoli was mildly tortuous. The Via Appia proceeded as far as Sinuessa, then turned inland to Capua; a branch highway, the Via Consularis Campana, diverged en route to Puteoli. Cumae, and the other coastal cities,

[10] Titus' remedial measures in Campania: Jones 160–62.
[11] For the Sacellum at Miseno and the equestrian bronze of Domitian/Nerva: Amalfitano 254–60.

had to rely on a deteriorating, hazardous road that traversed the marshy flatland of the Savo, Volturnus and Clanis rivers. Domitian's highway progressed from Aquae Sinuessanae across the Volturnus river and along the shore to the Savo river heading towards Miliarium XII at Volturnum (Castelvolturno); after crossing the Volturnus river on an arched bridge, it continued to Liternum (Miliarium XXIV), crossed the emissarium of Lago di Patria (Giugliano), continued between the Silva Gallinaria and reclaimed Lago di Licola, to Cumae (Miliarium XXX), entering the city from the north. Its city circuit passed alongside the later Antonine Baths, the Domitianic Capitolium, along the South Porticus to the municipal buildings at the Forum's east end, and exited at the Arco Felice. Thereafter the highway skirted Lake Avernus in the direction of Puteoli. A branch road at Croce di Cuma linked Cumae with Misenum.[12]

There were earlier precedents for Domitian's conquest of natural obstacles and regional improvements. Caligula's headstrong antics in the bay of Baiae had turned sea into land with a bridge of boats that rivalled Xerxes' bridge at the Dardanelles; torches and fires that illuminated Caligula's "triumphal" bridge turned night into day.[13] Nero's grand design, thwarted by his death, to provide an inland waterway from the Portus Julius to Ostia was meant to compete with Darius' cuttings through the Phlegraean promontories of the Chalcidike.[14]

[12] For the Highway, eulogized by Statius, *Silvae* 4.3: consult Coleman 1988, 13–21, 102–35; troublefree access to Cumae and the Phlegraean Fields, see Caputo 116–17; Clark 230 (map).

[13] Caligula's A.D. 39 spectacle: Dio 59.17.1–11; Suet. *Gaius* 19; D'Arms 90–91. Frederiksen (Purcell) 336: "This display was directed to some extent at oriental hostages who might be awed by the magnificence and populousness of Campania."

[14] Nero's A.D. 65–68 canal project: Tacitus, *Ann.* 15.42.2, 4; Suet. *Nero* 31.3; Statius, *Silvae* 4.3.7–8; D'Arms 98; Griffin 107–8; *Fossa*

Domitian's highway, like Aeneas' passage through the Avernian underworld, was marked by two monumental gates, "triumphal" arches: the first at Aquae Sinuessanae at the approach to the Volturnus bridge, the other at the cutting through Mons Grillus at Cumae. Statius evokes the Sibyl as welcoming "spirit" with triumphal laurel (her Apolline hallmark) at the coastal road's terminus. Thereafter the traveller could leave Caesar's Palace (Domus Augustiana) at dawn and, by accelerated stages, within fourteen hours witness the sunset behind the acropolis at Cumae.[15]

Statius' extended description of the entrance arch over the Volturnus river highlights its paraphernalia: bronze trophies of captured weapons and armor from the Chatti and Daci, and doubtless a cuirassed portrait of the Emperor, armed with a thunderbolt, as Jove's representative and victor on earth.[16] The Cumaean arch, called "Arco Felice," provided a three, possibly four-storeyed facade, with six (perhaps eight) niches designed to house honorific statuary. The single-bay brick arch (ca. 20 m high x 6 m wide) provided easy access to the Avernian region by enabling travellers to avoid the steep ascent of Monte Grillo between Puteoli and Cumae. Statius' and Juvenal's designation of

---

Neronis, Caputo 115–16; Frederiksen (Purcell) 336: "The project reflects a general concern at this period for communications between Campania and Rome, which by no means involved the by-passing of the Campanian ports but rather their closer links with the capital." Perhaps, as with the Flavian project, Nero's *fossa* would also have drained the coastal marshes and so would have provided new land for veteran settlement.

[15] Coleman 1988, 129: "Along the Via Domitiana it was 141 Roman miles from Rome to Puteoli. Only a traveller on horseback could have covered this journey in one day, and he would have to travel at the speed of a messenger conveying an emergency message."

[16] For the arch at the Volturnus crossing, see Coleman 1988; *Silvae* 4.3.67–96, pp. 120–27.

Cumae as "carefree" and as "gateway" to Baiae bespeaks personal experience.[17]

The attic is a mystery: did it carry a branch line of the Augustan Aqua Serino into the communities along the Tyrrhenian shoreline, or was it simply an overpass compensating the hill's division? Was it crowned by an attic group, the Emperor's triumphal chariot? Sixteenth century views of Cumae and the arch and travellers' notes provide no answer. Fears[18] suggests that the attic may have supported the emperor in military dress, holding Jove's thunderbolt, and crowned with the laurel wreath by Victory. Certainly coins of Domitian, between A.D. 85 and 96, portray him as a statuesque "Thunderer" (Tonans). Hypotheses aside, Kleiner has the final say: "when arches were erected within the secure frontiers of the empire and their stated purpose was not to celebrate the defeat of Rome's enemies but rather the paving of roads and bridging of rivers . . . tropaic statuary carried another message, namely that Roman victories could be won not only against men but against Nature herself."[19]

Stretches of the Via Domitiana have surfaced along its route, notably in the vicinity of the Arco Felice (where the one-time slippery surfaces of the lava paving blocks were treated to stippling three decades ago), in the Cumaean forum, and elsewhere in the environs.[20]

The downtown area of Cumae underwent major redevelopment in Domitianic times. The antique Samnite Jupiter "Flazius" temple, which Salmon argued was a Samnite

[17] Statius, *Silvae* 4.3.65; Juvenal, *Sat.* 3.1–5. Fears 1975, 1–4 challenges the scholar's conception of Imperial Cumae as a ghost town, a backwater provincial retreat.

[18] Quotation: Fears 1975, 8. For the Arco Felice: Amalfitano 308–9; Caputo 171–74.

[19] Kleiner 192.

[20] Coleman 1988, 115 (photos of paving at Arco Felice, Cuma).

"cathedral," had been erected during the 4th or 3rd century B.C.[21] The tufa structure with its hexastyle by 12 peripteral design was jettisoned by the Domitianic architect. The temple, which originally housed the Samnite Jupiter "Tonans," had been redesigned, probably during Sullan times, as a Capitolium, reflecting counterparts at Pompeii and Paestum. Uncertainty still attaches to the scale and appearance of the Republican edifice; its replacement, the newly designed Domitianic Capitolium (56.94 m x 28.50 m), is surpassed only by Rome's Capitoline temple (62.25 m x 53.50 m).

The upper structure, rebuilt and elevated, incorporated building blocks and elements from abandoned (or dismantled) acropolis buildings.[22] The porch was extended by an additional stepped platform at a lower level, and the cella was rebuilt to accommodate the Capitoline Triad. The construction technique in the rebuilt temple is characteristically Flavian: horizontal brick work (*opus latericium*) combined with *opus reticulatum*; marble facing was used generously in the cella and elsewhere. Colossal seated acrolithic cult images occupied the tripartite cella, with Jupiter central, Minerva on his left, and Juno on his right.

The impressive east facade, dominating the forum (50 m wide x 120 m long), competed with the Augustan Temple of Apollo on the citadel's lower terrace. The scenographic vision from the east end of the Cumaean Forum matched that of contemporary Rome's Palatine when viewed from the Forum Romanum. The six frontal Corinthian columns of the Capitolium's porch accented the gigantic structure. One magnificent marble capital survives. The stepped grandeur of the temple must have been stupefying: a central narrow flight of ten or more shallow steps led from the

[21] Salmon 1967, 165–66; Sgobbo 1977, 231–64.
[22] For the Capitolium: Amalfitano 303–4; Caputo 149–53, with axonometric drawing; Fears 1975, 5–6; Sgobbo 1977, 231–64.

forum level to an extensive lower podium furnished with sacrificial altars; from there another broad flight of steps led to the towering hexastyle porch and so to the cella with its Corinthian columnar room dividers; the three enthroned cult statues were installed in separate rooms at the rear, and the interior was enhanced by six pseudoperipteral columns on the cella walls; a side passageway led from the cella to a *posticum* where an Oscan mosaic inscription, now disintegrated, proclaimed a family's benefaction in days of yore. The west end of Cumae's forum, with the towering Capitolium, was a landmark for miles around.

From Greek and Samnite times, a yellow tufa porticus had shaded the southern side of the market area. During Sullan times (89–80 B.C.) the porticus was rebuilt in stuccoed grey tufa and crowned by a continuous frieze of arms, perhaps with a second level, possibly with a partner on the Forum's north side. The excavators believe that modifications were introduced during the triumviral period when Octavian and Agrippa were deeply involved with Cumae as a military defense centre, but the portico(es) survived into the Domitianic era.

Remains of a single bay triumphal arch survive on the north side of the Capitolium podium, after the pattern at Pompeii, where arches flank the sides of the Capitolium. A fountain house (*nymphaeum*) probably balanced the arch on the south side of the podium.

Excavation by M. E. Bertoldi (1971–1972) revealed an Italic style temple set within a porticoed precinct, measuring altogether 38.50 m x 26.20 m, oriented north-south and so perpendicular to the Capitolium.[23] The excavator assigned it to the reign of Augustus, and identified Demeter/Ceres as its resident, a cult long associated with Cumae's religious history. But the ascription has not found favor,

[23] Cf. Bertoldi 38–42; Fears 1975, 6–7; Caputo 153–56, with axonometric drawing.

and alternatives suggest either a Shrine of the Augustales, or a Temple of Deified Vespasian (and Titus).

The precinct is colonnaded on three sides, as tidy a containment as that of the Apollo Temple alongside the Forum of Pompeii, and is accessible from the Forum's southside portico. Three separate stepped entries pierce the precinct wall. The lateral porticoes are apsidal, recalling the design of the Building of Eumachia (rebuilt post A.D. 62) at Pompeii. The temple podium, which survives, had marble steps; the apsed cella is only partly extant. Contra Bertoldi, Johannowski and Fears date the temple and its construction techniques to the Domitianic period.[24] The building, which evidently surmounts a pre-Roman structure, certainly went through two building phases: the earlier version had twenty-four columns set inside the perimeter wall thereby providing a roofed "cloister" walk with facilities for rain water drainage; the side passages are apsidal and there are semicircular niches in the perimeter walls at the midway point, 1.20 m above the cocciopesto paving. The intercolumniations show screen walls in *opus reticulatum*. The perimeter walls which merge *opus latericium* and *opus reticulatum*, were faced with white stucco and "wall paper" disks in blue, yellow and deep red on the walls and on the apsidal end walls.

The cortile, within which the temple podium rests, was paved during its earlier phase with yellow tufa blocks. This earlier building resembles the Building of Eumachia at Pompeii, and the "Basilica" at Herculaneum. Caputo has identified the first century B.C. building as the Shrine of the Augustales, a collegial space resembling that of the recently reclaimed Sacellum at Misenum, with an open court providing space for sculptures, meetings, receptions and banquets.[25]

[24] Johannowski 972; Fears, n. 23 *supra*.
[25] Caputo 154, 156; for the Misenate shrine, n. 11 *supra*.

During the Julio-Claudian period, possibly Neronian, the Italic style temple was added inside the existing portico, and so transformed the earlier meeting space into a sanctuary. The original tufa block paving was replaced with travertine paving stones, framed by limestone blocks, and the intercolumnar screen wall was probably dismantled. The apsidal cella of the tetrastyle temple housed a cult statue base; the temple's interior dado was exclusively *opus reticulatum*. Of the original decoration some vestiges of the stuccoed interior walls survive with a series of square relief panels, together with portions of the marble threshold and doorpost. The design of the Flavian complex recalls the Temple of Apollo at Pompeii. The three-stepped entries are not aligned with the intercolumniations of the forum porticus. Fears is probably right in identifying it with the Temple of the Deified Vespasian at Cumae cited in *CIL* X, 3698. At Pompeii the Templum Divi Vespasiani rises behind the forum's porticus.

Identification of structures in the immediate environs of the Porticus Temple remains hazy, but the excavators believe that a large apsidal building, oriented north/south and raised above the forum level, immediately east of the Porticus Temple, may have housed the basilica. Its west side displays *opus reticulatum* faced with marble slabs.[26]

Cumae's Central Baths, rising on the east side of the Via Cuma-Licola, with a stretch of the Via Domitiana on their northern side, were romantically identified with the Sibyl's Tomb ("Sepolcro della Sibilla") by artists and travellers during the 18th and 19th centuries.[27] The Baths were a survival from Samnite days (3–2 c. B.C.). The main room is a large rectangular space with a barrel vault, and with stuccoed *opus incertum* walls. Rectangular niches, lined with

[26] Basilica (?): Caputo 156, 158.
[27] Cf. Amalfitano 306; Caputo 161–62.

cocciopesto and stuccoed, are almost certainly "lockers" appropriate to a changing room (*apodyterium*). The structure was modified in Flavian times, probably Domitianic, to provide a steam room with comparable "lockers." The rear (east) wall accommodated a large basin for ablutions, not unlike the basin set by local gentry into Pompeii's Forum Baths. Windows admitted light and air and a later addition provided a sunning space for bathers. Other barrel-vaulted rooms are located to the north and east of the main room but their function remains enigmatic. The remains are disappointing, but an unexpected dividend emerged in the shape of a fluted marble support for a basin (*labrum*) with an oscan inscription verifying that the Romanised building derived from an oscan-samnite bath-palaestra complex.

Efficient bathing facilities required adequate water and a constant supply. Prior to Augustan times when the Aqua Serino was inaugurated, Cumae's water supply depended on wells and cisterns, with times of plenty and dearth. The impressive Aqua Serino, which ran for some ninety-six kilometres, ended the uncertainty for a whole series of towns including Pompeii, Naples, and Puteoli, with branch lines to Nola, Atella (near modern Aversa), Cumae, Baiae, and Misenum.[28] Largesse notwithstanding, the Augustan facility was not infallible: cisterns appear repeatedly on the Cumaean acropolis and there is a cavernous one in the Crypta Romana. The city's Forum Baths, likely Antonine, modelled after Ostia's Forum Baths or Rome's Baths of Trajan, incorporated an enormous cistern which must have collected Serino aqueduct water fed directly into the tank.[29]

Government buildings appropriate to colonial towns are still wanting at Cumae. However, the so-called "Masseria

[28] Consult Sgobbo 1928, 75–97; D'Arms 79–80; Amalfitano 42; Keppie 73–74, 112–13.
[29] For the Antonine Forum Baths: Fears 1975, 9–10; Amalfitano 298–301; Caputo 141–44.

del Gigante," named after the colossal marble torso of the Capitolium's Jupiter found in 1758 in its environs, must equate with the Curia, the "senate house" of the local decurions. Facing the Capitolium which climaxed the Forum's west end, the "Farm House" had retained much of its original concrete vault as late as 1740 judging by an etching by the scrupulously accurate 18th century engraver, Filippo Morghen. The Flavian Senate House, probably Domitianic, constructed in *opus mixtum, opus latericium* and *opus vittatum*, is a farmer's storage space today, but it once towered above the Forum level. The plan, provided by the engraver Paolo Paoli in 1768, incorporates a central unit, the aforementioned barrel-vaulted apsidal hall, and two smaller rooms on either side, recalling the three units at the south end of the Pompeian forum.[30]

Cumae's city walls, originally Greek (8th–5th century), enclosed the acropolis (NW), the foot of Mons Grillus (E), pierced by Domitian's "Arco Felice," the marshy territory of Licola (N), and the hilly terrain where the Villa Vergiliana stands today (S).[31] The gates are hard to locate, but one certainly graced the southern wall at the Croce di Cuma, leading to the amphitheater, and two others opened along the northern stretch to provide access to the road linking Cumae and Capua (Cumis/Capuam), and to the port facility at Lago di Licola. The Licola Gate probably admitted the Via Domitiana into the city. There must also have been an earlier gate in the eastern stretch to provide access to Mons Grillus and the ascent to Lake Avernus.

Cumae's arena, coeval with Pompeii's, sits outside the south wall and the gate at the Croce di Cuma.[32] The *cavea*

---

[30] Cf. Amalfitano 304–6; Caputo 162–63.

[31] City walls: Pagano 847–71; Amalfitano 308; Caputo 107–9.

[32] Amphitheater: Beloch 189; Welch 73–75; Amalfitano 306–8; Caputo 168–69, and Frederiksen (Purcell) 339, 348 (social status and spectacle in the Cumaean amphitheater under Tiberius).

is framed by earth embankments. A circuit of arches and pilasters (E and S) with a facing of *opus incertum* crowns the *summa cavea*. The oval arena is oriented N-S on a major axis of ca. 90 metres; the seating is barely discernible today because of cultivation. A 19th century farmhouse marks the entry to the arena on its north side, balancing a portal on the south side; two minor entries opened on the east and west sides. It closely resembles the amphitheater at Pompeii (80 B.C.) and the late Republican arena at Puteoli.

Recent excavations have revealed that the amphitheater expanded during the 1st century A.D., possibly after the earthquake of 62 when the *summa cavea* of Pompeii's amphitheater was rebuilt; the latest expansion can be detected in Paolo Paoli's 1768 engraving, *Pianto del Circo a Cuma*.[33] The addition consisted of an outer ring wall providing attic accommodation (*maenianum summum*) and a colonnaded gallery with standing room only. Caputo associates the additions with urban expansion under Augustus, and with the Domitianic program at Cumae. The expansion after the eruption of A.D. 79, when the Pompeian amphitheater was *hors de combat* forever, met popular demand by offering a complement, maybe a measure of competition, to the Augustan arena at Puteoli and the Republican amphitheater at Capua.

The Villa Vergiliana, overseas academic center of The Vergilian Society, towers above the sunken arena on its north side. The Villa was constructed after 1906 by *Societas Cumana* (Stuttgart) on the remains of what appears to be a Domitianic temple, oriented N-S. When the temple, facing the amphitheater, was excavated in 1842, it was identified in local lore as Mercury's. Mercury as mercantile protector, or, given the underworld context, as psychopompus, seems plausible as tenant, but Grandgrind's facts are missing.

---

[33] Paoli, plate 33.

Records from 1842 indicate that the Roman temple displaced an archaic Greek temple at the site; the new "tempietto" had four Doric stuccoed brick columns on its facade, four attached pilasters in the rear, and seven pilasters on either flank. The pronaos measured 4.70 m deep, and the cella, measuring 13.48 m deep, had an altar with marble facing at its center.[34]

Robert Paget's mariner's eye detected what he regarded as two lighthouse foundations constructed in brick and mortar near the railway line of Mussolini's Ferrovia Circumflegrea.[35] But excavations in 1992 have dispelled Paget's conjectures: a sanctuary of Isis Pelagia (Marina) has surfaced unexpectedly in what purports to be the entry channel of Paget's hypothetical harbour south of the acropolis. Revision is in order, and the new Egyptian complex has now been associated with a coastal dune, a natural break-water and barrier for the harbour, which is also capable of supporting a sanctuary of the marine goddess and an adjacent pharos. The building remains include a low rectangular temple podium and a (Nile?) water basin surrounded by a portico some ten metres distant. Statuary finds, retrieved from the basin, all decapitated, include three Ptolemaic statuettes, an Isis and a priest of Osiris in basalt, and a sphinx in grey granite. The excavators argue that a late Republican complex (perhaps Triumviral), successor to an even earlier construction damaged by bradyseism, underwent modifications during the first and second centuries A.D. and that it was destroyed by Christians after 397. Both Herculaneum and Pompeii provide architectural and pictorial evidence for our understanding and reconstruction of the Cumaean example.[36] Flavian and

[34] Villa Vergiliana "tempietto": Beloch 189; Caputo 169.

[35] Portus Cumanus: Paget 159-66; Amalfitano 294-95.

[36] Isis sanctuary: De Caro 11-13; Caputo 174-76; Tinh, passim. On Campanian oriental cults: Amalfitano 101-3.

contemporary sympathy with the Isis cult is well documented: Otho, short-term emperor in A.D. 69, was a devotee; Domitian, in A.D. 69, according to Suetonius, owed his life "to priests of that somewhat questionable order." Domitianic alterations and enrichment of the Isis Sanctuary at Cumae are hardly debatable.

Sic Cumae veteres permanent. Work continues along the wave-pounded shores beneath the Apolline heights and the developing Parco Archeologico is gaining international attention. Domitianic and Antonine buildings have greatly enriched our understanding of Imperial Cumae. New finds along the littoral and on the foothills of the acropolis, the emerging amphitheater, the expanding program of excavations in the Forum and discoveries of roadside tombs[37] provide splendid complement to the antique glories of Greek and Samnite Cumae.[38]

Works Cited

Amalfitano, P., G. Camodeca, M. Medri. 1990. *I Campi Flegrei, un itinerario archeologico.* Venezia.

Anderson, J. C. 1981."Domitian's Building Programme. Forum Julium and Markets of Trajan. *ArchN* 10:41–48.

———. 1983. "Domitian's Building Programme." *Historia* 32:93–105.

———. 1984. *The Historical Topography of the Imperial Fora. Collection Latomus* 182. Brussels.

---

[37] Tocco 485–96.

[38] The foregoing essay is a token of respect and admiration for a scholarly *cicerone* who has enriched and stimulated the imagination and energy of countless students and teachers in Italy and elsewhere. Truly, *saxa loquuntur* more eloquently, more wittily, and more informatively when Paul MacKendrick shoulders the burden.

Beloch, J. 1890. *Campanien*. Breslau. Italian translation: Napoli 1989.

Bertoldi, M. E. 1973. "Recenti scavi e scoperte a Cuma." *BdA* 57:38–42.

Caputo, P., R. Morichi, R. Paone, R. Rispoli. 1996. *Cuma e il suo parco archeologico. Un territorio e le sue testimonianze.* Roma.

Clark, Raymond J. 1996. "The Avernian Sibyl's Cave: From Military Tunnel to Mediaeval Spa." *C&M* 47:217–43.

Coleman, Kathleen M. 1988. *Statius: Silvae IV.* Oxford.

———. 1986. "The Emperor Domitian and Literature." *ANRW* 2.32.5:3087–3115.

D'Arms, J. H. 1970. *Romans on the Bay of Naples.* Cambridge, Mass.

De Caro, S. 1995. "Novità isiache della Campania." In "Alla ricerca di Iside." *PdP* (Napoli):11–13.

De Iorio, A. 1814. *Guida di Pozzuoli e contorni.* Napoli.

Fears, R. 1975. "Cumae in the Roman Imperial Age." *Vergilius* 21:1–21.

———. 1981."The Cult of Jupiter and Roman Imperial Ideology." *ANRW* 2.17.1:3–141.

———. 1981. "Jupiter and Roman Imperial Ideology: The Role of Domitian." *ANRW* 2.17.1:233–45.

Frederiksen, M. (& N. Purcell). 1984. *Campania.* London.

Griffin, Miriam. 1984. *Nero: The End of a Dynasty.* London.

Hardie, Philip. 1986. *Virgil's Aeneid: Cosmos and Imperium.* Oxford.

Johannowsky, W. 1959. *EAA* 970–73. s.v. Cuma.

Jones, Brian. 1992. *The Emperor Domitian.* New York.

Keppie, L. F. J.1983. *Colonisation and Veteran Settlement in Italy, 47–14 B.C.* London.

Kleiner, Fred S. 1991. "The Trophy on the Bridge and the Roman Triumph over Nature." *AC* 60:182–92.

MacKendrick, Paul. 1960, 1976. *The Mute Stones Speak: The Story of Archaeology in Italy.* New York.

Morghen, Filippo. 1765. *Le antichità di Cuma e Baia.* Napoli.

Pagano, M. 1993. "Ricerche sulla cinta muraria di Cuma." *MEFRA* 105:847–71.

Paget, R. F. 1968. "The Ancient Ports of Cumae." *JRS* 58:152–69.

Paoli, P. A. 1768. *Antiquitatum Puteolis, Cumis, Bais existentium reliquiae.* Neapolis.

Robathan, D. M. 1942. "Domitian's Midas Touch." *TAPA* 73:130–44.

Salmon, E. T. 1967. *Samnium and the Samnites.* Cambridge.

Sgobbo, I. 1977. "Il maggior tempio del foro di Cuma e la munificenza degli Heii cumani in epoca sannitica." *RAAN n.s.* 52:231–64.

——. 1928. "L'acquedotto romano della Campania: Fontis Augustei Aquaeductus." *NSc* 6:75-97.

Stambaugh, John E. 1988. *The Ancient Roman City.* Baltimore and London.

Tinh, Tran Tam. 1964. *Essai sur le culte d'Isis à Pompei.* Paris.

Tocco, G. 1975. "Saggi di scavo nella città e nella necropoli di Cuma." In *Atti del XVI convegno di Studi per la Magna Grecia. Taranto 1975.* Napoli.

Welch, Katherine. 1994. "The Roman Arena in Late-Republican Italy: a New Interpretation." *JRA* 7:59–80.

Et Manu Papae:
Papal Subscriptions Written
Sua Manu in Late Antiquity

Ralph W. Mathisen
University of South Carolina

Official documents that were issued during Late Antiquity (traditionally, c. A.D. 260–640) sometimes contain addenda to the document qua document. In general, such addenda are known generically as *subscriptiones*, or subscriptions.[1] These subscriptions are well known from the late Roman legal corpora, such as the *Codex theodosianus*. Most were added by imperial clerks and are related to the circumstances—such as the the date and location—under which the documents were promulgated, recorded, or received. At other times, however, postscripts were written *sua manu* ("in their own hand") by the officials in whose names the documents were issued. The postscripts could be placed anywhere in the document—after the text, in the margin, or

---

[1] It should be pointed out, moreover, that in a Roman legal sense, the word *subscriptio* generally referred to words written at the end of a document.

on the other side—and as a result, they were often omitted from later copies of the documents.

These official postscripts played an important role, for in the world of late Roman officialdom documents had to be properly authorized before thay could take effect.[2] The autograph postscripts served this purpose. The most significant secular postscripts, of course, were those of the emperor himself. Common imperial postscripts took the form of what might be called "farewell salutations," that is, phrases such as *vale* so-and-so, *carissime nobis* ("farewell, so-and-so, most dear to us"), common in the late third and fourth centuries, or *bene valere te cupimus* ("we wish you to be well"). Beginning in the fourth century, emperors also used Christian farewells, such as *deus vos servet* ("god preserve you") or *divinitas te servet per multos annos* ("god preserve you for many years"); the last of these continued in use into the seventh century.[3] In the existing manuscripts, salutations of this type sometimes are preceded by a copyist's phrase, such as *et manu imperatoris, et manu divina*, or simply *et alia manu*.[4]

---

[2] For private documents, especially wills and testaments, see *CTh* 2.27.1.1, 4; 4.4.5, 5.9.2, 9.19.1–4; *Digest* 29.7.6.1; *CJ* 6.22.8.1, 6.22.10.1, 6.23.21[2], 6.23.28.6[3], 6.23.29.3,6; 6.30.22.26; 7.6.1.1c; 7.40.1.2; 7.41.1; 8.17.11; 8.48.6; 9.23.1, 2, 4, 6; 9.49.9; 10.25.1; 12.37.16.1, 5. For the emperors, note Ulpian (*Digest* 1.4.1.1–2: Ulpian *Inst.* 1, cf. Just. *Inst.* 1.2.6): quod principi placuit legis habet vigorem . . . quodcumque igitur imperator per epistulam et subscriptionem statuit vel cognoscens decrevit vel de plano interlocutus est vel edicto praecepit, legem esse constat. haec sunt quas vulgo constitutiones appellamus (the version in *Inst.* lacks *et subscriptionem*). See, in general, Millar, *Emperor*, 219–22.

[3] See J. Zepos and P. Zepos, eds., *Jus Graecoromanum*, vol. 1. In *Novellae et aureae bullae imperatorum post Justinianum*. Ed. C. E. Zacharias A. von Lingenthal (Athens, 1931; repr. Aalen: Scientia Verlag, 1962).

[4] Words following *et alia manu* can be identified as imperial only on the basis of their content. Other obviously non imperial phrases—such as even the date-and-place indicator—also can be introduced by *et alia*

In the church, meanwhile, the administration of the bishops of Rome came to look more and more like that of the imperial government. The popes had their own secretarial bureaux, or *scrinia*, that dealt with correspondence and records—one should not think that the popes sat down at their desks to write their own letters. A letter of Gregory the Great of 595, for example, concludes with the words, "I dictated this letter to be written by Paternus, a notary of our church."[5] As the papal chancery evolved, its documents looked more and more like imperial documents. Papal documents, too, preserve similar kinds of addenda, although they are less well studied than their imperial counterparts. This short study will investigate postscripts written in the pope's own hand.

The papal postscripts are sometimes clearly identified in the manuscripts by introductory formulae such as *et manu papae* or *et manu ipsius*. Like the imperial subscriptions, others are preceded by formulae such as *et alia manu* or *et subscriptio*.[6] But the insertion, or omission, of these formulae was strictly up to the scribe, and done according to no standard rules.

What, then, can these jejune papal postscripts tell us about papal activities, attitudes or policies? The most common papal postscript is also the first to appear. It reads, *deus vos incolumes custodiat, frater carissime* ("god keep you well, dearest brother"), or some variant thereof. The first extant use, by pope Julius (337–52), is found in a document

---

manu: cf. Zosimus, *Epist. Ex relatione fratris* (3 Oct. 418), *et alia manu: data quinto monas Octobris Honorio XII et Theodosio VIII augustis consulibus* (*PL* 20.679–80).

[5] See Greg.Mag. *Regesta* 5.29 (A.D. 595), *hanc autem epistolam Paterno notario ecclesiae nostrae scribendam dictavimus.*

[6] See *Et alia manu* in C. Silva-Tarouca, *Nuovi Studi sulle Antiche Lettere dei Papi, Gregorianum* 12 (1931) 3–56, 349–425, 547–98 (= Rome 1932, (with pages renumbered) 361[69]–374[82]).

written c. 341, and is in Greek.[7] Additional examples survive from the pontificates of Liberius (352–66), and many later popes.[8]

Two popes of the early fifth century used another kind of farewell salutation. Innocent (401–7) used the rather secular form, *bene valete, fratres carissimi* in letters to the Council of Toledo c. 404 and twice to African bishops in 417. And Zosimus (417–18) used the form *bene valete, fratres* in a letter to African bishops. Significantly, this form also was used by the contemporary emperors Honorius (395–423) and Theodosius II (408–50), and its use may reflect Innocent's and Zosimus' intent to ape their imperial counterparts.[9]

Indeed, given that all the extant papal examples of this formula occured in letters to groups of bishops in other provinces, that is, Africa and Spain, the use of the imperial salutation could suggest a desire to extend papal authority into these regions, à la the emperors. For in letters to individual bishops, Innocent reverted to the standard *deus vos incolumes custodiat* formula.[10]

---

[7] Athan. *Apologia secunda* 21.1 (Opitz 2.1 pp. 102–13), addressed to those who had signed the letter brought from from Antioch in 340; see L. Duchesne, *Early History of the Christian Church*, 4th ed. (London, 1920) 2.162–63.

[8] Liberius: Hil. Pict. *Collectanea antiariana parisina* 7.11.2: *CSEL* 62.172–73; Idem., *Hist.* fr. 6: D. A. B. Caillau, ed., *Collectio selecta ss. ecclesiae patrum*, vol. 27 (Paris, 1830) 179–80, 184; cf. also, e.g., Innocent *Epist.imp.* 41: *CSEL* 35.92–96.

[9] Honorius, c. 410, to the Spanish soldiers: *optamus commilitones nostros per multos annos bene agere. et alia manu: bene valete*: see H. S. Sivan, "An Unedited Letter of the Emperor Honorius to the Spanish Soldiers," *ZPE* 61 (1985) 273–87; Theodosius II, c. 420, to Egypt, *bene valere vos cupim[us: Pap.leidensis* Z, the only surviving autograph imperial postscript: see D. Feissel and K. A. Worp, "La requête d'Appion, évêque de Syene, à Théodose II: P. Leid. Z revise," *Oudheidkundige Mededelingen* 65 (1988) 97–111.

[10] Note the letters to five African bishops, Jan. 417, *et alia manu. deus*

Beginning with pope Leo (440–61), one sees an increasing degree of standardization in the papal farewell salutations. *Deus te incolumem custodiat* became virtually de rigueur, and was used by popes through Boniface IV (608–15) at least.[11] It is with the variations from this standard formula, therefore, that the remainder of this discussion will primarily be concerned. Leo's only extant variant occurred in a letter of 457 to the Council of Nicaea, where he reverted back to the old imperial usage, *bene valete, fratres carissimi*—with a *in domino* appended for ecclesiastical flavor. One might wonder whether Leo's anomalous use of this salutation might betray a bit of his own pseudo-imperial pretensions.

The primary variation from the *deus te* formula, however, occurred in papal letters to emperors and high-ranking *saeculares*. In such instances, popes apparently often felt the need to be rather more flowery, not to mention original, in their farewell salutations. Felix III, for example, subscribed to a letter to the emperor Zeno in 485, "May omnipotent god always guard your power in peace."[12] Pope John II was even more flamboyant in a letter to Justinian in 533. The postscript reads, "And with another hand: the grace of our lord Jesus Christ and the love of god the father and the communion of the holy spirit be with you always, most pious son. Likewise the subscription: may omnipotent god guard your kingdom and safety with perpetual protection, most glorious and clement son, emperor Augustus."[13] In

---

vos incolumes custodiat, fratres charissimi. data sexto Kalendas Februarias . . . (*Epist.* 31: *PL* 20.593–97); and to Aurelius of Carthage, 27 Jan. 417, *deus te incolumem custodiat, frater carissimus. data sexto Kalendas Februarias . . .* (*Epist.* 32: *PL* 20.597–98).

[11] Boniface *Epist.Merov.* 12 (*MGH Epist.* 3.453–55).

[12] *Omnipotens deus custodiet vestram potentiam in pace semper* (also cited in Greek). (*Epist., Convenit clementiae: PL* 58.917–22).

[13] *Et alia manu: gratia domini nostri Iesu Christi et caritas dei patris et*

this case, the pope for some reason felt the need to add two salutations. It may be that one was appended to the document itself, and the other was written on the cover. And a letter of John to the senate in the next year bears the subscription, "And with another hand: may our lord god keep Your Magnitude safe, most beloved sons, deservedly illustrious and magnificent."[14]

Popes were equally effusive in letters to barbarian kings. A letter of Pope Pelagius of 557 to the Frankish king Childebert, for example, ends, "May our god keep Your Excellency safe, lord son, most glorious and outstanding."[15] And Pope Boniface, in 613, subscribed to a letter to the Frank Theoderic II (596–613), "May the supernal grace keep Your Excellency well, lord son."[16] Apparently, in the papal scheme of status, secular lords warranted greater consideration, at least when it came to salutations, than ecclesiastical ones.

Some of the most interesting papal postscripts, however, are not farewell salutations at all. On rare occasions, popes added brief personal comments in their own hands at the ends of official letters, and they give us some precious in-

---

communicatio spiritus sancti sit semper vobiscum piissimi fili. item subscriptio: omnipotens deus regnum et salutem vestram perpetua protectione custodiat, gloriossisime et clementissime fili imperator Auguste, Epist., Reddentes honorem, embedded in a letter of Johannes Inter claras to Justinian (25 Mar. 534). The entire letter is the same as CJ 1.1.8; in manuscripts of the CJ, the et alia manu is rendered variously et subscriptio (C), item et subscriptio (R), and et haec subscriptio (M). The second et alia manu is omitted altogether in mss. CRB.

[14] Et alia manu: incolumem magnitudinem vestram deus noster custodiat, dilectissimi filii merito illustres atque magnifici: ACO 4.210.

[15] Incolumem excellentiam vestram deus noster custodiat, domine fili gloriosissime atque praecellentissime (Epist., Excellentiae vestrae = Epist.Arel. 51: MGH Epist. 3).

[16] Incolumem excellentiam vestram gratia superna custodiat, domine fili (23 Aug. 613) (Epist., Scripta excellentiae = Epist.Merov. 13: MGH Epist. 3.455–56).

sights into some of their personal cares and concerns.[17]
Liberius, for example, in 357, writing from exile, appended
a plaintive double postscript to Vincentius, bishop of
Capua, in a letter in which he asked Vincentius to intercede
with the emperor for his release. The full subscription
reads, "And with his own hand. God keep you well, brother.
Likewise, the page was inscribed in his own hand. I share
communion with all the eastern bishops and with you. I ab-
solve myself before god. You will see, if you allow me to lan-
guish in exile, that god will be the judge between me and
you."[18]

Such addenda, however, usually have a more positive
tone, and often refer to the receipt or granting of personal
favors. Leo of Rome in 454 appended to a letter to bishop
Juvenalis of Jerusalem the words, "I respectfully received
the particle of the holy cross along with the good wishes of
Your Devotion."[19] Likewise, a letter of 521 to Epiphanius of
Constantinople from Pope Hormisdas concludes, "And in
the hand of the pope: we received the jeweled golden cup,
the silver plate and the other silver cup, and the two veils
intended for the service of the basilica of the blessed
apostle Peter which were sent by Your Charity."[20]

---

[17] These kinds of matters also were transmitted as verbal messages.

[18] *Et manu ipsius: deus te incolumem custodiat, frater. item manu ipsius
pagina perscripta: cum omnibus episcopis Orientalibus pacem habemus et
vobiscum. ego me ad deum absolui. vos videritis, si volueritis me in exilio
deficere, erit deus iudex inter me et vos* (Hil. Pict. *Collectanea antiariana
parisina* 7.11.2: *CSEL* 65.172–73). Vincentius in the past had been a
papal legate to Constantius.

[19] *Particulam dominicae crucis cum eulogiis tuae dilectionis veneranter
accepi. dat prid nonas Septemb Aetio et Studio vv cc conss* (*Epist., Acceptis
dilectionis: ACO* 2.4.91–93). That this is a subscription is indicated by
the fact that it is included only in mss. PPII, but omitted in mss.
GEQLGamma, that is, it was not clearly part of letter per se, and therefore was not always seen fit to be included.

[20] *Et manu papae: suscepimus calicem aureum gemmatum, patenam*

A different kind of favor was extended by Pope Symmachus to Caesarius of Arles in 513. The pope's letter concluded with a papal postscript, "God keep you well, dearest brother," followed by the time and date indicator, and then a second papal postscript: "I grant only to Your Charity the right to wear the *pallium* throughout all the Gallic regions."[21] In this instance, a great personal honor was granted by the pope in his own hand, and this would have added even additional lustre to the distinction.

So far, the discussion has considered various ways in which the papal subscriptions were similar to the imperial ones. In one regard, however, they were different. Emperors never signed their names in the modern sense, but popes sometimes did. A letter of Pope Vigilius, in 540, to bishop Menas of Constantinople, concludes, "And in the hand of the lord pope: with the help of god, through his grace, I, Vigilius, bishop of the holy catholic church of the city of Rome, have reviewed and subscribed to these pages of the preceding letters, which I dictated with the help of god, and with his assistance."[22] This subscription also shows the papal clerical staff in action.

And speaking of the clerical staff, it might be useful to say a few words here about the reasons for the survival of

---

argenteam et alium calicem argenteum et vela duo ministerio basilicae beati Petri apostoli profutura a caritate tua directa (Epist.imp. 239: CSEL 35.738–39). The *Liber pontificalis* 54, which does list specific gifts sent by the emperor Justin, does not list these, which probably are to be lumped into the entry, "From Greece, many gold and silver vessels."

[21] *deus te incolumem custodiat, frater carissime. data VIII Idus Novembres, Probo viro clarissimo consule. caritati tuae tantummodo per omnes Gallicanas regiones utendi pallei concessimus facultatem (Epist., Hortatur nos = Epist.Arel. 26: MGH Epist. 3).*

[22] *et manu domni papae. deo iuvante per ipsius gratiam Vigilius epicopus sanctae ecclesiae catholicae urbis Romae has scidas epistolarum supra scriptarum, quas ego deo iuvante dictavi, ipso auxiliante recognovi atque subscripsi: Epist., Licet universa (Epist.imp. 93: CSEL 35.354–56).*

the autograph postscripts. For it would appear that the postscript usually was added only to the copy that was actually sent to the recipient, not to file copies that were kept in the papal archives. This explains why letters of Leo and Hilarus that were preserved in the *Epistulae arelatenses*, a catalogue of letters sent to the bishops of Arles, do contain papal postscripts, but the versions preserved in the papal archives themselves do not.[23]

And note the letter sent in 521 by Pope Hormisdas to the bishop of Constantinople, which survives in Latin and Greek versions. The Latin version, from the archives in Rome, concludes with the date, which would have been added by the Roman file clerk: *data VII Kal. Apr. Valerio cons.* But the Greek version, the one actually sent, concludes with the pope's farewell saluation, or the Greek version of it, "And in another hand: god keep you well, dearest brother."[24]

This brief investigation of papal postscripts has provided some additional insight not only into some of the personal activities and concerns of the popes themselves, but also into the operation of the papal chancery. But there is actually much more to the story. For the pope was not the only bishop who subscribed to documents. No, any bishop worth his salt had a chancery of his own, some large, such as those at Milan or Constantinople, and some very modest. And every bishop subscribed to his own letters and documents, in just the way that the pope did.[25]

---

[23] *MGH Epist.* 3.

[24] *Epist.imp.* 237: *CSEL* 35.722–33, the Greek version was inserted into the *acta* of the Council of Constantinople of 536, which may explain why it was translated.

[25] Note, for example, the subscription of a deacon of Milan of c. 382, *ego Sabinus diaconus Mediolanensis legatus de authentico dedi* (*PL* 13.347–49).

The Heracleotai of Athens

cↄↄↄↄↄↄↄↄ

Jon D. Mikalson
University of Virginia

This study of the Heracleotai in Athens involves a bit of epigraphy, of archaeology, of prosopography, and of history. I began work on it in Spring 1996 in the Blegen Library of the American School of Classical Studies in Athens, and I could not help but ponder how I came to be in that place and doing this subject, now thirty years after I, as a freshman, encountered Paul L. MacKendrick in my first college Latin course at the University of Wisconsin. He began to plant seeds that day and nourished them for four years. However it came to be, I now find myself working on the topics, in the ways, and in the places of Paul MacKendrick. It would not have happened without him, and I welcome the opportunity to offer him τροφεῖα on this occasion.

The turbulent politics of Heracleia on the Pontus in the fourth and early third centuries B.C., including the establishment of democracy and violent turns to an oligarchy, to a long and powerful tyranny, and to the reestablishment of democracy in 281, created a large group of exiles, and

many of these found their way to Athens. In fact, within the
foreign population of Hellenistic and Roman Athens the
Heracleotai stand out, initially by sheer numbers, second
only to immigrants from Miletos. From tombstones alone
we can identify in Athens, from the mid-fourth century B.C.
to the second century A.D., over 600 Heracleotai, approximately 450 men and 160 women.[1] All but thirty-two of
these gravestones have been given a date, almost exclusively on the basis of the letter forms, and they range pretty
evenly over the Hellenistic and Roman periods: roughly
16% come from the fourth century B.C., 13% from the
third, 22% from the second, 27% from the first, and 22%
are dated to the first or second century A.D. or, more generally, to the "Roman" period.[2] If we add to these tombstones
historical and epigraphical records of other Heracleotai in
Athens, we can start to develop a picture of the economic,
social, and religious life of such foreigners in Athens.

We begin with Clearchos, the historically most prominent
of all Heracleotai, who in 364 established the tyrannical dynasty which was to rule Heracleia Pontica until 284. In the
370s, himself then in exile for democratic sympathies, he
spent time in Athens in philosophical and rhetorical study,
especially under Isocrates, and he alone of the many
known Heracleotai received citizenship from Athens, a
grant not common then and no doubt motivated by his sta-

---

[1] The tombstones for Heracleotai in Athens are *IG* II² 8548–8825,
8572a, 8609a, 8636a, 8654a, 8778a, 8812a and *SEG* 12.191, 14.196–
200, 16.206 and 207, 19.279 and 280, 21.951–58, and 965, 24.246,
26.321 and 322, 29.223 and 224, 31.217, 32.298–300, 34.213, 37.168,
and 38.223. *IG* II² 8578 and 8579 are the same text (*AM* 67 [1942],
#351). The Heracleote tombstones recorded in *SEG* 1.34 and 43 and
2.31–34 are in fact *IG* II² 8797, 8634, 8738, 8772, 8647, 8786.

[2] Some of the inscriptions are dated, e.g., III/II B.C. or II/I B.C. For
the division into centuries, I have assigned half of such entries to the
earlier century, half to the later century.

tus as a pro-democratic exile, by his aristocratic family background, and by close associations with Isocrates and the general Timotheos.[3] When Clearchos turned, in 364, from democrat to tyrant he became alienated from Isocrates (*Ep.* 7.12–13), and he seems not to have visited Athens again nor to have made further use of his Athenian citizenship. Ca. 345 Isocrates renewed *xenia* with Clearchos' son and successor Timotheos and had regular visitors from Heracleia (*Ep.* 7.12–13). Ca. 315 Menander in his *Halieis* (frags. 13–24 Edmonds) attacked Dionysios, Clearchos' second son and Timotheos' successor, as a "fat pig" devoted to gluttony and pleasure—an apparently accurate description (Burstein 77, 80). According to Athenaios (12.549c) Menander devised the plot, set in Heracleia, "for the sake of some exiles from Heracleia," no doubt some of the very Heracleotai in Athens whom we discuss here. One can only imagine with what emotions these Heracleotai saw their oppressor represented and attacked in the theater of their new homeland.

S. Burstein has set forth in detail the ties between Clearchos, his successors, and Heracleia Pontica in general with Athens and with the Heracleote exiles in the early Hellenistic period. In our examination of the Heracleotai in Athens we leave these foreign policy matters largely aside, but do note that Heracleia became increasingly important to Athens as a place of production and transshipment of the grain desperately needed in Athens throughout the period. Several of the Heracleotai living in Athens were engaged in this or similar trading businesses. Pseudo-Demosthenes 52 tells of the substantial financial dealings in Athens of the Heracleote Lycon, a *xenos* of Aristonous of Deceleia and of Archebiades of Lamptrai, both of whom assisted him in his financial affairs. The case arose because

---

[3] Burstein 50.

Callippos of Lamptrai, the Athenian *proxenos* of Heracleia, had made claims (illegal and unjustified, according to the speaker) on Lycon's assets after his tragic death at the hands of pirates.[4] In the increasing difficulties of the grain supply, particularly ca. 307 B.C., at least three Heracleotai pitched in, as traders, shipowners, or contributors, to help Athens.[5] Other Heracleotai also assisted Athens in times of need, but also no doubt for their own profit, as, e.g., the Heracleote who in 307/6 contracted for rebuilding a stretch of the city wall.[6] He and another Heracleote metic, Onesimos, both enjoyed *isotelia*, the exemption from the usual metic taxes.[7]

The Heracleotai encountered thus far were probably all well-to-do, and among these well-to-do would also have been the family of Agathon, son of Agathocles. Already in the mid-fourth century he and his family had constructed a monumental grave *peribolos* in a prestigious location in the Cerameicos, on the Street of the Tombs just beyond and immediately adjoining the *peribolos* of the Athenian family of Dexileos.[8] In later times, from the end of the fourth century B.C. on, a marker of some social and financial prominence was the registration of one's sons in the *ephebeia*. By 123/2 the Athenians had opened their now venerable institution to select foreigners. No Heracleotai were among the

[4] Callipos himself was a powerful individual in Athens, like Clearchos a friend and student of Isocrates. See Burstein 41, 49.

[5] *IG* II² 408, 479, and 480. The occasion for the honors given a Heracleote in 318/17 is not known but may well be also related to the grain supply (*IG* II² 535 + *Hesperia* 8 [1939] 30–32, #8).

[6] *IG* II² 463 + *Hesperia* 9 (1940) 68, #9, line 124.

[7] *IG* II² 463 + *Hesperia* 9 (1940) 68, # 9, line 124, and *IG* II² 8652.

[8] The wall of the *peribolos* facing the street was eight meters in length. The *peribolos* included at least seven grave monuments and perhaps a small garden. The tombstones include *IG* II² 8550, 8551, and 11891. For a general description of the *peribolos* and bibliography, see Garland 135–38.

fourteen foreigners (including four Romans) in the first
such "mixed" class attested,[9] but in the class of 119/18
there were two Heracleotai among the seventeen foreigners
(*IG* II² 1008.115 and 119), in 117/16 at least one among
twelve foreigners (1009.112), in 107/6 two among the
twenty-four (1011.90 and 117), in 102/1 at least one among
the forty (1028.151), and, finally, in 39/8 at least one in a
now quite large group of foreigners (1043.117).

For the less prominent, less wealthy Heracleotai we must
turn to the tombstones. From them we know, for example,
the husbands of thirty-seven Heracleote women. Not surprisingly, three of these husbands were Heracleotai themselves,[10] and it is likely that in the seven instances where the
husband is given no ethnic he too was a Heracleote.[11] Individual Heracleote women also married men from Ephesos
(*IG* II² 8588), Laodiceia (8587), Ankura (8671), Antioch
(8686), Termessos (8734), Plataia (8818), Kibura (8820),
and a Mede (8728). Two were married to men from
Maroneia (8628 and 8793). Most importantly, sixteen of the
thirty-seven married Athenian citizens,[12] none certainly until the second century B.C. and many later. These Athenian
husbands have demotics but never patronymics, and this
makes positive identification impossible, but we may well
have the separate tombstones of both the Heracleote Kakis
and her Athenian husband, Alexis of Semachidai (*IG* II²
8693 and 7379) and of Proxena and her husband Polemon
of Kytheros (8768 and 6613). If the Sosipolis of Hama-
xanteia of *IG* II² 8735 and 8481 is the same man, he had a
taste for foreign wives, the Heracleote Nana and the
Edessan Eirene. Only one extended family emerges, that of

[9] *IG* II² 1006 as reedited by Reinmuth, 185–91.

[10] *IG* II² 8647, 8676, and 8825.

[11] *IG* II² 8584, 8612, 8649, 8653, 8694, 8774, 8802.

[12] *IG* II² 8549, 8578, 8581, 8606, 8609, 8688, 8693, 8695, 8735, 8757,
8768, 8773, 8781, 8785 and *SEG* 19.279 and 31.217.

Archianassa and her husband, Leukippos of Phrearrhioi. Her father was Nikandros, no doubt a Heracleote. Her son was named Nikandros after his grandfather, and this son's daughter, named Archianassa after her grandmother and no longer designated a Heracleote, married Antigonos of Kydathenaion.[13] This serves to remind us that the descendants, male and female, of these Heracleote women who married Athenians would no longer be "Heracleote," and that many more "Athenians" than we can know had some Heracleote "blood" in the second century B.C. and after.

The Athenian husbands of these Heracleote women do not seem a particularly distinguished lot. Of the sixteen only one may have left some record. Rhodion's husband, Apollonios of Eroiadai, may have been the *bouleutes* of 135/4.[14] Little more is known of their descendants. The son of Dionysia and Antipatros of Lamptai may have been an ephebe in the class of 123/2.[15] And quite probably Menestratos, the *bouleutes* of ca. 30 A.D., was the son of Strateia and her husband Kriton of Phlya.[16]

We have already noted some of the more distinguished Heracleote men, but details of some less prominent men emerge also. In the fourth century Olympos was a κυβερνήτης (*IG* II² 8755). In the third century Hermias, Sostratos, and Pasichares served as mercenary soldiers for the Athenians,[17] and in 218/17 Kteson, along with an Eretrian and an Argive, was a prominent soldier among the

[13] *IG* II² 8581, 7726, and 7721. Stemma in *PA* 9059.

[14] *IG* II² 8773 and *Agora* 15.243.118–19.

[15] *SEG* 19.279 and *IG* II² 1006.108.

[16] *IG* II² 8781 and *SEG* 28.95.38. Menestratos was also the name of Strateia's father, and it would seem that the Kriton of *SEG* 28.95.38 is more likely Strateia's husband than, as Trail (294) suggests, her grandson. Another Kriton of perhaps the same family was an *ephebe* ca. 110 A.D. (*IG* II² 2020.38).

[17] *IG* II² 1956.153–55 and 1957.15.

περίοικοι who manned the garrison at Rhamnous. But, to judge from the surviving mercenary lists, this type of service was not a favored career for Heracleotai. The proportion of their enrolment as mercenaries is much smaller than their proportion of the foreign population in general. On the artistic side, the Heracleote Spintharos wrote tragedy in Athens in the last quarter of the fifth century (Burstein 34). Baton was a sculptor ca. 200 B.C., and three of his signatures survive.[18] Dionysios, son of Simos acted in Athens at the City Dionysia ca. 251 B.C. and also, some years previously, at the Soteria in Delphi.[19] In 129/8 Apollonios was a "pipe player" (*SEG* 21.694), and, finally, in ca. 47–42 the Heracleote Antiochos served as one of the παιδευταί of the ephebes (*IG* II² 1040.41–42).

Clearchos had studied philosophy and rhetoric in Athens, and some of his countrymen attained prominence there as teachers and scholars, several in the following of Plato and Aristotle, including Amyclas, Bryson, Chamaileon, and Chion. Chion returned to Heracleia under Clearchos' rule and served in the court. Later, however, he turned against Clearchos, and in 352 participated in his assassination. For this he paid with his life. But the most famous Heracleote philosopher at Athens was Heracleides Pontikos. A student of Speusippos and Aristotle and a prolific writer himself, he was a fixture of the philosophical community in Athens until he too returned to Heracleia, in 339 B.C.[20]

For all Heracleotai, rich or poor, philosophers or mercenaries, it must have been very difficult to satisfy their religious needs. Participation in most Athenian state religious activities was, from earliest times, excluded for metics and other non-citizens. The few Heracleote boys who found

[18] *IG* II² 3858, 4280, and 4281.

[19] Ghiron-Bistagne 321.

[20] On these Heracleote philosophers in Athens, see Burstein 41, 61, 64, and 123 nn. 28 and 29.

their way into the *ephebeia* after 123 B.C. would have had
some official role in Athenian state cult, but how had their
fathers and grandfathers, mothers and grandmothers, and
all other Heracleotai worshipped the gods in Athens?

The Heracleotai did this, it appears, by eagerly participat-
ing in the variety of "foreign," non-Athenian cults available
in Attica. Such *thiasoi* were not numerous, and the evidence
for them is meager, but when we have such evidence, we
are likely to find a Heracleote there. Demophilos and
Dionysios were both officials of the cult of Pankrates in its
early times, in 300/299 B.C. (*SEG* 41.171 and 247E). In
299/8 Menis was honored by his fellow devotees of Zeus
Labraundos in Piraeus for being an honest and generous
treasurer of the *thiasos* (*IG* II² 1271). In 266/5 Kephalion
was a priest of one of the cults of the Mother of the gods in
Piraeus (*IG* II² 1271). In the first century, when most such
foreign cults had died out, Heracleotai turned elsewhere.
Ca. 50 B.C. Dorion served as the first known ζάκορος of the
state cult of Asclepios, an office modeled on eastern cults
and open in most cults in the Hellenistic period only to foreigners (*IG* II² 4466).[21] And, in 103/2 B.C., Zobios joined
one of the first cults in which we know Athenians and foreigners worshipped together, that oι Sabazios in Piraeus
(*IG* II² 1335).

Among these activities we can only guess at any pecu-
liarly "Heracleote" elements. Zeus Labraundos is certainly
distinctive. The cult of this Carian deity was centered at
Labraunda, about ten miles east southeast of Miletos. This
Zeus was worshipped also at Miletos,[22] and I strongly suspect, though evidence is lacking, that he was introduced to
Piraeus by Milesians and that Heracleotai shared in this
cult as they shared in other *thiasoi* with Milesians.[23] It would

---

[21] On Dorion and the ζάκορος of the Asclepios cult, see Aleshire 87.
[22] Laumonier 552.

seem improbable that Pontic Heracleotai worshipped him in their homeland and brought him from there. Equally distinctive is the cult of Pankrates in Athens. As early as 300/299 two Heracleotai and a Milesian were officers of the cult. The cult's location is familiar to American visitors to Athens, directly beneath Harry S. Truman on Leophoros Constantinou, and Pankrates has maintained himself, 2500 years later, as the eponym of this district of Athens called Pangrati. The cult featured Zeus and Heracles type figures and first appears in the second half of the fourth century, just at that time when Heracleote exiles first arrived in Athens.[24] When and if the material from the cult is fully published, we will probably find it to be the strongest and longest lasting of the foreign cults in Athens in the Hellenistic period, and it may have owed its prominence and durability to the many Heracleotai and Milesians living in Athens throughout the period. The reported participation of some Athenian men in this "foreign" cult, very unusual in this period, may have resulted from their intermarriage with Heracleote and Milesian women. Here we may have a cult founded by Heracleotai after their Heracles,[25] a cult in which Milesians also joined, or else a cult founded by Milesians (on the model of Zeus Labraundos?) in which Heracleotai found something akin

---

[23] Strabo (12.3.4) claims that Heracleia Pontica was a colony of Miletos and this would go far in explaining the Heracleote and Milesian joint ventures in Athenian cult, but Strabo is probably mistaken. The historical Heracleia was clearly a colony of combined elements from Megara and the Boeotian League, and Burstein (13–15) denies any Milesian involvement, early or late, in the colonizing of Heracleia.

[24] The sanctuary was discovered in 1953. Of the reportedly large number of inscriptions found in 1953 and 1954, only fourteen (collected in *SEG* 41.247) have received any form of publication whatsoever. For the many reliefs and for some very elaborate and highly speculative discussion of the origins of this cult, see Vikela.

[25] On Heracles in Heracleia, see Burstein 35 and 107 n. 44.

to the Heracles of their Heracleian homeland. Whatever the case, a relief dedicated to Heracles by a Heracleote (*IG* II² 4952) should probably be added to the fifty-two known and published reliefs of this cult and indicates that some Heracleotai were still devoted to Heracles in the Roman period.[26]

We thus have a large number of Heracleotai in Athens throughout the Hellenistic and Roman periods, pursuing careers and opportunities open to metics and foreigners, some attaining rather high levels of economic and social success. Some Heracleote women married Athenians and thereby established citizen political and religious rights for their future generations. The Heracleotai, in religious matters, initially were limited to their own domestic cults and to whatever few "foreign" religious associations they might join or found, but as soon as Athenian religious and social institutions were opened up to foreigners in the late Hellenistic period, the Heracleotai were among the first to seize the new opportunities and to integrate themselves further into Athenian life.

Works Cited

Aleshire, S. B. 1989. *The Athenian Asklepieion*. Amsterdam.

Burstein, S. M. 1976. *Outpost of Hellenism: The Emergence of Heraclea on the Black Sea*. University of California Publications: Classical Studies 14. Berkeley.

Garland, R. 1982. "A First Catalogue of Attic Peribolos Tombs." *ABSA* 77:125–76.

Ghiron-Bistagne, P. 1976. *Recherches sur les acteurs dans la Grèce antique*. Paris.

[26] For this relief see Oehler 47, no. 2 and pl. 94a. For helpful discussion of this relief I am indebted to Carol Lawton.

Laumonier, A. 1958. *Les cultes indigènes en Carie.* Paris.

Oehler, H. 1980. *Foto und Skulptur: Römische Antiken in englischen Schlössern.*

Reinmuth. 1972. "*I.G.*, II², 1006 and 1301." *Hesperia* 41:185–91.

Trail, J. 1978. "Greek Inscriptions from the Athenian Agora." *Hesperia* 47.269–326.

Vikela, E. 1994. *Die Weihreliefs aus dem athener Pankrates-Heiligtum am Ilissos, Mitteilungen des Deutschen Archäologischen Instituts.* Athenische Abteilung 16. Berlin.

The Dacian Walls Speak:
Plato in Moldavia

Helen F. North
Swarthmore College

Among the benefits conferred on lovers of the classical world by Paul MacKendrick there is one that may properly be called unique: his series of books on archaeological sites in countries settled by the Greeks and Romans, which have guided innumerable travelers since 1960, when *The Mute Stones Speak* first appeared. As a veteran of many Swarthmore Alumni Colleges Abroad in Mediterranean and Central European areas, as well as cruises sponsored by other organizations, not to mention individual travel over many years, I acknowledge a profound debt to the Roman, Greek, German, French, North African, Iberian, and Dacian *Stones*. My contribution to this *Festschrift* grows out of a visit to Romania, which began with a close study of *The Dacian Stones Speak*.

In October a year ago, after exploring the museums of Constantza and traveling to Adamclissi to make what we could of the remains of the Tropaeum of Trajan and its bizarre reconstruction, our party ventured outside MacKendrick territory and flew up to the Carpathians to visit three of the marvelously decorated monasteries of Moldavia, which, with their well-preserved exterior paintings, provide a fascinating glimpse of late Byzantine iconography as interpreted by Romanian artists of the sixteenth century. At two of the sites my eye was caught by the image of Plato (identified by name), richly dressed, crowned, holding in his hand a scroll inscribed in Old Church Slavonic, and bearing on top of his crown a coffin containing a skeleton (Illustration 1). Riveted by this emblem, I thought at once of *Republic* X, the *Phaedo*, and other dialogues that might have inspired such a conception, and it is this portrayal that I should like to elucidate, after a preliminary glance at the iconography of Plato at certain key periods since the fourth century B.C.

In spite of the warning of the Platonic Socrates that images lack the qualities possessed by their originals (*Crat.* 432b), Plato, like most founders of ancient philosophical schools, has never wanted for portraits. Olympiodorus in his *Life* of Plato says that they were set up everywhere (1.32 Westerman). True, there was no episode in his life-story comparable to Aristotle's apocryphal entanglement with Phyllis. Hence he did not enjoy the widespread popularity in mediaeval art that caused his pupil to be portrayed in so many satirical cycles depicting the enslavement of wise men to their courtesan-mistresses. There is always a certain sobriety about the representation of Plato, whether in sculpture, mosaics, painting, or manuscript illumination, comparable to the ὄγκος (dignity) and ὕψος (loftiness) recognized by ancient critics in the style of his dialogues. Nevertheless, the conception of the philosopher and his significance differs from age to age, as do the medium and the skill of the artist, and in each case the image tells us something about

Illustration 1. *Tree of Jesse, Sucevitza, detail (Plato).*
Photograph by the author.

how Plato was regarded at a given time and with what aspect of contemporary culture he was connected.

The earliest recorded image is the statue erected at the Academy. According to Diogenes Laertius (3.25) Favorinus in his *Memorabilia* records that Mithradates the Persian dedicated to the Muses a statue of Plato made by Silanion. Dating probably from around 370 B.C., it was evidently the source of many copies, sixteen or more portrait busts (not full-length statues) being accounted for, mostly of Roman manufacture in the first to third centuries of our era.[1] The expression is serious, even melancholy, and the closely cropped hair, the short locks combed down over the forehead, and the full beard determined the way Plato would be represented thereafter, whenever a serious attempt was made at portraiture.[2]

It was probably a bust derived from Silanion's statue to which Cicero gave an honored place both on the lawn of his Tusculan villa and in the *Brutus,* his dialogue on the history of Roman oratory that he set *in pratulo propter Platonis statuam* (*Brutus* 6.24) and in which he saluted Plato's eloquence. Who, Cicero asks, is richer in style (*uberior in dicendo*) than Plato? He quotes the familar saying that if

[1] See Boehringer for photographs of sixteen statues in ninety-two plates; Richter 2.165–67, figs. 903–75; Bernoulli 2.18–34 and plates IV–VI. For two portraits of Plato recently acquired by museums in Munich and Kassel see Zanker, figs. 24, 38, 39a, b.

[2] Plato's detractors accused him of being ill-disposed (δυσμενής) toward everyone (Athenaeus xi.506a) and of knowing how to do nothing but frown (σκυθρωπάζειν), raising his eyebrows haughtily like a snail (Amphis, fr. 13, Kassel and Austin). Winter attempts a sociological analysis of Plato portraits, including versions by Raphael, Rubens, and Rembrandt. Plate 6, 137–38, shows Plato as an ecstatic mystic, *flamine divino plenus.* See Zanker 40–43, 67–77 for modern interpretations of Plato's ancient portraits and for the conclusion that "Plato was depicted not as a philosopher, but simply as a good Athenian citizen" (76), i.e., not as a model for the portrayal of intellectuals.

Jove spoke Greek, he would speak like Plato and repeats the widely held belief that Demosthenes had been Plato's pupil, although admitting that the philosophic style, if used in court, would seem *pacatior*—too tame (31.120-21). Since Cicero aspired to combine philosophy and rhetoric, Plato was the ideal choice for a symbolic presence in the *Brutus*, even as the plane tree under which the dialogue *De Oratore* is conducted explicitly paid tribute to the setting of the *Phaedrus* (*De Or.* 1.28, *Phaedr.* 229a) and implicitly, according to one interpretation, to Plato himself, if the Greek name of the tree (πλάτανος) is a covert allusion to the philosopher.

In Hellenistic art Plato was associated with a wide range of other learned figures—philosophers, sophists, poets. At the Serapeion in Memphis an exedra dated to the time of Ptolemy I displayed statues of Plato, Thales, Heraclitus, and Protagoras amid a group of poets—Homer, Pindar, Hesiod—and others unidentified, eleven in all.[3] The standing statue lacks a head, but is identified by an ancient graffito on the base. The grouping represents an agglomeration of the best in various literary categories, poetry and prose, without exclusive attention to philosophy. It has been suggested that it originated in the Library of the Serapeion of Alexandria,[4] and if so it would be an early example of the vogue for adorning sections of a library with portraits of the authors whose works were kept there—a vogue that extended through the great libraries of the Middle Ages and the Renaissance even into modern times.

In Rome in the late Republic there was another vogue, this one for portraits of great men in every conceivable category (Pliny *NH* 35.2). Varro's *Imagines*, in fifteen books, contained 700 portraits, Greeks and Romans, statesmen,

---

[3] Lauer and Picard 120-47.
[4] Schefold 191 n. 1.

poets, philosophers, and this work became so popular that there was demand for an epitome in four books.[5] Varro's images were grouped in sevens (an alternative title was *Hebdomades*). What might be called vocational groupings were fashionable, and it was in gatherings of ancient thinkers that Plato is sometimes thought to have been represented, most often in mosaics. The Seven Wise Men, of whom Plato was not one, provided a model for such groups. He himself was the first to mention this canon (*Prot.* 343a), whose content varied enormously. It was the number, not the identity, of the members that remained constant, and if the names are not supplied, it is rarely possible to be sure who is included in a given group. A first-century mosaic from Torre Annunziata, now in the National Museum, Naples, showing seven typical philosophers and thought to be a copy of a Hellenistic painting has been variously identified as the Seven Sages, with Thales pointing at a sphere, a scene from the Academy, with Plato doing the pointing, and a scene from the Lyceum featuring Demetrius of Phaleron.[6] Another copy of the same Hellenistic painting, a second-century mosaic from Sarsina in Umbria, now in the Villa Albani, gives rise to the same conflicting theories. A Cologne mosaic, dating from the later third century after Christ, shows the busts of six figures, all sages or philosophers (except for Sophocles), grouped around Diogenes. One is identified as Plato, another as

[5] Rawson 199.

[6] Hanfmann 210, 226–27 nn. 25, 26; Bernoulli 34–38, figs 3, 4; Richter 1.81–91, figs. 316, 319; Elderkin 92–111. The existence of a sculptural group of Seven Wise Men in Athens is suggested by *Anth. Graec.* 16.332 (Zanker 355 n. 38). For portrait heads of philosophers and their pupils at Aphrodisias in the fifth century and a general discussion of late antique groups of intellectuals see Smith 127–55. Laurer and Picard 157 trace the Italian mosaics to the Memphis Serapeion by way of Hellenistic murals.

Aristotle, but the names are nineteenth-century restorations.[7]

One more trace of a statue of Plato erected before the end of antiquity is found in the *Ecphrasis* of Christodoros, who mentions a heterogeneous group of sixty bronzes standing in the Zeuxippos, a public gymnasium in Constantinople, where they were set up in the time of Septimius Severus. They include poets, prose-writers, gods, goddesses, and other figures from mythology, whom the poet describes in hexameter verses varying in length from two lines (Plato) to forty (Homer). His characterization of Plato gives no hint of the way he was portrayed: "There stood godlike Plato, who previously showed the Athenians the hidden ways of the heaven-taught virtues" (*Anth. Graec.* 2.97–98). The gymnasium was destroyed by fire shortly after the poem was written (A.D. 532), and there is no way of knowing whether any of the later representations of Plato derived from this statue, rather than from that by Silanion, or whether, indeed, this was Silanion's original, transported like so much Greek sculpture to Byzantium.

Of the surviving or reported ancient representations—statues, busts, mosaics—it may be said that all testify to the veneration accorded to Plato in antiquity as philosopher, rhetorician, or man of letters. Where he is associated with other figures they are persons of intellectual eminence, whether philosophers or not. The frequency with which ancient literary critics pair him with Homer[8] makes it understandable that he should be closely linked with the poet in art, as in the glass panels in *opus sectile* (c. 365–375) found at Kenchreai, where figures of Plato and Homer evidently

---

[7] Richter 1.81, figs. 351, 359, 360; Schefold 155, figs. 4, 5, 7–9; Parlasca 80–82.

[8] "Longinus" 13.3; Quintilian 10.1.81; Cicero, *Tusc.Disp.* 1.79 (Panaetius called Plato *Homerum philosophorum*).

formed a pair.[9] The popular grouping of the Seven Wise
Men doubtless inspired the inclusion of Plato with other
notable philosophers of the archaic and later periods, when
Roman householders commissioned mosaics, portrait
busts, or statues to demonstrate their cultural aspirations.

In the Middle Ages Plato is sometimes represented in
scenes involving another group of seven, this time the liberal arts. Although the famous portrayal of the arts and
their historical practitioners on the Royal Portal at
Chartres (1145–55) links with dialectic a figure generally
identified as Aristotle, there are miniatures from the 12th
century onward that show Plato too in the neighborhood of
this art. Katzenellenbogen calls attention to a French manuscript of about 1140 in which the commentary of Boethius
on Porphyry's *Isagoge* is preceded by an image of Dialectica
standing on a pedestal, with much smaller figures above
and below—Plato and Aristotle above her head, Socrates
and a contemporary dialectician, Magister Adam, at her
feet. All four are seated and make gestures with pointing
figures to indicate disputation.[10]

Plato could also be associated with the art of music, once
again in connection with Boethius. Katzenellenbogen discusses an English miniature of about 1160 in a manuscript
of Boethius' *De Musica* which, while not portraying Musica
herself, shows four philosophers engaged in activities connected with the practice or theory of music. Boethius and
Pythagoras play musical instruments, while Plato and
Nicomachus engage in disputation. Plato, described in the
margin as *summus philosophorum*, is said to teach (*edocet*).
While gesturing with the didactic index finger of his right
hand, he holds in his left a large book inscribed with the
word MUSICA. Nicomachus stands facing him, gesturing

[9] Ibrahim 164–78, figs. 33, 148–52; Zanker 324–25.
[10] Katzenellenbogen 39–55 and fig. 5.

with his right hand and holding in his left a much smaller book, also inscribed with the word *musica* (in smaller letters). Unlike Boethius and Pythagoras, who sit on chairs, Plato is enthroned on a sphere, presumably representing the world as described in the *Timaeus*.[11]

Not just one of the individual arts, but Philosophia herself is associated with Plato (and Socrates) in the intricate scheme devised by Herrad of Landsberg in the *Hortus Deliciarum* (late 12th century) to show the relation among philosophy, the liberal arts, the good philosophers, and the false arts. In a design suggesting a rose window a central circle is divided into unequal parts. In the larger, upper segment sits Philosophia enthroned, while in the lower, smaller segment sit Socrates and Plato, identified by the word *philosophi* on the bench on which they sit and by their names to the left of each head. They are engaged in writing. Inscriptions describe the achievement of the two philosophers: they taught at first ethics, then natural science, and finally rhetoric, and they were the sages of the world, the clerics of the gentiles.[12] Above the two seated philosophers is the more general statement that philosophy has taught how to investigate the nature of the universe. Here and elsewhere the fact that Socrates actually wrote nothing is ignored, in favor of the conventional method of representing teachers with scrolls or other writing materials.

In all these 12th-century portrayals Plato is honored for legitimate achievements—the teaching of dialectic, the discussion of musical theory, the study of philosophy—and in each of the miniatures analyzed by Katzenellenbogen he is shown teaching, disputing, or writing. But a well-known 13th-century manuscript in the Bodleian Library, Oxford (MS Ashmole 304) shows Plato in a totally new context, in-

[11] Katzenellenbogen, fig. 6.
[12] Katzenellenbogen 49 and fig. 9.

structing Socrates as he writes a treatise on fortune-telling.[13]

The historian Matthew Paris, monk of St. Albans, illustrated the *Prognostics of Socrates the King* by showing Socrates seated before a writing desk, dipping pen into inkpot, listening to Plato, who stands behind his chair. Above Socrates' head is his name, capitalized. Plato's name is also given, but without the capital. His left hand, index finger pointing, gestures in front of Socrates, who cocks his head to listen. Plato's right hand rests on the back of the chair, finger pointed as if to prod Socrates. His brow is corrugated, his expression anxious and intent. His position behind Socrates' chair and his attitude as of one giving instruction recall a scene familiar in ancient art, when a Muse, standing behind a seated figure, usually that of a poet, leans over him and points to a book that he is reading.[14]

Many who see the miniature express surprise that Plato is teaching Socrates, rather than Socrates Plato,[15] but surely the representation of Plato telling Socrates what to write testifies to a lingering memory of Plato as the true author of Socratic dialogues in which he himself does not take part. If so, it is a striking recognition of the haunting elusiveness of Plato's persona in his own writings. More surprising is the connection of the two philosophers with fortune-telling, but, as we shall see, the Middle Ages credited the pagan Wise Men with prophetic powers unknown in the classical period. We should not forget Virgil the magician.

---

[13] Hassall 73–75.

[14] For two examples see Knauer 13–46 and figs. 25, 27.

[15] See Derrida 13–14 for his reaction to the "révélation apocalyptique" of finding Plato behind Socrates. I am indebted to Professor Frederick J. Crosson for calling my attention to Derrida's typically bizarre discussion.

The most celebrated of all images of Plato, at the center of Raphael's School of Athens (1508–11), returns to the sobriety of the liberal arts tradition and portrays him, with Aristotle, in a context where the two philosophers are both thought to represent dialectic.[16] In the midst of groups suggesting the other liberal arts and containing figures who have been likened to their celebrated practitioners stand Plato and Aristotle. Tucked under his left arm Plato holds a book whose title, *Timaeus,* explains the gesture of his right hand, pointing upward towards the heavens. Aristotle holds the *Ethics,* and his gesture—right hand stretched out, palm downward—indicates that he is concerned with what is on earth. Socrates, the first of the Attic triad, is unmistakably present in the group representing rhetoric (a group that even includes what looks like the personified Rhetorica of Martianus Capella),[17] but Plato and Aristotle together occupy center stage, thus demonstrating the primacy of dialectic.

If we now return to the Dacian walls, we find that Plato continues to be a didactic figure linked with other philosophers, but his message is entirely different—shockingly so— and his philosophical peers, while still including Socrates and Aristotle, have become more numerous and much more heterogeneous. The painting at the monastery of Voronetz, corresponding to the one at Sucevitza that first captured my attention, uses the same gesture with the right index finger pointing upward as we have seen in the 12th-century miniatures and the School of Athens, while at both Voronetz and Sucevitza Plato holds a scroll proclaiming a message to the viewer. On the walls of both monasteries Plato and other pagan thinkers—including a Sibyl—are part of elaborate representations of the Tree of Jesse, and without exception their scrolls refer in some way to the doc-

[16] Garrard 372–73.
[17] Garrard 372.

trine of the Trinity, the Incarnation, the Redemption, or the honor due to the Blessed Virgin.

One of the glories of the Moldavian monastic churches is the painting of scriptural subjects that adorns their exterior walls, a 16th-century development that has been compared to the carving on Romanesque churches in the West.[18] Like the sculpture concentrated around the entrances of such churches, the Moldavian paintings would have provided instruction to the crowds of laypeople gathered outside the tiny monastic establishments. Their iconography, while in most respects faithful to Byzantine tradition, exhibits some characteristics peculiar to a small group of churches in Serbia, Bulgaria, Yugoslavia, and Mt. Athos, as well as Romania, in all of which the Tree of Jesse is prominent and is embellished with pagan thinkers as well as Hebrew prophets.

In the refectory of the Great Lavra on Mt. Athos in the sixteenth century the Tree of Jesse, surmounting a portrayal of the death of Abel, shows the sleeping Jesse framed by a frieze of philosophers and other ancient prophetic figures, six on the right, six on the left.[19] Their names are given: Philo, Cleanthes, Solon, "Dialid," Pythagoras, Socrates on the viewer's left, Homer, Aristotle, Galen, the Sibyl, Plato, and Plutarch on his right. All of them are gorgeously robed, some of them crowned, carrying scrolls whose message they emphasize with eloquent gestures. Plato, second from the end on the viewer's right, carries a scroll, but there is no sign of the coffin and skeleton. The theme of pagan prophets of the Incarnation actually appears much earlier (in 1310–13 at Prizren in Serbia), but the Great Lavra (c. 1536) is the first of these Eastern churches to exhibit the full iconographical scheme, parts

---

[18] Grabar 6.
[19] Millet, plate 151.3; Chatziakis, plate 33.

of which survive in some seventeen churches painted between the thirteenth and seventeenth centuries.[20]

The Jesse Tree normally adorns church interiors, but in Moldavia in the sixteenth century it moves to the outer walls, where in some cases it has survived to this day in a remarkable state of preservation, spectacular with its scrolling acanthus branches against a vivid green or blue background. Usually on the south wall, the Tree may have a frieze of philosophers underneath, on either side of Jesse, or they may serve as a kind of frame in a vertical band on one side or both. Thus at Voronetz, most famous for the magnificent Last Judgment on the west wall (painted around 1550), the south wall is occupied by a Tree of Jesse of the same date, to the right of which is the band of philosophers,[21] with Aristotle at the bottom and in ascending order Plato, the Sibyl, Pythagoras, Socrates, and a sixth figure at the top, difficult to identify.[22] Each figure holds a scroll with an inscription in Old Church Slavonic, but only Plato has the attribute that caught my eye at Sucevitza, the open coffin containing a skeleton just above his crowned head. Also above his head is an object resembling the sun in profile, much like a relief on a post-Byzantine plaque at the Great Lavra.[23] It is at this object that Plato is pointing (Illustration 2).

At Sucevitza, built in 1584, where the frescoes are dated to 1602-4, ten figures form a frieze beneath the Tree, some of them with puzzling names (found elsewhere also in this tradition). To Plato, Porphyry, Homer, Sophocles, Aristotle, and the Sibyl are added such mysterious personages

---

[20] Taylor 130. Consult this article for a detailed analysis of the tradition to which the Byzantine Jesse Trees belong.

[21] There may have been a corresponding band on the other side, now effaced.

[22] Taylor 135 n. 34, gives the name Thgilid.

[23] Kados 152, plate 82.

Illustration 2. *Tree of Jesse, Voronetz, detail (Plato). Photograph by Dan Grigorescu, from Petru Comarnescu, Voroneţ: 15th and 16th Century Frescoes (Bucharest 1959) plate 129.*

as Astakoe, Goliud, Vaso, Udin, Selum, and Saul. Plato, a dignified figure with long gray beard, clad in a gold-bordered red tunic over a dark green skirt, holds in both hands a scroll proclaiming that Christ will be born of Mary in the time of Constantine and Helen,[24] the same message as at Voronetz. On his head is a three-pointed crown, immediately on top of which is an open coffin containing a skeleton. There is no trace of a sun-disk.

A third Moldavian monastic church, at Moldovitza, was painted in 1537, earlier than Voronetz and Sucevitza. Here the philosophers, including Plato, Plutarch, Aristotle, the Sibyl, and the unidentifiable Astakoe, Thudi, and Omir (Homer?) are ranged in two vertical bands, to left and right of the Jesse Tree. Plato, standing below Aristotle, is shown in a frontal position, holding his right hand against his chest, his left grasping a scroll, which bears the same message as at Voronetz and Sucevitza. The object above his head, which looks like a plaque supporting the figure of an infant, must nevertheless be the Platonic emblem of the open coffin with skeleton, crudely rendered. Here too the sun-disk is lacking.

Not until 1936 was it pointed out that more than two centuries earlier than the Moldavian churches a Tree of Jesse carved in relief on the façade of the cathedral at Orvieto (c. 1305–8) included two rows of prophetic figures, one a Sibyl, another a male figure beside which is a large open coffin containing a skeleton. The scrolls flourished by the prophets, bearing no inscription, offer no aid to identification, but there can be no doubt about the presence here of Plato.[25]

[24] I am grateful to my colleague George Krugovoy and to Professors John F. Callahan and Ihor Ševčenko for help with the original Old Church Slavonic.

[25] Nava 363. See also Carli, plate 16.

The image of a skeleton in close proximity to a philosopher may remind us of the Boscoreale cups and the whole
tradition of skeletons as tokens of the inevitability of death,
even for the wise,[26] but the Orvieto façade and the
Moldavian churches are indebted to a different tradition,
or rather two traditions, one going back to the sixth century, the other to the ninth. The first leads to the association of the pagan thinkers with the Tree of Jesse, the second to the emblem of the sun, the coffin, and the skeleton
in proximity to a philosopher who prophesies the birth of
Christ. When the two traditions come together, we have
the Plato of the Moldavian churches.

First, the older tradition, that of pagans foretelling the Incarnation. While early Church Fathers celebrated the wisdom of certain Greek philosophers, especially Plato and
Aristotle, it was the Sibyls whom Lactantius and Augustine
credited with Messianic prophecies, believed to have prepared the Roman Empire for the birth of Christ.[27] To link
them with Hebrew prophets was to proclaim the parallelism of the Old Testament and pagan antiquity in the universal goodness of God (as later in the *Dies irae: teste David
cum Sibylla*), and it is not surprising that Sibyls made an
early appearance in representations of the Tree of Jesse, beginning in the 11th century.[28] In French stained glass windows portraying the Jesse Tree they are recorded first at S.
Denis and may still be seen at Chartres. The philosophers
who appear on the façade of the duomo in Siena in the
13th century (Plato and Aristotle as prophets of the Gen-

[26] Dunbabin 228–31. Cf. also the 15th-century "Rouen iconography" of the cardinal virtues, which gives Prudentia a coffin on her head
as a *memento mori*.

[27] Lactantius *Div. Inst.* 1.6.12, Augustine *De Civ. Dei* 18.23. For the
Sibylline oracles in Western Mediaeval literature and art, consult Parke
152–73, Ayrton 126–31.

[28] Watson 9, 20; Francovich 1.213 n. 245; Henry 233.

tiles along with the Erythraean Sibyl, beside the Hebrew prophets)[29] first enter the picture through collections of Prophecies (*Chresmoi* or *Theologiai*) of Greek Wise Men, in circulation from the sixth century and derived from the *Theosophia* of Aristokritos, wherein eminent Greeks and Hebrews foretold the birth of Christ.[30] In several manuscripts related to the *Chresmoi* Seven Sages, including Plato, utter such prophecies, and eventually they are coopted to support the Tree of Jesse.[31]

There grew up a tradition of painters' manuals providing instruction in how to represent the Tree of Jesse, the best known of which is the *Hermeneia* of Dionysios of Fourna, active on Mt. Athos c. 1730, which incorporated material from earlier sets of directions. Related manuals in Romania, often differing in the identity of the Sages and the text of their scrolls, were used by the Moldavian painters, who obviously knew a version in which Plato says that Christ will be born of the Virgin Mary in the reign of Constantine and Helen, the message invariably inscribed on his scroll.

A Romanian version of the *Hermeneia* specifies that this message was found on Plato's tomb,[32] and here the second tradition intersects with the first. In the 9th-century *Chronographia* of Theophanes the Confessor, the annals of the year 781, the first year of the joint reign of the Empress Irene and her son Constantine VI, record the discovery in the "Long Walls of Thrace" of a larnax containing the body of a man. On the sarcophagus was an inscription that said, "Christ will be born of Mary the virgin, and I believe in Him. In the time of the rulers Constantine and Irene, O Sun, you will see me again."[33] Although the occupant of the

[29] Ayrton, plates 97, 102 (Plato), 95 (Erythraean Sibyl).
[30] Francovich 1.213–19, Delatte 97–111.
[31] Mango 201–7, Taylor 141 n. 53, Henry 233–34, 274.
[32] Mango 205.
[33] 1.455, 12–17.

sarcophagus was not named by Theophanes and was variously identified as the story found its way into many Greek
and Latin chronicles (it was cited even by St. Thomas
Aquinas),[34] the name of Plato came to be most tenaciously
attached to the tomb, and thus we find the Moldavian
painters of the Jesse Tree endowing him with the open coffin and skeleton, and at Voronetz faithfully adding the detail of Helios looking upon the philosopher once again, as
predicted in the *Chronographia*. The message on his scroll is
identical with that recorded by Theophanes, except for the
substitution of Helen for Irene, presumably because in connection with the name Constantine that of Helen seemed
more impressive, and by the sixteenth century Irene and
her son were of little consequence.

It remains to ask why the pagan seers, including Plato
with his emblematic coffin, appeared in the fourteenth century at Orvieto and two centuries later in Moldavia, in each
case embellishing the Tree of Jesse. Michael D. Taylor,
whose study of the Orvieto Tree and its Balkan relatives
has solved many problems connected with this iconography, suggests that the archetype, now lost, was produced
around 1262–64 in northern Italy in reaction to heretical
doctrines such as those of the Cathars or Patarines, active
in Orvieto in the 13th century, which denied the human
nature of Christ. It was at this time that Pope Urban IV was
living in Orvieto and could have chosen, as a means to oppose this heresy, the Jesse Tree, which graphically demonstrated the descent of Christ through His Blessed Mother
from Jesse and six generations of Old Testament Kings, according to the prophecy of Isaiah XI.1–3. The testimony of

[34] *S. Theol.* pt. II–II q.2.a.7, where both the Sibyl and the discovery of
the sarcophagus are cited as examples of revelation to the gentiles.
Consult Mango 201–7 for references to the story and for the Romanian
redaction of the *Hermeneia* which connects the inscription with Plato's
tomb.

Hebrew prophets, normally pictured with the Jesse Tree, was now fortified by predictions ascribed to the pagan philosophers and "the wise Sibyl" as well—all available from the tradition of the *Chresmoi*. The hypothetical archetype gave rise, not only to the sculpture at Orvieto, but, carried across the Adriatic as early as c. 1268, to the Eastern variants, both on Mt. Athos and in the Romanian churches, where the persistence of Byzantine conventions in art caused the portrayal of the Jesse Tree to be replicated for centuries, long after competing types of iconography had reduced its appeal in the West.[35]

When I asked an Orthodox nun at Sucevitza why Plato was shown with the skeleton above his head, she replied, "Because he was always thinking about death." If we remember Plato's definition of philosophy as preparation for death, we must concede that there is a sense in which her explanation was correct, however innocent of the long, intricate history of the pagan Wise Men prophesying the birth of Christ or the origin of Plato's mysterious emblem.

Works Cited

Ayrton, Michael. 1969. *Giovanni Pisano Sculptor.* New York.

Bernoulli, Johann Jacob. 1969. *Griechische Ikonographie.* Vol. 2. Hildesheim.

Boehringer, Robert. 1935. *Platon: Bildnisse und Nachweise.* Breslau.

de Boor, Carolus G., ed. 1883–1885. *Theophanis Chronographia.* Leipzig. (Rpt. Hildesheim, 1963).

---

[35] Taylor 145–73; see 139 for the hypothetical stemma. The doctrine of Transsubstantiation depends on that of the Incarnation, and Taylor 150–51 notes that it was Urban IV who instituted the Feast of Corpus Christi in 1264 and caused the corporal involved in the Miracle of Bolsena to be moved to Orvieto.

Carli, Enzo. 1947. *Le Sculture del Duomo di Orvieto.* Bergamo.

Chatzidakis, Manolis. 1969–1970. "Recherches sur le peintre Théophane le Crétois." *Dumbarton Oaks Papers* 23–24:309–52.

Delatte, A. 1923. "Le declin de la légende des VII sages et les prophéties théosophiques." *Musée Belge* 27:97–111.

Derrida, Jacques. 1980. *La carte postale: De Socrate à Freud et au-delà.* Paris.

Dunbabin, Katharine M. D. 1986. "*Sic Erimus Cuncti . . .* The Skeleton in Graeco-Roman Art." *Jahrbuch des Deutschen Archäologischen Instituts* 101:185–255.

Elderkin, G. W. 1935. "Two Mosaics Representing the Seven Wise Men." *AJA* 39:92–111.

de Francovich, Geza. 1952. *Benedetto Antelami, Architetto e Scultore e l'Arte del Suo Tempo.* Milan and Florence.

Garrard, Mary D. 1984. "The Liberal Arts and Michelangelo's First Project for the Tomb of Julius II (with a Coda on Raphael's 'School of Athens')." *Viator* 15:335–404.

Grabar, André. 1963. *Painted Churches of Romania.* New York.

Hanfmann, George M. A. 1951. "Socrates and Christ." *HSCP* 60:205–33.

Hassall, A. G. and Dr. W. O. Hassall. 1976. *Treasures from the Bodleian Library.* New York.

Henry, Paul. 1930. *Les églises de la Moldavie du nord dès origines à la fin du XVIe siècle: architecture et peinture.* Paris.

Ibrahim, Leila, Robert Scanlon and Robert Brill. 1976. *Kenchreai: Eastern Port of Corinth: II. The Panels of Opus Sectile in Glass.* Leiden.

Kadas, Sotiris. 1979. *Mount Athos: An Illustrated Guide to the Monasteries and Their History.* Athens.

Katzenellenbogen, Adolf. 1961. "The Representation of the Seven Liberal Arts." In *Twelfth-Century Europe and the Foundations of Modern Society.* Eds. Marshall Clagett, Gaines Post and Robert Reynolds. Madison, Wisc. 39–55.

Knauer, Elfriede R. 1993. "Roman Wall Paintings from Boscotrecase: Three Studies in the Relationship between Writing and Painting." *Metropolitan Museum Journal* 28:13–46.

Lauer, J.-Ph. and Ch. Picard. 1955. *Les statues ptolemaïques du Serapieion de Memphis.* Paris.

Mango, C. 1963. "A Forged Inscription of the Year 781." *Recueil des travaux de l'Institut d'Etudes byzantines 8.* Mélanges G. Ostrogorsky. 201–7.

Millet, Gabriel. 1927. *Monuments de l'Athos: les peintures.* Paris.

Nava, A. 1936. "'L' Albero di Jesse' nella Cattedrale d'Orvieto e la Pittura Bizantina." *Rivista dell'Istituto d'Archeologia e Storia dell' Arte* 5.3:363–76.

Parke, H. W. 1988. *Sibyls and Sibylline Prophecy in Classical Antiquity.* Ed. B. C. McGing. London and New York.

Parlasca, Klaus. 1959. *Die römischen Mosaiken in Deutschland.* Berlin.

Rawson, Elizabeth. 1985. *Intellectual Life in the Late Roman Republic.* Baltimore.

Richter, G. M. A. 1965. *The Portraits of the Greeks.* London.

Schefold, Karl. 1943. *Die Bildnisse der antiken Dichter Redner und Denker.* Basel.

Smith, R. R. R. 1990. "Late Roman Philosophical Portraits from Aphrodisias." *JRS* 80:127–55.

Taylor, Michael D. 1980–1981. "A Historiated Tree of Jesse." *Dumbarton Oaks Papers* 34-35:125–76.

Watson, Arthur. 1934. *The Early Iconography of the Tree of Jesse.* Oxford.

Winter, E. K. 1930. *Platon: Das Soziologische in der Ideenlehre.* Vienna.

Zanker, Paul. 1995. *The Mask of Socrates: The Image of the Intellectual in Antiquity.* Tr. Alan Shapiro. Berkeley.

An Ordinary Aphrodisian Family: The Message of a Stone

૮૪૪૦૪૦૪

Joyce Reynolds
Newnham College, Cambridge

Stones can speak, as our honorand so happily demonstrated, but may need coaxing to give a useful message; which is of course, especially true of inscribed funerary stones, the most numerous category in our epigraphic *corpora* and the one most often written off as boringly monotonous. I offer, for his amusement I hope, a text from Aphrodisias, in essence a rather wordy assembly of formulae standard in the city's funeraries (although it contains one nugget of news), because it seems possible to coax out of it something about a family below the level of the élite who normally dominate our picture.[1] It will, I fear, seem very little and quite unsurprising.

[1] This is a detail from a larger work in progress, an attempt at analysis of the funerary inscriptions of Aphrodisias. All concerned with material discovered at Aphrodisias continue to owe a heavy debt to Professor Kenan T. Erim who excavated there, con amore, for so many

287

The text is cut on the lid of a marble pilaster-and-garland sarcophagus, in letters of a type common at Aphrodisias in the second and third centuries A.D., 0.02–0.03m. high; ΤΗ ligatured in l.4.[2] In the second line the letters ΙΚΟΣΟΠΡΟ and ΗΑΥΤΟΥΕ, in the third ΤΙΝΑΗΕΚΘΑ and ΒΗΣΚΑΙΕΠ are cut on projecting features of the lid; in l.4 ΘΕΩΑ and ΤΙΣΕΜ are cut on the projecting bases of the two central pilasters. A chip had removed the lower left hand corner of the base before the letterer began his work.

On the lid

    ἡ σορὸς καὶ ὁ τόπος καθ᾽οὗ ἐνκεῖται ἐστὶν Μάρκου
Αὐρηλίου Ζωτικοῦ τοῦ Διονυσίου εἰς ἣν σορὸν ταφή—
    σονται αὐτὸς Ζωτικὸς ὁ προγεγράμμενος καὶ Αὐρηλία
Τατία ἡ γυνὴ αὐτοῦ ἕτερος δὲ οὐδεὶς ἕξει
    ἐξουσίαν ἐνθάψαι τινα ἢ ἐκθάψαι τῶν προγεγραμμένων
ἐπεὶ ἔστω ἀσεβὴς καὶ ἐπάρατος καὶ τυμβωρύ—

On the base

    χος καὶ προσαποτείσει τῇ θεῷ ᾿Αφροδείτῃ ἀργυρίου *,ΒΦ᾽
καὶ τῇ σεμνοτάτῃ συντεχνίᾳ τῶν τε-
5   κτόνων *,Α ὧν τὸ τρίτον ἔστω τοῦ ἐγδικ(ήσα)ντος τῆς
ἐπιγραφῆς ἀπετέθη ἀντίγραφον εἰς χρεοφυλάκιον
    ἐπὶ στεφανηφόρου Ζήνωνος Μυλλέου τὸ β᾽μηνὸς Καισα-
ρεῶνος   *vacat*

The date is deducible from the nomenclature of ll.1, 2. Both husband and wife are Aurelii, but the husband's filiation is given in the Greek manner and seems to imply that his father was not a Roman citizen; it is very likely then that the pair were enfranchised following the *Constitutio Antoniniana* of A.D. 212. An approximate dating in the later

---

years. I am also, of course, indebted to his successors, Professor R. R. R. Smith and Dr C. Ratté.
    [2] For the type of sarcophagus see Asgari 345–49 and Isik; for the lettering, Reynolds 1982, 33.

years of the first quarter of the third century follows from this; the decoration and lettering are consonant.[3]

The sarcophagus was found in 1993–94 by the Director of the Aphrodisias Museum, along with others of a similar type, to the east of the city in a location distant from any known tombs of members of the civic élite.[4] In any case it betrays itself, even to a casual glance, as a somewhat pretentious piece of an ancient equivalent of mass production;[5] and either defective from the start or shop soiled—there is no telling how and when it lost its lower left corner, only that the letterer had to allow for that. It cannot have been exactly cheap even so, but it lacks the finesse of craftsmanship which would have made it expensive and, indeed, any individuality except in so far as the purchaser caused the inscription to be added. For the inscription he employed a reasonably competent letterer;[6] but given the space available, he could not avoid spoiling the aesthetic effect of the relief sculpture, without producing either an easily legible or a pleasing example of epigraphic art.[7]

[3] The non-Roman status implied by the name of the stephanephorus in l.6 is not contrary evidence, since a number of rich Aphrodisians are known to have bequeathed money to finance post mortem tenures of the stephanephorate which are not always indicated as such. Zenon was presumably stephanephorus for the first time before 212 and for the second post mortem and after that year.

[4] Such evidence as exists suggests that the élite tombs were nearer the city, the few that can be placed being beside the main roads as they left it; but study of Aphrodisian tombs is bedevilled by the fact that, in the immediate vicinity of the city, the structures above ground were apparently destroyed (possibly by an earthquake) around the middle of the fourth century A.D., after which their blocks were extensively used in the city-wall, see Roueché 1989, 43–44.

[5] See Isik.

[6] But one whose mind seems to have strayed from the job, see the uncorrected error in l.4.

[7] We might fairly deduce that it mattered very much to have the text

There is a considerable number of sarcophagi of similar date, similarly inscribed, at Aphrodisias. Three examples will help to define the range of persons to whom they belonged. The first is a rather better piece of work than ours, with some individuality since it includes portrait busts, while the inscription implies a larger and more monumental setting; it belonged to a city councillor and his brother—not, I should guess, of very high rank (judging by their names) but in the governing class. The second is again of rather better workmanship than ours, and probably a little grander, but not so very much so; its owners were a sculptor (who need not have been more than a hack-worker) and a *pigmentarius*, a man who sold paints—a couple of tradesmen in fact; the third was found near ours and is again rather better in quality and marked notably by an industrial scene among its reliefs, perhaps to be interpreted as glass blowing; the process shown was presumably the trade of the owners' family, although there is no reference to it in the inscription.[8] We are certainly being pointed in the direction of a modest society of reasonably prosperous tradesmen. Our owner's personal name confirms this, for while his father and his wife have names which are attested at all known levels of Aphrodisian society, his own name, Zoticus, has never appeared for a member of the élite. It occurs, however, on an unpublished sarcophagus of quality much like his own, found in the same area; and still more strikingly on the long inscription of Aphrodisian Jews and sympathisers with Judaism, where it is borne by one Jew and two sympathisers.[9] At the head of the list of sympathisers is a small group of city councillors (not, on the evidence of their names, very high in the civic hierarchy),

---

on the tomb, but that frequent or serious readers were not expected.

[8] MAMA VIII.575, 574; Smith and Ratté 27–29 with fig. 23.

[9] Reynolds and Tannenbaum 5–7.

but thereafter, both among the sympathisers and among the Jews themselves, a marked number of men are identified by their trades, some of which are quite humble ones like that of carder/fuller; but if I am right to interpret this inscription as a list of donors, no one on it can have been anything like poverty-stricken. It may also be relevant that Zoticus' wife is given no filiation; wives without filiation can be found in other funeraries at Aphrodisias but it seems more usual to give them one, even in modest families;[10] its absence here suggests that Zoticus set no store by his connection with her family.

Can the inscription tell us more? The text begins with a statement of ownership of a kind that is found on many Aphrodisian tombs[11]—the sarcophagus and the place on which it stands belong to M. Aurelius Zoticus. For sarcophagus Zoticus uses σορός, the preferred word at Aphrodisias, together with the colourless τόπος in a phrase which seems to mean simply the ground on which the sarcophagus stands. Many other Aphrodisians described or implied more elaborate contexts for their sarcophagi;[12] this is about as simple as it could be. Nevertheless he continued with lengthy provisions of a type that appears on many very grand Aphrodisian tombs as well as on other modest ones; he and his wife are the only persons who have a right to be buried in the sarcophagus—there is no reference to children nor to dependents, so this was perhaps an elderly couple with no offspring nor expectations of any[13] and no dependents in the household.[14] Anyone else who buries in

[10] Thus MAMA VIII.576.

[11] For the language of Aphrodisian funeraries see Kubinska 1976; the material is also presented in Kubinska 1968 where it is integrated into a wider study.

[12] Thus MAMA VIII.574, 581, 582.

[13] They may, of course, have had a married daughter whose husband was providing tomb-space for her.

[14] In some funeraries there is provision for θρέπτοι and/or for

it or removes the authorised bodies is to be impious, accursed and a tomb breaker and in addition to pay specified sums to two named institutions, out of which one third is to go to the successful prosecutor.[15] He adds that a copy of the document had been deposited in the civic Property Archive in a named month of a named year.[16] In essence Zoticus followed a local convention which is, with mild variants, widely attested in Asia Minor. His sentence is a little less formally constructed than in many other examples, for having stated that no one else has a right to use his sarcophagus and introduced a new clause with ἐπεί, he omits the hypothesis ("if anyone does so") and passes straight to the apodosis ("he is to be impious, etc."). We may argue that he is not a very literary type, but the omission is not unparalleled and the meaning not in doubt. It seems that it was a matter of individual choice how much the specified penalties should be and to whom they should be paid. Zoticus specified penalties of *3500—fairly low down in the Aphrodisian scale but not at the bottom of it.[17] Comparisons, however, are not wholly fair, since so few Aphrodisian funerary texts can be precisely dated or connected with the tomb complexes to which they referred, although the value

---

named persons of unclear status, perhaps dependents (thus MAMA VIII. 575); we do not know where household slaves were normally buried.

[15] It would be inappropriate to discuss here either the legal basis for these provisions or the frequency of prosecutions undertaken in accordance with them. What matters is that Zoticus thought it worth making and recording them—and (see below) was not entirely following convention in the manner in which he did so.

[16] LSJ originally glossed a χρεοφυλάκιον as an archive of public debts, but in its 1996 supplement withdraws the word "public"; in fact at Aphrodisias the bulk of the documents known to have been deposited in it were concerned with rights in property. The formula for the deposit shows that the documents were filed in monthly batches for each year.

[17] Thus *2500 in MAMA VIII.567, *3000 in 553, 10,000 in 545, 546.

of money certainly changed over time and the size and grandeur of the monuments must have been relevant to the sums specified. In the choice of institutions to receive the penalties Zoticus shows—on present evidence—his one sign of individuality. It was very common indeed to specify the civic deity, or the imperial treasury, or even the treasury of the Roman People; and a fair number of people named two recipients.[18] Zoticus paired the civic deity with the Tradesmen's Association of the τέκτονες (carpenters, joiners, but the word seems sometimes to be used for many kinds of makers, even builders). This is not quite the first time that a Tradesmen's Association has appeared as a recipient of a funerary penalty at Aphrodisias, but in the one earlier case the name of the trade has been lost.[19] It is the first time both that the full formula has survived and that the Association of Carpenters etc. has appeared there. It may well be that Zotikus was himself a member of the Association, despite the silence of his inscription;[20] but whether he was or not he certainly regarded its members as persons in whose goodwill he felt some faith. They were, we may conjecture, among his neighbours and "his kind of men."

The existence of a number of Tradesmen's Associations in Aphrodisias has come to light recently, mainly from inscribed seats in the civic stadium.[21] Clearly these Associa-

[18] Thus Aphrodite in MAMA VIII.565, 567, the imperial treasury in 538, 545, the treasury of the Roman People in 556b, 567; the city and the imperial treasury in 542, Aphrodite and the imperial treasury in 576.

[19] Reinach, no. 186, where I propose συν]τεχνίᾳ for Reinach's odd κακο]τεχνία; there is no doubt that the word stands within the prescription of a recipient of a funerary penalty.

[20] Compare the silence of the inscription on the sarcophagus figuring an industrial scene, p. 290 above.

[21] Published and discussed by Roueché 1993, 83–98, 112, 124. The basic work on the Tradesmen's Associations is Waltzing; a new discussion concentrating on the evidence from the eastern provinces (poorly

tions were publicly recognised and their members consti-
tuted, in virtue of their membership, a mildly privileged
section of the citizen body, joining in appropriate public
occasions as such. Zoticus describes the Association of Carpenters etc. as σεμνοτάτη, which may well be an official title
for a publicly recognised Tradesmen's Association at
Aphrodisias, although it is not yet attested for any others of
them.[22] The quality of σεμνότης attributed was dignity and
propriety of behaviour, which appears quite often in decrees of official praise of members of the élite[23]—it was an
attribute of the "establishment." No doubt the city fathers
hoped for dignified behaviour from their tradesmen—we
have no idea whether they always got it. Zoticus, however,
who used this adjective of an Association, and so many conventional words and phrases in his funerary arrangements,
seems to show himself acceptant of élite mores; and, I suggest, illustrates that again by pairing the Tradesmen's Association with Aphrodite herself, the goddess in whose service the élite of Aphrodisias were deeply involved.

For the private activities of these Associations Aphrodisias has so far produced very little information, and all
concerned with funerary matters. In addition to the inscription under discussion, and the one mentioned above
that has lost the name of its association, there is a quite
modest tombstone for an emporiarch (the modesty of the
stone warning us not to overestimate his status) who is represented as greeting the Association of Linenworkers as

---

represented in Waltzing) will be found in Van Nijf. I am most grateful to
him for showing me the text before its publication.

[22] Waltzing, vol. IV, 575 cites it in use for the leather-workers at
Cibyra and for the purple-dyers and the fullers at Hierapolis, both
neighbours of Aphrodisias and known to have had connections with
her.

[23] Thus MAMA VIII.408, 409.

well as other passers-by from his tomb.[24] It suggests the proximity of some place regularly visited by the Association, in the circumstances perhaps a communal tomb for members who had none of their own. It might be conjectured that Associations also carried out regular rites at members' tombs or others entrusted to their care, as is well-attested at Hierapolis—but of this kind of thing there is, so far, no trace at all at Aphrodisias.

I return to Zoticus and his wife. They seem to have been a pair with no apparent family, some substance though hardly what would count as wealth, a modest status; people who liked to make a bit of a show, but were not very sensitive to aesthetics or literary style, conformist, on the face of it at least, to the ethos of the élite; like the betters whom they accepted , anxious to ensure the sanctity of their remains after death, but in the absence of descendants seeking for that the help not only of the goddess of the élite, the city goddess, but of their own kind, the tradesmen who must have been the company that they kept in their lifetime. It is not a startling message to claim to have coaxed from a stone; but since the city could not have been built or maintained without people of their kind it is perhaps worth struggling even for such a scrap.

Works Cited

Asgari, N. 1977. "Die halbfabrikate Kleinasiatische Girlandensarkophage und ihre Herkunft." *AA*:329–80.

Calder, W. M., and J. M. R. Cormack, *Monumenta Asiae Minoris Antiqua*. Manchester 1962. [= MAMA VIII]

[24] Reynolds 1995.

Isik, F. 1981/2. "Kleinasiatische Girlandensarkophage mit Pilaster oder Säulenarchitektur." *JÖAI, Beiblatt* 53:29–146.

Kubinska, J. 1968. *Les Monuments funéraires dans les Inscriptions de l'Asie Mineure.* Warsaw.

———. 1970. "Les Tombeaux d'Aphrodisias d'après les Inscriptions." *Études et Travaux du Centre d'Archéologie Mediterranéenne de l'Académie polonaise des Sciences* 4:114–18.

Reinach, Th. 1906. "Inscriptions d'Aphrodisias." *REG* 19:79–150, 201–98.

Reynolds, J. 1982. *Aphrodisias and Rome.* London.

———. 1995. "The Linen-market of Aphrodisias in Caria." In *Arculiana, Recueils d'hommage offerts à Hans Bögli.* Eds. F. E. Koenig and S. Rebetez. Avenches.

Reynolds, J., and Tannenbaum, R. 1987. *Jews and Godfearers at Aphrodisias.* Cambridge.

Roueché, C. 1989. *Aphrodisias in Late Antiquity.* London.

———. 1993. *Performers and Partisans at Aphrodisias in the Roman and Late Roman Periods.* London.

Smith, R. R. R., and C. Ratté. 1996. "Archaeological Research at Aphrodisias in Caria, 1994." *AJA* 100.1:5–33.

Van Nijf, O. 1997. *The Civic World of Professional Associations in the Greek East.* Amsterdam.

Waltzing, J. P. 1895–1900, *Étude historique sur les Corporations professionelles chez les romains.* Louvain.

Sarcophagus of M. Aurelius Zoticus of Aphrodisias

Cicero, Bibulus, and Caesar's Agrarian Bills of 59 B.C.E.[1]

L. Richardson, jr
Duke University

When Julius Caesar entered office as consul on the first of January 59 B.C.E. a land reform bill stood high on his list of priorities; this was common knowledge. Such bills were no novelty to the Romans; they had been proposed repeatedly and at close intervals since the tribunate of Tiberius Gracchus in 133 B.C.E.[2] They always aimed at a redistribution of the *ager publicus*, in effect taking the vast abusive holdings that had been amassed by many of the very rich and converted into *latifundia* and breaking them up into smaller farmsteads for distribution to army veterans and the urban poor and landless, especially families with children who could be counted on to work them.

---

[1] The literature on this subject is very extensive; the most important and most recent discussions are those of Shackleton Bailey 406–8, Mitchell 1991, 98–102, and Wiseman 1994b, 368–75. There the interested reader will find references to the pertinent literature.

[2] Plutarch, *TG* 8.7–9.5. On the agrarian problem in general and its development, see Lintott 53–59.

Ager publicus was land that had been won in war by Rome
from its enemies. As part of the peace settlement with a
city or nation Rome would exact some portion of its territory. The amount varied, depending on the circumstances.
It seems usually to have been a third or a half of the existing *ager publicus* of a city, but in the case of Capua, which
had not only sheltered Hannibal but flagrantly aided and
abetted him, it was the whole amount. Some part of this
might be put up for sale to produce cash for the coffers of
the treasury, but part seems always to have been reserved
to become a Roman possession in perpetuity. This was
then divided into small parcels to make farms to be let at a
very nominal rent to the poor and land-hungry. As a social
program this was laudable, and it carried with it a perva-
sive romanization of the newly allied territory that
strengthened Roman control, an important consideration.

But as richer and more powerful Romans began to see
the economic advantages of large estates that could be
farmed by cheap slave labor, vast holdings that could be
turned into sheepwalk, olive orchard, and vineyard in large
scale operations, they first began to offer higher rents that
would drive out the small farmers and poorer farmers and
gradually pieced together estates that often extended for
many miles, for which they paid only a pittance in rent. The
viciousness of this development having early become apparent, among the Licinio-Sextian rogations of 367 B.C.E.
was a law forbidding the holding of more than 500 *iugera* of
ager publicus, about 330 acres, by any single individual.[3]
This checked the expansion of *latifundia* only briefly; by using the names of the various members of a *familia*, includ-

---

[3] Rotondi 216–18. Many scholars today believe that this legislation
belongs rather to the time of Cato the Censor in the second century
B.C.E.; see Tibiletti 191–96.

ing freedmen and even sometimes invented identities, es-
tate-holders got around the law to make additions to their
holdings and subsequently transferred these openly into
their own names. Abuses were rife and condoned; every
senatorial family seems to have been more or less openly
deeply involved. In the middle of the second century B.C.E.
Gaius Laelius, the close friend of Scipio who was noted for
his probity, attempted to introduce measures to eliminate
such abuse and correct the situation but was dissuaded
from pursuing this by the pressure of influential friends
and the threat of physical violence (Plutarch, *TG* 8.4).

By the late 60s the situation had become acute, with the
swelling ranks of the landless urban poor increasingly
ground by debt and tightness of money, veterans of a succession of successful armies clamoring for land as part of
their well-earned rights, and the ill-got wealth of Sulla's fa-
vorites in which the confiscations from the proscribed figured large flaunted before everyone's eyes. The college of
tribunes of 63, led by P. Servilius Rullus, had attempted to
pass a bill calling for the radical use of public funds accru-
ing from Pompey's conquests in the East for the purchase
of land from its present holders on terms highly favorable
to them, plus the *ager publicus* of the *ager Campanus* and adjacent *campus Stellas*, which would then be redistributed to
alleviate the crisis.[4] Sulla's confiscations would remain un-
touched, but public land abroad would be sold, and new
colonies could be founded. It was an ambitious scheme that
offered advantages to many of the senatorial class, those
who had suffered most from the decline in land values provoked by the turbulence that was racking Italy. And the
board of land commissioners with praetorian authority
lasting five years that was proposed to be elected held out
promise of great wealth and *dignitas* for the successful can-

---

[4] On Rullus' bill, see Cicero, *Agr. passim*; Mitchell 1979, 184–205.

didates. But Cicero was alarmed at the power this would offer to an ambitious and likely unscrupulous few and the
reckless squandering of enormous treasury funds. He mus-
tered strength among the more conservative elements in
Rome, won one of the tribunes, Caecilius Rufus, to an-
nounce that he would veto Rullus' bill if it were promulgated, and attacked the bill in a series of brilliant speeches,
first in the senate and then before the people, and succeeded, not without rhetorical guile, in defeating the measure. It is now generally believed that the real author of the
bill was not Rullus but Julius Caesar and that it was designed not only to win favor for him with the *plebs* by relieving poverty but to limit the power of Pompey, who was to
be, in effect, excluded from becoming one of the land commissioners. It would also have consumed a considerable
proportion of Pompey's spoils. A similar bill, introduced
early in 60 by the tribune L. Flavius, was also defeated.[5]

Whatever Caesar's part in the maneuverings of 63 may
have been, everyone was aware that on his entrance into his
consulship he would propose a land bill. Probably it had
figured large in his campaign for office the previous summer, for Cicero and Lucullus are reported to have worked
strenuously through the remainder of the year to mount
senatorial opposition to such a bill, in which they would
have had the support of the other consul-designate,
Calpurnius Bibulus, and his brother-in-law, Cato (Plutarch,
Cat. Mi. 31.4–5). Caesar, however, repeatedly assured the
optimates that he would propose no measure that was not
to their advantage, and in December he sent Cornelius
Balbus to Cicero to try to persuade him to lend his support
to the legislation (Cicero, *Att.* 2.3.3–4). In his interview
with Balbus Cicero may have been sounded out as to his

[5] On Flavius' bill, see Cicero, *Att.* 1.19.4, 2.1.6–8; Cassius Dio
37.50.1–4; Wiseman 1994a, 365.

willingness to join the other members of the so-called First Triumvirate, and much was made of Pompey's interests and the advantages that would accrue to Cicero. This would mean abandoning not only certain close allies but also his political creed; still Cicero was impressed by Balbus' arguments, at least as far as the agrarian legislation was concerned. Cicero wrote to Atticus that he felt he must debate both sides of the question at length and in detail.

So when in January Caesar, as the first candidate to be elected consul, had the fasces, he presented to the senate a bill with which no one could find fault, although the great majority of the senators disliked and disapproved of it. It provided for the redistribution of all the *ager publicus* in Italy, except for the *ager Campanus* and *campus Stellas*, which had figured prominently in Rullus' and Flavius' bills and evidently proved a major obstacle to their acceptance, and the purchase of such additional land as might be required only from owners willing to sell and at the price at which it had been assessed in the tax rolls. For this purpose the booty of Pompey's conquests in the East and the new tributes and taxes recently established there provided a great deal of surplus money, so there would be no drain on the treasury. The program was to be administered by a board of twenty land commissioners, chosen among the most suitable men, from whose number Caesar himself would be excluded from consideration. This bill was read in the senate, and Caesar offered to alter or eliminate any clause with which any senator found fault. No criticism was offered, or apparently could be offered, but the senators were by and large depressed and unhappy with the provisions and seem to have made their unhappiness perceptible. Caesar then asked them individually and by name to comment and clarify their objections. They then embarked on a filibuster, promising to pass the bill and finding no fault with it, but offering distractions and delays. Cato

made a long and particularly irritating speech in which he
urged that they abide by the existing state of affairs on general principles. His dogged persistence on this point ultimately so exasperated Caesar that he threatened to imprison Cato and was on the point of dragging him out of
the curia when so many senators volunteered to accompany
him to prison that the gesture had to be abandoned
(Plutarch, *Cat. Mi.* 33.1–2; Cassius Dio 38.3.1–3).

What would have been the provisions of a bill that could
not be criticized but distressed the optimates? Like all such
bills it aimed at correcting abuses; the most flagrantly abusive *latifundia* would be broken up and made into small
farms for proper cultivation. But some form of adequate
compensation must have been offered, if no criticism was
possible. That compensation must have been land of
greater extent and greater value carved from the new ac-
quisitions of *ager publicus* in the East. At this time the veterans and urban poor were asking for land in Italy, and it
would not be until the next generation that land and colonies even on the frontiers of Italy would be considered acceptable in land bills, but senatorial and equestrian wealth
had a long history of investment abroad. Offered more
than they were losing, the optimates could not object to disadvantage in the redistribution of their abusive holdings,
and for some the chance of a place on the board of commissioners would have meant important power and prestige. Much as they might prefer land in Italy for its familiarity and convenience, the same factors weighed heavily with
the poorer classes, and settlement abroad for these would
mean, in effect, surrender of the franchise that they had
fought so hard to win. Cato's opposition was irrational, the
natural reaction of one of his birth and upbringing:
changes in the *mos maiorum* must be resisted.

Where did Cicero stand on the question? Unfortunately
we have no letters of his from late December in 60 (Cicero,

Att. 2.3), when he was looking forward to political activities in Rome in January, to early April in 59 (Cicero, *Att.* 2.4), at which time he was at Antium. In his April letter he mentions that Clodius has been offered an embassy to Tigranes of Armenia, presumably in connection with the ratification of Pompey's disposition of eastern affairs, and although the text of the letter presents difficulties at a crucial point, it is clear that Cicero regards this as Clodius' reward for his efforts on Caesar's behalf and considers himself equally deserving. In his next letter he sees a mission to Alexandria for himself as a distinct possibility (Cicero, *Att.* 2.5), which could only be in connection with the efforts of Ptolemy Auletes to have himself declared a friend and ally of Rome in order to secure his rule in Alexandria in the face of increasing unrest among his subjects (Cassius Dio 39.12.1). Ptolemy had shown himself disposed to spend large sums for such recognition, and the embassy to fetch the money to Rome would be conspicuous and lucrative. Eventually the price was set at nearly six thousand talents, obtained in the names of Julius Caesar and Pompey (Suetonius, *Jul.* 54.3). Cicero admits to Atticus that he would be delighted to visit Alexandria and Egypt, not least because it would take him away from Rome and a political scene in which his own stand was increasingly out of favor with the triumvirate and their supporters on the one hand and the old guard senatorial faction on the other (Cicero, *Att.* 2.5.1). Also among his considerations must have been that it would take him away from his personal enemy, Publius Clodius, and his attacks on an important and illustrious mission for which Clodius himself had at one time been considered as a possible leader (Cicero, *Att.* 2.7.3).

This overture to Cicero must have been his reward for his not only not opposing Caesar's land bill, but actually speaking in its favor. And if Caesar's friend Cornelius Balbus had failed to persuade Cicero of the excellence of the bill, then

Pompey had succeeded with arguments about the advantages to him. For it was from Pompey's spokesman
Theophanes that Cicero expected further word. But the offer never came, and if Cicero was chagrined at this, he
cloaked his disappointment in scorn for those who seemed
more likely to be so honored (Cicero, *Att.* 2.7.2).

How long Cicero remained in Rome at the beginning of
59 is not clear, but since he had the defence of Antonius
Hybrida to attend to, and it would have taken almost the
whole of January to put the land bill through, given the
mixed reception it received and the delay required between
promulgation and ratification by the comitia, and the
month of February was reserved for the reception of foreign embassies by the senate, during which time we must
presume the representatives of Ptolemy would have presented his petition for recognition yet once more, and that
this brought the question again to public attention and discussion from which the possibility of an official mission to
Alexandria emerged, we may not be far wrong in imagin-
ing that Cicero was in Rome most of the time from which
there are no letters, through which period he offered no
opposition to the legislative program of the triumvirate. At
this time he was not privy to the counsel of Pompey, although he seems to have tried to sound him out on the
more important issues and been answered vaguely and gently rebuffed (Cicero, *Att.* 2.9.1; 2.16.2). It was probably in
bewilderment and frustration, as well as from realization
that he had compromised himself in the eyes of Cato and
Lucullus (Cicero, *Att.* 2.4.4; 2.5.1; 2.6.2), that he had left
Rome for an extended tour of his estates and those of
Terentia. By early April he was at Antium and had been
away from Rome long enough to have inspected a splendid
and extensive property of Terentia's, a *saltus* that he com-
pares to Epirus, and at this time he was projecting travels
that would keep him away from Rome past the beginning

of May (Cicero, *Att.* 2.4.5–6), although he found little to do at Antium but read and meditate (Cicero, *Att.* 2.6.1). He is both anxious for news of what is happening in Rome and determined not to let it affect him (Cicero, *Att.* 2.5.3; 2.6.2). One deduces that he would prefer not to have to defend his recent actions to Cato (Cicero, *Att.* 2.4.1). In fact, he would like to put it all behind him for the present and devote himself entirely to literary and philosophical concerns (Cicero, *Att.* 2.5.2; 2.6.1–2). He is whistling in the dark.

By mid-April his plans had crystallized. He would go to his villa at Formiae for the Parilia, then leave Formiae at the beginning of May, returning to Antium for the games there that lasted until the sixth of May. Thereafter he would go to Tusculum and Arpinum, returning to Rome by the beginning of June (Cicero, *Att.* 2.8.2). The sojourn at Formiae was probably projected with a view to an interview with Pompey, who also had a villa there, but no interview is mentioned in his letters from Formiae in late April. It was there that on the last day of April Cicero received a letter from Atticus that shocked him out of his indifference (Cicero, *Att.* 2.16). Caesar had proposed a new land bill that would include the *ager Campanus* among the lands to be redistributed. Whether he had found the available *ager publicus* insufficient for the land commissioners, or too few owners were willing to sell their lands at the price quoted is not clear; one may suspect that Caesar had had it in mind to take the *ager Campanus* all along and was only waiting for the work of the land commissioners to gather the impetus of popularity necessary to overcome the objections of the optimates. Cicero fulminates against Pompey, who has found excuses for defending Caesar's program up to this point, the first agrarian bill, the recognition of Ptolemy, and the relief of the equestrian *publicani*, but who surely cannot find a fair defence for this (Cicero, *Att.* 2.16.2). But he sees that he is helpless, that it would be futile to try to

mount opposition to the bill, given his strained relationship
with the old guard.

Many of our sources confuse the two land bills and tele-
scope them into one (e.g., Appian, *BC* 2.2.10–12; Cassius
Dio 38.1.1–6.4), but it is clear from Cicero's letters that
there were two bills, one in January and one in May, and
that it was the second bill that excited active, even violent
opposition. In a *contio* that became famous Caesar somehow brought Bibulus before the people and urged him to
offer criticism of any of the provisions of the bill. When
Bibulus replied only that he would not allow any innovation
during his consulship, Caesar begged him and got the assembled crowd to beg him to relent and accept the bill.
Bibulus then lost aplomb and hotly denounced the proceedings, saying that he would not allow this bill to be presented even if all Rome wanted it, and then left the rostra.
Caesar then brought forward Crassus and Pompey, both of
whom spoke in favor of the bill, Pompey making the famous statement that if anyone lifted a sword against it, he
would come to its defence with a sword and shield (Cassius
Dio 38.4.1–5.5). This must have been very close to the day
on which the bill would normally be presented to the
comitia for a vote, perhaps the day before, certainly not
more than two or three days earlier.

On the day of the vote Caesar's adherents filled the forum before dawn, and many of them brought concealed
weapons in the expectation of violence (Appian, *BC*
2.2.10–11), but soldiers were not in evidence, perhaps in
deference to the Roman abhorrence of force that smacked
of monarchical despotism. Caesar had the apparatus for
voting set up at the temple of Castor, presumably in front
of the speaker's platform, and the voting urns to receive the
ballots there.[6] Probably this equipment had to be brought

---

[6] Cerutti.

from the comitium at the opposite end of the forum and had been arranged in advance with a view to removing the voting as far as possible from the curia and the possibility of interference by magistrates, senators, or tribunes of senatorial sympathy. Caesar was in the process of delivering a speech, presumably in the *contio* preliminary to putting the measure to a vote, when Bibulus appeared in the forum with such support as he could muster, including Cato, Lucullus, and three tribunes. This company made its way to the temple of Castor, perhaps all the way from the comitium, the crowd falling back in deference to their indignation and authority, although someone is reported to have emptied a basket of filth over Bibulus's head along the way (Plutarch, *Pomp.* 48.1). Bibulus was allowed to mount the platform beside Caesar, but when he attempted to speak and interpose his veto, he was unceremoniously hustled off the platform, and a riot ensued. Bibulus' fasces were broken to pieces; two of the tribunes with him were seriously injured; and he himself was bundled off by friends to the safety of the temple of Jupiter Stator. Cato attempted to save the day and interpose his dignity and authority, but when he attempted to speak, he was twice lifted up bodily and carried from the forum by Caesar's adherents (Appian, *BC* 2.2.11; Cassius Dio 38.6.1–3). So the bill was passed.

The following day Bibulus, undaunted by the events of the previous day, appeared in the senate and tried to persuade that body to invalidate the new law, but the senators, intimidated by the wild enthusiasm of the populace for the measure, were reluctant, and the Caesarian tribune Publius Vatinius then intervened and arrested Bibulus, threatening to imprison him. Praetorian tribunals were hastily put together to make a semblance of the voting platform and bridge in front of the rostra, presumably because the proper apparatus was still at the temple of Castor at the opposite end of the forum, and poor Bibulus was led over these, exposed to the derision and insults of the mob, in a cruel mockery of the voting procedure (Cicero, *Vat.* 21). During this disgraceful charade not a single senator moved to come to Bibulus' assistance, and eventually it was other tribunes who came to the rescue, and by their intervention saved Bibulus from incarceration (Cassius Dio 38.6.4-6). Cato and Lucullus, we must presume, were not present, possibly indignant at the failure of other senators to rally to the cause, or perhaps attending to cuts and bruises received on the previous day.

It was only after this betrayal by the very optimates for whom he had labored long and hard that Bibulus withdrew to the comparative safety of his house and announced that he would be watching the heavens on every comitial day for the eight months remaining in his term of office, an announcement reissued as each day came that technically invalidated all legislation but to which Caesar paid no heed. Bibulus has been accused of being cowardly and foolish, but he was neither. He had risked his life repeatedly in public in the first months of 59 (Plutarch, *Caes.* 14.6), and it was only after the senate refused to support him that he forsook the arena of the forum. Even then he continued to fight for what he saw as right and legitimate with all the means available to him, edicts that were posted on the rostra and men crowded to read. They were also gleefully copied and widely disseminated (Cicero, *Att.* 2.19.5).

How was Cicero occupied during this turmoil? In a letter to Atticus from Antium in the middle of April he had proposed to go to Tusculum in early May, on the Nones or thereabout, but not to Rome (Cicero, *Att.* 2.9.4). From Tusculum he would go to Arpinum and return to Rome about the first of June. His plans then changed, and he extended his stay at Formiae from late April into May, although he complained that Formiae was as bad as Rome for interruptions. It was there on the last day of April that he learned from a letter of Atticus' of Caesar's new land bill, but he did not let it lure him back to Rome to oppose or support it. Ultimately he went to Arpinum about the tenth of May, having arranged to meet Atticus there, and there apparently they devoted their days to long philosophical discussions, possibly even the dialogues from which Cicero was later to fashion the setting of the *De Legibus*. We have no letters of Cicero's between early May and sometime well into June, by which time Caesar's bill had been voted into law, together with a clause requiring every candidate for office in the coming elections to swear to uphold this law (Cicero, *Att.* 2.18.2). Cicero was then in Rome and writing to Atticus, who was off on a business trip to Greece and avid for news. What is interesting is that Caesar has offered Cicero a place as one of his *legati* on his proconsular staff, or a *legatio libera voti causa*, in order to protect him from the machinations of Clodius (Cicero, *Att.* 2.18.3). What form the latter might take is not clear, since Cicero thought it would be scotched by Clodius in the senate or else offer insufficient immunity; presumably it would have entailed taking Cicero away from Rome for the duration of Clodius' tribunate. So if Clodius' transition to the plebs was Caesar's angry and vindictive response to Cicero's criticism of the triumvirate in his defence of Antonius Hybrida, as Cicero himself believed (Cicero, *Dom.* 41, *Sest.* 16, *Prov.* 41–42), then Caesar must have had second thoughts and relented, and the offer of a *legatio* must have been in recognition of Cicero's services, reward for his not having opposed either of the land bills. Ultimately Cicero's pride led him to refuse the offer; even though he knew from bitter experience that he could not rely on the support of the optimates, he thought he could fight fire with fire. For Bibulus it was different; it was the optimates who had seen to his election and given him a program. Then, Cicero included, they had pulled the rug from under him.

Works Cited

Cerutti, Steven M. 1997. "P. Clodius and the Stairs of the Temple of Castor." *Latomus* 56:forthcoming.

Lintott, Andrew. 1994. "Political History, 146–95 B.C." *CAH* 9^2:40–103.

Mitchell, Thomas N. 1979. *Cicero, The Ascending Years.* New Haven and London.

——. 1991. *Cicero, The Senior Statesman.* New Haven and London.

Rotondi, Giovanni. 1912. *Leges publicae populi romani.* Milan. (Repr. Hildesheim 1990.)

Shackleton Bailey, D. R. 1965. *Cicero's Letters to Atticus 1.* Cambridge.

Tibiletti, G. 1948. "Il possesso dell' *ager publicus* e le norme *de modo agrorum* sino ai Gracchi." *Athenaeum* 26:173–236.

Wiseman, T. P. 1994a. "The Senate and the *populares*." *CAH* 9^2:327–67.

——. 1994b. "Caesar, Pompey and Rome, 59–60 B.C." *CAH* 9^2:368–423.

Survey Archaeology around Fordongianus (*Forum Traiani*), Sardinia

Robert J. Rowland, Jr.
Loyola University New Orleans

Stephen L. Dyson
State University of New York at Buffalo

In 1987 the authors initiated a long-term research project on Romanization in selected areas of west-Central Sardinia (fig. 1) aimed at utilizing site survey to reconstruct the impact of the Roman conquest on settlement patterns in the lowland-upland transitional area east of modern Oristano. In the first phase of the project (1987–89), we studied the territory bounded by the modern communes of Bauladu and Fordongianus (Roman *Forum Traiani* [Zedda; Rowland 1976, 460–61; Zucca 1986a; Meloni 1988, 533–34; 1990, 302–6]), concentrating in the first instance on the persistence or reutilization of prehistoric sites in and into the Roman period (Rowland and Dyson 1988, 1989). In the first season we undertook some sporadic searches for Roman villa and farmstead sites in the lowlands around

313

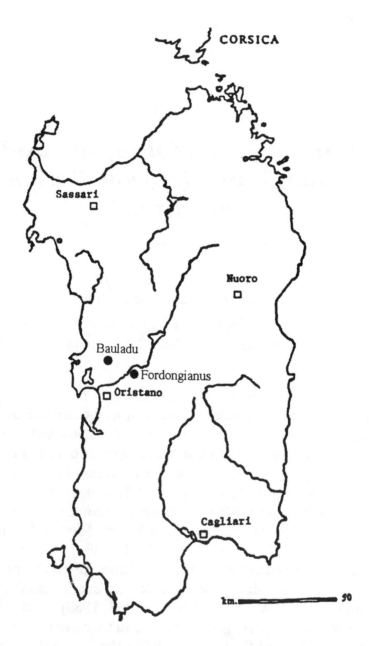

Fig. 1 *Map of Sardinia showing provincial capitals, Bauladu and Fordongianus*

Bauladu, but none were found. However, this region is relatively far from any known major Roman settlement, so the pressure for reorganizing the countryside on a Roman model would have been severely limited. Because such would not have been the case for the rural areas around the administrative center of *Forum Traiani*, we conducted an intensive survey in the summer of 1988.

Using information on the likely location of Roman rural sites derived from research on mainland Italy (cf. Dyson 1982; Barker and Lloyd), we developed a highly opportunistic survey strategy that was designed to maximize the recovery of Roman sites around Fordongianus. Five weeks of intensive work produced almost none, which suggests that the Romans did not develop an extensive villa-farmstead system in the hinterland of *Forum Traiani*. The evidence from the two parts of our research fits nicely into a picture of rural conservatism. Recent research has placed greater emphasis on the survival of native cultural systems in other parts of the Roman Empire (e.g., Millett; Barker 1995, 249). The Sardinian countryside around Bauladu and Fordongianus, with its contrast between the high level of continuity at native sites and minimal rural romanization, provides an extreme example of that situation (Dyson and Rowland 1990, 1991, 1992). What follows is a presentation of what we did find in that survey season (fig. 2).

The modern community of Fordongianus is situated about thirty meters above sea level on the left (south) bank of the Tirso River some twenty-six kilometers from its mouth. It is strategically located at the interface between the lowlying alluvial valley to its west and southwest and the mountainous interior: Busachi, about seven kilometers upriver as the crow flies, is more than 400 meters above sea level. The soil in the immediate vicinity of the Tirso and its tributaries is old alluvium; otherwise, the territory of

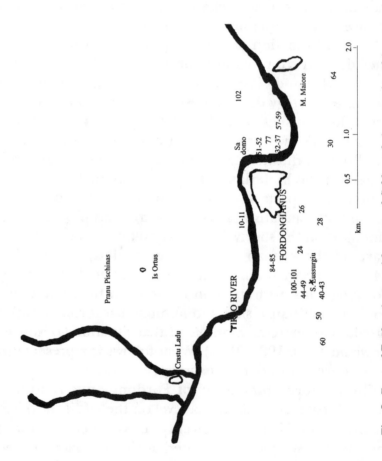

Fig. 2. *Zone of Fordongianus with surveyed fields and sites mentioned in text*

Fordongianus is virtually encompassed by basaltic lavas and, to the immediate south and southwest, trachitic tuffs.

Prior to our survey, evidence for the early prehistoric periods (i.e., prenuragic: see below) around Fordongianus was exiguous in the extreme: specifically, two sets of rock cut tombs (*domus de janas*) in the regions Gulari and Domigheddas (Angius 752; Pinza 41–44; Taramelli 490–91). What we have been able to add, while still not extensive, is not without significance. One of the earliest human settlements so far identified in the interior of Sardinia is marked by a widespread obsidian scatter on the summit of a plateau known as Crastu Ladu, an ideal site for an open-air settlement about two kilometers downstream from Fordongianus, 150 meters from the river and between two tributaries, the Riu Pitziu and the Riu Canale Mannu. One piece of obsidian from Crastu Ladu provided a hydration date of 5614 ± 164 B.C. (Dyson et al. 26, 39) which coheres very nicely with the range of 5700–5300 B.C. for the Cardial Early Neolithic suggested by C-14 (Tykot 5). Another neolithic date near Fordongianus, 5263 ± 133 B.C. (Dyson et al. 26, 38), overlaps the late Cardial period and its successor, early Filiestru (5300–4700 [Tykot]). The obsidian yielding this date was found in field number 58, a vineyard in the region Campu 'e Putzu about 250 meters north of the Tirso upriver from town.

About 500 meters southeast of field 58 across the Tirso is a plateau similar to Crastu Ladu, Monte Maiore, about 100 meters from both the Tirso and a tributary, the Riu Funtana Roia. The earliest date provided by obsidian from Monte Maiore is 2894 ± 176 B.C. (sub-Neolithic [Ozieri]/ Early Copper Age [Tykot]), but nearly fifty samples from there remain undated, so the possibility remains open that it too had an early open-air settlement. Two pieces of obsidian from field 50, in the region Pranu Casteddu at the 115 meter contour about 350 meters uphill from the church of

S. Lussurgiu (see further below), yielded dates of 2508 ± 148 B.C. and 1340 ± 128 B.C. (Dyson et al. 26f., 38). Together with another third millenium date, 2301 ± 145 B.C., provided by a piece of obsidian found in field 60, about 150 meters further uphill (ibid.), these objects allow one to speculate on the possibility of a protonuragic site followed by a nuragic one on the summit of the hill. A similar date (2322 ± 124 B.C.) was provided by obsidian found in field 64 in the region Perdu Meano about 300 meters northeast of the road from Fordongianus to Allai and Samugheo at about 2.4 km, near the only water sources in the area (ibid.).

Although there are relatively few nuragic structures within the boundaries of the territory of Fordongianus itself, there is an impressive number in the broader Fordongianus catchment area. Excavations at nuraghi have tended to demonstrate that it is unlikely that these structures were occupied continously from the time of their construction (cf., e.g., Webster), and it is possible that some nuraghi were intended *ab initio* to be utilized only seasonally. Our survey did not actually discover any nuraghi that were previously unknown: the significant result is a reemphasis on the continuous utilization or reutilization of nuragic sites into and in the Roman period (Dyson and Rowland 1990, 1991, 1992; cf. Webster and Teglund). Clearly, the zone was well populated in the second and first millennia B.C. to about the time of Punic expansion into the interior (Barreca 1978; Rowland 1982). After the Roman conquest, a general absence of republican period pottery suggests, but does not prove, a population decline, some of it no doubt due to warfare and forced translocation (cf. Rowland 1988); other factors creating population fluctuations, attested in historic periods, may also have been at work (Day 1973, 1987a, b; Terrosu Asole; Tangheroni). It is easy, moreover, to exaggerate the extent of depopulation and disclocation because of our ignorance of late nuragic ceramics (Rowland 1992) and because excavation or resurvey at any one of the sites we examined could produce examples of materials currently lacking, a phenomenon which Graeme Barker has frequently likened to "a blinking traffic signal" (most recently 1996, 195). Throughout the area, the presence of Roman imperial pottery, particularly African Red Slip Ware, at nuragic sites surely documents an increase in setttlement during that period. Present-day rural road networks suggest that communications and exchanges between the various nuraghi were relatively easy (Rowland 1990).

The best known site in Fordongianus, and one of the major Roman monuments in Sardinia, is the Roman baths, dating to the first century A.D. with second/third century restructuring, mentioned by Fara in the sixteenth century when the baths (called *semidirutae*) apparently were still partially functioning (*termae inprimis tota Sardinia celeberrimae ad sudandum et varios morbos depellendum efficaces*: Fara 74)—indeed, the water of the thermal spring is still used by the townsfolk for washing clothes. The site was excavated by Taramelli between 1899 and 1902 (Taramelli 1903). It was known to Ptolemy as *Hydata Hypsitana* (*Aquae Hypsitanae*) (*Geog.* 3.3.7), and an early first century A.D. inscription indicates that the center served as place where the local tribes, the *civitates Barbariae*, gathered to pledge loyalty to Rome and the emperor (*AE* 1921, 86 = Sotgiu 1961, nr. 188; cf. also *CIL* 14.2954; 10.5859–60, 7863). There is some evidence that the springs had been utilized during the Punic period (Barreca 1986, 298)

The community was presumably elevated early in the second century to the status of Forum by the emperor whose name it then bore (Meloni 1988, 253–55; 1990, 302–6). Evidence for an amphitheater has been attested (Zedda 20; Zucca 1986a, 17–18), along with traces of an aqueduct

(Spano 168; Zucca 1986a, 29–30). In time the town was large and important enough to have a martyr (S. Luxurius: cf. below) and a bishop (Meloni 1990, 423–26, 438–39; Rowland 1984). By the sixth century, the town was the seat of the military governor of the island and had been defended by a wall, traces of which were still visible in the last century (Procop. *Aed.* 6.7.343b; Georg. Cypr. *Descr. Orb. Rom.* 682; *Notit. episcop. orient.* [Migne, *PG* 107.344]; Zedda 19). Over the centuries, sporadic archaeological finds from the town and the countryside have been reported (summarized in Rowland 1981, 46–47). Angius (750) provides a hint of how much must have been lost to scholarship:

> Quando scavasi dentro il paese e nella prossima zona trovasi qualche cosa di più che le fondamenta, camere coperte, vasi, utensili, pezzi d'architettura, ecc. e si può benissimo determinare di quanto ne' secoli trascorsi siasi levato il terreno. Molti oggetti pregievoli vennero di tempo in tempo dissotterrati, ma venuti in mani barbare furono annientati o venduti allo straniero.

One of the more interesting of these last is the report that in 1365 the governor and reformer of Cagliari, D. Alberto Satrillas, instructed Francesco de Corrallo, administrator of the royal rights, to pay a rich merchant of Cagliari, one Eximeno di Torrente, 300 gold florins for various pieces of jewelry that had been found at Fordongianus in a marble sarcophagus containing also the remains of a woman; by order of the king, Satrillas sent these objects, along with others from elsewhere, to the royal court (Spano 163).

A late republican/early imperial tomb (erroneously called "'late Roman" in *PECS* 338) in the region Is Ortus (Taramelli 485) was part of "una più vasta necropoli" (Zucca 1986b, 172 n. 68) about two kilometers northwest of Fordongianus. Is Ortus ("the gardens") is a well-watered region (largely by the Funtana Is Ortus) with fertile soil of volcanic origin within about a kilometer of both the Tirso and the Riu Marcu. The plateau above Is Ortus, Pranu Pischinas, is the findspot of the tombstone of two individuals, "Bflsa" (i.e., Belsa or Beisa), wife of Caritus, and Benit[us?] (Sotgiu 1961, nr. 186; 1988, nr. 196). Another hypogeum "ad arcosolio" has been reported from the area Sa Domo de sa Señora on the right bank of the Tirso immediately to the northeast of town; it is dated on typological grounds and by the presence therein of lamps with biblical scenes to the late ancient/early Christian period (Zucca 1986a, 30; 1989, 127 n. 11).

In addition to the baths, the other significant standing monument around Fordongianus is the church of S. Luxurius (Santu Lussurgiu), a twelfth-century structure (with later modifications) over a pre-existing crypt and martyrium about 1.2 km west-southwest of town. On the basis of the mosaics found there, the deposition of the remains of the martyr seems to have occurred early in the fourth century, and the crypt was renewed in the fifth. Excavations undertaken between 1985 and 1987 revealed another restructuring in the sixth century, a collapse and rebuilding early in the seventh, and, probably, yet another collapse before the new church was constructed (Zucca 1989, 130–36). It had long been known that the cemetery around S. Lussurgiu "potrebbe risalire ad età preconstantiniana" (Zucca 1986b, 178), but there was no more precise chronological information or data available before our survey.

In July 1988, part of our crew surveyed the fields immediately adjacent to the church (fields 40–49), and the directors resurveyed the area in October 1988 (fields 40–49, 100A and B, and 101). No prehistoric, Punic, republican or (except for a single sherd of *terra sigillata*) early imperial material was found in any of these fields. Roman utilitarian and storage wares abounded, as did fragments of roof tiles attesting to the funerary nature of the zone. There were a few pieces of glass, a "medallion," a dagger blade (perhaps not ancient), and a coin of Maxentius. There were also twenty-seven pieces of datable African Red Slip Ware, including sherds of Hayes 196 (A.D. 100–200), 8A (A.D. 80–200), 9A (A.D. 100–60), 5A (A.D. 60–100), 27 (A.D. 150–250), and several pieces of A ware (A.D. 75–250). Clearly, the zone which later became a memorial to Saint Luxurius was already functioning as a necropolis in the second century, perhaps even as early as the late first century—or, unfortunately on the basis of a single sherd, the early first century.

Most of our field surveys around Fordongianus, however, as already noted, produced almost no Roman material. One area which did yield Roman material was a series of fields between Strada Statale 388 and the right bank of the Tirso directly across the river from the town, proceeding eastward through Campu 'e Putzu and Campu Bingias. Fields 51 and 52, adjacent hayfields, are probably to be considered a single site, 150 to 200 meters from the Tirso. Here, there was a large concentration of roof tiles (on the order of several hundred fragments) and pottery to the northeast of a small rounded plateau (a threshing area?). In addition to Roman utilitarian and late-imperial included ware (cf. Dyson and Rowland 1992, 212), there were seven identifiable sherds of African Red Slip ware: one each of A (A.D. 75–250), C (A.D. 200–400) and D (A.D. 320–660) wares along with two of Hayes 50A (A.D. 230–360), and one each of Hayes 6A/B (A.D. 80–200) and Hayes 91B/C (A.D. 450–525). About 200 to 250 meters to the east-southeast, two adjacent vineyards, fields 35 and 36, probably also formed a single site. Here, in addition to Roman material, were found two sherds of burnished nuragic pottery and artefacts of obsidian and basalt, undoubtedly a continuation of the scatter found in fields 32, 33 and 34 to the east; the three dated pieces from these fields yielded hydration dates of 1216 ± 107 B.C., 470 ± 126 B.C. and 70 ± 100 B.C. (Dyson et al. 38). A single piece of obsidian, collected in field 37, a vineyard just below fields 35 and 36, is probably part of the same assemblage. Another small scatter was found in field 77, closer to the river. The Roman material is consistent with what was found in fields 51 and 52: Roman utilitarian and storage vessels, roof tiles, and African Red Slip Ware, the datable sherds of which were of Hayes 199 (2d c. A.D.), 81B (A.D. 450–500), 58–61 (A.D. 290–450), 9A (A.D. 100–60), D (A.D. 320–660), 196 (A.D. 100–200), 50A (A.D. 230–360), 58B (A.D. 290–375), 59 (A.D. 320–420) and 182 (A.D. 150–250).

About 500 meters north of S. Lussurgiu, fields 84 and 85, about 200 meters northwest of the Campo Sportivo, seem to have contained a small cemetery; the terrain appeared to have been bulldozed to form a plateau where there is currently a children's playground. Artefacts included amphora and tile fragments along with sherds of African Red Slip Ware (Hayes 104B [570–600], 197 [100–425], 23 [75–425] and D [320–660]). None of these sites approaches anything resembling a "villa" and should rather be considered small rustic farmsteads or their associated burial grounds.

Field number 10 had a single roof tile imbedded in the farmer's wall between it and field 11. Field 24, adjacent to the southwest side of the Campo Sportivo, yielded twenty-five fragments of Roman roof tiles; no other artefacts were present. Field 26, a vegetable garden in the region Su Muntigu about 300 meters south of town, yielded one sherd of Roman utilitarian pottery, one rim of late imperial included ware, two sherds of uncertain date and four modern ones. Field 28, a little further uphill to the south, although overgrown with thistles, provided from a single plowed furrow two worn, undiagnostic sherds of African Red Slip Ware. Field 30, a hayfield between the Riu Mannu and provincial highway 49, southwest of the region Perdu

Meano, yielded ten pieces of medieval glazed wares. Fields 57, 58 and 59, vineyards in the southwestern portion of Campu Bingias near the river, provided a single piece of Roman utilitarian ware (in 57) along with small scatters of basalt and obsidian. Field 102, across highway 388 from Campu Bingias, at the 27.6 km marker, yielded a handle and a body sherd of Roman utilitarian ware. Some of these findspots might not even rise to the level of being sites— were the tile fragments at the Campo Sportivo rubble hauled in from elsewhere?—and are not particularly informative about settlement around Forum Traiani in the Roman period.

Clearly, an extensive villa-farmstead system analogous to what one finds in the Ager Cosanus, for example, did not develop around Fordongianus during the Roman period; just as clearly, pre-existent settlement patterns around the nuraghi persisted into, and through, the Roman period in this area as elsewhere in Sardinia. In this province, the Romans were content to leave the native social and economic systems largely intact since they were well suited to the ecology of the region and to a productive system which combined agricultural and pastoral activity. The nuragic sites that survived were examples of natural selection in a land that was, and is, harsh indeed. Sardinia thus provides an excellent example both of rural conservatism and of the Romans' flexibility in adapting to special environments and traditions in their large and complex empire.

Works Cited

Angius, V. 1840. "Fordongianos." In *Dizionario geografico storico-statistico-commericale degli stati di S. M. Il Re di Sardgega*. Vol. 6. Ed. G. Casalis. Torino. 744–52.

Day, J. 1973. *Villaggi abbandonati in Sardegna dal trecento al settecento: inventario*. Paris.

——. 1987a. "L'insediamento precario nei secoli XII–XVIII." In *Uomini e terre nella Sardegna coloniale*. Turin. 127–39.

——. 1987b. "Villaggi abbandonati e tradizione orale." In ibid. 141–73.

Barker, G. 1995. *A Mediterranean Valley: Landscape Archaeology and Annales History in the Biferno Valley*. Leicester.

——. 1996. Review of M. Torelli, ed., *Atlante dei siti archeologici della Toscana*. In *JRS* 86:194–95.

Barker, G., and J. Lloyd. 1991. *Roman Landscapes: Archaeological Survey in the Mediterranean Region*. British School at Rome, Monograph 2. Rome.

Barreca, F. 1978. "Le fortificazioni fenicio-puniche in Sardegna." In *Atti del primo Convegno italiano sul Vicino Oriente antico*. Rome.

——. 1986. *La civiltà fenicio-punica in Sardegna*. Sassari.

Dyson, S. L. 1982. "Archaeological Survey in the Mediterranean: A Review of Recent Research." In *American Antiquity* 47:87–98.

Dyson, S. L., and R. J. Rowland, Jr. 1990. "Survey and Settlement Reconstruction in West-Central Sardinia (1987-1991)." *AJA* 96:203–24.

——. 1991. "Continuity and Change in Roman Rural Sardinia: The Maryland-Wesleyan Survey." In *Arte militare e architettura nuragica: Nuragic Architecture in its Military, Territorial and Socio-economic Context*. Proceedings of the First International Colloquium on Nuragic Architecture at the Swedish Institute in Rome, 7-9 December 1989. Stockholm. 53–63.

——. 1992. "Survey and Settlement Reconstruction in West-Central Sardinia (1987-1991)." *AJA* 96:203–24.

Dyson, S. L., L. Gallin, M. Klimkiewicz, R. J. Rowland, Jr., and C. M. Stevenson. 1990. "Notes on Some Obsidian

Hydration Dates in Sardinia." *Quaderni della Soprintendenza archeologica per le Provincie di Cagliari e Oristano*
7:25–42.

Fara, G. F. 1835. *De Chorographia Sardinia.* Libri duo. Ed. A.
Cibrario. Torino.

Meloni, P. 1990. *La Sardegna romana.* 2d ed. Sassari.

———. 1988. "La Sardegna romana. I centri abitati." In
ANRW II.11.1. Berlin. 491–551.

Millet, M. 1990. *The Romanization of Britain.* Cambridge.

Pinza, G. 1901. *Monumenti primitivi della Sardegna.* MAL 11.
Rome.

Rowland, R. J., Jr. 1976. "Aspetti di continuità culturale
nella Sardegna romana." *Latomus* 36:460–70.

———. 1981. *I ritrovamenti romani in Sardegna.* Rome.

———. 1982. "Beyond the Punic Frontier in Sardinia." *American Journal of Ancient History* 7:20–39.

———. 1984. "La cristianizzazione della Sardegna fino al 600
circa dopo Cristo." *Quaderni Bolotanesi* 10:117–28.

———. 1988. "Preliminary Etymological Observations on the
Romanization of Sardinia," *Annali della Facoltà di Lettere e
Filosofia dell'Università di Cagliari* 45:243–47.

———. 1990. "Appunti sulla romanizzazione attorno a
Forum Traiani (Fordongianus)." *L'Africa Romana* 7:533–
36.

———. 1992. "When Did the Nuragic Period in Sardinia
End?" In *Sardinia Antiqua: Studi in onore di Piero Meloni.*
Cagliari. 165–75.

Rowland, R. J., Jr., and S. L. Dyson. 1988. "Survey Archaeology in the Territory of Bauladu: Preliminary Notice."
*Quaderni della Soprintendenza archeologica per le Provincie
di Cagliari e Oristano* 6:129–39.

———. 1989. "Survey Archaeology in the Territories of Paulilatino and Fordongianus: Preliminary Notice." *Quaderni della Soprintendenza archeologica per le Provincie di Cagliari e Oristano* 7:157–85.

Sotgiu, G. 1961. *Iscrizioni latine della Sardegna.* Vol. 1. Padova.

———. 1988. "L'epigrafia latina in Sardegna." In *ANRW* II.11.1. Berlin. 552–739.

Spano, G. 1860. "Fordongianus." In *Bollettino Archeologico Sardo* 6:161–68.

Tangheroni, M. 1983. "Per lo studio dei villaggi abbandonati a Pisa e in Sardegna nel Trecento." In *Sardegna Mediterranea.* Rome. 211–32.

Taramelli. 1903. "Fordongianus. Antiche terme di Forum Traiani." In *Notizie degli Scavi.* 469–92. Rome.

Terrosu Asole, A. 1974. *L'insediamento umano medioevale e i centri abbandonati tra il secolo XIV e il secolo XVIII.* Rome.

Tykot, R. 1993. "Radiocarbon Dating and Absolute Chronology in Sardinia and Corsica." In *Radiocarbon Dating and Italian Prehistory.* Eds. R. Skeates and R. Whitehouse. London. 1–22.

Webster, G. 1996. *A Prehistory of Sardinia, 2300–500 B.C.* Sheffield.

Webster, G., and M. Teglund. 1992. "Toward the Study of Colonial-native Interactions in Sardinia from ca. 100 B.C.– A.D. 456." In *Sardinia in the Mediterranean: A Footprint in the Sea.* Studies in Sardinian Archaeology Presented to Miriam S. Balmuth. Eds. R. Tykot and T. Andrews. Sheffield. 448–74.

Zedda, A. 1906. *Forum Traiani.* Cagliari.

Zucca, R. 1986a. *Fordongianus.* Sassari.

———. 1986b. "Ricerche storiche e topografiche su Forum Traiani." In *Nuovo Bollettino Archeologico Sardo* 3:167–87.

———. 1989. "Forum Traiani alla luce delle nuove scoperte archeologiche." In *Il suburbio delle città in Sardegna: persistenze e trasformazioni.* Atti del terzo Convegno di studio sull'archeologia tardoromana e altomedievale in Sardegna (Cuglieri, 28–29 giugno 1986). Taranto.

What Is a Classic?
Answering Mr. Eliot's
Question, Fifty Years Later

cononono

Harry C. Rutledge
The University of Tennessee

On the 16th of October 1944 T. S. Eliot delivered his presidential address before the newly founded Virgil Society of Britain. The lecture had the title, "What Is a Classic?" The address was one of the most eloquent hymns to Vergil ever written.[1]

That T. S. Eliot should be inaugural president of the Virgil Society would have surprised no one. Famous for the learned notes that accompanied an early publication of *The Waste Land* in 1922 with their emphasis on sources in Ovid and for the epigraph to his beautiful poem of the Prufrock collection of 1917—the poem, "La Figlia che Piange," the

---

[1] An earlier version of this paper was presented at the University of Georgia in October, 1995. The standard critical editions of Horace have been used, with the special annotative help of E. C. Wickham, *The Works of Horace* I (Oxford, 1896.)

329

epigraph, *O quam te memorem virgo, Aeneid* 1.327—Eliot's *The Family Reunion* of 1939, based on Aeschylus' *Oresteia*, was the work of a Classical scholar. Meanwhile, his essays under the title, *The Sacred Wood* (1920) are drenched with Classicism, beginning with the epigraph from Petronius. It was in 1948 that Eliot received the Nobel Prize for literature, but his friends in the Virgil Society could have seen it coming. The homage of the presidency was laud, honor and prescience on the part of the British Virgil Society. Eliot responded with his incomparable paper, quickly published by the house of which he was a director.[2]

The human mind has ever loved lists of great achievements. These lists range from the Alexandrian "Seven Wonders of the World" to Hadrian's Villa, with its reconstruction of the emperor's favorite buildings and sites in the Greek East. The powerful financier, J. P. Morgan, became an omnivorous collector, wanting one of each of everything. His monument is his library in New York City; the rest went to the Metropolitan Museum of Art, whose classical collections, though grand, will never equal the display of the Louvre or, above all, the British Museum. In this century, later than Morgan, we have the remarkable collecting effort of William Randolph Hearst who specialized in Greek pottery for the adornment of his mansion overlooking San Simeon, California, and a special favorite of mine, the wonderful collection of American furniture and decorative arts at the late Miss Ima Hogg's home, "Bayou Bend" in Houston.

With regard to these collections of the arts of painting, sculpture and decoration, our question, "What Is a Classic?," is reinforced by Kenneth Clark's essay of 1979, *What Is a Masterpiece?* Clark, one of Bernard Berenson's last stu-

---

[2] For a positive word among the mixed reviews see M. R. Ridley, *CR* 59:64.

dents, posed his question and answered it in a slender but rich essay, the 1979 Thames and Hudson lecture in memory of the house's founder, Walter Neurath.

The concluding words of Kenneth Clark's essay have a broad significance:

> "Although many meanings cluster round the word master-piece, it is above all the work of an artist of genius who has been absorbed by the spirit of the time in a way that has made his individual experiences universal. If he is fortunate enough to live in a time when many moving pictorial ideas are current, his chances of creating a masterpiece are greatly increased. If, to put it crudely, the acceptable sub-jects of painting are serious themes, touching us at many levels, he is well on his way. But in the end a masterpiece will be the creation of his own genius." (Clark 44)

T. S. Eliot in his famous paper has as a guiding light the word and concept of *maturity*. As Eliot lays out his points in this lecture,[3] he is at his most vatic in phrasing and manner. Surely one of the most exalted pieces of writing in English of this century is his much earlier study, "Tradition and the Individual Talent" of 1920, wherein the poet remarks on "the historical sense," observing

> "The historical sense compels a man to write not merely with his own generation in his bones, but with a feeling that the whole of the literature of Europe from Homer and within it the whole of the literature of his own country has a simultaneous existence and composes a simultaneous order." (*Sacred Wood* 49)

[3] As later collected, Eliot's paper was briefly noted by some re-viewers of *On Poetry and Poets*. The anonymous reviewer (as then was the custom in *TLS*) observed: ". . . we are left with a term and a concept whose usefulness seems very limited, except perhaps as a way of indi-cating generally, with a minimum of particular reference . . . the merits of Virgil." (Citations following from *OPP*.)

Having established his central theme of maturity, President Eliot proceeds to elaborate. Maturity is first of all the maturity of the mind (WIC 55) and then maturity of manners (WIC 56). Maturity of manners comes in "an age when society has achieved a moment of order and stability, of equilibrium and harmony . . ." (WIC 57). On then we go to a consideration of the development of maturity of language. Eliot is heading towards Vergil, nodding to Catullus, Propertius and Horace along the way as inferior artists.

Eliot brings us to Vergil by way of Aeneas' encounter with the shade of Dido in Book 6 (450–76). Eliot calls this "one of the most civilized passages in poetry" (WIC 63). Eliot observes: ". . . Aeneas does not forgive himself—and this, significantly, in spite of the fact of which he is well aware, that all that he has done has been in compliance with destiny, or in consequence of the machinations of gods who are themselves, we feel, only instruments of a greater inscrutable power" (WIC 64).

Eliot moves on, pausing briefly for a recapitulation, proceeding to add to his criteria for the Classic two new conditions, "comprehensiveness" (WIC 69) and "universality" (WIC 69). He declares, "The classic must, within its formal limitations, express the maximum possible of the whole range of feeling which represents the character of the people who speak that language" (WIC 69).

From this point to the end of his lecture the "American Magus," as Marion Montgomery crowned him in his fine monograph of 1970, moves into the general language that belongs to high praise, pronouncing that "our classic, the classic of all Europe, is Virgil" (WIC 73).[4]

---

[4] For related studies of Eliot the Vergilian see Donker and Rutledge. Reeves' dissertation has major chapters on *The Waste Land* and *Four Quartets*. Reeves treats *W I C* from the standpoint of the influence on Eliot of Haecker (101–36).

Eliot's magnificent praise of Vergil is the admiration of one erudite artist for another. His criteria for the recognition of greatness, leading up to universality, are impeccable. Today, however, we see the curious limits of Eliot's study. Except for a fleeting reference to Turnus (WIC 64), the essay is entirely concerned with Vergil's masterpiece in the old fashioned terms of the first six books. When I began my career at The University of Georgia in 1960, following the deepest possible introduction to Rome by Professor Paul MacKendrick in the summer of 1958 at the American Academy, the study of Vergil was not at all the scholarly industry that it has come to be since 1965 and few scholars were concerned with the second half of the *Aeneid*.

The accomplishment of Vergil in the second half of the *Aeneid* is to discern triumph and tragedy, as did Winston Churchill in his extraordinary history of World War II, the sixth and final volume of which had this dark phrase as its title.

Vergil, working in the luxuriant form of the epic poem, pursues several themes in Books 7–12 of the *Aeneid*. Aeneas as a newcomer to Italy is as Achilles, an invader of Troy-land. Vergil dilates on rural, forested Italy, especially in Book 8, just as Horace does throughout his poems. I think of 1.9, the "Soracte Ode" where Horace and a friend have a warming cup of wine in a snowscape, but especially 1.17 where the poet invokes a hot summer day; up in the hills Tyndaris plays on a flute; all of this *in reducta valle* (*Odes* 1.17.17), a secret garden.

Youth is so important in the second half of the *Aeneid*. There is Pallas, Evander's son and so admired by Aeneas. His death on the battlefield is brutal and sad; his funeral, where his corpse is wrapped in tapestries woven by Dido (*Aeneid* 11.72–75) pains the reader. And there is Lavinia, tossed like the top in *Aeneid* 7.378–84, among her mother and her suitor Turnus, and the patiently awaiting Aeneas, for whom she is destined by Fate. That Lavinia is an object of desire is made clear in Book 12 when she so wonderfully—because it's a unique description by Vergil—blushes as she hears her mother and Turnus discussing her future (12.64–66).

But most delightful of the young people in *Aeneid* 7–12 is Ascanius, Aeneas' son, who enters the poem as a boy and becomes Captain of the Fort when his father has to go to the field. This was my subject before the 1987 Institute of the American Classical League. I later repeated the lecture before the Texas Classical Association, published in the TCA Bulletin of 1991. Such a wonderful young man! The sweet boy of *Aeneid* 1 grows up. Time passes and he is capable of being his father's regent in the Italian war (*Aeneid* 9.257–74). *Arma virumque*. All of the just mentioned plot and *gloria* are not Eliot's concern.

Today's probing interest in the whole poem, with special stress on Books 7–12 and, above all, on the ambiguous ending of the poem, was given special emphasis at a conference held at Florida State University in December 1992 in honor of Professor Lynette Thompson's fifty years of teaching. Philip Hardie, William Anderson, Christine Perkell were a few of the fine scholars on the program. Terms such as "intertextuality" and "privatization," terms that are a laser beam as compared with Eliot's courtly critical terms were the style—such was the spirit, the mode of interpretation and dialogue at the Florida meeting. And so, with no disparagement of Eliot's deeply sensitive lecture, we find ourselves fifty some years later asking, "Well then, what *is* a Classic, now?"

My answer to Eliot's great question will be Book 4 of Horace's *Odes*, published in approximately 13 B.C. As I lay out my argument, let me at the outset acknowledge the value and help of Michael C. J. Putnam's Townsend Lectures at Cornell University, published in 1986 as *Artifices of*

Eternity: *Horace's Fourth Book of Odes*. My approach will be to lay out the structure of Horace's fourth book, only fifteen poems, and then discuss them in terms of Eliot's magisterial criteria of the famous lecture. I want to keep my presentation rather more of general interest, less of the technical terminology and point of view of the brilliant conference in Tallahassee.[5]

The fourth book of Horace's *Odes* is majestic and solemn in tone. There is praise for the commonwealth of the Augustan Empire. There is concern for youthful beauty and the inexorable approach of old age. Horace has presented these themes before, but now his palette is that of a deep silvery lake at twilight. Lalage is still beautiful, her hair becoming gray.

If we assume that the world of Caesar Augustus was at its height in 13 B.C. (generally agreed, cf. Armstrong 138–39), the latest collection of Horace's poetry, with its imperial inspiration, could only reflect that world. It was what Wendell Wilkie called *One World*, and Michael Putnam rightly connects the fourth book with the supreme Augustan sculptural creations of the Ara Pacis and the Forum Augustum. With regard to the Forum, Putnam underscores the materials of the building (Putnam 335), and thus the stones are equal to the words.

Eliot was concerned with maturity, comprehensiveness and, finally, universality. With maturity he associated mind, manners and language.

The fourth book of Horace's *Odes* has its beginning, middle and end. The first Ode of the fifteen is a quiet meditation. Horace is too old for the arrows of love. Venus, please! It is young men such as Paulus Fabius Maximus,

---

[5] The critical spirit and mode of discourse of the Florida conference are captured by Gregson Davis in his *Polyhymnia: The Rhetoric of Horatian Lyric Discourse*. See especially 133–43 for *Odes* 4.

later to be consul, who are fair prey for the goddess. Our bard is beyond all of this. But, there is the Ligurinus of this world (1.33–40), the arrestingly handsome young man, of whom Horace—*senex*, in general—deeply dreams.

The center of the book should be the eighth ode, the hymn to Italian artistry in general and the celebratory poem in particular. In a word, praise for Horace's special inspiration, the Muses of Calabria. But it's not that neat because the Muses of Calabria are richly framed by Ode Seven, a poem about the changing seasons and a mélange of associated references to Aeneas, Tullus and Ancus (7.15) and to Hippolytus and Theseus (7.26–27). The ninth Ode is a glorification of Greek literature with stress on Homer and assorted Greek lyric poets. In the midst of this festival comes Lollius, whose troubled career did not cost him the friendship of Caesar Augustus. In a miracle of panegyric, Horace's Lollius becomes the heir to all the ages. Thus, Odes 7, 8 and 9 are an encapsulation of the Greco-Roman achievement, as the discerning Horace could well appreciate as the first century B.C. glided to its majestic, Augustan end.

And so it is certainly appropriate to Horace's mature world-view that Ode 15 would proclaim . . . *tua, Caesar, aetas* (15.4) the era of Augustus, and end with the imperial salute of *progeniem Veneris canemus* (15.32) "We will hymn the race of Venus."

So far, we are certainly seeing Horace's own maturity of mind, his understanding of manners in the world that has become the Augustan Empire, and the clear maturity of his own language, both majestic and crystalline. We began with the very personal poem of the first Ode, on to the central trio of poems where the high culture of Greece embraces the Muses of Calabria. Ode 15 is paean to the one-world of Rome.

How does the rest of the collection work with the beginning, middle and end of Horace's fourth book? What are the dynamics, the undulations of both art and sensibility in this masterpiece?

Ode 2 praises Pindar, the grand lyricist of Greece. Horace despairs of writing either grandly or of the grandeur of the Augustan Age. In Ode 3 our author protests that he is neither soldier nor athlete. Is there hope? Can Horace be the "minstrel of the Roman lyre" (3.23)? In Ode 4 Horace rallies: he goes through the Punic Wars; the great triumph over Carthage. This poem is truly a backward glance, with the artist in full control of the Roman achievement. And so, easily to Ode 5, the brilliance and the blessing of Augustus' reign.

The fourth book of *Odes* needs a rest. We pause in Ode 6 to contemplate Vergil's brilliant but remote divinities, Apollo and Diana. Then the powerful center of the book, Odes 7, 8, 9—Greco-Roman culture, the Muses of Calabria, and the bards of combined yore with the military commander Lollius, Augustus' friend, and, I would note, not a perfect hero—the heir to all the ages.

Ode 10, we pause and reflect. Ligurinus ages. So does the old admirer of spring and youth. But then, there's a jar of Alban wine. Silver vessels, a wreathed altar. It is a birthday poem to Maecenas. Maecenas, although the ostensible recipient of the poem is Phyllis. But Phaëthon is also invoked and his *avaras . . . spes* (11.25–26)—greedy hopes. Maecenas, one of the architects of the Augustan Empire, did not deserve such a jolt from Horace, whose Thaliarchus of the wonderfully hospitable Soracte Ode, 1.9, is surely Maecenas on a country visit to his friend in the country. There are slips in these panegyrics. No one is perfect. Great ones have frailties. Phaëthon will always be the figure of ambition. Meanwhile there is the *plenus Albani cadus*.

The jug of Alban wine. Horace and Maecenas have their putative birthday visit, Caesar Augustus notwithstanding.

Maecenas, once the great aide to Augustus and the chief representative of the old Etruscan aristocracy whose endorsement Augustus coveted for tradition and prestige, had, in fact, been dismissed from Augustus' inner circle some years (beginning in 23 B.C. Syme 409) before *Odes* 4 was published. But Maecenas lived until 8 B.C. Ode 11 is not the welcome of an older man to Phyllis. The welcome is to Maecenas, whether he can come or not. The ancient friendship has been moved to a rather distant level—the poems in the fourth book mainly herald Augustus. Of course Horace would be the soul of discretion in a reference to Maecenas. But such a friendship, and Horace's eternal gratitude to his patron, are conditions of life symbolized by silver vessels and an altar. There are many gods in Horace's heaven, Maecenas not the least.

Ode 12 of Book 4 opens with mention of the fate of Itys, the tragic child surrounded by Tereus, Procne and Philomela, swooningly evoked by Aeschylus in the *Agamemnon*. As the sacrificial mother became a bird, so the reference to country life brings the poet and his readers to Arcadia and to Vergil. The language is that of a ritual. Horace and Vergil would be symposiasts, celebrants, Vergil bringing to the ceremony the aromatic spikenard. Vergil has been dead for six years. Horace's poem, literally drenched with affection, suggests the paintings from Paestum, now in the museum there, where Youth drowns.

Ode 13 moves more deeply into old age. Cinara, Horace's emblem for feminine beauty, is gone, now Lyce follows, a too young older woman. The final image of the poem is ashes.

Ode 14 returns to the imperial theme. The power of Augustus is the power of war. But the Pax Augusta has had its price. The mood of the poem is more dark than triumphant and we find ourselves recalling the ruined sacred tree of Faunus in *Aeneid* 12, around whose mournful stump Aeneas and Turnus have their last battle. The Nile, the Danube and Britain's Ocean are evoked by Horace in grandiloquent language, *compositis . . . armis*—"with arms laid to rest." The triumph, in the eyes of a person like Horace, so bittersweet, as many today would view the recent accord with the country of Vietnam. The darkness of these imperial events will never be invisible.

And so, after what I take to be the guarded glory of Ode 14, we come to the concluding poem of the collection. As I have already observed, this poem is the grandest possible salute to the Pax Augusta.

T. S. Eliot has the criteria, beyond maturity, of comprehensiveness and universality. Horace's fourth book presents the worlds of Homer and Greek tragedy; he honors the lyric poets. He does not mention Socrates, but we feel Socrates and his generous view of life and love throughout the book. The builders of empires are not mentioned, Alexander the Great and Julius Caesar. But Augustus Caesar and his aides are both the successors and the embodiment of those predecessors who also envisioned One World. I have used the phrase more than once in this study, "heir to all the ages." It comes from Henry James' enraptured description of Milly Theale, his ill-fated heroine in *The Wings of the Dove* (1.109). The phrase suits Eliot's theme of "universality," the literary theme of Vergil through Book 8 of the *Aeneid*, the concluding book of Ovid's *Metamorphoses* and, certainly, Horace's fourth book of *Odes*.

Eliot triumphantly observes before the Virgilians of Great Britain, "Our classic, the classic of all Europe, is Virgil" (WIC 73). But Eliot did not even try to contend with the dark world and the dark fate of Turnus. On Horace's side, by the time he collected his fourth book, his was the universe, the One World, of the Augustan Peace. Horace would have known the price of this creation, as well as the value.

The fourth book of Horace's *Odes* answers Eliot's question especially well because its themes move into the Augustan Empire that could only have been imagined by Vergil at his premature death in 19 B.C. From the point of view of theme, Vergil's poem is universal as of 19 B.C. and certainly embraces the themes of the Greek masters before him. Homer obviously and Euripides and Plato loom over, feed and furnish Vergil's *Aeneid*. Vergil is an heir to all the ages. The influence on him of the earlier Roman poet-historians and Lucretius cannot be described enough.

Horace, writing in the more dense, tighter, more vatic style, genre of the ode, both surveys and encapsulates the Greco-Roman world. Vergil saw the outlines, the foundations and the direction of the Augustan Age. Horace saw a vision materialize. In Eliot's terms of maturity and the concomitant universality, Horace's final work, though slender, must be regarded as the fuller answer to Eliot's arresting question.

Works Cited

Anon. 1957. "Out of the Sacred Wood." *Times Literary Supplement* 18 Oct. 624.

Armstrong, David. 1989. *Horace*. New Haven.

Clark, Kenneth. 1979. *What Is a Masterpiece?* London.

Davis, Gregson. 1991. *Polyhymnia: The Rhetoric of Horatian Lyric Discourse*. Berkeley.

Donker, Marjorie. 1974. "*The Waste Land* and the *Aeneid*." *PMLA* 89:164–71.

Eliot, T. S. 1971. *The Complete Poems and Plays*. New York.

——. 1928. *The Sacred Wood: Essays on Poetry and Criticism.* London.

——. 1945. *What Is a Classic? An Address Delivered before the Virgil Society on the 16th of October 1944.* London.

——. 1957. "What Is a Classic?" In *On Poetry and Poets.* New York.

Haecker, Theodor. 1934. *Virgil: Father of the West.* Tr. A. W. Wheen. London. (Rpt. 1970.)

James, Henry. 1922. *The Wings of the Dove.* New York.

Montgomery, Marion. 1969. *T. S. Eliot: An Essay on the American Magus.* Athens, Ga.

Putnam, Michael C. J. 1986. *Artifices of Eternity: Horace's Fourth Book of Odes.* Ithaca.

Reeves, Gareth E. 1981. *T. S. Eliot and Virgil.* Ann Arbor.

Rutledge, Harry C. 1966. "Eliot and Vergil: Parallels in the Sixth *Aeneid* and *Four Quartets.*" *Vergilius* 12:11–20.

Syme, Ronald. 1952. *The Roman Revolution.* Oxford.

Wickham, E. C. 1896. *The Works of Horace* I. Oxford.

Wilkie, Wendell. 1943. *One World.* New York.

Aphrodite and the *Satyrica*[1]

ဢဢဢဢ

Gareth Schmeling
University of Florida

The penultimate chapter of the *Satyrica* opens with an introduction of Philomela (140.1): *matrona inter primas honesta*. The reader immediately thinks back to the episode of the Widow of Ephesus (111.1): *matrona quaedam Ephesi tam notae erat pudicitiae*. Both the Widow and Philomela manipulate others to obtain what they desire. Eumolpus is the *auctor* of the Widow story and *actor* in the Philomela episode. Though he introduces himself (83.3) *ego . . . poeta sum*, he is in fact a poet *manqué* (90.1: *ex is, qui in porticibus spatiabantur, lapides in Eumolpum recitantem miserunt*), but an extraordinary raconteur, and the stories he tells and the stories told about him are couched in a thick literary texture.

---

[1] It is probable that no one outside the immediate MacKendrick family owes more to Paul MacKendrick than do I. For me he was *magister optimus*. That I was later seduced by the Siren voices of literary criticism could not have been foreseen by Paul: better was expected of a good Lutheran boy. In order of preference I suppose that he hoped for an epigrapher, archaeologist, or historian: *peccavi*.

Philomela has a high social standing (*honesta* is not a moral description) and belongs to the local aristocracy of Croton, i.e. she represents the best, that small part of society which excludes the masses. She holds a social position to which every Roman woman aspires and of which every Roman man approves. On the other hand she prostitutes her young daughter and son to wealthy, childless individuals in hope of being included in their wills. The noble and resourceful Philomela is worthy of praise from the Roman establishment, but because of her current actions she must be socially damned by that Roman establishment. It is the same Philomela, but interpretation is everything. Philomela and her situation are an example of syllepsis, the "master trope"[2] which distinguishes the ancient novel. The figure of rhetoric, in which a word or situation is used only once, but the context suggests ambiguity and at least two different meanings, is generally referred to as syllepsis.

The concluding chapters (116–41) of the *Satyrica*, which take place in Croton, are concerned with a narrative which focuses on the social phenomenon of *captatio* (116.6: *nam aut captantur aut captant*). The motif of *captatio* had been dealt with many times in the past and was familiar to the Roman reader. What is special about Petronius' treatment of the motif here is that the *captatores* themselves are the victims of an elaborate deception planned by the storyteller Eumolpus.[3] (Who better to perpetrate a complex fraud than a writer of fiction?)[4] The inner story of *captatio*

[2] D. Selden, "Genre of Genre," in *The Search for the Ancient Novel.* Ed. J. Tatum (Baltimore 1994) 51.

[3] J. P. Sullivan, *The Satyricon of Petronius: a Literary Study* (London 1968) 66ff.; P. G. Walsh, *The Roman Novel* (Cambridge 1970) 104ff.; V. Tracy, "*Aut captantur aut captant,*" *Latomus* 39 (1980) 399–402; C. Panayotakis, *Theatrum Arbitri: Theatrical Elements in the Satyrica of Petronius* (Leiden 1995) 182ff.; G. B. Conte, *The Hidden Author: An Interpretation of Petronius's Satyricon* (Berkeley 1996) 135ff.

[4] T. P. Wiseman, "Lying Historians: Seven Types of Mendacity," in

is wrapped inside of an outer story of deception by Eumolpus, which in turn is wrapped in the literary framework of a mime. And Eumolpus is made director of a real-life play (117.4): *"quid ergo" inquit Eumolpus "cessamus mimum componere? facite ergo me dominum."* The mime has spread from the theater, and life in Croton, which had earlier been a thinly veiled illusion, becomes now a hoax of a deception. The terminology and structure of the hoax belong to the theater, and life in Croton, at whatever level, turns into a fiction. Instead of creating a story, Eumolpus prefers to live in one which he created. We need not impose a literary flavor on this episode: the text proudly displays it.

In hope of securing a legacy Philomela sets her plans into motion by handing over her son and daughter not to Eumolpus but to his *bonitas* (140.2), so that he might educate them. He chooses to begin the education of the young girl (*filia speciosissima*) first, not that of the young boy (*doctissimus puer*), and promptly invites her *ut sederet supra commendatam bonitatem* (140.7). Not only is there high[5] literary texture of satire and theater here, but also low punning.

At 140.5 there is another pun, but this one is more elaborate and lies obscured in textual problems:[6] *Eumolpus . . .*

Lies and Fiction in the Ancient World. Eds. C. Gill, T. P. Wiseman (Exeter 1993) 122–46.

[5] Conte (n. 3) *passim.*

[6] In finding new sexual meanings in the *Satyrica* I risk yielding to that American weakness noted by M. L. West, "Melica," *CQ* 20 (1970) 209 n. 3: "The desire to find hitherto unsuspected sexual meanings in ancient literature frequently seems to blind American scholars to all considerations of relevance, style, and common sense." Not only do American scholars come in for chastisement from Professor West, America itself is derided for being so far from civilization. M. L. West, *Textual Criticism and Editorial Technique* (Leipzig 1973) 9: "Most classical manuscripts are now in European libraries or museum collections, but some are in monasteries (particularly in Greece) or private owner-

non distulit puellam invitare ad † *pigiciaca* † *sacra*. There are difficulties with *pigiciaca*, and scholars have turned their attention to the word.[7] But the key to the solution, I believe, rests with *sacra* in conjunction with *pigiciaca*.

The limited manuscript evidence is laid out by Bücheler and Müller:[8] pigiciaca *L:* pygesiaca πυγησιακὰ *margo l.* Bücheler adds *requiro* ΑΦΡΟΔΙCΙΑΚΑ, *nam* πυγή *et* πυγίζειν *ab hoc loco alienissima*, and prints *pigiciaca*. Müller (1961) prints † *pigiciaca* † and then in later editions prints *Aphrodisiaca*.

It seems clear that the two greatest editors of Petronius reject the basic reading πυγ—and the implication of the word, sodomy—in this case heterosexual sodomy, a practice otherwise known in the Roman novel.[9] Eumolpus earlier in the *Satyrica* had shown marked homosexual proclivities, but here he clearly chooses for sex the *filia speciosissima* and passes over the *ephebus* (140.4): he joins the other characters in the *Satyrica* in bisexuality.

I would like to suggest that the manuscript reading is correct and, as unlikely as it seems, the interpretation of Bücheler and Müller is also on the mark. Though the young girl is summoned *ad pigiciaca sacra*, she is invited to vaginal intercourse, the sacred rites of Aphrodite, that is, an Aphrodite of Sicily, known as Καλλίπυγος Ἀφροδίτη. The story is told by Athenaeus (12:554 c–e): the two daughters of a farmer argue about which of them has the more lovely

---

ship, and some are in such places as Istanbul or Jerusalem, or in America."

[7] B. Baldwin, "*Pigiciaca sacra*: a Fundamental Problem in Petronius," *Maia* 30 (1978) 119–21; E. Campanile, "Interpretazioni Petroniane," *SSL* 4 (1964) 115–26.

[8] F. Bücheler, ed., *Petronii Saturae* (Berlin 1958 [1862]); K. Müller, ed., *Petronii Arbitri Satyricon* (Munich 1961); idem, *Petronius Satyrica* (Munich 1983³).

[9] Apuleius, *Met.* 3.20.

buttocks (ποτέρα εἴη καλλιπυγοτέρα) and hit on a plan of standing by a highway and exposing their finer qualities to passing, handsome men. The two young women attract the attention of the two sons of a wealthy man, who reluctantly agrees to their marrying these less socially acceptable women—the locals nickname the sisters καλλίπυγοι, who in turn found Καλλιπύγου 'Αφροδίτης ἱερόν. I would propose then that *pigiciaca sacra* are rites performed in honor of Καλλίπυγος 'Αφροδίτη, but structured by Petronius in the narrative as syllepsis. As the farmer's daughters seduced the wealthy man's sons by exposing their natural beauty, so Philomela (*floris extincti*) exposed her young daughter.

Encolpius, the narrator, along with the brother of the girl, observes at least part of the *pigiciaca sacra* through the keyhole of the bedroom door. In several ways the episode at *Satyrica* 140 is an echo of the Quartilla episode at 25–26: the act of sexual intercourse is performed within the ritual of a *pervigilium Priapi* (21.7), the young woman's name is Pannychis (a pun on *pervigilium*), and Encolpius observes the erotic rites through a chink in the door. Both episodes display heterosexual acts in a religious context.

Milton's *in Quintum Novembris, anno aetatis 17* (1626): Choices and Intentions

Dana F. Sutton
University of California, Irvine

Although *in Quintum Novembris* was the youthful Milton's longest and most ambitious Latin work, in general it is lightly esteemed. The author of a recent survey of Milton's Latin poetry explained why:[1]

> Its chief interest for the modern reader lies in its fore-shadowing of *Paradise Lost*. Satan in 'In Quintum Novembris' is a brief but not incompetent sketch for the gigantic

[1] Condee 63f. A similar appraisal can be found at Tillyard 30. Neglect is as common as disparagement. In a lengthy study of Milton's early works, by Hanford, two sentences are devoted to *in Quintum Novembris* (101). Even this is better than Bradner's discussion of Milton's Latin works (111–18): he failed to mention it at all! It is doubtless for this same reason that the scholarship devoted to this poem is very thin on the ground. There exists only one study of fundamental importance, by Cheek. Clearly something is very wrong, either with the poem—or with us.

figure of *Paradise Lost*. Both poems use many of the epic conventions—the adventurous journey, the council (of Cardinals in 'In Quintum Novembris,' of devils in *Paradise Lost*), the rousing speech to the indolent follower, the supernatural being in disguise, and so on.

But 'In Quintum Novembris' is marred by several flaws. Perhaps the most important is the poorly managed conclusion: for the first 169 lines the poem has an enthusiastic if melodramatic drive; suddenly at 170 Fama appears and twenty-three lines of the poem are devoted to describing her. Then within thirty-three lines she saves England by revealing the fact of the conspiracy. After such elaborate preparations for England's downfall we might justifiably expect more heroic efforts would be needed to save her. A Satan who would be foiled by these last thirty-three lines of the poem doesn't resemble the *ferus ignifluo regnans Acheronte tyrannus, / Eumenidum pater,* "the fierce tyrant who controls Acheron's flaming currents, the tyrant who is father to the Furies" (7–8), who dominates the beginning of the poem. One suspects that the seventeen-year-old poet tired after 150 or so lines and simply finished off the poem as quickly as he did.

At least if one begins with the same set of initial expectations and assumptions as did this writer—more about these in a moment—these remarks are, if anything, exceedingly gentle. Regarded as a narrative poem, perhaps even as a miniature historical epic, *in Quintum Novembris* is sadly botched. As a recounting of the facts of the Gunpowder Plot, even if we make every allowance for the consideration that Milton was writing poetry rather than history, it seems a total failure. Where one expects to find some kind of factual narrative with human actors, one gets little more than mythmaking. Who else but Milton has ever managed to write about the Plot without mentioning Guy Fawkes? A modern reader ignorant of the facts of the Plot comes away from the poem in something like complete bewilderment.

Then is it a hopeless failure? Even the youthful Milton was still Milton, and possibly the fault is not in the poem itself, but in the misguided way we read it. If one "deconstructs" the above-quoted remarks, one sees that their author has approached *in Quintum Novembris* with a heavy baggage of preconceptions. First, he identifies it as a miniepic, differing from genuine epic principally in terms of length—as if length were a dispensable feature of that genre. Then, on the basis of that identification, he permits himself to assume that the poem should conform to certain canons of behavior characteristic of epic. Paramount among these are narrative coherence and proportion: whatever else an epic may be, whatever conventions it may follow, it is a poem that tells a story, and hence that ought to display the characteristics of good storytelling. Frustrated that *in Quintum Novembris* does not fulfill his expectations, he adopts a dismissive attitude.

In Quintum Novembris is of course not an epic. Its length disqualifies it from any such categorization. Another classificatory term seems more appropriate, epyllion.[2] Since an epyllion is a short hexameter poem,[3] the invocation of this word dispenses with the length problem. But this maneuver does not address the major difficulty of narrative coherence. Let us see if we can do better. With an eye to such items as Marlowe's *Hero and Leander* and Shakespeare's

---

[2] *In Quintum Novembris* has in fact been identified as such (Rand 116). But Rand unhelpfully—and wrongly—defined an epyllion as a "mock-epic" and did not investigate any of the consequences of this classification.

[3] Typically between about 250 and 500 lines. The genre probably had its origins in the more self-contained books of Homer and the longer of the *Homeric Hymns*, and in antiquity it probably fostered the development of this form that an epyllion was of a satisfactory length to occupy a not-too-unwieldy papyrus roll.

Venus and Adonis, modern English scholars write about the Ovidian epyllion. This genre has recently been described:[4]

> Unlike an epic such as the *Aeneid*, Ovid's [*Metamorphoses*] conveniently divides into numerous discrete episodes involving perennially fascinating topics such as frustrated passion, incest, rape, and murder, all of which, including the last, are aspects of its erotic character. In addition, the overall theme of transformation or change of identity makes for keen psychological interest. With Ovid the epic's customary sphere of action broadens to include something of a more reflective dimension, so that the poet seems not merely to be presenting a startling event but also musing on what may underlie its occurrence.

The trouble is, of course, that epyllia of the sort this writer has in mind may lack such epic conventions as adventurous journeys, rousing speeches, councils, and divinities in disguise (as well as many others one could enumerate), but they are still narrative poems, and so, in this most fundamental sense of all, are to be judged by the same criteria as epics.

But the genus of the classical epyllion (together with its neoclassical imitations) is in turn divisible into two distinct species, each having its own aims and methods. If the Ovidian epyllion is one species, the Alexandrian epyllion is a very different one. Writing of Callimachus' *Hecale* Alban Lesky wrote:[5]

> By calling the *Hecale* an epyllion we do not only indicate its small size, but also a specific method of narrative different from the larger epic. Certain episodes, mostly not the central ones, are taken from the context of old legends and are lovingly reshaped, while the remaining themes are left at

---

[4] Roe 15.
[5] Lesky 715f.

the fringe. . . . The *Hecale* had an extraordinary influence; poems of the Roman neoterici, such as the *Io* of Licinius Calvus or the *Smyrna* of Helvius Cinna are modeled upon it; Catullus' poem on the *Marriage of Peleus and Thetis* and the *Ciris* from the Appendix Vergiliana also bear testimony to this influence.

Elsewhere the same author speaks of "the delight of Hellenistic epyllia in depicting little scenes."[6] The genre is characterized by verbal scene-painting, focus on piquant details, and creation of atmospherics, with the writer gliding hastily over everything else if he treats anything at all. The author of an epyllion of the Alexandrian type is under no obligation to present the reader with a coherent narrative; indeed, to do so would be to violate the rules of the particular game he has chosen to play. In consequence, such an author has a right to have his work measured by appropriate yardsticks.

We suddenly find ourselves on more solid ground. One of the very things for which Tillyard and Condee criticized *in Quintum Novembris*—its abrupt ending—is a typical generic feature of the Alexandrian epyllion. Another characteristic of this form is scene-painting, often at the expense of narrative flow, what would normally be regarded as proper proportion and overall coherence. *In Quintum Novembris* certainly contains a lot of scene-painting. Cheek analyzed the poem into four principal "movements" consisting of Satan's initial flight over England and thence to Rome, a description of Rome as the lair of the evil Pope, the consistory convened by the Pope on the following morning at which the Plot is hatched, and the scene in which Rumor's tower is elaborately described[7] and in which

<hr>

[6] Lesky 640.

[7] This passage is heavily indebted to Ovid's description of the house of Rumor at *Metamorphoses* 12.39ff. At the same time, it is very reminis-

she published news of the Plot in time for it to be fore-
stalled.[8]

Things are beginning to look more optimistic. If we are
not yet quite sure what Milton was trying to do, we can at
least clear the ground for a more profitable consideration
of the poem by discovering what he was *not* trying to do.
But if the observation is to be made that *in Quintum
Novembris* is to be read and judged as an Alexandrian
epyllion, a major qualification must immediately be made.
By tradition, the genre is essentially playful: as exemplified
by such classical specimens as Catullus' sixty-fourth poem,
and by latter-day imitations like the fourth Eclogue of Thomas Watson's *Amintae Gaudia* (1592), its purpose is to pur-
vey beguilement and delight with its charming descriptive
set-pieces. Milton, however, put the form to an unexpected
use by giving it a deeply serious purpose.[9] He was unin-
terested in retelling the familiar story of the Gunpowder
Plot, its discovery, and the fate of the Plotters. As a fundamental item of early Stuart dynastic mythology, this was a
most familiar tale, and had been treated in several previous
Plot poems, as we are about to see. Rather, he uses *in
Quintum Novembris* as an instrument for revealing the Plot's
ethical and theological foundations.

To comprehend this, it is necessary to understand the position of *in Quintum Novembris* within the context of a spe-

---

cent of one of Spenser's emblematic "house" descriptions in *The Faerie
Queene.* Obviously, these Spenserian descriptions are very congenial to
the scene-painting of Alexandrian epyllion (Thomas Campion's *ad
Thamesin,* described in a note below, contains several such passages).

[8] Cheek 175f.

[9] He was not the first to do so. Thomas Campion's *ad Thamesin*
(1595) has been criticized on precisely the same grounds as *in Quintum
Novembris:* Bradner 53f. and Davis 359f. It too is an Alexandrian
epyllion, put to the serious purpose of showing that the motive that led
to the launching of the Armada was the same as that of the Spanish
conquest of America: insane greed.

cialized tradition of Anglo-Latin quasi-epic, and Milton's debts to his immediate predecessors.[10] Like them, he took his cue from the official governmental representation of the Plot and its meaning.

What actually transpired in the Gunpowder Plot will always be a subject of intense historical debate.[11] All we really know depends on information put out by the government, which was scarcely behindhand in issuing its version of events. This was first promulgated by Attorney General Edward Coke in his prosecution speeches against the surviving Plotters. Then it was publicized in two "white papers" issued soon after the discovery of the conspiracy, *A true and perfect relation of the proceedings at the severall arraignments of the late most barbarous Traitors* and *A Discourse on the maner of the discouery of this late Intended Treason*. The latter's status as virtually a state document was emphasized by the fact that it was printed in the same volume with King James' 1605 address from the throne.[12] These items are very similar: they present a series of carefully selected documents (confessions of the accused and extracts from Coke's trial speeches, linked by a suitably clucking narrative). The account that was fashioned in this way became a political myth fraught with ideological and theological implications.

The myth's first component involved the Jesuits. The idea for exploding Parliament and thus killing James and his heir-apparent Prince Henry, and of setting up one of his younger children as a compliant figurehead in order to

[10] This has been partially realized and explored by Haan 1992 and 1993.

[11] The Plot has generated a fairly large literature, which unfortunately appears to be dominated by amateurs, apologists, conspiracy theorists, and cranks. Two recent works free of such faults can be recommended, those of Nichols and Fraser. But the best treatment remains Donald Carswell's volume in the Notable British Trials Series.

[12] *His majesties speach in this last session of Parliament etc.*

gain toleration for Catholicism, was hatched by a small circle of English malcontents. Father Henry Garnet, the Jesuit Superior for England, and several other members of the Order were to some degree privy to the Plotter's plans, and it was at least alleged that they apprised the Vatican of their efforts. The government account exactly inverted this situation so as to make the Anglo-Catholic conspirators the instruments of the international Jesuit octopus, acting under Garnet's instructions. This construction of the facts was greatly facilitated by such points of Jesuit doctrine as Cardinal Allen's argument that the killing of heretical sovereigns was morally justified, and the theory of equivocation, supposedly preached to the Plotters by Father Garnet, according to which it was acceptable for Catholics to lie to the authorities about their faith. Repeated in subsequent Plot literature, this portrayal of the Jesuits acquired a greater measure of plausibility because of Ravillac's assassination of Henri IV in 1610.

The second and equally important point had to do with King James himself. As the official version went, the conspiracy came to light because the Plotters had qualms about killing Catholic peers in the general explosion they were planning. Hence an anonymous letter was sent to one such peer, Lord Monteagle, cryptically urging him to avoid the impending meeting of Parliament. Puzzled and deeply disturbed, he rushed to some of the King's ministers and showed them the mysterious letter. As they could make no sense of it, they awoke James, and thanks to his sagacity—and, at least in some literary accounts, thanks to divine guidance—he perceived that a plot was afoot, and ordered a search of Parliament's cellars. Guy Fawkes was arrested, and his confession led to the uncovering of the Plot. Whether or not this account was truthful—it neglects, for example, the fact that Monteagle received the letter and showed it to the ministers over a week prior to Fawkes' arrest—it served to stress James' superior intellect and remind his subjects that he enjoyed a special relation with the Almighty.

The origin of the specialized tradition in which Milton was working can be located in a remarkably influential Latin poem, the *Pareus* of 1586, probably written by George Peele.[13] I say remarkably influential because in several crucial respects *Pareus* served as the prototype for a number of later literary presentations of the Gunpowder Plot, including *in Quintum Novembris*.

The execution of Dr. William Parry for an alleged conspiracy to assassinate Elizabeth elicited a governmental "white paper," *A True and Plaine Declaration of the Horrible Treasons Practiced by William Parry*, that in terms of intention, content, and structure, served as a model for Gunpowder Plot "white papers." It set forth an official account of events, together with a prescription with what loyal Englishmen should think and feel about them. *Pareus* stands in precisely the same relationship to this work as later Gunpowder Plot literature does to the latter documents.

More specifically relevant to Milton's poem is that the author of *Pareus* devised a literary formula with powerful political and theological implications. At the beginning of the poem a Pluto who manages to combine many attributes of the classical Pluto and the Christian Satan delivers himself of a wrathful speech, out of frustration that Protestant England is baffling his attempt to dominate the world. He sends for Deception and instructs her to travel to Rome. She is to inspire the Pope with the idea of assassinating Elizabeth. Deception flies to the Vatican and pours this message in the ear of the sleeping Pope. When he awakens he summons Cardinal Como, his Secretary of State, and orders him to find some human instrument to carry out the

---

[13] Edited by Sutton 151–219.

plan. Como recruits Parry, who goes to England but is arrested before he can perform his mission.

This narrative pattern accomplishes several things. With its chain reaction, whereby the movement begins in Hell and operates through the Church, it conveys both that England's immediate enemy is an agent of Rome, and that the Catholic Church is charged with the mission of preserving and extending Satan's earthly empire, an exact inversion of the Church's claims. Thus the local disruption created by Parry is made to appear part of the Church's worldwide machinations, which in turn are a manifestation of an ongoing Manichaean struggle of cosmic proportions between the forces of good and evil. Just as the Pope is cast in the role of Satan's supreme agent on earth, so the English sovereign is represented as God's special champion. The formula mythologizes contemporary history and quite literally demonizes both the Church and Parry himself.

Peele, if he was responsible for this extraordinary work, concocted it partially on the basis of Vergilian elements. The anger his Pluto displays towards England is modeled on the wrath of Juno towards the Trojans, and his ranting speech takes its cue from Juno's speech at *Aeneid* 1.37ff.[14] The episode in Book 7 of the *Aeneid*, in which Juno commands the Fury Allecto to fly to Italy and fill the hearts of Turnus and his mother Amata with hatred of the Trojans, and Allecto appears to the sleeping Turnus to rouse him to action are powerful stimulants: hence the war between the Trojan immigrants and the native forces of Italy. He also introduced into English literature a new kind of lord of the Underworld, a hybrid Pluto-Satan, combining the traditional attributes of both. His model for this figure was the

---

[14] Although this is not the case in *Pareus*, later writers working in the tradition it began frequently set similar speeches in the context of an infernal council (as did Milton).

Pluto of Canto 4 of Tasso's *Gerusalemme Liberata,* or more precisely (as several verbal resemblances show) of this same figure as he appeared in the partial Latin translation of this Canto, published at London in 1584 by Scipio Gentili under the title *Plutonis Concilium ex Initio Quarti Libri Solymeidos.*[15]

This powerful mythologizing formula proved enormously influential, for the direct or at least indirect influence of *Pareus* is visible in a good deal of literature written over the next few decades.[16] Even before the Gunpowder Plot, it was an established narrative pattern. Its appeal lay in its flexibility: it could readily be adapted to fit a variety of historical situations.

William Alabaster [1568–1640] was highly esteemed in his own lifetime. At *Colin Clouts Come Home Again* (1595) 400ff., Spenser lavishly praised his abortive attempt to write the Great Patriotic Epic for his times, the *Elisaeis.*[17] In Book 1—all Alabaster ever wrote, because he subsequently converted to Catholicism—Satan gives an angry speech about the progress of the Protestant cause in England, and then goes to Rome to goad Papacy (the Church personified) into action. Papacy in turn goes to England, where she appears to the evil Bishop Stephen Gardiner in a dream and inspires him to fill the newly enthroned Queen Mary with fear and hatred of her younger sister Elizabeth. Mary

---

[15] Thus a link is established between Tasso's new ruler of the Underworld and Milton's Summanus (whom is often said to be a kind of prototype for Satan in *Paradise Lost).*

[16] Not just the items discussed in this article: variations on the new Satan-Pluto show up in the sixth Eclogue of Thomas Watson's *Amintae Gaudia* (1592) and Thomas Campion's *ad Thamesin* (1595). Perhaps John Donne's *Ignatius his Conclave* (1611) was also influenced by Peele or one of his literary successors, since it is written around the idea of an infernal council.

[17] Edited by O'Connor.

responds by having Elizabeth put under arrest, and at the end of the book she is brought to the Tower.

What we have of the *Elisaeis* was scarcely meant to stand on its own, as is revealed by its dissatisfactory ending which leaves Elizabeth stranded in the Tower. The future participle in the title page statement *in duodecem libros tribuendi liber primus* shows that we have here the fragment of a work never continued. The poet's unfulfilled plans are sketched in the proem (40ff.):

> hic, regina, tuum genus, aetatisque tenellae
> sacra rudimenta, et raptos de sorte triumphos
> instituam: castamque deo tutante salutem,
> et meritam sarta de relligione coronam.
> addam urbes Scotiae domitas Gallumque repulsum,
> et coniuratas vano conamine turmas.
> atque hic ferventem bello, vastisque latentem
> caedibus Oceanum: et magna de classe ruinas,
> atque incestatos Hispano sanguine fluctus.

It is tempting to suppose that Book 2 would have described the Marian persecutions; the poet would then have moved on to Mary's death and Elizabeth's triumphant accession. On the basis of the passage just quoted we can see that the epic would have narrated campaigns against Scotland and France, as well as such conspiracies against the queen as the Babington Plot, and would, naturally enough, have presented the defeat of the Armada as its grand climax. In Book 1 Alabaster does not keep his promise to tell of Elizabeth's lineage and early upbringing. Unless he decided to omit this material as he progressed with his writing, this may hint that he planned on some sort of flashback to Elizabeth's childhood. The proposed distribution of this material into twelve books reveals his intention. His idea was presumably to be a Vergil for his times, writing a national epic with Elizabeth as its heroine. Hence, no doubt, the admiration for this work expressed by Spenser, who nursed kindred ambitions. This intention is underscored by the numerous sidenotes in some of the manuscripts which preserve the text of Book 1, in which parallels with the *Aeneid* are carefully recorded, for the poem is liberally peppered with Vergilian tags. Satan may have been intended to play the role of the Queen's constant enemy, as Juno was Aeneas' in Vergil, so that a series of his malevolent interventions would have served to propel the plot. This might be inferred from 53, *atque deam variis vitae obiectare procellis* and also from the author's sidenote on 8f. which mentions Satan's wrath. Possibly the idea of narrating Elizabeth's career within the cosmological context of an ongoing duel between Satan and God and their subordinate agents would have served as the equivalent of the divine machinery of classical epic. How the poet proposed to distribute his account of Elizabeth's career over twelve books, or how he imagined it would provide sufficient material to fill them, is a subject fit only for conjecture.[18] The

---

[18] There are reasons for thinking that the young Milton read and learned from the *Elisaeis*. O'Connor stated that this was so but (in the course of a monograph-length study!) excused himself from reciting the evidence, noting only the verbal parallel of *El.* 500 to *Q.N.* 133. Considerably more important parallels are visible. When Milton's infernal Summanus flies over England and looks down on the white cliffs of Dover (25f.), this replicates the similar view seen by flying Papacy at *E.* 294f. In both poems a rather satirical description of the Vatican is combined with the chain-reaction narrative sequence inherited from *Pareus* (compare *E.* 153–99 with *Q.N.* 48–67). Milton's description of the hideous place to which the Pope summons his agent (139ff.) is ultimately based on Vergil's description of Hell gate surrounded by personified abstractions (*Aeneid* 6.273ff., also imitated by Spenser at *Faerie Queene* 2.7.21ff.) Alabaster imitates the same model, with some quite similar details, in his description of Papacy's home at *E.*153ff. and the picture of the interior of St. Peter's at *Q.N.* 60f. resembles that given at *E.* 203ff.).

way that Book 1 is excessively padded out with epic similes suggests he would have had difficulty.

In Quintum Novembris is one of no less than five narrative poems about the Gunpowder Plot that adapts the narrative, ethical, and theological formula of *Pareus*–at least if one extends the concept "narrative" to embrace more or less mythologized accounts as well as realistic historical ones. The Plot was of central importance for the ideology, or even the official mythology, of James' reign, and so both it and the Oath of Allegiance that it engendered produced a tremendous amount of literary effort and pamphleteering (not excluding some efforts along the latter line by James himself). The items described here because they adopt *Pareus'* formula are in fact only a fraction of the poetic effusions written in response to the Plot.[19] The substance and tone for all loyalist accounts of the Plot was initially set by Attorney General Coke. Although our five poems exhibit important differences in terms of intentions and length, in essence they adopt the same strategy: they present a more or less fictional account whereby events are mythologized in a way highly congenial to Coke's view. This is done by combining his demonized account with the narrative pattern of *Pareus*. These two forms of myth-making were highly supportive of each other: to marry them, all one had to do was revise the formula of *Pareus* so as to create room for the Jesuits as Satan's prime agents on earth.[20] It would appear that the credit for this revision be-

---

[19] Binns 457 n. 31, presents a list of such works, but even this is incomplete: omitted, for example, are a lost narrative on the subject attested by William Gager in the course of his 1608 *Pyramis* (168ff.), and Francis Herring's *Venatio Catholica* and epigrams included with the second edition of *Pontificia Pietas* (1609).

[20] This appears to be new: in English anti-Catholic literature not much attention was paid to the Jesuits prior to the Gunpowder Plot.

longs to the Scottish poet Michael Wallace (Latinized as Valesius on the title page of his poem).

This work, printed in 1606, has the rather daunting title *In Serenissimi Regis Iacobi Britanniae Magnae, Galliarum, Hiberniae etc. Monarchae ab Immanissima Papanae Factionis Hominum Coniuratione Liberationem Faelicissimam Carmen* Ἐπιχάρτικον.[21] Angry at the peace and prosperity of England under the rule of King James, Pluto convenes a hellish council where he makes his complaint in a wrathful speech. The devil Abaddon responds with the advice that Pluto should employ the services of the Jesuits to rectify the situation. Abaddon, disguised as a Jesuit, appears at Rome, where he recruits Guy Fawkes with a speech remarkably like that of Cardinal Como to Parry in *Pareus* (175ff.), urging him to explode Parliament when the royal family is present. Fawkes complies, but the Gunpowder Plot is foiled when God perceives it and intervenes. A mysterious letter is sent to Lord Monteagle; he discloses it to the government; James in his wisdom deciphers the letter, and the Plot is foiled. The poem concludes with praise of the King and an exhortation to exterminate all Anglo-Catholics.

Francis Herring's *Pietas Pontifica* was also printed at London in 1606.[22] Lucifer sired the devil Falsus on the Great Whore (the Church). Now that Falsus has grown to maturity, the Whore delivers a speech to him complaining about having lost England to Protestantism. She urges him to go to England to rectify the situation. Arriving there disguised as Guy Fawkes, he recruits many men to his cause and manages to become a member of the Court. Ultimately he plants among his confederates the idea of blowing up Parliament; the plan goes forward until God looks down, sees it, and sends an angel to set in motion the train of events that unmasks the Plot. The poem ends with an exhortation

[21] Edited by Haan 1993, 368–401.
[22] Edited by Haan 1992, 221–95.

to James similar to that of Wallace, including the advice that Anglo-Catholics should be exterminated.

Unlike Wallace's work, Herring's poem proved popular and went through several printings and two English translations.[23] Inspired by his literary success, Herring issued a much more ambitious version in 1609, dedicated to Prince Henry, and prefaced by a long prose essay about the Plot, and accompanied by a sequel (really a Book 2 with a separate title), *Venatio Catholica*, about the apprehension of the conspirators. The most important alteration is that the names of Falsus and Robert Catesby have been exchanged at a crucial point, giving to Catesby the proposal to explode Parliament, and Falsus an answering speech in praise of this suggestion. This change was presumably made in the interest of historical accuracy, for Catesby was the prime mover of the Plot. But it was ruinous to the literary effect Herring originally strove to create. Since the Plot's central idea is now hatched by a mortal rather than by the agents of Hell, Fawkes-Falsus is now demoted from a demon to the status of a minor imp and, although Herring's infernal machinery is retained, it is rendered largely pointless.

Save for the strong Puritan coloration of Herring's poem—which perhaps helps account for its popularity, together with the simplicity of his Latin—these two works are obviously so similar in conception, narrative contents, and even some details, that one must have been based on the other. We cannot be quite sure which came first.[24] Neither

[23] *Pietas Pontificia* was reprinted in its expanded version, in 1609, and also received the compliment of a pirate printing two years later. In addition, it was twice translated into English verse, by "A. P." in 1610 and, in a "very much dilated" version, by John Vicars in 1617. This latter translation was reprinted as late as 1641.

[24] One consideration suggests the priority of Wallace's work. He Latinizes Guy Fawkes' surname as *Fauxius*, while Herring employs the

poem provides a satisfactory historical account of the Plot. In Herring's case, for example, the poem's flaws as a narrative are probably more apparent to a modern reader than to an audience that is already familiar with the facts. Thus, for example, his description of the conspirators' digging activities at 195ff. is confusing because he does not explain that they first rented a nearby house and tried to drive a tunnel into the cellar of Parliament. Similar complaints can be made about Wallace's effort. A second defect is shared by both works: those human actors in the story who are neither demonized (like Fawkes) nor heroized (like the king) are thrust into the background and become shadowy lay-figures. Lifelike and interesting rendition of character has no place in this kind of fictionalized history. Likewise, since the reader is presumed to be familiar with the facts, characters are often inadequately introduced when they first appear.

What we find instead of realistic narrative, obviously, is heavy mythologization, the sources for which are somewhat clearer in the case of Herring. *Pareus* and the *Elisaeis* both use a rather complex narrative move whereby a chain of characters act on each other sequentially to produce a historical result. Thus in *Pareus* we have the sequence Pluto > Deception > The Pope > Cardinal Como > William Parry, and the *Elisaeis*, in obvious imitation, has Satan > Papacy > Stephen Gardiner > Mary.[25] Both begin with the ruler of

---

form *Falsus*. The direct transformation of Fawkes into *Falsus* is neither natural nor self-evident, and only makes sense if a pun on the French *faux* is involved. So it would appear that Wallace created this initial pun and that Herring's *Falsus* is a secondary elaboration on it. [It may be worth poining out that Milton also Latinized Fawkes' name as *Fauxus* in line 2 of a short Latin poem entitled *In Proditionem Bombardicum* written at about the same time as *in Quintum Novembris*.]

[25] Probably motivated by a delicate reluctance to criticize a sovereign, Alabaster represents Mary as a weak and pliable tool in Gardiner's hands, not as savage Bloody Mary.

Hell, operate by means of the Catholic Church, and end with an English catspaw recruited to execute the infernal scheme in question. In both poems there is a passage describing the king of the Underworld's fear and loathing of the advance of Protestantism and of English peace and prosperity. In *Pareus* this takes the form of a speech by Pluto, while in the *Elisaeis* an equivalent passage is cast in third-person narrative. In both cases, too, at the point which Deception and Satan arrive at Rome we find a set-piece describing the Vatican. *Pietas Pontificia* simplifies this pattern, but its main outlines are still recognizable. Lucifer begets the fiend Falsus on the Great Whore (the Catholic Church personified), and she sends him into the world to do his dirty work with a speech quite similar to that of Pluto in *Pareus*. Thus Herring adheres to the pattern somewhat more closely than does Wallace. Equally self-evident is the similarity in conception of Papacy and the Great Whore. Making Fawkes-Falsus the demon himself, rather than a human agent similar to Parry or Gardiner, is the chief deviation from the established scheme. This decision had a certain basis in fact insofar as, although Fawkes was a native of York, he had spent a number of years on the Continent fighting for the Spanish, and so it must have seemed to his contemporaries as if he had popped up out of nowhere. Further details also seem to reflect *Pareus*: at 81ff. there is a wildly unhistorical passage in which Falsus insinuates himself at Court. This seems to echo Peele's description of Parry worming himself into Elizabeth's good graces.

Phineas Fletcher [1582–1650], the elder son of the poet-diplomat Giles Fletcher, was educated at Eton and Cambridge and then obtained a fellowship at Kings College, which gave him the opportunity to develop his poetical talents. *Locustae* exists in several manuscripts as well as in printed form. Two early ones can be dated respectively to 1611 and 1612, and a third (which introduces substantial changes and gives the poem a more satirical cast) must have been written prior to 1621. This recension more closely resembles the printed version, issued in 1627.[26]

Dis (whose home, interestingly, is in Virginia) convenes an infernal council and complains of the lapse of Catholicism around the world. A devil named Aequivocus[27] responds by urging Dis to rely on the Jesuits. Aequivocus himself volunteers to go to Rome to inspire the Pope. There follows an excursus in which the effects of the Jesuits' subversive activities on various nations are recounted. Aequivocus comes to Rome and finds the Pope. Another excursus traces the rise of the papacy. The Pope, himself distraught by the decline of Catholicism, convokes a council and delivers a complaining speech, placing particular emphasis on the situation in England. Inspired by Aequivocus, a senior Jesuit speaks up and advises the Pope to work by stealth. He then sketches a plan for blowing up Parliament and the royal family. This advice is greeted with cheers. The Pope agrees to adopt the plan. The Jesuit recruits the members of the Gunpowder Plot, who set about their work. God looks down, sees the crime about to occur, and sends one of His eagles down to earth to intervene. The Plot is revealed thanks to the Monteagle letter, and the poem ends with praise of God and King James. Especially in its final printed version, *Locustae* is filled out with a good deal of embellishment, as the author looks at Jesuit machinations in other countries and provides a highly unfriendly thumbnail history of the Church.

---

[26] An edition (without English translation) may be found in Boas, volume 2. In his introduction Boas explains the history of the text and presents a collation of recensions. There appeared simultaneously with *Locustae* a very free English translation by the author himself, printed under the title *The Apollyonists*.

[27] A name calculated to evoke the doctrine of Equivocation preached by Father Garnet.

The conception of *Locustae* is sufficiently similar to that of the poems of Wallace and Herring that Fletcher must be presumed to have been familiar with one or both of them. Indeed, the alternative title *Pietas Iesuitica* itself serves to establish familiarity with Herring's *Pontificia Pietas*. On the other hand, the poem begins with an infernal council such as had been portrayed by Wallace, whereas there is no equivalent scene in Herring. Though he might have acquired this idea directly from Tasso (perhaps with a little help from John Donne), there is no similar ambiguity about the indebtedness of his demon Aequivocus to Wallace's Abaddon, a character conceived in very much the same way, and who performs exactly the same function in the story. Likewise, the description of the House of Parliament and the prospective session there, coupled with the speaker's advice about blowing it up, at 554ff. resembles *in Serenissimi Regis Iacobi* 202ff. rather more closely than the equivalent passage at *Pontificia Pietas* 168ff. It therefore appears that Fletcher was familiar with both earlier printed Gunpowder Plot poems. At least in its final form, his work may perhaps be described as an expanded rehash of those of his two predecessors, with a great deal more interest in showing how the Plot fit in with the international strivings of the Jesuits.

Thomas Campion's *de Pulverea Coniuratione* is preserved in Sidney Sussex College, Cambridge, ms. 59. and has only recently been edited.[28] The date of the poem cannot be fixed with precision: although its editors thought it later, a more likely estimate is prior to November 1616.[29]

[28] Lindley and Sowerby.

[29] Because of the prominence given to the marriage of Princess Elizabeth to Prince Frederick of the Rhine in 1613, coupled with the eulogy of her former guardian, Lord Harington, who died in the same year (2.109ff.), as if both events were recent and newsworthy, and because of the small notice taken of Prince Charles (who is only referred to by the word *dux* at 1.153, although the published translation misses

In Book 1 Satan, angry at the decline of Catholicism, calls an infernal council and delivers his now-familiar speech. A nameless hooded devil urges him to employ gunpowder to destroy king and Parliament. At Satan's instigation False Religion appears to Robert Catesby as he is sleeping and recruits him to organize the Plot. He in turn recruits the other Plotters. They become involved with the Jesuits, who second their efforts. Fawkes is brought into the conspiracy. They make their preparations and the Plot moves forward. In a scene set at Elizabeth's tomb in the Abbey, True Religion prays to God to preserve Britain from the Plotters. God responds by inspiring James to prorogue Parliament. After a delay, when the day for Parliament's convocation is at hand, God sends an angel, who delivers the mysterious letter to Lord Monteagle, James deciphers its meaning, and steps are taken to foil the Plot. Book 2 narrates the capture of the surviving Plotters by the sheriff's posse at Holbeach House.

Writing nearly a decade later, and considering the requirements of a readership in whose minds historical details were no longer so clear, and perhaps also entertaining some thought of bequeathing the memory of these important events to posterity, Campion made good the defects of his predecessors and tried to combine a mythologized version of events with a coherent account of the Plot and with characterizations that are considerably more than perfunctory. To a certain extent this attempt was successful. Certainly, any modern reader who has not already familiarized himself with the facts of the Plot from other sources will find small enlightenment in the poems of Wallace, Herring, and Fletcher, and much in them will seem enigmatic. *De Pulverea Coniuratione* poses no similar problem, and so

---

the allusion), which would have been extremely improbable in a poem written after his investiture as Prince of Wales in November 1616.

can be read today with considerably more profit and enjoyment. And so, for all its mythmaking, the poem approaches the stature of genuine historic epic in a way its predecessors do not. A significant sign of its realism is that Campion correctly represents Percy and Catesby as the ringleaders of the Plot, Guy Fawkes is relegated to his true role of technical advisor, and reasonably realistic portraits are sketched of all the principal players in the drama.

But this statement requires immediate qualification, for the poem contains a serious flaw. In an attempt to paint the story of the Plot against a cosmic background, and also to imitate the divine machinery of classical epic, Campion so overloads his poem with interventions by powers both infernal and supernal that his characters are scarcely allowed any thoughts or feelings, let alone actions, of their own. With the partial exception of James, perhaps, they are reduced to the status of marionettes, which deprives them of a good deal of their potential dignity and stature as literary figures. Campion set himself the problem of balancing historical narration against mythmaking, but did not solve it as adequately as had Alabaster.

Campion's insistent denial (2.13ff.) that there was any unusual portent on the night of November 4th, especially of a celestial nature, invites interpretation as a response, and quite likely as an implied rebuke, to Wallace's entirely fictitious description of a solar eclipse at lines 279ff. of his poem. Other signs of familiarity with that work also exist. Campion's nameless hooded Jesuit who advises Satan that Parliament ought to be blown up (1.95ff.) bears a strong resemblance to Wallace's Abaddon, as do the speeches these two characters deliver. His pun on the name of *Ignitius* Loyola at 1.305 is borrowed from line 159 of *in Serenissimi Iacobi*. An outburst of indignation at the Plotter's misuse of the sacrament of Communion to seal their compact at 1.282ff. looks like an elaboration on a similar expostulation by Wallace (255f.). Taken in combination, such resemblances appear to admit no room for doubting that Campion had read and learned from Wallace's poem.

Catesby's speech at 1.184ff., in which he reproves a confederate for being insufficiently daring and stresses the need to wipe out the entire royal family, rather than just James, appears modeled on Falsus' similar advice at Herring's *Pontificia Pietas* 148ff. Other details suggest familiarity with that work. The description of Fawkes' trip to Belgium in May 1605 (1.563ff.) finds a match in Herring's poem (116ff.), but this transaction is not mentioned in that of Wallace. The unhistorical detail (1.679f.) that the pretext for searching the Whynniard house was to hunt for some garments that had been stolen from Queen Anne looks indebted to *Pontificia Pietas* 355f. The same may be true of the expression of anxiety that the Abbey might have been damaged in the explosion (2.30ff.), for Herring gives voice to a similar sentiment (250f.). More generally, the articulation of Campion's poem into two books resembles that of Herring's expanded second version. We have seen that Herring's narrative falls into two parts. The first deals with the hatching of the Plot and the arrest of Fawkes, and the second with the fate of the rest of the Plotters. It is probably no accident that Campion distributes his material according to the same scheme. Though the two works are quite different in detail (Herring's sequel is far more mythologized and, like its predecessor, is largely devoted to anti-Catholic rhetorical excursions) they both contain some parallel episodes: Digby's feigned hunt, and the fate of the Plotters when run to earth at Holbeach.

Like Fletcher's *Locustae*, therefore, albeit in a very different way, *de Pulverea Coniuratione* is an expanded and elaborated rewriting of these two works. In part, this was accomplished by the addition of a welter of extra heavenly and infernal interventions in the course of the story. But the chief novel ingredient was a new fidelity to the historical record, coupled with far more detailed and realistic characterizations. In this sense, it looks as if Campion's intent was to correct and improve upon his predecessors.

Following the chronological order of the poems in this series, we now get back to Milton, and by now it is clear that he was working in what was by his time a well-established tradition of Anglo-Latin historical epic with its own set of specialized conventions and narrative moves. The conclusion seems inevitable that he was consciously operating within this tradition, observing its conventions, and satisfying its reader expectations. In comparison with this discovery, the question of precisely which previous items in the tradition exerted influence on him assumes only a secondary significance.[30] It is an especially difficult question to assess, since, as the number of authors in the tradition multiply, so do the choices confronting the scholar bent on *Quellenforschung.* Nevertheless, even if we let the matter rest at the level of genre, certain interesting things become evident. The most salient characteristics of Milton's poem do not result merely from personal artistic choice, miscalculated or not; they are inherited from the specialized *traditio* in which he was working. To one degree or another, most of these poems substitute mythmaking for history and consequently suffer from precisely the kind of defects for which *in Quintum Novembris* is criticized.

Campion tried to remedy such deficiencies by increasing the admixture of factual historical narrative and realistic character-portrayal. One may think his project foredoomed

---

[30] It has already been investigated by Haan 1992 and 1993 (although she only took into account Wallace, Herring, and Fletcher). Cf. also Sutton 221–28. It is conventional wisdom among Miltonists that the primary source was Fletcher, but I cannot discern any signs at all of Milton's knowledge of that work. Internal evidence suggests Campion (see the next note).

to failure—probably no poet could aspire to be Vergil and Lucan at the same time—but he deserves credit for producing a far more satisfactory Stuart epic than did his predecessors. Milton perhaps perceived the same deficiencies as had Campion,[31] and likewise sought to improve upon them. But he took the opposite tack by dispensing altogether with history and human characters (a very idealized James excepted), and presented a pure distillation of the tradition's mythological component. His object was to focus the reader's attention unswervingly on the ethical and theological implications of the Gunpowder Plot, in the form already incorporated in the Plot literary tradition, rather than on the surface play of events—and selection of Alexandrian epyllion rather than epic as his genre gave Milton an appropriate literary vehicle for doing this. As dissatisfactory as this strategy may seem from the viewpoint of the modern reader in need of a history lesson, this work

---

[31] He was possibly familiar with *de Pulverea Coniuratione* (which is preserved in a Cambridge manuscript). There are certain evident similarities between that work and *in Quintum Novembris*. Hope's bedside speech to Catesby at *P.C.* 1.162ff. bears a strong resemblance to Summanus' similar one to the Pope at *Q.N.* 92ff., considerably more so than the beginning of the only other bedside speech in this series of poems, Alabaster's *Elisaeis* 346ff. When Deception appears to the sleeping Pope in Peele's *Pareus* there is no speech, and the poems of Wallace and Herring do not contain equivalent scenes. (Campion's editors suggested that for both the source may be Mercury's speeches to Aeneas at Vergil, *Aeneid* 4.265ff. and 560ff. It is true that both speeches begin with an echo of 4.560-62. Nevertheless in terms of dramatic situation, the actual prototype for both Peele and Campion is Allecto's address to the sleeping Turnus at 7.421ff., which also begins with a rousing question.) And the monkish disguise adopted by Summanus at *Q.N.* 79ff. distinctly recalls the appearance of the nameless hooded fiend of *P.C.* 1.85ff. (although, as is well known, this description is indebted to the description of St. Francis by the Scots poet George Buchanan); the physical resemblance is considerably closer to this figure than to Wallace's Abaddon or Fletcher's Aequivocus.

was, after all, conceived for the benefit of knowledgeable contemporaries, not for us. The poem behaves the way it does, in short, because of the deliberate artistic choices Milton has made. It it is unhelpful to invoke such "explanations" as youth, incompetence, or flagging enthusiasm in the course of composition. *In Quintum Novembris* behaves the way it does because of purposeful artistic decisions: it is precisely what its author, very much in control of his material and aware of what he was doing, wanted it to be.

Works Cited

Binns, J. W. 1990. *Intellectual Culture in Elizabethan and Jacobean England: The Latin Writing of the Age.* Leeds.

Boas, Frederick S. 1909. *The Poetical Works of Giles Fletcher and Phineas Fletcher.* Cambridge.

Bradner, Leicester. 1940. *Musae Anglicanae: A History of Anglo-Latin Poetry 1500–1925.* New York. (Rpt. New York, 1966.)

Carswell, Donald. 1934. *The Gunpowder Plot.* London.

Cheek, Macon. 1957. "Milton's 'In Quintum Novembris': An Epic Foreshadowing." *Studies in Philology* 54:172–84.

Condee, R. W. 1974. "The Latin Poetry of John Milton." In *The Latin Poetry of English Poets.* Ed. J. W. Binns. London and Boston. 58–92.

Davis, Walter H. 1967. *The Works of Thomas Campion.* New York.

Fraser, Antonia. 1996. *Faith and Treason.* London.

Haan, Estelle. 1992. "Milton's *In Quintum Novembris* and the Anglo-Latin Gunpowder Epic." *Humanistica Lovaniensia* 41:221–95.

——. 1993. "Milton's *In Quintum Novembris* and the Anglo-Latin Gunpowder Epic, Part II." *Humanistica Lovaniensia* 42:368–401.

Hanford, J. W. 1925. *Studies in Shakespeare, Milton and Donne.* Ann Arbor.

Lesky, Albin. 1966. *A History of Greek Literature.* Tr. James Willis and Cornelis de Heer. London and New York.

Lindley, David, and Robin Sowerby. 1987. *Thomas Campion: de Pulverea Coniuratione.* Leeds.

Nichols, Mark. 1991. *Investigating the Gunpowder Plot.* Manchester and New York.

O'Connor, Michael. 1979. "The 'Elisaeis' of William Alabaster." *Studies in Philology* monograph 76.

Rand, E. K. 1922. "Milton in Rustication." *Studies in Philology* 19:109–35.

Roe, John. 1992. *The Poems: Venus and Adonis, The Rape of Lucrece, The Phoenix and the Turtle, The Passionate Pilgrim, A Lover's Complaint.* Cambridge.

Sutton, D. F. 1995. *Oxford Poetry by Richard Eedes and George Peele.* New York.

Tillyard, E. M. W. 1930. *Milton.* Cambridge.

E. S. Beesly
and the Roman Revolution

T. P. Wiseman
University of Exeter

The name of Edward Spencer Beesly (1831–1915) is best known to historians of the Labour movement.[1] He was an energetic supporter of the early trades' unions, both helping them with practical advice and forcefully stating the justice of their case for middle-class readers in the main-stream journals.[2] He arranged and presided over the inau-gural meeting of the International Working Men's Associa-tion in 1864 (the "First International"), and thereafter was in regular contact with Karl Marx, though his own Comtean Positivism was not to Marx's taste. As Beesly him-

[1] See Davidson 168–78; Kent 53–58; Harrison 1965, 251–345, "The Positivists: a Study of Labour's Intellectuals." There will be a biography of him in the *New Dictionary of National Biography* (publication sched-uled for 2004).

[2] E.g., Beesly 1861b, 1867, 1870. Beesly was a regular contributor to the *Bee-Hive* weekly ("A Journal of General Intelligence, Advocating In-dustrial Interests"), which was the mouthpiece of the Trades Council. See Harrison 1960.

self somewhat wryly put it, "Dr. Marx and I were always good friends; to the end of his life I had a great esteem and regard for him: and I am sure that he considered me to be a well-meaning person—which was more than he was willing to allow with regard to most people who differed with him."[3]

But Beesly was also an academic historian. His first job after graduating in *Literae Humaniores* at Oxford (1853) was as assistant master in history at Marlborough College; in 1859 the political influence of John Bright, and the prolonged industrial dispute in the London building trades, brought him to the capital; the following year he was appointed to the Professorship of History at University College, and that of Latin at Bedford College, posts which he held until 1893 and 1889 respectively. His combined professorial income was £300 a year, representing something like £15,000 by today's values.[4] But the duties were not demanding: at University College he had to give lectures only once or twice a week, and he sometimes took the opportunity to abandon the University of London syllabus and lecture "on wide fields and long periods of history, a practice, in my opinion, much more appropriate to the Chair, and more useful educationally."[5]

For a follower of Auguste Comte's "secular religion," history had to be understood according to the Positivist creed of progress, as humanity evolved from theological to abstract (or metaphysical) interpretations of experience, and

[3] Harrison 1959, 32, quoting a letter in *Christian Socialist*, March 1884.

[4] Kent 54; cf. Jenkins 4, "the best working rule I have been able to devise is to multiply all nineteenth-century values by a factor of fifty in order to turn them into late-twentieth-century terms." Beesly himself (in Ker 36–37) describes his university income as "insignificant"; he clearly had private means.

[5] Beesly, in Ker 36–37; I am very grateful to Michael Crawford for tracking down the Ker volume for me.

from there to positive scientific understanding.[6] One can imagine the college authorities having a different view of what the history curriculum required.

It so happened that in the very year of Beesly's appointment the Professor of Modern History at the University of Cambridge published his inaugural lecture. This was the Rev. Charles Kingsley, author of *Alton Locke*, *Hypatia* and *Westward Ho!*, Chaplain in Ordinary to the Queen, and Rector of Eversley, Hampshire; the title of the lecture was *The Limits of Exact Science as Applied to History*. Beesly gave it a withering thirty-two-page review:[7]

> We know what it is that goeth before destruction, or we should be amazed that, not content with uttering this stuff before a select audience, Mr. Kingsley should have surrendered it irrevocably to the handsome type and substantial binding of Messrs Macmillan. . . . The lecture is a bad one, from the title-page to the conclusion—bad in conception and in execution, in argument, in style, and even in grammar.

Beesly insisted, against the novelist's idea of history as "the history of men and women, and nothing else," that there are indeed laws which the course of civilisation has followed and will continue to follow:[8]

> The most important laws that govern human progress are few, simple, and beyond our interference. The heat of a southern summer, the cold of a northern winter, are influences which we cannot alter. Englishmen *must* consume more nutritious food than Neapolitans, they *must* be better housed and clothed, they *must* use more fuel. The labour necessary for procuring all these comforts *must* have a cer-

[6] Convenient summaries in Harrison 1965, 251–54; 1960, 206–10.
[7] [Beesly] 1861a, 305–36, quotations from 320 and 336. The review is unsigned.
[8] Ibid. 310–11.

tain effect upon their character. Again, such statical laws as
the preponderance of the affective faculties in the individual over the intellectual, of the personal instincts over
the social, are facts in our nature which we must accept.
Comte's great dynamical law of the three stages through
which the various branches of human knowledge have
passed is, in our opinion, no less universally true.

An acquaintance with these and such like general unifor-
mities in the course of nature is the first requisite for useful
speculation on social questions. Taken by themselves, indeed, they would be but poor guides of action. We could
not construct from them a complete deductive science of
society, as geometry is, based upon a few axioms and postu-
lates. But when we compare them with the observed facts
of history, we can distinguish, with more or less exactness,
certain derivative laws, and these again, by the aid of such
specific observation as the nature of the case may admit,
will give us rules for action in the present and expectation
as to the future; not, indeed, *exact* rules, but such as we can
have no hesitation in accepting as the only rational basis of
all efforts for the amelioration of our condition.

That final phrase sums up his position. History, as properly
understood, is useful for the present. It is a "guide of
action."

In the latter part of his review, Beesly addressed the
"great men" conception of history. Kingsley had argued
that their will alone was sufficient to determine events. The
Positivists had a subtler view: "men of genius, whether
speculative or active, influence their age precisely in proportion as they comprehend and identify themselves with
its spirit."[9] Let Julius Caesar illustrate the point:[10]

Never before or since has human being exhibited in so high
a degree all the qualities, noble as well as useful, of a born

[9] Ibid. 324.
[10] Ibid. 326–27.

ruler of men. Never had a great man a grander *rôle* to play. To preside over the most important crisis in the history of the most important branch of the human race—this was a task which could not but fall to a great man. It fell to the greatest. Here then, if anywhere, we shall see destiny shaped and bent by human genius. For once the future of a nation, or rather of the world, is bound up in the life of an individual.

But Caesar was assassinated. His old enemies of the aristocracy destroyed him. "The game is played over again, with hardly a variation in the moves; and at Philippi the reactionists are at length made to comprehend that they are beaten. How far was the history of Rome altered by the murder of Julius?" Caesar's great design was simply carried out by Augustus, "a man every way his inferior."

And what was that design, the achievement of which Beesly identifies as the most important crisis in the history of the most important branch of the human race?[11]

From early manhood, nay, almost from boyhood, has the great plan been maturing in the splendid calm of that self-contained, self-counselling mind. For nearly half a century he has marked the signs of the political horizon. No word has he breathed of his inner purpose. . . . [T]he Empire— the combination of the dictatorial and tribunitian powers, to be wielded in the interest, not of Rome nor of Italy, but of the world—that is an idea which one brain alone has grasped.

Beesly was a convinced republican, an admirer of Mazzini and of Abraham Lincoln; he saw the Union victory in the American Civil War as giving "a vast impetus" to republican sentiments which would shake "the tottering edifice of

[11] Ibid. 327.

English society."[12] Why should he exult in the coming of the Roman Empire?

* * *

In March 1865 a new journal was launched, with the purpose "of aiding Progress in all directions." Its editor, G. H. Lewes, invited Beesly and his friend Frederic Harrison to contribute to the first issue, on any topic "short of direct attacks on Christianity."[13] Beesly's offering was an article on Catiline as a party leader. Marx read it, and was quite impressed:[14]

> Professor Beesly hat vor einigen Wochen in der *"Fortnightly Review"* einen Artikel über Catilina, worin dieser als Revolutionsmann vindiziert wird. Es ist allerlei Unkritisches darin (wie von einem Engländer zu erwarten, z.B. Falsches über die stellung Cäsars zur damaligen Zeit), aber die intensive Wut über die Oligarchie und die "Respektabeln" ist hübsch. Auch die Hiebe auf den professionellen englischen "dull littérateur."

> Professor Beesly has an article on Catiline in the *Fortnightly Review* a few weeks ago, justifying him as a revolutionary. There's all sorts of uncritical stuff in it (as you'd expect from an Englishman, e.g. he's wrong on Caesar's position at that time), but the intense rage at the oligarchy and the "respectable" is nice. Also his digs against the professional English "dull littérateur."

It was followed by "Cicero and Clodius" in 1866 and "The Emperor Tiberius" in 1867–68, a trilogy later published in

---

[12] Beesly 1865b, q.v. for the death of Lincoln: "Since the great Julius fell under the daggers of the Roman aristocrats, perhaps no death so sad has thrown a gloom over the world." For Beesly's splendid speech at John Bright's rally of working-class support for Emancipation (St. James' Hall, 26 March 1863), see Harrison 1965, 69–77.

[13] Vogeler 58.

[14] Letter to Engels, 19 August 1865: Marx and Engels 145.

book form.[15] Read against his political preoccupations at the time, these polemical essays give a vivid picture of Beesly's qualities as a historian. They may also cast some light on the origin of the title of Sir Ronald Syme's master-piece—an incomparably greater work, but one which similarly grew out of contemporary political realities.[16]

In telling the story of Catiline "calmly and consistently with common sense," writes Beesly,[17]

> I protest, by anticipation, against the supposition that I am amusing myself by maintaining a paradox. My sole desire is to do something towards the elucidation of a much misunderstood period of Roman history. I care nothing about the memory of Catiline, except so far as he was the representative, for a time, of the revolution which it is sought to blacken through him, just as the French revolution is blackened by calumniating Danton and Robespierre.

In itself, the idea of a Roman revolution was not new. The Abbé de Vertot's history of the revolutions of the Roman Republic was one of the most widely read historical works of the eighteenth century. For him, however, the revolution *par excellence* was the achievement of Roman freedom in the early Republic;[18] the word was used, quite casually, in the

[15] Beesly 1865a, 1866a, 1867-68. Reprinted as Beesly 1878, "Catiline," 1-37; "Clodius," 38-83; "Tiberius," 84-148.

[16] Syme ix: "It has not been composed in tranquillity . . . [T]he theme, I firmly believe, is of some importance." See Galsterer, esp. 12 on Syme's use of "revolution."

[17] Beesly 1865a, 168 = 1878, 3-4.

[18] Vertot d'Aubeuf 1719 (7th ed. 1778), 1720 (6th ed. 1770). The *Discours préliminaire* begins: "L'amour de la liberté a été le premier objet des Romains dans l'établissement de la république, et la cause ou le prétexte des révolutions dont nous entreprenons d'écrire l'histoire. Ce fut cet amour de la liberté qui fit proscrire la royauté, qui diminua l'autorité du consulat, et qui en suspendit le titre en différentes occasions."

same context by Nathaniel Hooke in his *Roman History* of 1738, while the translator Thomas Gordon even attributed it to Sallust in his excursus on the establishment of the Republic.[19]

Hooke's use of the word is particularly relevant, since his *History* was consciously "byass'd to the popular side" in order to counter the influence of Vertot, who was "devoted to the aristocratical faction."[20] His work is cited with approval by one of Beesly's radical predecessors, John Thelwall (1764–1834), in his *Rights of Nature, Against the Usurpations of Establishments.*[21] Hooke and Thelwall were agreed that "after the *Gracchi*, there never arose a tribune, or any other magistrate, honest and generous enough to espouse the true interests of the people . . . till at length *Sylla*, having seized the dictatorship, changed the very form of the Republick, almost annihilated the tribunitian power, and reduced the government to an aristocracy."[22]

For Beesly, on the other hand, the Gracchi were the *beginning* of revolution.[23] His introduction continues with an explanation of the phrase:[24]

---

[19] Hooke I iii, 115 (Decemvirs and Tarquins respectively); Gordon 6, rendering *Sed ea tempestate* (Sall. *Cat.* 7.1) as "Upon this Revolution, . . ."

[20] Hooke I ii–iii.

[21] Reprinted in Claes 389–500; see 488–89 on the "band of Ruffian Senators" (Hooke's phrase) who "extinguished Roman liberty in the blood of [Tiberius] Gracchus."

[22] Hooke II 560. Cf. Thelwall (Claes 489 n.): "Genuine Republican Rome expired with the Gracchi. The atrocious contests that ensued, between Sylla and Marius, and Caesar and Pompey, were mere struggles of individual ambition—or at least of *Monarchic and Aristocratic factions.*"

[23] Beesly 1865a, 170 = 1878, 8 (133 B.C. as "the commencement of the revolution") and 171 = 9: "The Roman revolution was inaugurated by the Gracchi. Never had a good cause more noble champions." The fourth book of Mommsen's *History of Rome* (1856; Engl. tr. 1866), covering the period from Ti. Gracchus to Sulla, is entitled "Die Revolution."

[24] Ibid. 168 = 4, 170–71 = 9.

Let us first endeavour to get some true conception of what the Roman revolution was, and what its course had been before Catiline became a prominent actor in it. It did not, like the French revolution, owe its birth to the growth of ideas and the progress of speculation. It was purely a revolt against intolerable practical evils. No government has been such a scourge to the governed, as was that of the Roman oligarchy during the last century of its existence.

There follows a lengthy analysis of the nexus of political corruption and provincial extortion in the age of Verres. It was an

infamous system of government maintained by the nobility for the most selfish and sordid ends. This was the system round which the respectable friends of order (*optimates*) rallied, the Catos, the Ciceros, and the Catuli. This was the system which the irreverent advocates of reform (*populares*), the Gracchi, the Catilines, the Caesars, strove to beat down. The reformers were not all pure-minded patriots, not all men of stainless lives. But if we would deal them even-handed justice, let us never forget what that thing was that they were labouring to destroy and their opponents to keep alive.

It was "the systematic, the methodical torture inflicted by the Roman oligarchy on the Roman world."

Note, the *world*. In his Kingsley review Beesly had welcomed the Empire because the emperor's powers were to be wielded "in the interest, not of Rome nor of Italy, but of the world." As a young man he had harangued the Oxford Union on the motion "that our foreign policy as dictated by the governing classes is selfish, shortsighted, and unworthy of a free people"; as a professor of history, he wrote that England's maritime power was marked by "flagrant violation of the simplest principles of morality, by contemptuous disregard of the rights of the weak and by an assumption of superiority intolerably wounding to the legitimate dignity of our neighbours"; as a petitioner to Parliament, he would soon be deploring the atrocities committed by the British army in Ireland, India and the West Indies.[25] Beesly had no objection to imperial rule as such, but it had to rest "on the only true basis for any government, the welfare of the community, and the consent of the large majority of the governed"—and that is what he believed the Roman revolution brought about.[26]

That may help to explain his otherwise baffling description of Gaius Gracchus:[27]

> The first really great man that Rome in six centuries had produced, imperial in his aims, fearless in his choice of means, he gathered up the whole force of the revolution in his single arm and smote the oligarchy with a mortal blow . . . [His policy] was in effect to incorporate the Italians with Rome, and to substitute a single ruler responsible directly to the people for the sham Republic.

No evidence or argument is offered for this extraordinary idea. But if the revolution was the pursuit of a single aim, its result must necessarily have been intended from the beginning.

Much more convincing is Beesly's running theme of the symmetry of political violence. The revolution was begun by Tiberius Gracchus; "the nobles beat his brains out in the street." Saturninus resorted to violence; "but how could he do otherwise when the nobility were ever ready to meet constitutional action by the bludgeon and the dagger?"

[25] Kent 54; Beesly 1866b, quotation from 196 (= 2nd ed., 131); *Hansard*, Commons 3 May 1867 (3rd series, 186.1929–33).

[26] Beesly 1867–68, 28 = 1878, 144.

[27] Beesly 1865a, 171 = 1878, 10. Cf. 172 = 12 on Sulla, "too fond of ease and self-indulgence to care for empire."

Livius Drusus, an honest aristocrat, tried to shame the oligarchy into reform; "he was assassinated. He had fully expected it." Next came Sulpicius; "the conservatives [were] eternally prating about order and the laws, while they knocked on the head every man who attempted reform by constitutional means. They had appealed to the sword, and so would he."[28]

The same applied to Catiline. He, Beesly insists, was the popular leader in Rome in the absence of Pompey:[29]

> Sallust tells us so in so many words, "Cuncta plebes Catilinae incepta probabat." Let us once understand this clearly, and Catiline's position becomes perfectly simple. He was the successor in direct order of the Gracchi, of Saturninus, of Drusus, of Sulpicius, and of Cinna, and was recognised as such both by friends and enemies. The popular cause, it must be owned, might have been in better hands; but . . . [i]t is fit and proper that when a Gracchus or a Drusus is murdered, the murderers should have to deal with a Catiline.

Beesly constantly, and rightly, stresses the unreliability of Cicero's rhetorical allegations about Catiline.[30] But he does not dispute the charge of attempted murder:[31]

> That Catiline may at this time have laid plans against the life of Cicero is probable enough. He was not a man whom

[28] Ibid. 171–72 = 9–11.

[29] Ibid. 175 = 18–19, quoting Sall. *Cat.* 37.1. (In fact, Sallust's very sweeping analysis includes at 38.3 the assertion that ideology counted for nothing, and that the people's champions were no less motivated by lust for power than those of the Senate.)

[30] Ibid. 176–78 = 20–24. This is the context of the phrase Marx noticed: "Our dull littérateurs have adopted [these libels] as serious facts, rather than confess how little we really know of ancient history beyond its broad features" (177 = 23).

[31] Ibid. 181 = 30.

we could expect to rise superior to the manners of his class. The nobility had never shrunk from assassination where it served their purpose; and Cicero, though he disliked it as applied to himself, could applaud it loudly where a Gracchus or a Caesar was the victim. Assassination is a form of crime which has always been especially characteristic of oligarchic manners.

Catiline was, of course, a patrician: "his ancestors had been consuls and decemvirs when the Metelli and the Domitii were clapping their chopped hands and throwing up their sweaty nightcaps on the Aventine or Mons Sacer."[32] So Beesly can have his cake and eat it: in so far as Catiline *was* a villain, it was because he was an aristocrat!

The real point, however, is not obscured by this sleight of hand. Catiline "did not mean to be knocked on the head like the Gracchi or Saturninus, whose cases Cicero was always quoting as wholesome precedents,"[33] and he knew that that was a real possibility. So do we, if we read our sources carefully enough. When Catiline walked out of the Senate on 20 October 63 B.C., "Cicero . . . had hoped that he would be murdered on the spot";[34] "Cicero distinctly states that he would have had it done if he had thought that his single death would have broken up the revolutionary party";[35] and when Catiline asks Catulus to protect his wife and daughter, "even while he writes he learns that the assassins are on his track."[36]

---

[32] Ibid. 176 = 19.

[33] Ibid. 180 = 28.

[34] Ibid. 180 = 29 on Cic. *Mur.* 51, *quem omnino vivum illinc exire non oportuerat.*

[35] Ibid. 181 = 30 on Cic. *Cat.* 1.4–6 and 12 (Beesly's note gives the false reference "IV 12").

[36] Ibid. 182 = 32 on Sall. *Cat.* 35.5, *plura quom scribere vellem, nuntiatum est vim mihi parari.*

That sort of insight, achieved by reading the sources "against the grain," seems to me the mark of a serious historian. It is clear enough, I think, that what made Beesly sensitive to Catiline's situation was his own experience of radical politics. Two generations earlier, he might easily have found himself (as Thelwall did in 1794) in the Tower of London on a charge of high treason. Even in mid-Victorian England the risks were serious. His close friend Frederic Harrison warned him about his outspokenness: "I take it that if you were ever drawn into a notorious religious or political fracas (and what is to prevent it?) it would avail you little in the world being a scholar and a gentleman."[37]

Beesly very soon was drawn into just such a "political fracas," and it was one which directly involved his two themes of imperial misgovernment and the violence of authority.

* * *

On 11 October 1865 there was a riot at Morant Bay, Jamaica, in which eighteen people were killed and thirty-one wounded. It gave rise to a rebellion, and on 13 October Governor Edward Eyre declared martial law. The rebellion was contained, but during the thirty days of martial law 439 people were shot or hanged, over six hundred were flogged, and about a thousand houses and cottages were burned down. The most conspicuous victim was G. W. Gordon, a member of the colony's legislature. He was arrested on 17 October, tried for high treason on the 21st, and executed two days later.[38]

News of the affair quickly reached England. Indignation at Eyre's actions was focussed in the creation in December

[37] Letter to Beesly in 1864, quoted by Harrison 1965, 280.
[38] Dutton 214–307 (a sympathetic but not uncritical biography of Eyre).

1865 of the "Jamaica Committee," with the aim of having him recalled to face trial for murder. John Bright, J. S. Mill and Charles Darwin were its leading lights; Beesly was one of the junior members. In January 1866 a Royal Commission of Enquiry was appointed. Its report, published in June, found that Gordon's guilt was not proved, and that Eyre had acted with "unnecessary rigour." The Governor was replaced, and left Kingston in July amid great demonstrations of support. As he sailed home, a rival committee was formed, to give him a hero's welcome and raise funds for his defence. Prominent among its members were Tennyson, Carlyle, Ruskin, Dickens, and Beesly's *bête noire* the novelist-professor Charles Kingsley.[39]

Beesly's attitude to the Eyre controversy is seen most clearly in a letter he wrote to a left-wing weekly protesting at the middle-class bias of magistrates:[40]

> It has at last come to this, that when a quiet and unoffending man is half-killed by a policeman and makes his complaint to justice, the magistrate coolly refuses to administer the law, and tells the injured man that he should have kept out of the way. Perhaps the London workmen can now begin to understand what took place in Jamaica. . . .
>
> Let those who have made themselves conspicuous recently on the popular side look out for themselves. Some day it will be their turn. Nay, unless an example is made of Mr. Eyre, I fully expect that Mr. Bright himself may one day be treated with no more ceremony than Mr. Gordon. . . .
>
> If a serious riot should take place in Lancashire a few years hence, and martial law be proclaimed—a very conceivable supposition—I have not the smallest doubt that the country gentlemen and officers of the army would take the opportunity to get rid of Mr. Bright, though he might have neither said or done anything stronger than he has at the

[39] Dutton 308-64.
[40] Beesly 1866c.

present time. No doubt the Tory Minister of the day would deplore it as a most unfortunate occurrence, and admit that the evidence had been quite insufficient to justify a conviction. Perhaps even a magistrate might be dismissed, and a colonel cashiered. But the deed would have been done, and Lord W. G. Osborne would go round with the hat.

Presumably Osborne was one of the fund-raisers of the Eyre Defence Committee.

The return of Eyre seems to have made Beesly reflect on the exile and return of Cicero. In July 1866 the *Fortnightly Review* carried his article on "Cicero and Clodius."[41] Once again, he insists that the conventional interpretation has got it all wrong:[42]

> We are asked to believe that, stained with the blood of the popular leaders, Cicero was respected and beloved by the vast majority of Roman citizens, and that the troubles which subsequently befell him were simply the result of a personal quarrel with Clodius. To maintain this paradox—for paradox it must appear to any one accustomed to reflect on political phenomena—*ex parte* statements of the least trustworthy of ancient writers have been adopted by modern historians as sober truth; his carefully cooked narratives have been cooked over again till the basis of fact has entirely disappeared. . . .

How has this come about? Partly because of "the credulous unphilosophical spirit, the ignorance of practical politics, the conservative tone of mind, and the literary *esprit de corps* too common among historians." But it is also because Cicero satisfies the modern writer's longing for "a full and vivid representation of events, with ample details as to the actors, and warm, sensational colouring for his scenes." And that is the fault of people like Charles Kingsley.

[41] See n. 15 above.
[42] Beesly 1866a, 421 = 1878, 39–40.

Beesly repeats Kingsley's dictum that "history is the history of men and women, and of nothing else," and contemptuously dismisses it:[43]

> We might be well content . . . to leave the trivial details about "men and women" to scholars, gossips and antiquaries, if they could indulge their taste without a serious perversion of such important passages in history as the Roman Revolution. There we must resist them, and establish the truth, even though in doing so we have to shock an amiable spirit of hero-worship.

(Note that the revolution has now attained the dignity of capital letters.[44]) Literary historians' sympathy for Cicero had already attracted Beesly's irony in a splendid passage at the end of his Catiline essay:[45]

> The little army of Catiline died round their leader like the Spartan Three Hundred round Leonidas at Thermopylae. . . . The world has generally a generous word for the memory of a brave man dying for his cause, be that cause what it will. But for Catiline none. The execrations of nineteen centuries lie piled on the grave of the successor of the Gracchi and the forerunner of Caesar. It is not good to make a literary man your enemy. . . .
> An unequal struggle. The man of letters has had the ear of the world ever since, and has told his story without contradiction. More than that, the literary men have stood by one another, as they always do—like game-preservers or Whitechapel thieves.

[43] Ibid. 421–22 = 41; cf. n. 8 above.

[44] Cf. ibid. 436 = 71: "My aim is not to persecute the memory of an individual, but to set the Roman Revolution in a clear light, and strip off the false colours with which the anecdote-mongers have bedaubed it." The same point, and the same capitals, at 1866a, 441 = 1878, 82 and 1867–68, 635 = 1878, 86.

[45] Beesly 1865a, 183, 184 = 1878, 34–35, 36.

It was surely a sign of the sharpening of the topical issues—all those literary giants lining up behind Eyre—that Beesly now directed his polemic at "Professor Kingsley" by name.

Once again, his mastery of the source material enables him to see behind the Ciceronian facade. "I have no doubt that the father of his country was universally hooted by the mob"; and the evidence is there, in the letter where Cicero tells Atticus about the time it didn't happen.[46] Of course Cicero was hated by the people, and his exile was the proper punishment for what he had done in 63; but "if there is a childish way of explaining a political movement, a literary man will generally adopt it."[47] His return from exile was voted by the wealthy in the *comitia centuriata*, and even there the custody of the ballot-boxes was entrusted to members of the Senate: "If this was merely the statement of a Clodian partisan, I should not ask any one to believe it. But it rests on the authority of Cicero himself, who mentions it twice."[48]

The most elegant of Beesly's demolitions comes at the critical point, where Clodius proposes the bill restating exile as the punishment for putting Roman citizens to death without trial:[49]

> Now [Cicero] might be seen in a squalid dress, followed by a train of crest-fallen aristocrats, and pelted with mud and stones while he strove to excite the compassion of his fellow-citizens. He tells us that "twenty thousand men" (*senatus hominumque viginti milia*) went into mourning with him.

[46] Beesly 1866a, 432–33 = 1878, 64–65 (Cic. *Att.* 1.16.11, *sine ulla pastoricia fistula*); cf. 422 = 42, "the lower orders of Rome, who had loved and trusted Catiline, exhibited a constant and determined hostility to the man who had hunted their hero to death to please the oligarchy."

[47] Ibid. 434 = 67.

[48] Ibid. 440 = 80; Cic. *Post red. in Sen.* 28, *Pis.* 36 (*vos diribitores, vos custodes fuisse tabularum*).

[49] Ibid. 435 = 69–70; Cic. *Post red. ad Quir.* 8.

Sanguine as he was of obtaining the applause of posterity, he perhaps hardly expected that the historians would solemnly one after the other repeat his wild exaggeration, as a reliable statistical fact.

Plutarch specified "twenty thousand young men"; Conyers Middleton in 1741 made that "the young nobility to the number of twenty thousand"; Cicero's latest biographer, William Forsyth Q.C., was now writing of "twenty thousand of the noblest youths of Rome." Beesly comments drily in a footnote: "London is nearly ten times as large as Rome in the time of Cicero; but 'twenty thousand noble youths' would be rather difficult to get together even in the height of the season."[50]

The enemy of the people, the man who committed murder under the guise of martial law, suffered "a most just retribution."[51] Would that happen to Eyre? Perhaps not. After all, the Senate reversed Cicero's exile by bringing in the country gentlemen:[52]

[L]arge numbers of Italians were collected in Rome on an appointed day, and under cover of these bands the Senate passed a resolution that any tribune exercising his constitutional right to impede the bill for the recall of Cicero, should be treated as a public enemy—in other words, knocked on the head.

It was just a month after the essay was published, and a week after Eyre had landed at Southampton, that Beesly wrote his letter about the danger to John Bright, and others "conspicuous recently on the popular side."[53]

---

[50] Ibid. 435 = 70 n. 1; cf. Plut. *Cic.* 31.1; Forsyth I 198.
[51] Ibid. 422 = 42.
[52] Ibid. 440 = 79–80.
[53] See n. 40 above.

* * *

In March 1867 Eyre was prosecuted as an accessory to murder, and the Shropshire magistrates dismissed the case. In the same month a Royal Commission began the investigation of Trades' Unions. On 27 March Beesly lectured in Bradford on the emperor Tiberius.

He began by explaining to his working-class audience what sort of regime had been overthrown by Caesar and Augustus:[54]

> Now I must first ask you to dismiss from your minds all those prepossessions in favour of the Republican Government which are derived from its name. It was no Republic. It was that worst of all governments, the monopoly of power by a privileged class. You know what that means. A single man ruling with despotic power must take some thought for the well-being of his subjects, or his reign will not last long. But a privileged class with immense landed property ... can perform with security feats of injustice and oppression from which a despot would recoil with dismay.

Then he told them what had happened to this "convenient instrument for aristocratic misrule:"[55]

> The people carried Julius Caesar to power, in order that he might crush privilege and establish something like equality. That was the leading idea of the Imperial system as carried out by Julius, Augustus, and Tiberius, its three great founders. They were, in fact, tribunes and champions of the people against the nobility, and of the provinces against Rome. Only, instead of relying upon oratory, and agitation, and street demonstrations, and monster meetings, they carried a sharp sword. So, at length, the aristocracy was tamed.

[54] Beesly 1867–68, 635–66 = 1878, 86–87.
[55] Ibid. 637 = 90; cf. also 20 = 126–27.

The subtext comes across loud and clear. Later that year, in Bradford again, Beesly would be drafting proposals for an independent political movement, the embryo of a Labour party.[56]

Most of the lecture was a defence of Tiberius' character, against Tacitus and "the *servum pecus* of modern writers."[57] But he focussed in particular on the political trials:[58]

> The fact is that the state trials of Tiberius afford the clearest indication of the basis on which his power rested. He crushed a lawless nobility, and dragged to justice governors who had been guilty of oppression and outrage in the provinces, and who found sympathy among their own class as similar criminals do now.

That was the result of the Roman revolution. One day, perhaps, it might happen in England, too.

In June that year William Broadhead, secretary of the Sheffield Sawgrinders' Society, admitted to the Royal Commission that he and his fellow-members had organised assaults on non-union workers, some of which had been fatal. A mass meeting of trade-unionists was held in Exeter Hall on 2 July to dissociate the movement from these crimes. Beesly was horrified at the revelations,[59] but in his speech at the rally he urged the unions not to be defensive. "Murder by trade unionists is no better and no worse than any other murder." What about Eyre, the darling of the middle

[56] See Harrison 1960, 228–29, who quotes Beesly's comment to a fellow-Positivist: "There will be little harmony between us and Bright henceforth, I fear."

[57] Beesly 1867–68, 642 = 1878, 101 n. 1; contrast 645 = 105 n. 2 on Velleius, with his "freedom and heartiness of style."

[58] Ibid. 26–29 = 139–47, quotation from 27 = 141–42.

[59] Davidson 176: he had urged the unions to "ferret out any member guilty of a breach of the law and drag him to justice." Cf. Harrison 1965, 279.

class, whose hands were red with the blood of more than four hundred men? "This man committed his crimes in the interests of his employers as Broadhead committed his in the interest of the workmen of Sheffield."[60]

There was a howl of venomous indignation in the press, and the President of the Senate of University College urged the dismissal of Beesly as being unfit to instruct students. When that attempt narrowly failed (thanks to George Grote), Beesly wrote to Marx: "The combat is only adjourned. In some shape it must sooner or later be renewed, for when duty calls I hope I shall never be silent."[61]

A brave man and an honest man, Beesly continued to speak out when he thought he could do some good,[62] but he had no more to say in public about Roman history. Even so, his trilogy of essays on the Roman revolution is a document of some importance. From one point of view, it illustrates the dangers to a historian of having an *a priori* pattern to demonstrate. What but the Comtean dogma could have brought this enthusiastic republican to praise "the splendid calm of two centuries, unparalleled hitherto in the history of the world, which followed the battle of Actium"?[63] On the other hand, his experience of the reality and the dangers of radical politics enabled him to read the Ciceronian evidence with a sensitivity to *popularis* thinking unparalleled in any historian before or since.

* * *

Paul MacKendrick's view of Cicero could hardly be further removed from Beesly's. But he too is a scholar and a gentle-

---

[60] *The Times*, 4 July 1867, p. 9; Harrison 1960, 226–27.
[61] Harrison 1959, 38–39.
[62] See for instance Harrison 1971, 37–117.
[63] Beesly 1866a, 441 = 1878, 82.

man, well able, as he showed with Kipling,[64] to be sympathetically discriminating about nineteenth-century attitudes. And perhaps he will not wholly disapprove of a man who admired the United States. "America," wrote Beesly in 1865, "is a standing rebuke to England. Her free institutions . . . are in too glaring a contrast with our own condition to be forgiven."[65]

Works Cited

[Beesly, E.S.] 1861a. "Mr. Kingsley on the Study of History." *Westminster Review* 19:305–36.

Beesly, E. S. 1861b. "Trades Unions." *Westminster Review* 20:510–42.

——. 1865a. "Catiline as a Party Leader." *Fortnightly Review* 1.2:167–84.

——. 1865b. "The Republican Triumph." *Bee-Hive* 185 (29 April 1865): 4.

——. 1866a. "Cicero and Clodius." *Fortnightly Review* 5.4:421–44.

——. 1866b. "England and the Sea." In *International Policy: Essays on the Foreign Relations of England*. London. 153–222 (= 2nd ed., 1884:103–49).

——. 1866c. "The Trial of Mr. Eyre." *Bee-Hive* 253 (18 August 1866): 4.

——. 1867. "The Trades Union Commission." *Fortnightly Review* 8.1:1–18.

——. 1867–68. "The Emperor Tiberius." *Fortnightly Review* 8.6:635–48 and 9.1:14–30.

——. 1870. "The International Working Men's Association." *Fortnightly Review* 14.5:517–35.

[64] MacKendrick 67–76.
[65] Beesly 1865b.

———. 1878. *Catiline, Clodius and Tiberius*. London.

Claes, Gregory, ed. 1995. *The Politics of English Jacobinism: Writings of John Thelwall*. Penn State.

Davidson, J. M. 1880. *Eminent Radicals in and out of Parliament*. London.

Dutton, Geoffrey. 1968. *The Hero as Murderer*. Sydney.

Forsyth, William. 1864. *Life of Marcus Tullius Cicero*. London.

Galsterer, H. 1990. "A Man, a Book, and a Method: Sir Ronald Syme's *Roman Revolution* after Fifty Years." In *Between Republic and Empire: Interpretations of Augustus and his Principate*. Eds. K. A. Raaflaub and M. Toher. Berkeley. 1–20.

Gordon, Thomas. 1744. *The Works of Sallust*. London.

Harrison, Royden. 1959. "E. S. Beesly and Karl Marx." *International Review of Social History* 4:21–58 and 208–38.

Harrison, Royden. 1960. "Professor Beesly and the Working-Class Movement." In *Essays in Labour History in Memory of G. D. H. Cole*. Eds. Asa Briggs and John Saville. London. 205–41.

Harrison, Royden. 1965. *Before the Socialists: Studies in Labour and Politics 1861–1881*. London.

Harrison, Royden, ed. 1971. *The English Defence of the Commune 1871*. London.

Hooke, Nathaniel. 1738–71. *The Roman History, from the Building of Rome to the Ruine of the Commonwealth*. London.

Jenkins, Roy. 1995. *Gladstone*. London.

Kent, Christopher. 1984. "Beesly, Edward Spencer (1831–1915)." In *Biographical Dictionary of Modern British Radicals II: 1830–1870*. Brighton. 53–58.

Ker, W. P. 1898. *Notes and Materials for the History of University College, London*. London.

MacKendrick, Paul. 1956. "Kipling and the Nature of the Classical." *CJ* 52:67–76.

Marx, Karl, and Friedrich Engels. 1965. *Werke*. Band 31. Berlin.

Syme, Ronald. 1939. *The Roman Revolution*. Oxford.

Vertot d'Aubeuf, Aubert de. 1719. *Histoire des révolutions arrivées dans le gouvernement de la république romaine*. Paris.

———. 1720. *The History of the Revolutions that Happened in the Government of the Roman Republic*. London.

Vogeler, Martha S. 1984. *Frederic Harrison: the Vocations of a Positivist*. Oxford.